Medical Terminology made Incredibly Easy!®

3rd
edition

Wolters Kluwer | Lippincott Williams & Wilkins
Health

Philadelphia • Baltimore • New York • London
Buenos Aires • Hong Kong • Sydney • Tokyo

Staff

Executive Publisher
Judith A. Schilling McCann, RN, MSN

Editorial Director
David Moreau

Clinical Director
Joan M. Robinson, RN, MSN

Art Director
Mary Ludwicki

Electronic Project Manager
John Macalino

Senior Managing Editor
Jaime Stockslager Buss, MSPH, ELS

Clinical Project Manager
Lorraine M. Hallowell, RN, BSN, RVS

Editors
Karen Comerford, Liz Schaeffer

Copy Editor
Dorothy Terry

Designer
Georg W. Purvis IV

Illustrator
Bot Roda

Digital Composition Services
Diane Paluba (manager), Joyce Rossi Biletz, Donna S. Morris

Associate Manufacturing Manager
Beth J. Welsh

Editorial Assistants
Karen J. Kirk, Jeri O'Shea, Linda K. Ruhf

Indexer
Barbara Hodgson

The clinical treatments described and recommended in this publication are based on research and consultation with nursing, medical, and legal authorities. To the best of our knowledge, these procedures reflect currently accepted practice. Nevertheless, they can't be considered absolute and universal recommendations. For individual applications, all recommendations must be considered in light of the patient's clinical condition and, before administration of new or infrequently used drugs, in light of the latest package-insert information. The authors and publisher disclaim any responsibility for any adverse effects resulting from the suggested procedures, from any undetected errors, or from the reader's misunderstanding of the text.

 Printed in China. For information, write Lippincott Williams & Wilkins, 323 Norristown Road, Suite 200, Ambler, PA 19002-2756.

MedTermIE3010608-050815

Library of Congress Cataloging-in-Publication Data
Medical terminology made incredibly easy!. — 3rd ed.
p. ; cm.
Includes bibliographical references and index.
1. Medicine. — Terminology. 2. Medical sciences. — Terminology. I. Lippincott Williams & Wilkins.
[DNLM: 1. Terminology as Topic. W 15 M4887 2009]
R123.M394 2009
610.1'4--dc22
ISBN-13: 978-0-7817-8845-8 (alk. paper)
ISBN-10: 0-7817-8845-5 (alk. paper) 2008011400

RRS1506

Contents

Contributors and consultants

Helen Christina Ballestas, RN, MSN, CRRN, PHD[C]
Nursing Faculty
New York Institute of Technology
Old Westbury

Kim Davis, MSN
ICU Nurse Manager
Ralph H. Johnson VA Medical Center
Charleston, S.C.

Vivian C. Gamblian, RN, MSN
Nursing Faculty
Baylor University
Louise Herrington School of Nursing
Dallas, Tex.

Donna Headrick, RN, MSN, FNP
Taft Community College
Advanced Cosmetic Dermatology
Bakersfield, Calif.

Shelley Huffstutler-Hawkins, DSN, APRN-BC, FNP, GNP, FAANP
Post Doctoral Fellow
University of North Carolina – Chapel Hill School of Nursing

Julia Anne Isen, RN, BS, MSN, FNP-C
FNP-C Primary Care
University of California, San Francisco

Hope Siddons Knight, RN, BSN
Nursing Faculty
Redlands Community College
El Reno, Okla.

Megan McClintock, RN, BSN
Nursing Faculty
Redlands Community College
El Reno, Okla.

Aaron Pack, RN, BSN
Nursing Informatics Specialist
Redlands Community College
El Reno, Okla.

Noel C. Piano, RN, MS
Instructor/Coordinator
Lafayette School of Practical Nursing
Williamsburg, Va.
Adjunct Faculty
Thomas Nelson Community College
Hampton, Va.

Angela R. Roughley, RN
Registered Nurse – Critical Care Unit
Deaconess Hospital
Oklahoma City, Okla.

Donna Scemons, RN, MSN, FNP-C, CNS, CWOCN
Nurse Practitioner
Healthcare Systems, Inc.
Castaic, Calif.

Marilyn D. Sellers, APRN, BC, MSN
FNP – Behavioral Science/Mental Health
VA Medical Center
Hampton, Va.

Connie K. Smith, RN, MS
Clinical Education Coordinator
Memorial Hospital of Union County
Marysville, Ohio

Jennifer K. Sofie, APRN, MSN
Adjunct Assistant Professor & Nurse Practitioner
Montana State University
Bozeman

Benita Walton-Moss, APRN, BC, DNS
Associate Professor
Johns Hopkins University School of Nursing
Baltimore, Md.

Not another boring foreword

If you're like me, you're too busy caring for your patients to have the time to wade through a foreword that uses pretentious terms and umpteen dull paragraphs to get to the point. So let's cut right to the chase! Here's why this book is so terrific:

It will teach you all the important things you need to know about medical terminology. (And it will leave out all the fluff that wastes your time.)

It will help you remember what you've learned.

It will make you smile as it enhances your knowledge and skills.

Don't believe me? Try these recurring logos on for size:

Pump up your pronunciation—charts at the beginning of each chapter that help you "talk to the walk" by sounding out the most difficult terms

Anatomically speaking—anatomic images that bring you face to face with the structures you're trying to pronounce

Beyond the dictionary—sidebars on the origins of words, which can help you remember and dissect their meanings

The real world—tidbits on more informal terminology that you may hear used in daily practice.

See? I told you! And that's not all. Look for me and my friends in the margins throughout this book. We'll be there to explain key concepts, provide important care reminders, and offer reassurance. Oh, and if you don't mind, we'll be spicing up the pages with a bit of humor along the way, to teach and entertain in a way that no other resource can.

I hope you find this book helpful. Best of luck throughout your career!

Joy

1

Key concepts of medical terminology

Just the facts

In this chapter, you'll learn:

- dissection of medical terms
- meaning determination of medical terms using roots, prefixes, and suffixes.

Dissecting medical terms

Because many medical terms derive from Greek and Latin, learning medical terminology is like learning a new language. Understanding these terms can be easier if you know how to analyze key elements and identify word associations.

Deciphering medical terminology requires deduction, my dear Watson.

Take it apart

Most medical terms are a combination of two or more parts. If you can successfully interpret each part, you can usually grasp the essential meaning of the word. Thus, interpreting the meaning of a medical term requires knowledge of common medical roots, prefixes, and suffixes.

Root it out

A root is the essential component of a word. Many medical roots signify a disease, procedure, or body part. Some roots appear at the beginning of a word, whereas others appear after a prefix, before a suffix, or between a prefix and a suffix. In addition, two or more roots may be combined to form a word, as in ***cardi-o-pulmonary*** and ***cardi-o-vascular***. The letter ***o*** is the most commonly used combining vowel.

Here are some examples of roots used in different positions:

- a root at the beginning of a word—***angi***oedema (***angi*** is a root that means *vessel*)
- a root in the middle of a word—en***cephal***ic (***cephal*** is a root that means *head*)
- a root at the end of a word—sclero***derm***a (***derm*** is a root that means *skin*)
- a combination of roots—***phototherapy*** (***photo*** is a root that means *light;* ***therapy*** is a root that means *treatment*).

If you can understand the building blocks, then you'll have the foundation for learning even the most complicated medical terminology.
CYAN
O
SIS

In the beginning

A prefix consists of one or more letters attached to the beginning of a root. Many prefixes used for medical terms are also applied to standard English vocabulary. To determine the meaning of a prefix in a medical term, consider a familiar word that begins with the same prefix. For example, the prefix ***anti-*** has the same meaning—*against*—in both *antislavery* and *antihistamine,* literally *against slavery* and *against histamine* (the compound that produces allergic reactions).

At last

A suffix is one or more letters attached to the end of a root. When a suffix begins with a consonant, a combining vowel, such as ***o,*** is placed before the suffix. Common use of suffixes in medical terminology includes adding a ***-y*** to a word to denote a procedure, such as *gastroscop****y,*** which means *endoscopic examination of the stomach.* Similarly, adding ***-ly*** to a word denotes an act or process; for example, *splenomega****ly,*** which means *the abnormal enlargement of the spleen.*

Break it down; build it up

With a bit of practice, you'll quickly discover how easy it can be to interpret the parts of a medical term and then combine them to identify the term's meaning. For example, in *acrocyanosis,* the root ***acr*** *(extremities)* and the vowel ***o*** are combined with the root ***cyan*** *(blue)* and the suffix ***-osis*** *(condition)* to form a term that means *a condition characterized by blue extremities.* (For another example of how to dissect a medical term to decipher its meaning, see *'Dem bones.*)

Beyond the dictionary

'Dem bones

A specialist in **osteopathology** studies bone diseases. The root ***oste*** is the Greek word for *bone.* A second root, ***patho,*** is derived from ***pathos,*** meaning *disease.* The suffix ***-logy*** is derived from the Greek root ***logia,*** meaning *the study of.* Put these parts together and you have the definition for **osteopathology**—*the study of bone diseases.*

At the root of disease?
A branch of medicine called **osteopathy** contends that skeletal misalignment impinges on adjacent nerves and blood vessels, causing disease.

Forming plural words

Plural words in English are usually formed by adding ***s*** or ***es*** to the end of a noun. The rules for forming plurals of many medical terms are different because of their Greek and Latin roots. Generally, plural words derived from these two languages are formed by adding or substituting vowels or syllables at the end of the word.

Examples of plurals of medical terms are:

- *maculae* (singular: *macula*)
- *adenomata* (singular: *adenoma*)
- *glomeruli* (singular: *glomerulus*)
- *pelves* (singular: *pelvis*).

Pronouncing medical terms

Medical terms can be difficult to pronounce if you've never heard them spoken. In this book, we'll show you how to pronounce words by placing them in all capital letters, with the syllable receiving the greatest stress appearing in tall capitals and the remaining syllables in smaller capitals. For example, in the word **cancer,** the stress is on the first syllable, so it would appear as follows: CAN-CER.

Here are some additional tips for pronunciation:

• only the ***s*** sound in ***ps*** is pronounced, as in *Pseudomonas*
• only the ***n*** sound in ***pn*** is pronounced, as in *pneumococcal*
• ***g*** and ***c*** assume the soft sounds of ***j*** and ***s***, respectively, when used before ***e***, ***i***, and ***y***; examples are *gene*, *gingivitis*, *cycle*, and *cytology*
• ***ph*** sounds like ***f***, as in *phlegm*
• ***x*** sounds like ***z***, as in *xeroderma* (pronounced ZEE-ROH-DER-MAH)
• ***g*** and ***c*** have hard sounds in front of other letters, such as *gangrene*, *gastritis*, *cornea*, and *cortex*
• ***ae*** and ***oe*** are pronounced ***ee***, as in *fasciae*
• ***i*** at the end of a word usually denotes a plural and is pronounced ***eye***, as in *fasciculi*
• ***es*** at the end of a word may be pronounced as a separate syllable, as in *nares*, pronounced NEH-REEZ.

Because phonetic spelling isn't used in medicine, it's important to consult a dictionary when in doubt about pronunciation. Also, some terms sound the same but are spelled differently and refer to different things. For example, *ileum* and *ilium* are pronounced alike, but the first term is part of the intestinal tract and the second one is a pelvic bone.

Be careful! Words like **ileum** and **ilium** sound the same but have different meanings.
Caution!

Understanding eponyms

An eponym is a medical term that's derived from the name of a person, usually the scientist who discovered the corresponding body part or disease. Many procedures and tests are also named after the persons who invented or perfected them.

Name that condition

Examples of eponyms for medical conditions include:
• **Addison's disease,** a syndrome resulting from insufficient production of hormones from the cortex of the adrenal gland
• **Alzheimer's disease,** a type of irreversible dementia
• **Cushing's syndrome,** a syndrome resulting from the production of excess cortisol from the adrenal cortex

- **Parkinson's disease,** a progressive degeneration of the nervous system that causes weakness, rigidity, and tremors
- **Stokes-Adams syndrome,** a heart condition characterized by sudden loss of consciousness.

Famous body parts

Parts of the body named for their discoverers include:
- **Bartholin's glands,** located in the female perineum
- **Cowper's glands,** located beneath a portion of the male urethra
- **Wernicke's center,** a speech center in the brain.

Featured procedures

Examples of eponyms for medical procedures include:
- **Allen's test,** a test for occlusion of radial or ulnar arteries
- **Belsey Mark IV operation,** a procedure to correct gastroesophageal reflux
- **Heimlich maneuver,** a technique for removing foreign objects from the airway of a choking victim.

What's in a name?

Medical devices such as catheters (tubes passed through body channels) are often named for their inventors; for example:
- the **Foley catheter** is an indwelling urinary catheter
- a **Hickman catheter** is a central venous catheter inserted for long-term use
- a **Malecot catheter** is a tube used for gastrostomy feedings
- a **Swan-Ganz catheter** is threaded into the pulmonary artery.

Recognizing word components

Words can be made up of roots, prefixes, and suffixes. (See *Common prefixes, roots, and suffixes*, pages 6 to 13.)

At the root of it all

A root is just what the word implies—where it all starts. A root can be a whole word or part of a word. Roots come from many different languages (such as Greek, Latin,

(Text continues on page 14.)

Common prefixes, roots, and suffixes

Knowing these common prefixes, roots, and suffixes will help you decipher unfamiliar medical terms.

Word component	Meanings	Examples
Prefixes		
a(n)-	absence, without	anuria (lack of urine output)
ab-	away from	abduct (move away from)
ad-	toward	adduct (move toward)
ambi-	both sides	ambidextrous (using both hands)
ante-	before, forward	anterior (front of the body)
anti-	against	antibody (immune response to an organism)
apo-	away from	apophysis (growth or protuberance)
aut(o)-	self	autoanalysis (self-analysis)
bi-	two	bigeminy (occurring in pairs)
diplo-	double	diplopia (double vision)
dys-	difficult, painful	dysuria (painful urination)
ec-	out of	ectopic (out of place)
end(o)-	inward	endoscope (a device used to examine a body cavity)
eu-	normal, health	euthyroid (normal thyroid function)
ex-	outside	exfoliation (peeling of layers)
hetero-	other, different	heterogeneous (different characteristics)
hyper-	above, beyond	hypernatremia (excess sodium)
hypo-	below	hypotension (low blood pressure)
infra-	beneath	infra-axillary (below the axilla)
intra-	within, into	intramuscular (into the muscle)
juxta-	near	juxta-articular (near a joint)
macr(o)-	large, long	macromastia (excessive breast size)
mal-	bad, abnormal	malformation (abnormally formed)
mega-	great, large	megacolon (enlarged colon)

Common prefixes, roots, and suffixes *(continued)*

Word component	Meanings	Examples
Prefixes *(continued)*		
meta-	beyond, change	metaphase (second stage of cell division)
micr(o)-	small	microbe (tiny organism)
mono-	one	monochromatic (having only one color)
morph(o)-	shape	morphology (study of the form and structure of organisms)
multi-	many	multifocal (arising from many locations)
olig(o)-	few, little	oliguria (too little urine)
par(a)-	near, beside, accessory to	paracentesis (puncture of a cavity for aspiration of fluid)
peri-	around	pericecal (around the cecum)
pico-	one-trillionth	picornavirus (extremely small RNA virus)
poly-	much, many	polydipsia (excessive thirst)
post-	behind, after	postoperative (after surgery)
pre-	before, in front	preanesthesia (before anesthetic is given)
pro-	favoring, supporting, substituting for, in front of	procoagulant (promotes coagulation)
pseudo-	false	pseudocyst (a cavity resembling a true cyst)
re-	back, contrary	recurrent fever (fever that returns after a remission)
retr(o)-	backward	retroauricular (behind the auricle)
semi-	half	semiflexion (position of a limb midway between extension and flexion)
sub-	under	subclinical (without symptoms)
super-	above	supercilia (the eyebrow)
supra-	above, upon	supraorbital (above the orbit)
tetra-	four	tetralogy (group of four)
trans-	across, through	transdermal (entering through the skin)

(continued)

Common prefixes, roots, and suffixes *(continued)*

Word component	Meanings	Examples
Roots		
abdomin(o)-	abdomen	abdominopelvic (abdomen and pelvis)
acou-	hearing	acoustics (the science of sounds)
acr(o)-	extremity, peak	acrodermatitis (inflammation of skin of the extremities)
aden(o)-	gland	adenocele (cystic tumor in a gland)
adipo-	fat	adipose (fatty)
alb-	white	albumin (protein found in the blood)
andr(o)-	male	androgen (male sex hormone)
angi(o)-	vessel	angiography (X-ray of a vessel)
ankyl-	crooked, fusion	ankylosis (consolidation of a joint)
bili-	bile	biliary (pertaining to bile or the gallbladder)
blast- or -blast	embryonic state	blastocyte (embryonic cell)
blephar(o)-	eyelid	blepharitis (inflammation of the eyelid)
brachi(o)-	arm	brachial artery (artery of the upper arm)
brady-	slow	bradycardia (slow heart rhythm)
calc-	heel	calcaneus (heel bone)
carcin(o)-	cancer	carcinoma (malignant growth)
cardi(o)-	heart	cardiac muscle (heart muscle)
caud-	tail	caudal (toward the tail)
cephal(o)-	head	cephalalgia (pain in the head)
cerebr(o)-	cerebrum	cerebral embolism (occlusion of a cerebral vessel by a blood clot)
cervic(i)(o)-	neck	cervical plexus (network of cervical nerves)
chol(e)-	bile	cholecystitis (inflammation of the gallbladder)
chondr(o)-	cartilage	chondritis (inflammation of cartilage)
col(i)(o)-	colon	colitis (inflammation of the colon)

Common prefixes, roots, and suffixes *(continued)*

Word component	Meanings	Examples
Roots *(continued)*		
cost(o)-	rib	costochondral (relating to a rib and its cartilage)
cut-	skin	cutaneous (relating to skin)
cyan(o)-	blue	cyanotic (blue colored)
cyst(i)(o)-	bladder	cystitis (inflammation of the urinary bladder)
cyt(o)-	cell	cytology (study of cells)
derm- or -derm	skin	dermatitis (skin inflammation)
dors(i)(o)-	back	dorsiflexion (upward bending of hand or foot)
enter(o)-	intestine	enterocolitis (inflammation of the intestines and colon)
erythr(o)-	red	erythrocytes (red blood cells)
fasci-	bundle	fasciae (bundles of muscle fibers)
febri-	fever	febrile (feverish)
fil-	threadlike	filament (fine thread)
galact(o)-	milk	galactose (sugar obtained from milk)
gastro-	stomach	gastritis (inflammation of the stomach)
ger(o)- or geront(o)-	aging	gerontology (study of aging)
gest-	carry	gestation (pregnancy)
gloss(o)-	tongue	glossitis (inflammation of the tongue)
glyc(o)- or gluc(o)-	sweet	glycogen, glucogen (forms of sugar)
gyn(o)-	woman, particularly female reproductive organs	gynecology (study of women's reproductive organs)
heme(a)(o)- or hemato-	blood	hematology (study of blood)
hepat(o)-	liver	hepatitis (inflammation of the liver)
hist(i)(o)-	tissue	histography (process of describing tissue and cells)
hydro-	water, hydrogen	hydrops (excess watery fluid)
hyster-	uterus	hysterectomy (surgical removal of the uterus)

(continued)

Common prefixes, roots, and suffixes *(continued)*

Word component	Meanings	Examples
***Roots** (continued)*		
ile(o)-	ileum	ileostomy (surgical opening in the ileum)
ili(o)-	ilium, flank	iliac muscle (muscle that allows thigh movement)
ischi(o)-	hip	ischiopubic (pertaining to the ischium and pubes)
jejun(o)-	jejunum	jejunectomy (excision of the jejunum)
kerat(o)-	horny tissue, cornea	keratectasia (a thin, scarred cornea)
kine(t)(o)-	movement	kinetic (pertaining to motion)
labio-	lips	labiograph (an instrument that records lip movement)
lact(o)-	milk	lactation (secretion of milk by the breasts)
laryng(o)-	larynx	laryngectomy (surgical removal of the larynx)
latero-	side	lateroflexion (flexion to one side)
leuk(o)-	white	leukocytes (white blood cells)
lip(o)-	fat	lipedema (excess fat and fluid in subcutaneous tissue)
lith(o)-	stone	lithocystotomy (surgical removal of bladder stones)
mamm(o)-	breast	mammogram (breast X-ray)
mast(o)-	breast	mastectomy (surgical removal of breast tissue)
melan(o)-	black	melancholia (depression)
meno-	menses	menostaxis (prolonged menstrual period)
ment-	mind	mental illness (psychiatric disorder)
mio-	less, smaller	miosis (excessive contraction of the pupil)
mito-	threadlike	mitochondria (rod-shaped cellular organelle)
my(o)-	muscle	myocele (hernia of muscle)
myc(o)-	fungus	mycology (study of fungi and fungal diseases)
myel(o)-	marrow, spinal cord	myelalgia (pain in the spinal cord)
myx-	mucus	myxoid (resembling mucus)

Common prefixes, roots, and suffixes *(continued)*

Word component	Meanings	Examples
***Roots** (continued)*		
nas(o)-	nose	nasolabial (between the nose and lip)
nephr(o)-	kidney	nephritis (kidney inflammation)
ocul(o)-	eye	oculomotor (eye movement)
ophthalm(o)-	eye	ophthalmia (inflammation of the eye)
orchi(o)-	testes	orchitis (inflammation of the testes)
oro-	mouth	oronasal (mouth and nose)
oss- or oste(o)-	bone	osteomyelitis (inflammation of bone and muscle)
ot(o)-	ear	otitis (ear inflammation)
ox(y)-	oxygenation	oxyhemoglobin (hemoglobin combined with molecular oxygen)
path(o)-	disease	pathogen (disease-causing organism)
ped(o)-	child	pediatrics (care of children)
pharmaco-	medicine	pharmacotherapy (treatment with medication)
pharyng(o)-	pharynx	pharyngitis (sore throat)
phleb(o)-	vein	phlebitis (inflammation of a vein)
phot(o)-	light	phototherapy (treatment by exposure to light)
plasm(o)-	liquid part of blood	plasminogen (protein found in tissues and body fluids)
pleur(o)-	pleura, rib, side	pleurisy (inflammation of the pleura)
pneum(o)-	lung	pneumonia (inflammation of the lung)
pod(o)-	foot	podiatry (care of the foot)
proct(o)-	rectum	proctectomy (excision of the rectum)
prote(o)-	protein	proteinemia (excess protein in the blood)
psych(o)-	mind	psychiatry (study and treatment of mental disorders)
pulmo(n)-	lung	pulmoaortic (pertaining to the lungs and aorta)
pyel(o)-	kidney	pyelonephrosis (disease of the kidney and renal pelvis)

(continued)

Common prefixes, roots, and suffixes *(continued)*

Word component	Meanings	Examples
Roots *(continued)*		
pyr(o)-	heat	pyrogen (an agent that causes fever)
ren(o)-	kidney	renography (X-ray of the kidney)
rhin(o)-	nose	rhinitis (inflamed mucous membranes of the nose)
rub(r)-	red	bilirubin (bile pigment)
sangui-	blood	sanguineous drainage (bloody drainage)
sarc(o)-	flesh	sarcoma (a highly malignant tumor made of connective tissue cells)
scler(o)-	hard	sclerosis (hardening of tissue)
scolio-	crooked	scoliosis (curvature of the spine)
sensi-	perception, feeling	sensory (pertaining to the senses)
sep-	decay	sepsis (infection in the bloodstream)
soma- or somat(o)-	body	somatization (psychiatric condition expressed through physical symptoms)
sten(o)-	narrow	stenosis (narrowing of a body passage)
tachy-	rapid, swift	tachycardia (rapid heart beat)
therm(o)-	heat	thermometer (instrument for measuring temperature)
thorac(o)-	chest	thoracotomy (surgical opening of the chest wall)
thromb(o)-	clot	thrombectomy (excision of a clot from a blood vessel)
toxi(o)-	poison	toxicosis (poisoning)
trache(o)-	trachea	tracheobronchitis (inflammation of the trachea and bronchi)
ur(o)-	urinary, urine	uropoiesis (formation of urine)
vas(o)-	vessel	vasospasm (spasm of a blood vessel)
ven(i)(o)-	vein	venosclerosis (sclerosis or hardening of the veins)
vesic(o)-	bladder	vesicospinal (pertaining to the urinary bladder and spine)

Common prefixes, roots, and suffixes *(continued)*

Word component	Meanings	Examples
Suffixes		
-algia	pain	neuralgia (nerve pain)
-ectomy	surgical removal	splenectomy (removal of the spleen)
-itis	inflammation	colitis (inflammation of the colon)
-lys(i)(o)	breakdown	fibrinolysis (breakdown of a clot)
-oma	tumor	blastoma (cancer composed of embryonic cells)
-osis	condition	fibrosis (formation of fibrous tissue)
-phob	abnormal fear	agoraphobia (fear of open spaces)
-plasia	growth	hypoplasia (incomplete development)
-plasty	surgical repair	angioplasty (surgical repair of blood vessels)
-plegia	paralysis	paraplegia (paralysis of lower body)
-pnea	breathing	apnea (absence of breathing)
-poiesis	production	hematopoiesis (production of blood cells)
-praxia	movement	apraxia (inability to perform purposeful movement)
-rrhea	fluid discharge	diarrhea (frequent soft or liquid bowel movements)
-scope	observe	endoscope (tool for observing the interior of body organs)
-stomy	opening	colostomy (portion of the colon is opened and brought through the abdominal wall)
-taxis	movement	ataxia (uncoordinated movements)
-tomy	incision	thoracotomy (surgical opening of the chest wall)
-tripsy	crushing	lithotripsy (crushing stones in the bladder, kidney, gallbladder, or other organs)
-trophy	growth	hypertrophy (overgrowth)

Arabic, French, and German) and find their way into English.

Perfect prefix

A prefix is a word component or whole word that attaches to the front of a root. A prefix can drastically change the meaning of a word. For example, the prefix ***extra-*** changes the word *ordinary* into *extraordinary.*

Super suffix

A suffix is a word component that attaches to the end of a root. Among other feats, a suffix can change the form of a word from an adjective, for instance, into an adverb. So you could add the suffix ***-ly*** to *extreme* to make *extremely* (as in *extremely interesting*).

Prefixes and suffixes are important, but focus on the root of the word to get the meaning quickly.

Memory jogger

To remember where a prefix goes and where a suffix goes, you can do two things:

- Think of the word *prefix:* **Pre-** means *before,* so a prefix is a word or word component that's "fixed" to the word "before" the root. If the prefix comes before the root, then the suffix comes afterwards.
- If that doesn't jazz you, just use the alphabet: ***P*** comes before ***S*** in the alphabet, so a prefix comes before a suffix—and before a root, for that matter, which starts with ***R.*** so now you have ***PRS*** (pretty riveting stuff?).

systole
parietal

Vocabulary builders

At a crossroads

Completing this crossword puzzle will help you get to the root of medical vocabulary. Good luck!

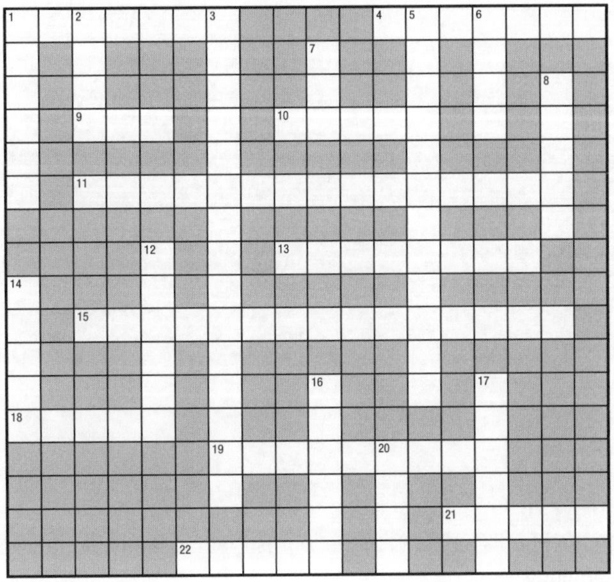

Across

1. Suffix meaning *production*
4. Root for *cancer*
9. Root for *decay*
10. Root for *fat*
11. Suffix in ***splenectomy*** means this (two words)
13. An eponymic maneuver
15. An eponymic speech center in the brain (two words)
18. Root for *male*
19. Root for *eye*
21. Root for *water*
22. Root for *bone*

Down

1. Syllable attached to the beginning of a word
2. Suffix for ***inflammation***
3. ***Pro-*** means this (two words)
5. ***Phobia*** is a root meaning this (two words)
6. Second root in ***erythrocyte*** means this
7. Root of ***pediatric***
8. Meaning of root in 7 down
12. Root for *heart*
14 .Prefix meaning *upon*
16. Prefix meaning *different*
17.Term for a word derived from a person's name
20. Root for *vessel*

Answers are on page 18.

Match game

Match the following roots and prefixes to their correct meanings.

Clues	Choices
1. Super	A. Rapid
2. Tachy	B. Stone
3. Thrombo	C. Above
4. Thermo	D. Large
5. Poly	E. Heat
6. Post	F. After
7. Oxy	G. Clot
8. Mono	H. Oxygen
9. Lith	I. Many
10. Mega	J. One

Finish line

Fill in the blanks below with the words that correctly identify key concepts of medical terminology.

Generally, plural words derived from Latin and Greek are formed by adding or substituting ________ (1) or syllables at the end of the word.

A ________ (2) consists of one or more letters attached to the beginning of a root.

In the word *oliguria*, the prefix ***olig*** means ________ (3).

A ________ (4) is the essential component of a word.

The term *Alzheimer's disease* is an example of an ________ (5).

A ________ (6) is one or more letters attached to the end of a root.

The plural of *pelvis* is ________ (7).

Answers are on page 18.

Talking in circles

Use the clues below to fill in the blanks with the appropriate word. Then unscramble the circled letters to find the answer to the question posed below.

1. ___ (◯) ___ ___ ___ (◯)
2. (◯) ___ ___ ___ ___ ___
3. (◯) ___ ___ ___ ___
4. ___ (◯) ___ (◯)
5. (◯) ___ ___ (◯) ___
6. (◯) ___ (◯) ___ (◯) ___ ___ ___

1. This root means *mental health.*
2. This root means *growth.*
3. This prefix means *backward.*
4. This prefix means *against.*
5. *Stone* is the meaning of this root.
6. If your patient has a sore throat, you may have to use this root and the suffix ***-itis*** to describe the condition.

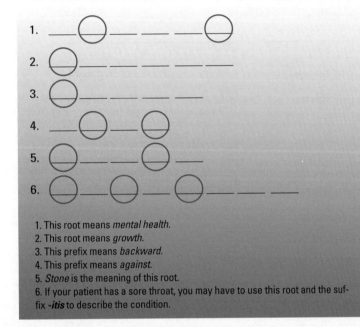

You look like you bumped your nose. Do you know what I think you need?

Answers are on page 18.

Answers

At a crossroads

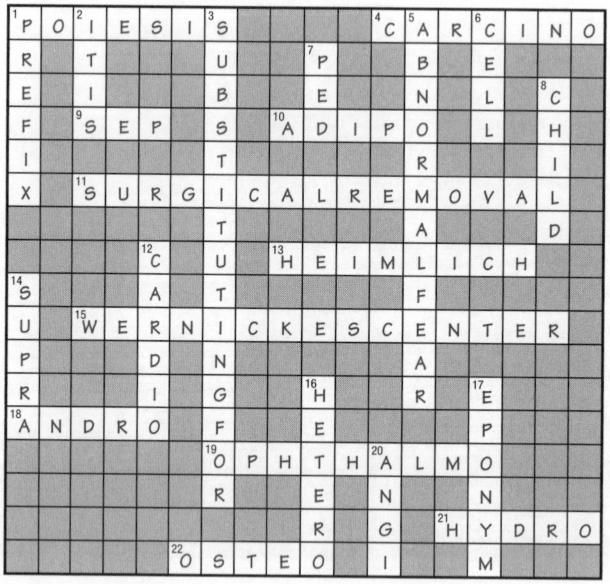
1 POIESIS
4 CARCINO
9 SEP
10 ADIPO
11 SURGICALREMOVAL
13 HEIMLICH
15 WERNICKESCENTER
18 ANDRO
19 OPHTHALMO
21 HYDRO
22 OSTEO
1 PREFIX
2 ITI
3 SUBSTITUTINGFOR
5 ABNORMALFEAR
6 CELL
7 PED
8 CHILD
12 CARDIO
14 SUPRA
16 HETERO
17 EPONYM
20 ANGI

Match game

1. C; 2. A; 3. G; 4. E; 5. I; 6. F; 7. H; 8. J; 9. B; 10. D

Finish line

1. Vowels; 2. Prefix; 3. Little; 4. Root; 5. Eponym; 6. Suffix; 7. Pelves.

Talking in circles

1. Psycho; 2. Trophy; 3. Retro; 4. Anti; 5. Litho; 6. Pharyngo
Answer to puzzle—Rhinoplasty

2

Body structure

Just the facts

In this chapter, you'll learn:

- terminology related to cells, organs, and tissues
- terminology related to the systems of the body
- terminology related to the directions, regions, and positions of the body.

Cells: Nature's building blocks

The cell is the body's basic building block and the smallest living component of an organism. In the late 1600s, British physicist Robert Hooke first observed plant cells with a crude microscope. He decided that the structures reminded him of tiny prison cells—hence the name **cell.** (See *Pronouncing key terms related to the cell*, page 20.)

Cells like me are the basic building blocks of the body.

Specialized units

The human body contains millions of cells grouped into highly specialized units that function together. Large groups of individual cells form tissues, such as muscle, blood, and bone. Tissues in turn form organs, such as the brain, heart, and liver. Organs and tissues are integrated into body systems—such as the central nervous system, cardiovascular system, and digestive system.

A peek inside the cell

Cells are composed of many structures, or **organelles,** that each have a specific function. The word **organelles** is from the neo-Latin word ***organella,*** an altered form of

Pump up your pronunciation

Pronouncing key terms related to the cell

Below is a list of key terms, along with the correct way to pronounce them.

Adenosine	UH-DEEN-OH-SEEN
Cytokinesis	SEYE-TOE-KUH-NEE-SIS
Epithelial	EH-PEH-THEE-LEE-UL
Golgi (as in Golgi apparatus)	GAWL-JEE
Meiosis	MEYE-OH-SIS
Mitochondria	MEYE-TOE-KAHN-DREE-UH
Ribonucleic acid	REYE-BOH-NOO-KLAY-IK AS-ID
Squamous	SKWAY-MUHS

organum, which means *organ.* (See *Just your average cell.*)

Cyto surroundings

Organelles live in **cytoplasm**—an aqueous mass that's surrounded by the cell membrane. ***Cyto-*** is from the Greek root ***kytos,*** which means *container* or *body*; it denotes a relationship to a cell. The **cell membrane,** also called the **plasma membrane,** encloses the cytoplasm and forms the outer boundary of each cell.

Nuclear power

The largest organelle is the **nucleus,** a word derived from the Latin word ***nuculeus,*** which means *kernel.* The nucleus is the control center of the cell. It stores deoxyribonucleic acid (DNA), which carries genetic material and is responsible for cellular reproduction or division.

The typical animal cell is characterized by several additional elements:

Anatomically speaking

Just your average cell

The illustration below shows the components and structures of a cell. Each part has a function in maintaining the cell's life and homeostasis.

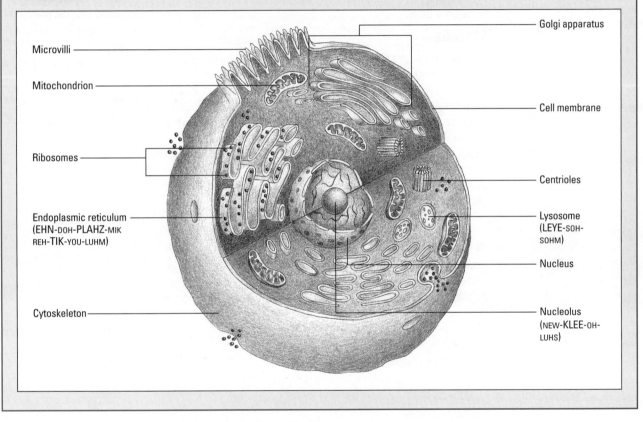

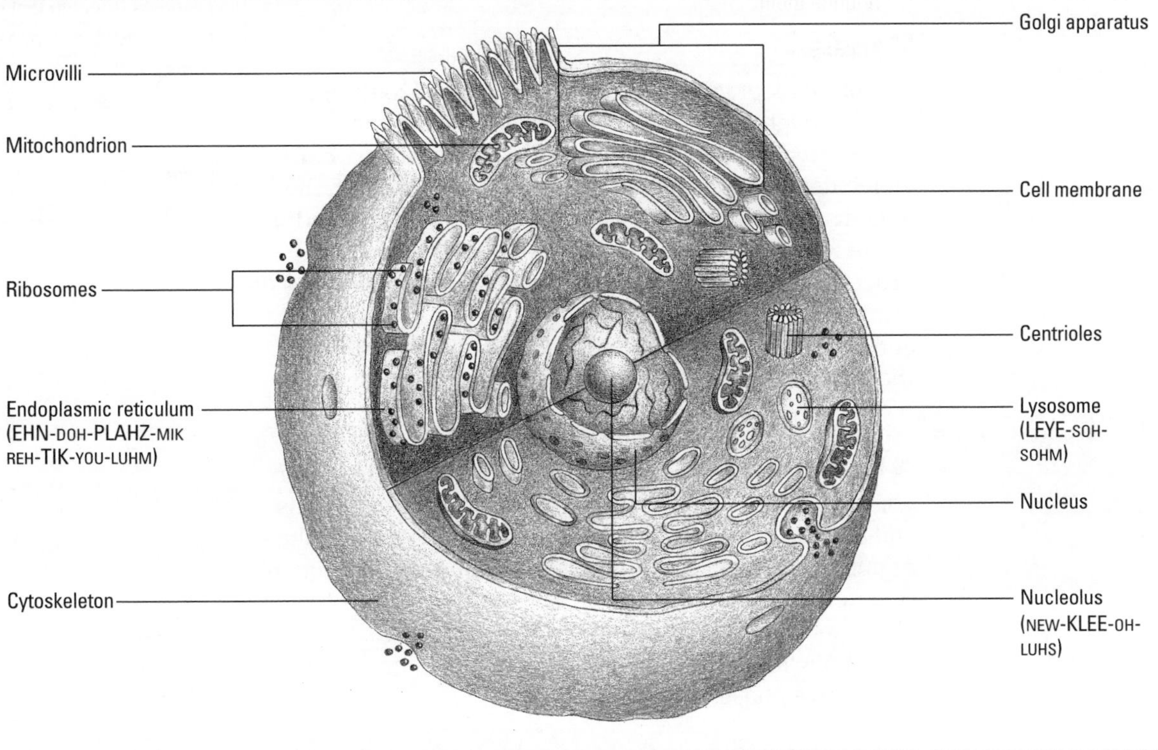
Golgi apparatus
Microvilli
Mitochondrion
Cell membrane
Ribosomes
Centrioles
Endoplasmic reticulum
(EHN-DOH-PLAHZ-MIK
REH-TIK-YOU-LUHM)
Lysosome
(LEYE-SOH-
SOHM)
Nucleus
Cytoskeleton
Nucleolus
(NEW-KLEE-OH-
LUHS)

- **Adenosine triphosphate,** the energy that fuels cellular activity, is made in the **mitochondria,** the cell's power plant.
- **Ribosomes** and the **endoplasmic reticulum** synthesize proteins and metabolize fat within the cell.
- The **Golgi apparatus** holds enzyme systems that assist in completing the cell's metabolic functions.
- **Lysosomes** contain enzymes that allow cytoplasmic digestion. (See *Why call it a lysosome?* page 22.)

Cell division and reproduction

Individual cells are subject to wear and tear and must reproduce quickly to replace themselves. Genetic information passes from one generation of cells to the next in an intricate process that is vital to survival. Mistakes here can lead to lethal genetic disorders, cancer, and other conditions.

Mitosis

All cells except gametes (ova and spermatozoa) reproduce through a process called **mitosis** (from the Greek root ***mitos,*** which means *thread,* with the suffix ***-osis,*** which denotes *an action or state*). During mitosis, the nucleus and genetic material of the cell divide, resulting in the formation of two separate daughter cells. The process is completed when the cell body completes its division (called **cytokinesis,** from the Greek root ***kytos*** and the Greek word ***kinesis,*** which means *movement).* (See *Divide and conquer: Five stages of mitosis.*)

Ready? Set? Divide

Cell division consists of one inactive phase and four active phases. Before a cell can divide, it must double in mass and content. This begins during the inactive growth phase of mitosis, called **interphase.** At this phase, **chromatin** (the network of small, slender rods in the nucleus that give it its glandular appearance) begins to form.

Replication and duplication of DNA occur during the four active phases of mitosis:

- prophase
- metaphase
- anaphase
- telophase.

Prophase

During **prophase,** the chromosomes coil and shorten and the nuclear membrane dissolves. Each chromosome is made up of a pair of strands, called **chromatids.** Chromatids are connected by a spindle of fibers called a **centromere.**

Beyond the dictionary

Why call it a lysosome?

The term **lysosome** comes from the Greek word ***lysis,*** which means *dissolution.* In plain terms, ***lysis*** means *destruction by enzymatic digestion.*

Memory jogger

As a way to remember the processes of mitosis, think of the phrase "I pulled my act together":

Interphase

Prophase

Metaphase

Anaphase

Telophase.

Divide and conquer: Five stages of mitosis

Through the process of mitosis, the nuclear content of all body cells (except gametes) reproduces and divides. The result is the formation of two new daughter cells.

Interphase

During *interphase*, the nucleus and nuclear membrane are well defined, and the nucleolus is visible. As chromosomes replicate, each forms a double strand that remains attached at the center by a centromere.

Prophase

In *prophase*, the nucleolus disappears and the chromosomes become distinct. *Chromatids*, halves of each duplicated chromosome, remain attached by the centromere. Centrioles move to opposite sides of the cell and radiate spindle fibers.

Metaphase

Metaphase occurs when chromosomes line up randomly in the center of the cell between the spindles, along the *metaphase plate.* The centromere of each chromosome then replicates.

Anaphase

Anaphase is characterized by centromeres moving apart, pulling the separate chromatids (now called *chromosomes*) to opposite ends of the cell. The number of chromosomes at each end of the cell equals the original number.

Telophase

During *telophase,* the final stage of mitosis, a nuclear membrane forms around each end of the cell and spindle fibers disappear. The cytoplasm compresses and divides the cell in half. Each new cell contains the diploid (46) number of chromosomes.

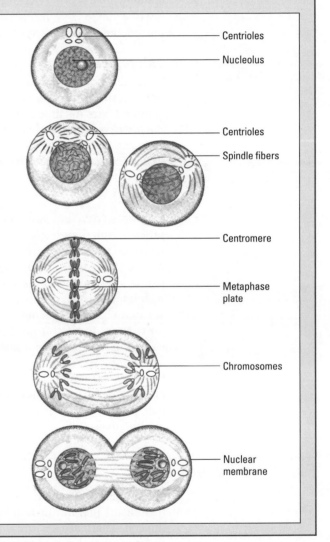

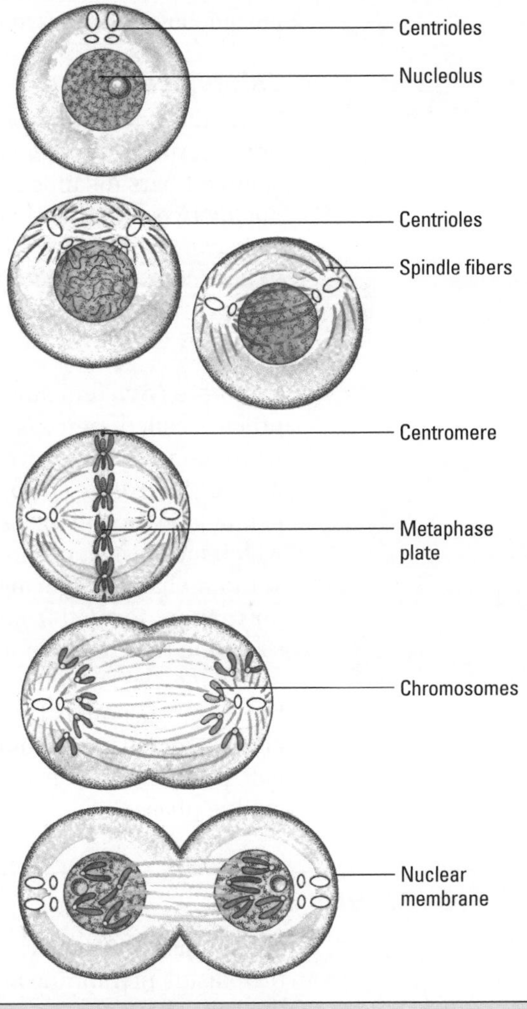
Centrioles
Nucleolus
Centrioles
Spindle fibers
Centromere
Metaphase plate
Chromosomes
Nuclear membrane

Metaphase

During **metaphase,** chromosomes line up in the center of the cell. The centromeres then replicate.

Anaphase

At the onset of **anaphase,** centromeres begin to separate and pull the newly replicated chromosomes toward opposite sides of the cell. The centromere of each chromosome splits to form two new chromosomes, each consisting of a single DNA molecule. By the end of anaphase, 46 chromosomes are present on each side of the cell.

Telophase

In the final step of mitosis—**telophase**—a new membrane forms around each set of 46 chromosomes. The spindle fibers disappear and the cytoplasm divides, producing two new identical "daughter" cells. Each of these cells can grow and develop, perhaps becoming a mother to new cells. (See *Tell me about telophase.*)

> ***Beyond the dictionary***
>
> **Tell me about telophase**
>
> The prefix ***telo-*** in **telophase** is derived from the Greek word ***telos,*** which means *an ultimate end.* Telophase marks the end of mitosis, yielding two daughter cells.

Meiosis

Gametes (**ova** and **spermatozoa**) reproduce through a process called ***meiosis*** (Greek, meaning *lessening*). The word **gamete** comes from the Greek root ***gamet,*** which means either *wife **(gamete)*** or *husband **(gametes)*** depending on its ending. **Ova** is the plural form of **ovum,** which means *egg*; both words come directly from Latin without change. **Spermatozoa** is the plural form of **spermatozoon,** formed from the Greek ***spermat,*** meaning *seed,* and the Greek root ***zôion,*** meaning *animal.*

In meiosis, genetic material between similarly structured chromosomes is intermixed and the number of chromosomes in the four daughter cells diminishes by half. Meiosis consists of two divisions separated by a resting phase.

Fluid movement

A cell must shuttle various molecules in and out through the plasma membrane and between compartments inside the cell. There are several different ways fluids and **solutes** (dissolved substances) move through membranes at the cellular level.

Going with the flow

In **diffusion,** solutes move from an area of higher concentration to an area of lower concentration. This movement eventually results in an equal distribution of solutes within the two areas. Diffusion is known as **passive transport** because no energy is needed to make it happen. Like fish traveling downstream, solutes involved in diffusion just go with the flow.

Letting fluids through

Osmosis (from the Greek root ***osm,*** meaning *to push*, and the Greek suffix ***-sis,*** which is used to form a noun from a word that was originally a verb) is another passive transport method. Unlike diffusion, osmosis involves the movement of a water (solvent) molecule across the cell membrane from a dilute solution, one with a high concentration of water molecules, to a concentrated one, one with a lower concentration of water.

Osmosis is influenced by the **osmotic pressure** of a solution. Osmotic pressure reflects the water-attracting property of a solute. It's determined by the number of dissolved particles in a given volume of solution.

Sometimes you need to work at it. Active transport requires energy, like swimming upstream.

Energy required

Unlike passive transport, **active transport** requires energy. Usually, this mechanism moves a substance from an area of lower concentration to an area of higher concentration. Think of this as swimming upstream. When a fish swims upstream, it uses energy.

Against the grain

The energy required for a solute to move against a concentration gradient comes from a substance produced and stored within the cell, **adenosine triphosphate,** or **ATP.** ATP supplies the energy for solute movement in and out of cells. Some solutes, such as sodium and potassium, use ATP to move in and out of cells in a form of active transport called the **sodium-potassium pump.** Other solutes that require active transport to cross cell membranes include calcium ions, hydrogen ions, amino acids, and certain sugars.

Body tissues: Holding it all together

Tissues are groups of similar cells that perform the same role; each tissue has at least one unique function. Tissues are classified by structure and function and are divided into four types: epithelial, connective, muscle, and nervous.

Epithelial tissue

Epithelial tissue (the **epithelium**) is a continuous cellular sheet that covers the body's surface, lines body cavities, and forms certain glands. It contains at least two types of epithelial cells.

Endothelium and mesothelium

Epithelial tissue with a single layer of squamous cells attached to a basement membrane is called **endothelium.** Such tissue lines the heart, lymphatic vessels, and blood vessels. Tissue that lines the surface of serous membranes, such as the pleura, pericardium, and peritoneum, is called **mesothelium.** Epithelial tissue is classified by the number of cell layers it has and the shape of the cells on its surface.

Layer upon layer

Depending on the number of cell layers, epithelial tissue may be simple or stratified:

- **Simple** epithelial tissue contains one layer of cells.
- **Stratified** epithelial tissue has three or more layers.

Classified by shape

Based on the shape of its surface cells, epithelial tissue may be characterized as squamous, columnar, cuboidal, transitional, or pseudostratified columnar:

- **Squamous** epithelial tissue has flat surface cells.
- **Columnar** epithelial tissue has tall, cylindrical, prism-shaped surface cells.
- **Cuboidal** epithelial tissue has cube-shaped surface cells.
- **Transitional** epithelial tissue has a unique arrangement of cell shapes in a stratified (layered) sheet. This type of tissue can stretch, such as the bladder does when it's full.
- **Pseudostratified columnar** epithelial tissue has one layer of oddly shaped columnar cells.

I swear it's true. The prefix ***pseudo-*** means *false.*

Connective tissue

Connective tissue is classified by structure into one of the following four categories: fibrous, bone, cartilage, or blood. Connective tissue is found in or around almost every organ of the body. Its function is to support, connect, and transport.

Fibrous

Fibrous tissue can be dense, loose, or adipose.

Cut loose

Loose connective tissue has large spaces that separate the fibers and cells. It contains much intercellular fluid.

Dense support

Dense connective tissue provides structural support. It has a greater fiber concentration.

Who are you calling fat?

Adipose tissue (fat) is a specialized type of loose connective tissue in which a single fat droplet occupies most of the cell. It cushions internal organs and acts as a reserve supply of energy. (See *Where* adipose *comes from.*)

Beyond the dictionary

Where *adipose* comes from

Adipose tissue is sometimes referred to as fat. The word **adipose** is derived from ***adiposus,*** a word with Greek and Latin origins: the Latin prefix ***adip-*** and the Greek root ***aleipha,*** which mean *fat* or *oil.*

Bone

Bone is hard, dense tissue with a calcified matrix.

Cartilage

Cartilage is a flexible matrix with a gristlelike gel.

Blood

Blood is a liquid matrix that contains red and white blood cells.

Muscle tissue

The three basic types of **muscle tissue** are striated, cardiac, and smooth.

Striated muscle tissue

Striated muscle tissue gets its name from the striped, or striated, appearance it has when viewed under a microscope. All striated muscle tissue capable of voluntary contraction is called **skeletal muscle tissue.**

Cardiac and smooth muscle tissue

Cardiac muscle tissue is striated but it contracts involuntarily. **Smooth** muscle tissue lacks the striped pattern of striated tissue; it consists of long, spindle-shaped cells.

Its activity is stimulated by the autonomic nervous system and isn't under voluntary control. Smooth muscle tissue lines the wall of many internal organs and other structures, such as the walls of arteries and veins.

Check out my dendrites. They receive and conduct impulses.

Nervous tissue

The main function of **nervous tissue** is communication. Its primary properties are **irritability** (the capacity to react to various physical and chemical agents) and **conductivity** (the ability to transmit the resulting reaction from one point to another). Nervous tissue cells may be neurons or neuroglia.

Neurons consist of three parts: dendrites, the cell body, and axons. Like tiny antennas, **dendrites** receive impulses and conduct them into the cell body. **Axons** carry impulses away from the cell body.

Neuroglia form the support structure of nervous tissue, insulating and protecting neurons. They're found only in the central nervous system.

Organs and systems: The specialists

When a group of tissues handles a more complicated task than any one tissue could perform alone, they're called **organs.**

Organs combine to form **systems,** which perform a more complex function than any one organ can manage on its own. The body depends on these systems in the following ways:

- The **immune system** protects the body from disease and invading organisms.
- The **nervous system** and **sensory system** process incoming information and allow the body to respond.
- Reproduction and urine excretion are managed by the **genitourinary system.**
- The **gastrointestinal system** digests and absorbs food and excretes waste products.
- Blood is transported by the **cardiovascular system.**
- The **respiratory system** maintains the exchange of oxygen and carbon dioxide in the lungs and tissues and regulates acid-base balance.

- The **integumentary system**—which includes skin, hair, nails, and sweat glands—protects the body and helps regulate body temperature. (See *Why call it* integumentary?)
- The **muscular system** allows the body to move.
- The **skeletal system** supports the body and gives muscles a place to attach.
- The **endocrine system** consists of glands that secrete regulating chemicals called **hormones.**
- The **circulatory system** consists of the heart and blood vessels. Oxygen and other nutrients are transported throughout the body via this system.
- The **reproductive system** includes the organs of reproduction, such as the gonads (testes in the male and ovaries in the female), which produce germ cells and manufacture hormones.

Beyond the dictionary

Why call it *integumentary?*

It's easy to see why **integumentary** is the term for a body system that includes the hair, skin, nails, and sweat glands. The origin of this word is the Latin word ***integumentum,*** which means *to cover.*

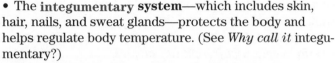

Directions, regions, and positions

Determining directions within the body is essential to accurately pinpoint the locations of structures. Terms that describe body planes, cavities, and regions are also useful.

Giving directions

Specific terms are used to define the relationship between body areas and the locations of structures. These terms describe the body in **anatomic position**—standing erect with arms hanging to the side, and palms facing forward:

- **Superior** means *above;* for example, the knees are superior to the ankles.
- **Inferior** means *below;* for example, the feet are inferior to the ankles.
- **Anterior** means *front* or *in front of;* for example, the sternum is an anterior structure. **Ventral** is sometimes used instead of anterior.
- **Posterior** means *back* or *in back of;* for example, the spine is a posterior structure. **Dorsal** may be used instead of posterior.
- **Medial** (midline) means *toward the center.*
- **Central** means *in the center.*
- **Peripheral** means *away from the center.*
- **Lateral** refers to the sides, or *away from the midline.*
- **Proximal** means *nearest to.*

- **Distal** describes a point farthest from the point of origin.
- **Superficial** describes a point nearest the body surface.
- **Deep** means *away from the surface.*

Body planes and sections

The body is theoretically divided into three areas called the sagittal, the frontal (coronal), and the transverse planes. (See *Body reference planes.*)

Sagittal plane

The **sagittal plane** runs lengthwise from front to back and divides the body into right and left sides. A **median sagittal** cut produces two equal halves, each containing an arm and a leg. (Don't try this at home!)

Plainly speaking, the body is divided into three planes: sagittal, frontal, and transverse.

Frontal plane

The **frontal plane** runs lengthwise from side to side, dividing the body into **ventral** and **dorsal** (front and back) sections.

Transverse plane

The **transverse plane,** also called the **horizontal plane,** cuts the body into upper and lower parts. These are known as the **cranial** (head) and the **caudal** (tail) portions.

Body cavities

A **cavity** is a hollow space within the body that usually houses vital organs. The two major cavities are the ventral cavity and the dorsal cavity. They're divided into smaller spaces for the internal organs. (See *Locating body cavities*, page 32.)

Ventral cavity

The **ventral cavity** contains the thoracic (chest) cavity and the abdominopelvic cavity. The **thoracic cavity,** located above the diaphragm, contains the heart, lungs, and large blood vessels that join the heart. The **abdominopelvic**

Body reference planes

Body reference planes are used to indicate the locations of body structures. Here are the median sagittal, the frontal, and the transverse planes, which lie at right angles to one another.

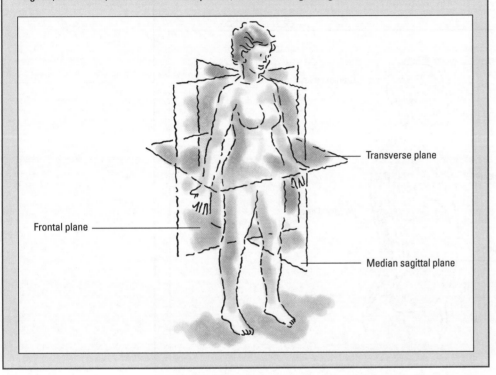

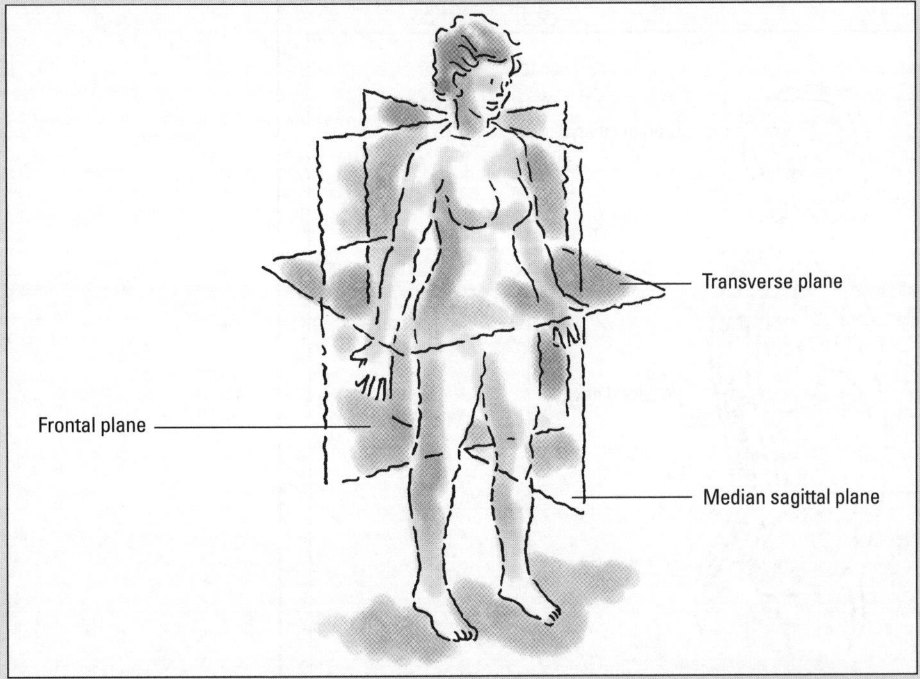
Transverse plane
Frontal plane
Median sagittal plane

cavity, located below the diaphragm, consists of the **abdominal cavity** (stomach, most of the intestines, kidneys, liver, gallbladder, pancreas, and spleen) and the **pelvic cavity** (urinary bladder, rectum, and internal parts of the reproductive system).

Dorsal cavity

The **dorsal cavity** includes both the cranial and spinal cavities:

- The **cranial cavity** is relatively small; it houses and protects the brain.
- The **spinal cavity** contains the spinal column and spinal cord.

Locating body cavities

The dorsal cavity, in the posterior region of the body, is divided into the cranial and vertebral cavities. The ventral cavity, in the anterior region, is divided into the thoracic and abdominopelvic cavities.

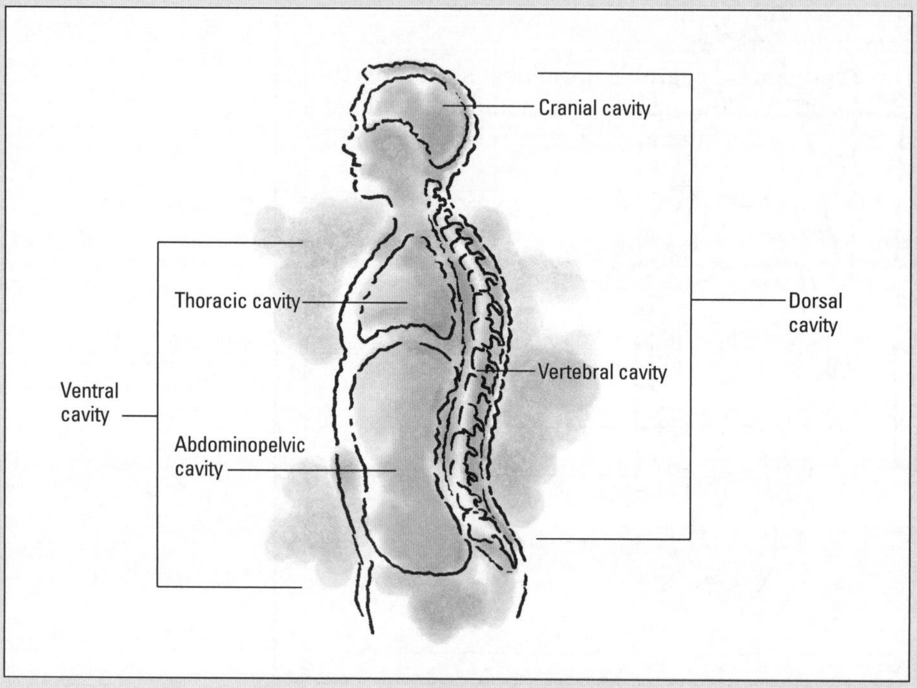
Cranial cavity
Thoracic cavity
Dorsal cavity
Vertebral cavity
Ventral cavity
Abdominopelvic cavity

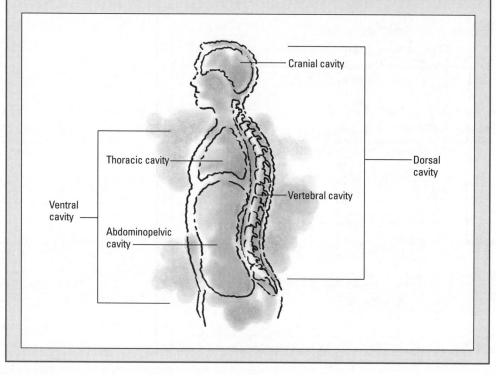

Abdominal regions

So many organs and structures lie inside the abdominal and pelvic cavities that special terms are used to pinpoint different areas. Nine regions are identified from right to left and top to bottom:

- The **right hypochondriac region** contains the right side of the liver, the right kidney, and a portion of the diaphragm.
- The **epigastric region** contains the pancreas and portions of the stomach, liver, inferior vena cava, abdominal aorta, and duodenum.
- The **left hypochondriac region** contains a portion of the diaphragm, the spleen, the stomach, the left kidney, and part of the pancreas.

- The **right lumbar region** contains portions of the large intestines and the right kidney.
- The **umbilical region** contains sections of the small and large intestines and a portion of the left kidney.
- The **left lumbar region** contains portions of the small and large intestines and a portion of the left kidney.
- The **right iliac (inguinal) region** includes portions of the small and large intestines.
- The **hypogastric region's** prominent structures include a portion of the sigmoid colon, the urinary bladder and ureters, and portions of the small intestine.
- The **left iliac (inguinal) region** contains portions of the small and large intestines. (See *Anterior view of the abdominal regions*, page 34.)

Positions

Patients may be placed in several positions for examination, testing, and treatment. (See *Picturing positions*, page 35.) These positions are described by many terms. The most frequently used include:

- **Fowler's**—head of bed raised 45 to 60 degrees, with knees slightly flexed
- **lateral recumbent,** or **Sims'**—lying on the left side with the right thigh and knee drawn up
- **lithotomy**—lying on the back with the hips and knees flexed and the thighs abducted and externally rotated
- **supine**—lying flat on the back
- **prone**—lying face down
- **Trendelenburg's**—lying flat with the head lower than the body and legs
- **knee-chest**—on knees with the chest resting on the bed.

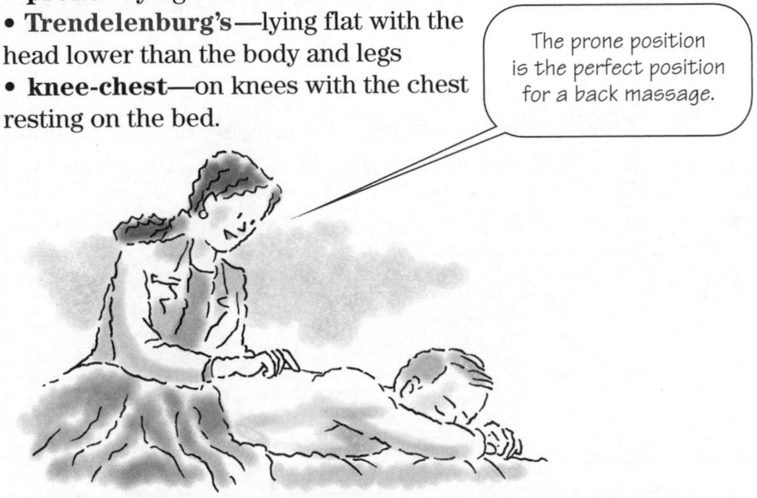
The prone position is the perfect position for a back massage.

Anterior view of the abdominal regions

This illustration shows the abdominal regions from the front.

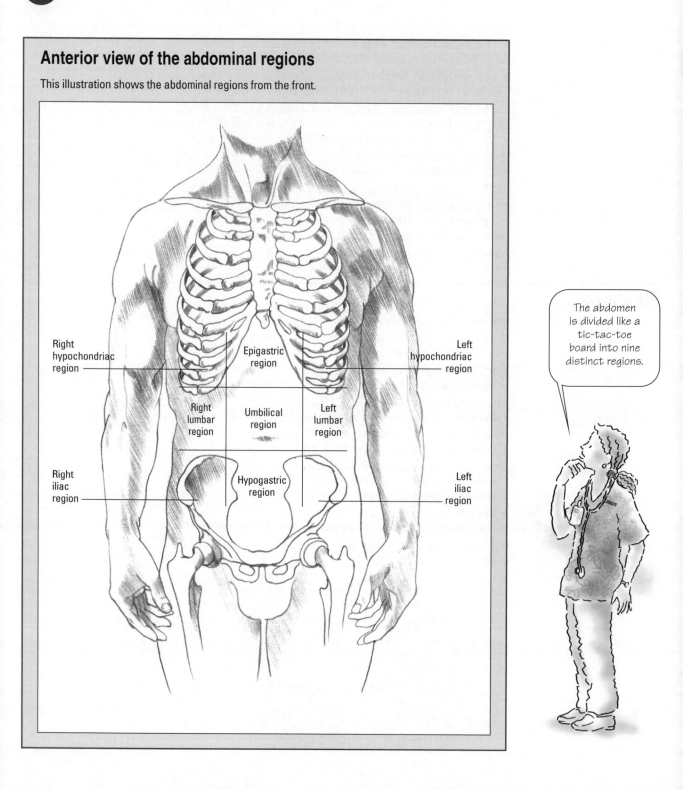

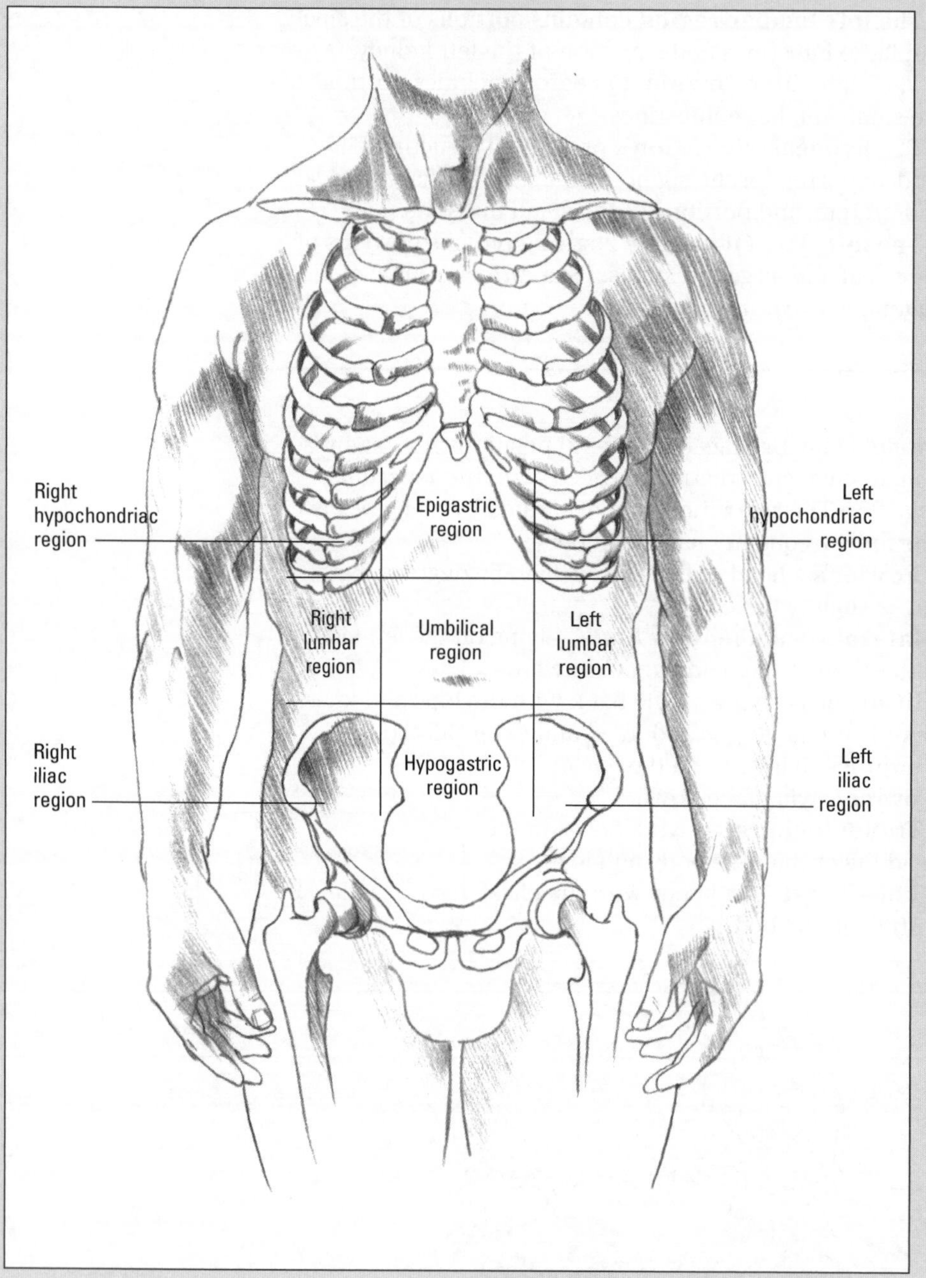
Right hypochondriac region
Epigastric region
Left hypochondriac region
Right lumbar region
Umbilical region
Left lumbar region
Right iliac region
Hypogastric region
Left iliac region

The abdomen is divided like a tic-tac-toe board into nine distinct regions.

Picturing positions

The illustrations below depict the various positions that the patient may be placed in for examinations, testing, and treatments.

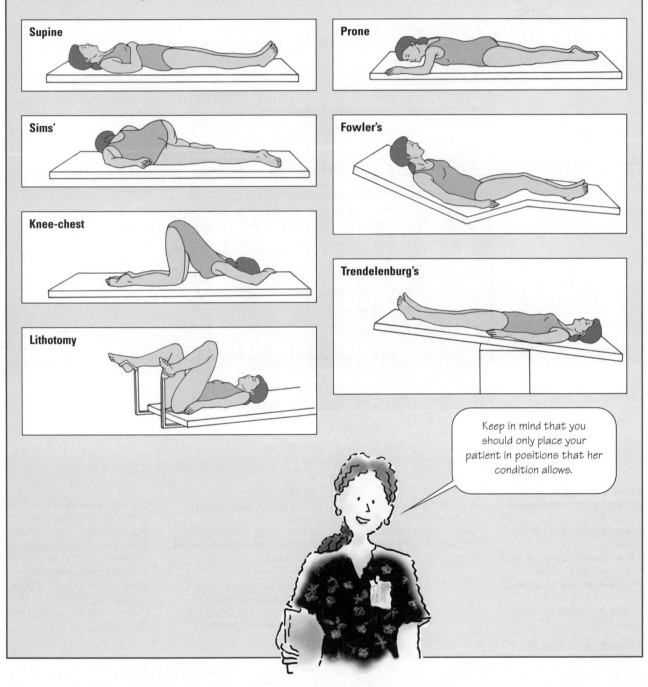

Supine

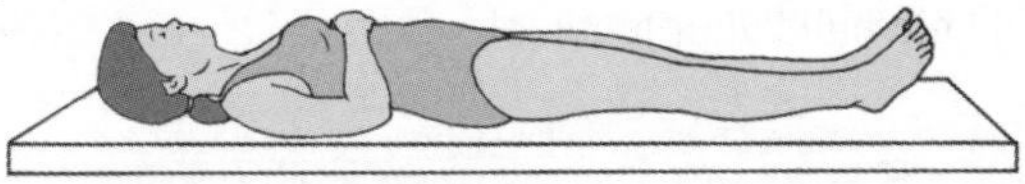

Prone

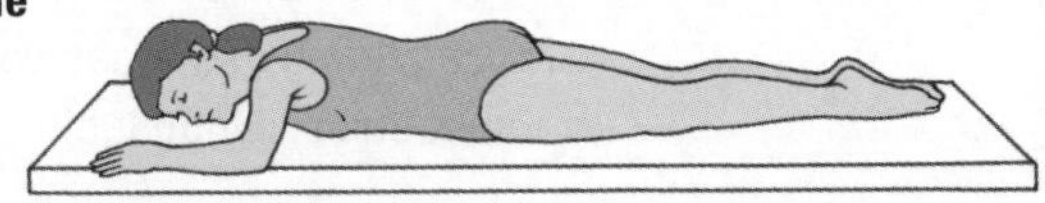

Sims'

Fowler's

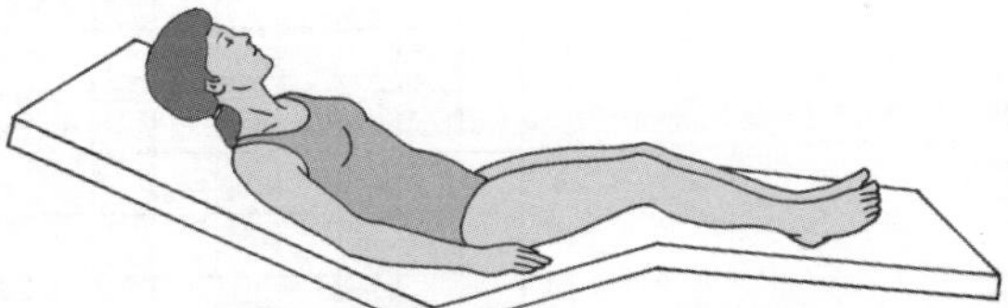

Knee-chest

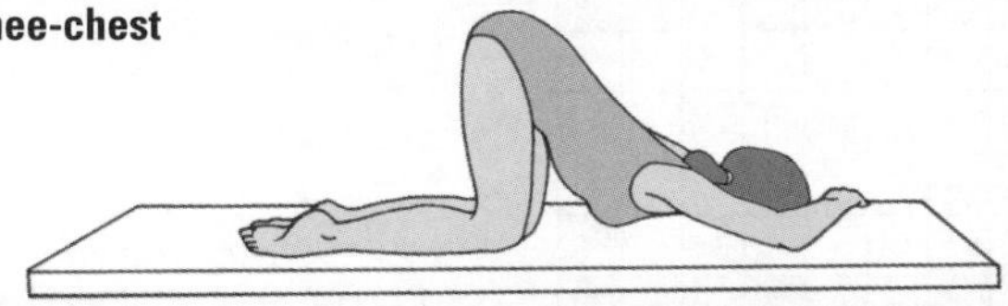

Trendelenburg's

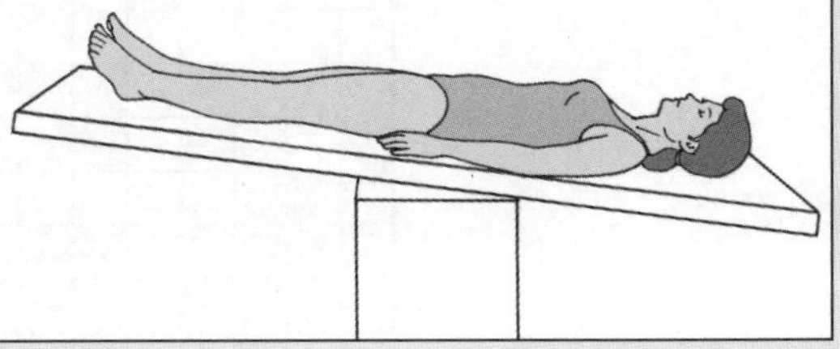

Lithotomy

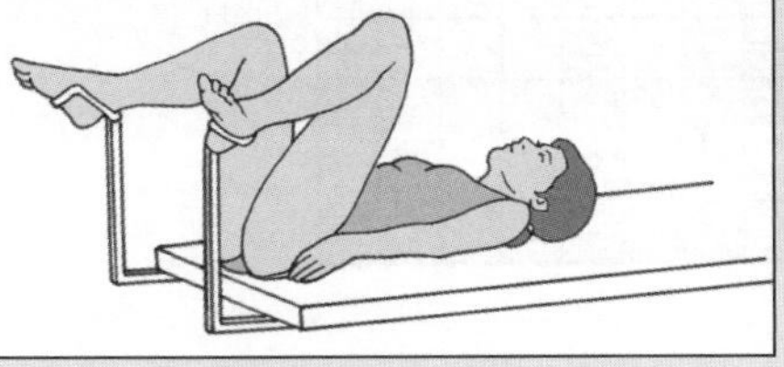

Keep in mind that you should only place your patient in positions that her condition allows.

systole

Vocabulary builders

At a crossroads

Completing this crossword puzzle will help build your medical vocabulary. Good luck!

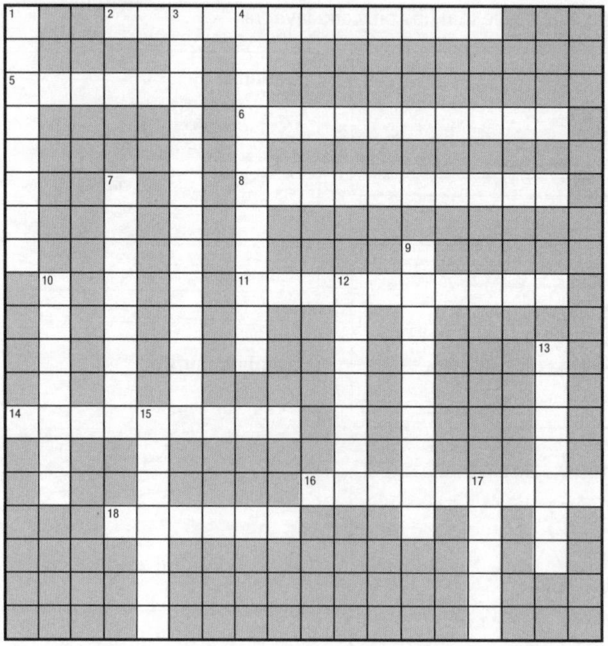

Across

2. Site of adenosine triphosphate production
5. Only type of cell that undergoes meiosis
6. Name for the structures of a cell
8. Growth phase of mitosis
11. Type of epithelial tissue that has three or more layers
14. Support structure of nervous tissue
16. The final step of mitosis
18. Eponym for a position in which the head of the bed is raised and the patient's knees are slightly flexed

Down

1. One of three body reference planes
3. Eponym for a position in which the patient's head is lower than his body or legs
4. Cell movement
7. Word that means *in front of*
9. When solutes move from an area of higher concentration to an area of lower concentration
10. Largest organelle
12. Type of tissue in which a fat droplet occupies most of the cell
13. Process of cell division from the Greek word for *thread*
15. Passive transport method whose root comes from the Greek word meaning *to push*
17. Physicist to first coin the term *cell*

Answers are on page 40.

Match game

Tissues are groups of similar cells that perform the same role. Each tissue also has at least one unique function. Match each clue to the correct type of tissue.

Clues

1. Tissue that lines the surface of serous membranes, such as the pleura, pericardium, and peritoneum
2. Epithelial tissue that has only one layer of cells but appears to have more
3. Tissue that has cube-shaped surface cells
4. Tissue that has large spaces that separate the fibers and cells and contains a lot of intercellular fluid
5. Tissue with a striped appearance
6. Nervous tissue that consists of three parts: dendrites, cell body, and axons

Choices

A. Loose connective
B. Mesothelium
C. Neurons
D. Pseudostratified
E. Cuboidal
F. Striated muscle

Knowing the different tissue types brings you one step closer to mastering anatomy.

Answers are on page 40.

O see, can you say?

Sound out each group of pictures and symbols below to reveal a term that was reviewed in the chapter.

1.

M
DRIA

2.

S
KUH

3.

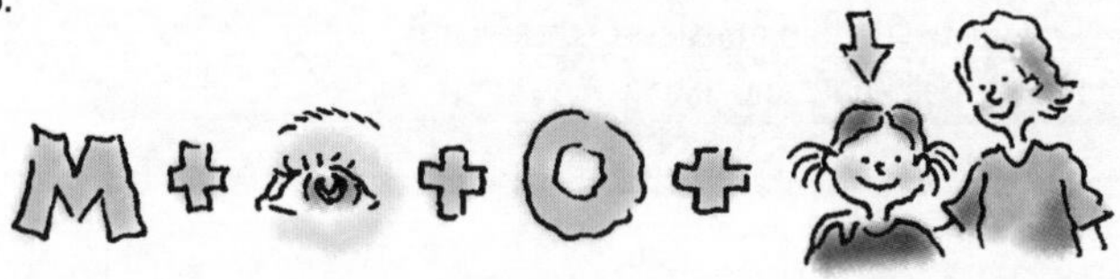
M
O

This is easy! Even long, medical words are simply a sum of their parts.

Answers are on page 40.

Talking in circles

Use the clues below to fill in the blanks with the appropriate word. Then unscramble the circled letters to find the answer to the question posed below.

1. __ (◯) __ __ __ __ __ __ __
2. (◯) __ __ (◯) __ __ __
3. __ __ __ __ __ (◯) __ __ __
4. __ __ __ __ __ __ (◯)
5. (◯) __ __ __ __ __ __ __
6. __ __ (◯) __ __ (◯)

1. This is an aqueous mass that is surrounded by the cell membrane.
2. Only gametes (ova and spermatozoa) undergo this type of reproduction.
3. Particles or solutes move from an area of higher concentration to an area of lower concentration in this type of movement.
4. The cavity that houses and protects the brain.
5. This plane runs lengthwise front to back and divides the body into right and left sides.
6. This prefix means *false.*

I'm hungry...and I need something other than a knife and fork! Which organelle is responsible for helping me digest foreign material?

Answers are on page 40.

Answers

At a crossroads

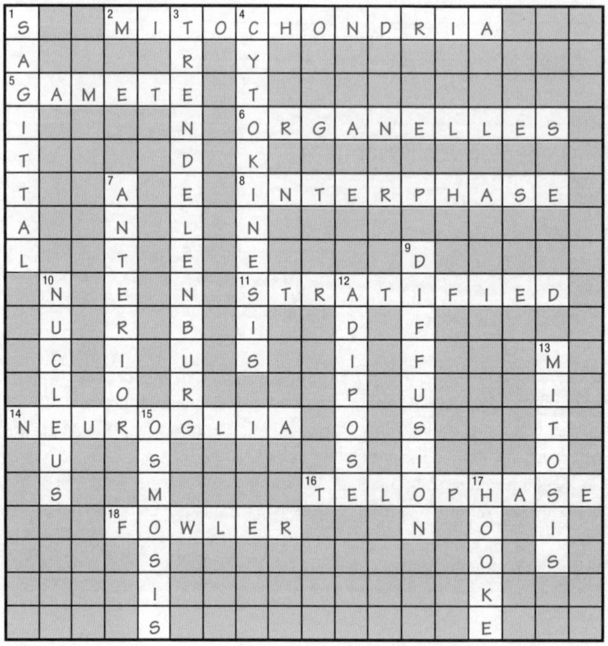
1 SAGITTAL
2 MITOCHONDRIA
3 TRENDELENBURG
4 CYTOKINESIS
5 GAMETE
6 ORGANELLES
7 ANTERIOR
8 INTERPHASE
9 DIFFUSION
10 NUCLEUS
11 STRATIFIED
12 ADIPOSE
13 MITOSIS
14 NEUROGLIA
15 OSMOSIS
16 TELOPHASE
17 HOOKE
18 FOWLER

Match game

1. B; 2. D; 3. E; 4. A; 5. F; 6. C

O see, can you say?

1. Mitochondria; 2. Cytokinesis; 3. Meiosis

Talking in circles

1. Cytoplasm; 2. Meiosis; 3. Diffusion; 4. Cranial; 5. Sagittal; 6. Pseudo
Answer to puzzle—Lysosome

3

Skeletal system

Just the facts

In this chapter, you'll learn:

- terminology related to the anatomy of the skeletal system
- terminology needed for physical examination of the skeletal system
- tests that help diagnose skeletal system disorders
- disorders of the skeletal system and their treatments.

Anatomy of the skeleton

The 206 bones of the skeletal system carry out six important anatomic and physiologic functions:

1. They protect internal tissues and organs; for example, the 33 vertebrae surround and protect the spinal cord, brain, and heart.

2. They stabilize and support the body.

3. They provide surfaces for muscle, ligament, and tendon attachment.

4. They move through lever action when contracted.

5. They produce red blood cells (RBCs) in the bone marrow (a process called **hematopoiesis,** from the Greek ***haima,*** or blood, and ***poiesis,*** meaning *making* or *forming*).

6. They store mineral salts; for example, approximately 99% of the body's calcium. (See *Pronouncing key skeletal terms*, page 42.)

Pump up your pronunciation

Pronouncing key skeletal terms

Below is a list of key terms, along with the correct way to pronounce them.

Acetabulum	AS-UH-TAH-BYOU-LUHM
Arthrocentesis	AR-THROH-SEN-TEE-SIS
Arthrodesis	AR-THROD-UH-SIS
Astragalus	AS-TRAG-UH-LUHS
Calcaneus	KAL-KAY-NEE-UHS
Canaliculi	KAN-UH-LIK-YOU-LEYE
Cartilaginous	KAR-TUH-LAJ-UH-NUHS
Coccyx	KOK-SIKS
Costochondritis	KOS-TOH-KON-DREYE-TIS
Hematopoiesis	HEE-MUH-TOE-POY-EE-SIS
Hyaline	HEYE-UH-LIN
Kyphosis	KEYE-FOH-SIS
Lambdoid	LAM-DOYD
Malleolus	MAH-LEE-OH-LUHS
Medullary	MED-UH-LAIR-EE
Occipital	OK-SIP-UH-TUHL
Periosteum	PER-EE-OS-TEE-UHM
Xiphoid process	ZEYE-FOYD PRAH-SESS

Bones-r-us

The skeleton is divided into two parts: the **axial** (from the Latin ***axis,*** meaning *axle* or *wheel*) and **appendicular** (from the Latin ***appendare,*** meaning to *add* or *append*). The **axial skeleton** forms the body's vertical axis and contains 74 bones in the head and torso; it also includes 6 bones of the middle ear, for a total of 80 bones. (See *The body's bones.*)

Anatomically speaking

The body's bones

The human skeleton contains 206 bones; 80 form the axial skeleton and 126 form the appendicular skeleton. The illustrations below show some of the major bones and bone groups.

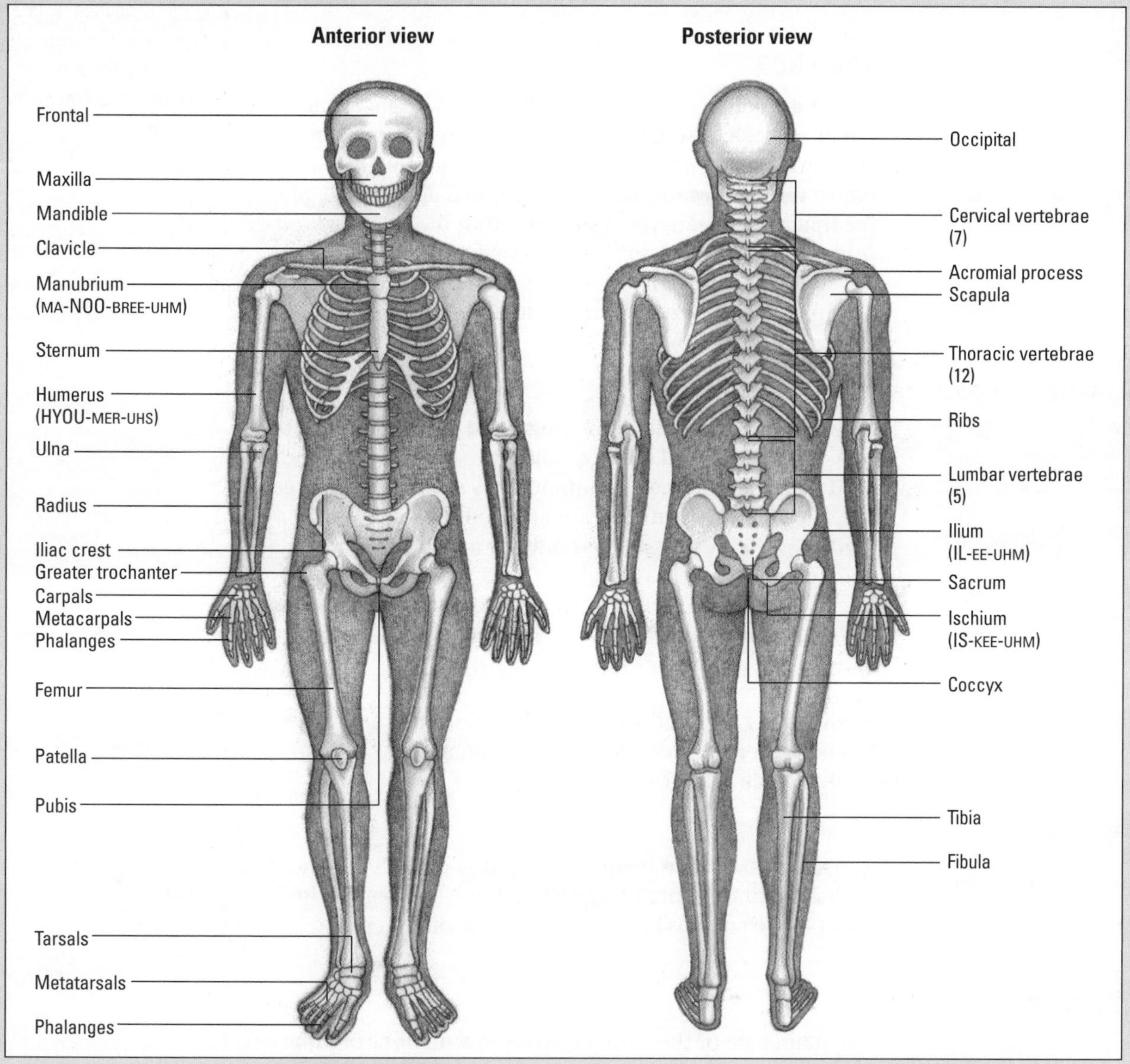
Anterior view
Posterior view
Frontal
Maxilla
Mandible
Clavicle
Manubrium (MA-NOO-BREE-UHM)
Sternum
Humerus (HYOU-MER-UHS)
Ulna
Radius
Iliac crest
Greater trochanter
Carpals
Metacarpals
Phalanges
Femur
Patella
Pubis
Tarsals
Metatarsals
Phalanges
Occipital
Cervical vertebrae (7)
Acromial process
Scapula
Thoracic vertebrae (12)
Ribs
Lumbar vertebrae (5)
Ilium (IL-EE-UHM)
Sacrum
Ischium (IS-KEE-UHM)
Coccyx
Tibia
Fibula

The **appendicular skeleton** contains 126 bones and includes the body's **appendages,** or upper and lower extremities.

The axial skeleton

The axial skeleton forms the long axis of the body and includes bones of the skull, vertebral column, and rib cage.

The skull

The **skull** contains 28 irregular bones in two major areas: the brain case, or **cranium** (from the Greek ***kranion,*** meaning *upper part of the head*), and the **face.** Eight bones form the cranium, 14 bones make up the face, and the inner ears contain 6 **ossicles** (from the Latin ***ossiculum,*** meaning *bone*), or 3 small bones in each ear. The jaw bone, or **mandible** (from the Latin ***mandibula,*** meaning *jaw*) is the only movable bone in the skull. (See *Bones of the skull.*)

Getting it together

Sutures are immobile joints that hold the skull bones together. The **coronal suture** unites the frontal bone and the two parietal bones. In infants, this suture isn't closed, leaving a diamond-shaped area (called the **anterior fontanel**), which is covered only by a membrane. This soft spot closes between ages 10 and 18 months. At the back of the head of infants, the **posterior fontanel** closes by age 2 months. (See *Little fountain.*)

A real airhead

Sinuses are air-filled spaces within the skull that lessen the bone weight, moisten incoming air, and act as resonating chambers for the voice.

Up front

The sinuses, the forehead, and the area directly behind it are part of the **frontal bone.** This bone also forms the **orbits** (eye sockets) and the front part of the cranial floor.

Take it from the top

The main part of the skull consists of a number of bones sutured together:

Beyond the dictionary

Little fountain

Fontanel, also spelled ***fontanelle,*** derives from French and means *little fountain.* It can also refer to any membrane-covered area between two bones.

- The **coronal suture** connects the frontal bone with the parietal bones.
- Two **parietal bones** crown the head, forming the roof and the upper part of each side of the skull.
- The **squamous suture** connects the parietal bones with the temporal bones.
- **Temporal bones** form the lower part of the sides of the skull and part of its floor. They contain structures of the middle and inner ear and the **mastoid sinuses**.

Anatomically speaking

Bones of the skull

The skull is a complex bony structure. It's formed by two sets of bones, the cranial bones and the facial bones.

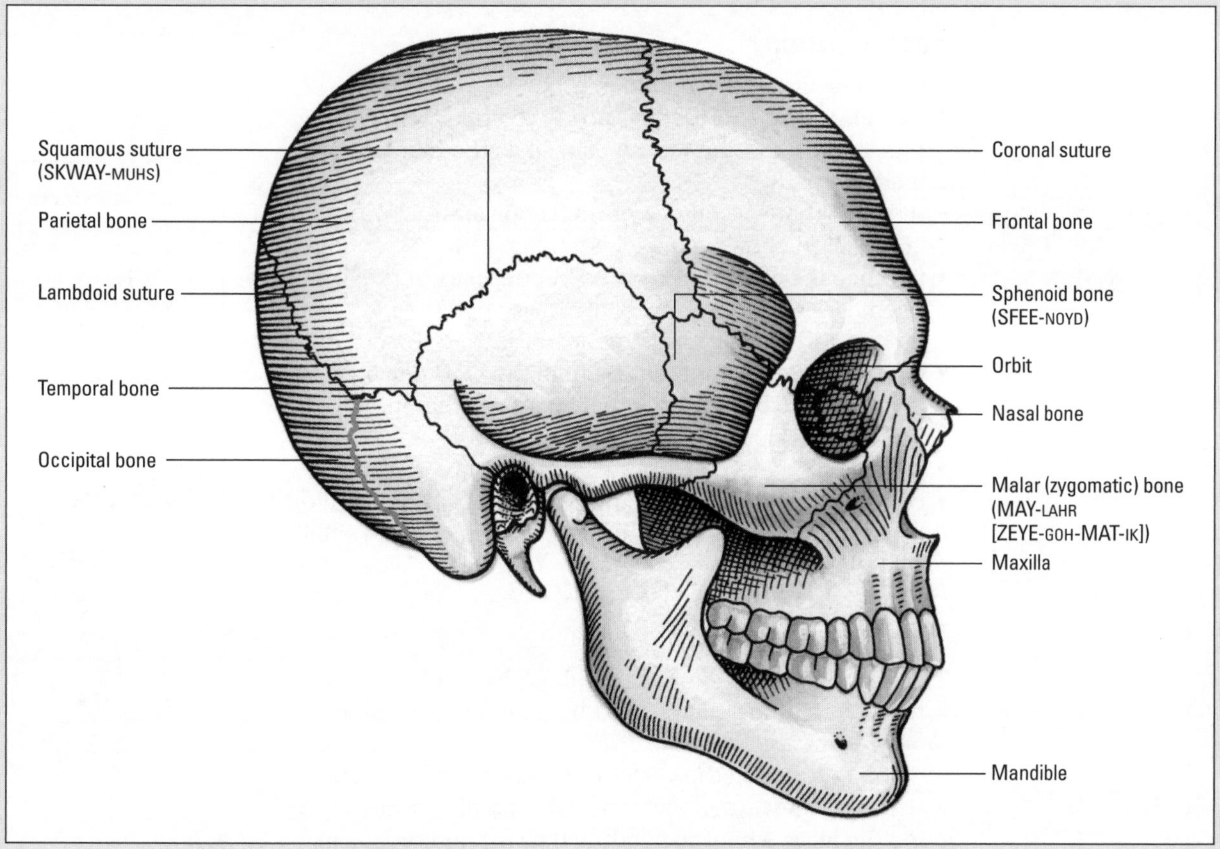
Squamous suture
(SKWAY-MUHS)
Parietal bone
Lambdoid suture
Temporal bone
Occipital bone
Coronal suture
Frontal bone
Sphenoid bone
(SFEE-NOYD)
Orbit
Nasal bone
Malar (zygomatic) bone
(MAY-LAHR
[ZEYE-GOH-MAT-IK])
Maxilla
Mandible

• The **lambdoid suture** connects the parietal bones to the occipital bone.
• The **occipital bone** forms the rear portion and the base of the skull and forms a movable joint with the first cervical vertebra.
• A large opening at the base of the occipital bone, called the **foramen magnum** (meaning *large hole*), allows the spinal cord to pass from the encephalon into the spine.

Memory jogger

As a way to remember the bones of the skull, use your head and think "part of man":

PARietal

Temporal

Occipital

Frontal

MAlar

Nasal.

A bat in the belfry

The **sphenoid bone** looks like a bat with outstretched wings and legs extended to the back. Located in the cranial floor, this bone is an anchor for the frontal, parietal, occipital, and ethmoid bones. It also supports part of the eye sockets and forms the lateral walls of the skull. The **sphenoid sinuses** are large air-filled spaces within the sphenoid bone.

Facial bones

The bones of the face include:
• two **maxillary bones** that form the upper jaw, nose, orbits, and roof of the mouth as well as the **maxillary sinuses**
• the cheekbones, called **zygomatic** or **malar bones,** that attach to chewing muscles
• two **nasal bones** that form the upper part of the bridge of the nose (**cartilage** forms the lower part)
• the **mandible** that forms the lower jaw
• two **lacrymal bones** that contain the lacrymal bag (part of the conduit through which tears drain in the nasal cannula)
• the **vomer** that's part of the nasal septum
• two **palatine bones** that form the posterior portion of the hard palate, lateral side of the nasal cavity, and small part of the orbit.

Joints between the vertebrae allow forward, backward, and sideways movement. Not all at once, though!

The spinal column

The flexible spinal column contains 24 **vertebrae** (plural of **vertebra**), the **sacrum**, and the **coccyx.** (See *Some thorny words of the spine.*)

Joints between the vertebrae allow forward, backward, and sideways movement. The spinal column supports the head while suspending the ribs and organs in

Beyond the dictionary

Some thorny words of the spine

Spine comes from the Latin word ***spina,*** which means *thorn,* and is related to **spike** as well. Latin writers likened the thorn to the prickly bones in animals and fish and, thus, the word also became the designation for the vertebral column.

Vertebra and spondylo

Also from Latin, ***vertebra*** derives from a verb meaning *to turn.* Therefore, it formerly connoted any joint—not just those of the spine. A Greek word, ***spondylos,*** has the same meaning as **vertebra.** It shows up in words like **spondylitis,** which is an inflammation of the vertebrae.

Sacrum and coccyx bringing up the rear

The **sacrum** was formerly known as the **os sacrum,** literally the *holy bone,* so called because it was thought to be a particularly choice bit and so was offered to the gods in sacrifice. The **coccyx** derives its name from the Greek word for the cuckoo, ***kokkyx.*** The Greek anatomist Galen thought this triangular bone resembled the shape of the bird's bill.

front. It also anchors the pelvic girdle and provides attachment points for many important muscles. The spinal column contains:

- seven **cervical** (neck) vertebrae, which support the skull and rotate
- twelve **thoracic** (chest) vertebrae, which attach to the ribs
- five **lumbar** (lower back) vertebrae, which support the small of the back
- the **sacrum,** a single bone that results from the fusion of five vertebrae and attaches to the pelvic girdle
- the **coccyx,** or tailbone, which is located at the bottom tip of the spinal column and is a single bone formed from the fusion of four or five vertebrae.

The spinal column is curved to increase its strength and make balance possible in an upright position. The vertebrae are cushioned by intervertebral disks composed of cartilage. (See *A look at the spinal column,* page 48.)

Anatomically speaking

A look at the spinal column

The 33 vertebrae of the spinal column surround and protect the spinal cord. They're divided into five sections: cervical vertebrae, thoracic vertebrae, lumbar vertebrae, sacrum, and coccyx.

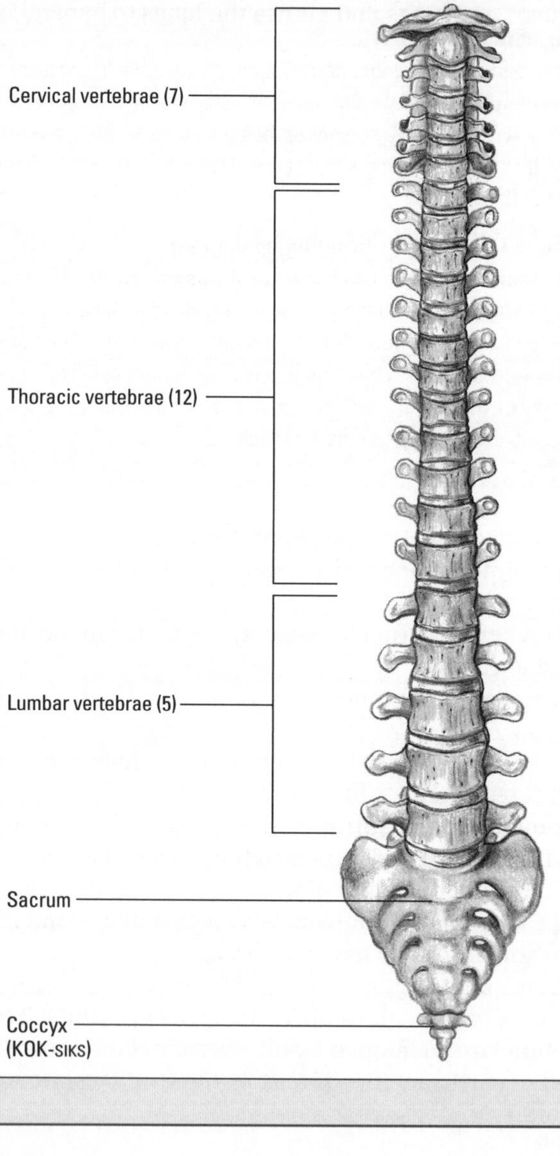
Cervical vertebrae (7)
Thoracic vertebrae (12)
Lumbar vertebrae (5)
Sacrum
Coccyx
(KOK-siks)

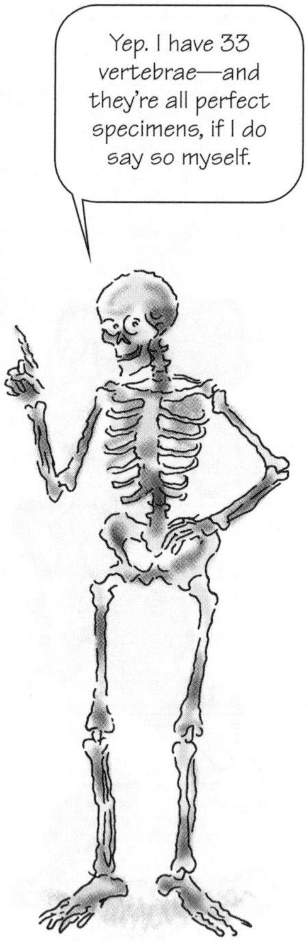
Yep. I have 33 vertebrae—and they're all perfect specimens, if I do say so myself.

Sternum

Located in the center of the chest, the **sternum** is a flat, sword-shaped bone that's attached to the **clavicles** (collarbones) and the innermost part of the first two pairs of ribs.

Caged in

The sternum, ribs, and thoracic vertebrae form a protective enclosure around the vital organs. Known as the **thoracic cage,** or **thorax,** this flexible structure protects the heart and lungs and allows the lungs to expand during respiration.

Ribs

The flat, curved bones attached to the thoracic portion of the spinal column are called **ribs.**

Ribs—true or false?

The term **costal** refers to ribs. The first seven pairs of ribs are attached to the sternum by **costal cartilage;** they're called **true ribs.** The remaining five pairs of ribs are called **false ribs** because they aren't attached directly to the sternum. All ribs are independently attached to the spinal column.

Appendicular skeleton

The appendicular skeleton includes the upper and lower extremities.

The ulna and the radius articulate with the humerus to form the elbow joint.

The upper extremities

The **clavicles,** or collarbones, are two flat bones attached to the sternum on their anterior side and to the **scapulae** (shoulder blades) laterally. This forms the **sternoclavicular joint.**

The scapulae are a pair of large, triangular bones that are located at the back of the thorax. These bones, plus the clavicles, form the shoulder girdles.

Armed and dangerous

The **humerus,** or upper arm bone, is a long bone with a shaft and two bulbous ends. The two long bones of the lower arm are the **ulna,** located on the little finger side of the humerus, and the **radius,** on the thumb side. These

Anatomically speaking

Bones of the hand

A view of the right hand, illustrating the positions of the carpals, metacarpals, and phalanges.

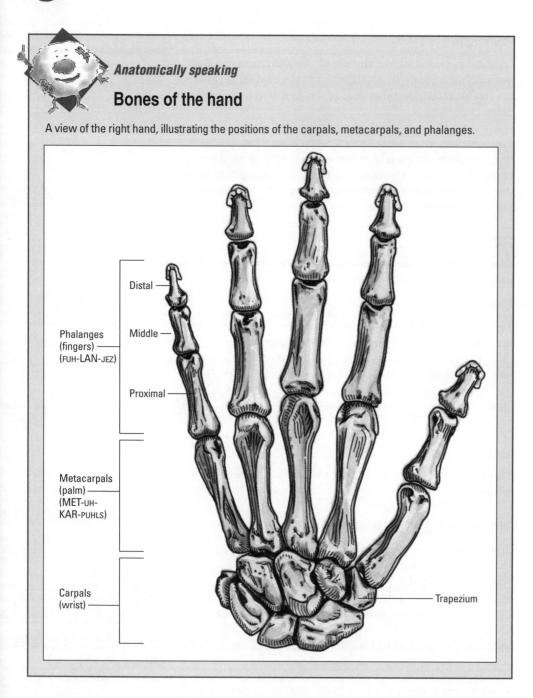

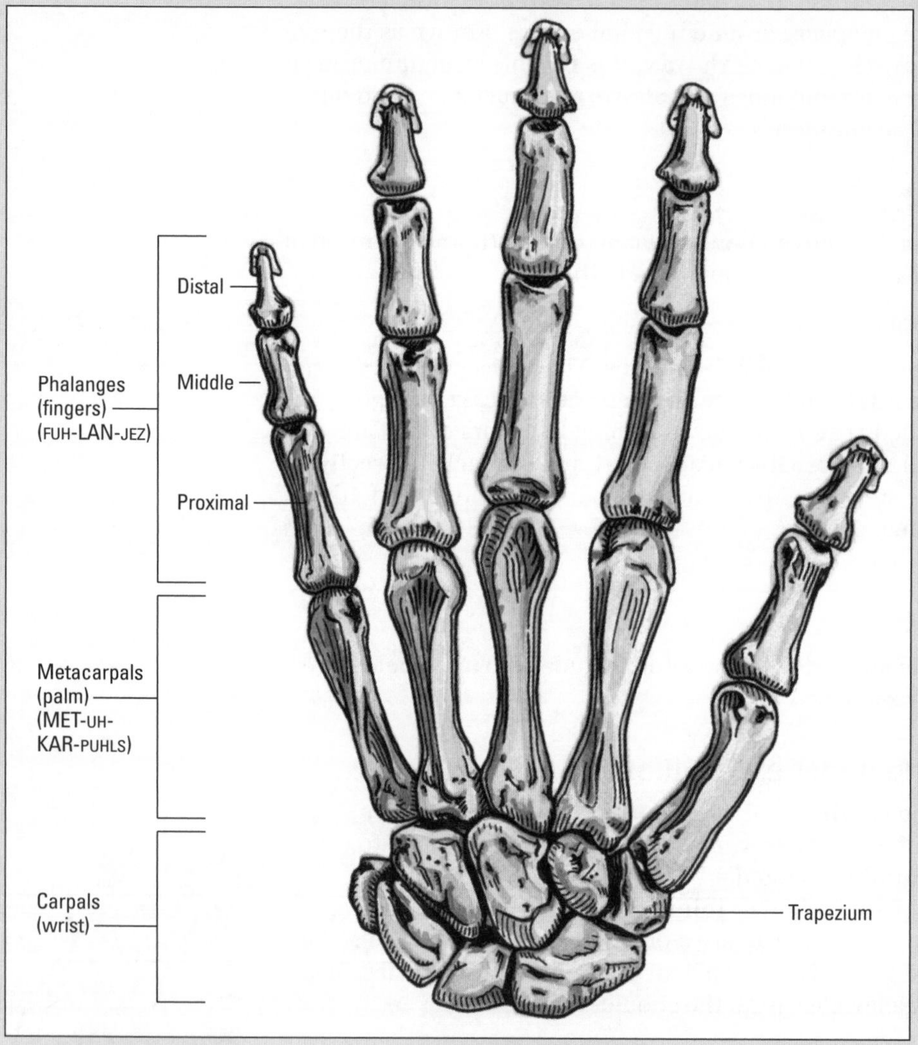
Distal
Middle
Phalanges (fingers) (FUH-LAN-JEZ)
Proximal
Metacarpals (palm) (MET-UH-KAR-PUHLS)
Carpals (wrist)
Trapezium

bones articulate with the humerus to form the elbow joint. The **wrists** are composed of eight small, irregular **carpal** bones aligned in two rows. Ligaments bind the carpals together.

A handful of terms

The bones of the hand are comprised of metacarpal bones and phalanges. (See *Bones of the hand.*)

The way these bones come together enables movement of the hand:

- Five small long **metacarpal** bones attach to the carpals and form the palm of the hand.
- **Phalanges,** or finger bones, are miniature long bones. Each finger has three phalanges, while the thumb has two. (See *A phalanx of phalanges.*)
- The thumb **metacarpal** has a freely movable joint, allowing a wide range of movement between the thumb metacarpal and the **trapezium,** the carpal at the base of the thumb.

Beyond the dictionary

A phalanx of phalanges

Phalanges is the plural of the Greek word ***phalange,*** or ***phalanx***. The latter term was applied to Greek and Roman army troop formations, noted for their closely joined and unified maneuvers.

Lower extremities

The lower extremities contain bones of the hip, thigh, leg, ankle, and foot.

Girdle words

Three pairs of bones fuse during childhood to form the **pelvic girdle,** the broadest bone in the body. This bone supports the trunk, protects the abdominal organs within its basin, and attaches the lower extremities to the body. The three pairs of fused bones include the **ilium,** which is the largest and uppermost of the three; the **ischium,** the lower and strongest set of bones; and the **pubis,** a pair of anterior bones that meet at the **symphysis pubis**—a cartilaginous joint.

It says here that the word **patella,** for kneecap, is a Latin word that means a *small, flat dish*—just what the kneecap looks like.

Give 'em a leg up

The two **femurs,** or upper leg bones, are the longest and heaviest bones in the body. They connect at the proximal end with the hip, articulating with the **acetabulum,** or hip socket. The femurs connect with the **tibia** at the distal end. The kneecap, or **patella,** is a small, flat bone that protects the knee joint and overlaps the distal end of the femur and the proximal end of the tibia.

Below the knee

The **tibia,** sometimes called the **shinbone,** is the largest and strongest of the lower leg bones. It articulates with the femur at the proximal end and meets the fibula and the talus at the distal end. The **fibula** connects with the tibia at its proximal and distal ends. The fibula's distal end also articulates with the talus. The articulation of the fibula, tibia, and talus bones creates the bony prominence on the outside of the ankle, called the **lateral malleolus.**

Now, fleetly, to the foot

The foot bones form a strong, stable arch with lengthwise and crosswise support. Strong ligaments and tendons of the leg muscles help the foot bones maintain their arched position:

- Seven short **tarsal bones** structurally resemble the wrist, and they articulate with the tibia and fibula:
  - The **talus bone (astragalus)** forms part of the ankle joint.
  - The heel, called the **calcaneus,** is the largest tarsal bone.
  - The **scaphoid bone** is also called the **navicular** because of its boat shape.
  - The **cuneiforms** (the **lateral, intermediate,** and **medial**) are three wedge-shaped bones that form the arch of the foot.
  - The **cuboid bone** articulates in the front with the metatarsal bones.
- Five **metatarsal bones** form the foot and articulate with the tarsal bone and the phalanges.
- The fourteen **phalanges** (toes) are similar to fingers, with three bones in each toe except the great toe, which, like the thumb, contains only two bones.

Words will never hurt me. But let's keep sticks and stones out of it!

Anatomy of bones

Bones are classified according to their shape:

- **Long bones** are the main bones of the limbs, except the patella, and those of the wrists and ankles.
- **Short bones** are the bones of the wrists and ankles.
- **Flat bones** include the sternum, scapulae, and cranium, among others.
- **Irregular bones** include the vertebrae and hip bones.

Boning up on bone material

All bones consist of two types of bone material: an outer layer of dense, smooth **compact bone** and an inner layer of spongy, **cancellous** (porous) bone. Compact bone is found especially in the shaft of long bones and in the outer layers of short, flat, and irregular bones. Cancellous bone fills the central regions of the epiphysis (the end of a long bone where bone formation takes place) and the inner portions of short, flat, and irregular bones.

Along the long bones

Long bones contain a number of visible, common structures:

- **diaphyses** (singular: **diaphysis**)—the long, narrow shaft of the bone contains the bone marrow and has two irregular ends
- **epiphyses** (singular: **epiphysis**)—the bulbous ends of long bones that provide a large surface for muscle attachment and give stability to joints
- **articular cartilage**—a thin layer of hyaline cartilage that covers and cushions the **articular** (joint) surfaces of the epiphyses
- **periosteum**—a dense membrane that covers the shafts of long bones; it consists of two layers: a fibrous outer layer and a bone-forming inner layer containing **osteoblasts** (bone-producing cells) and **osteoclasts** (bone-destroying cells)
- **medullary cavity**—a cavity filled with bone marrow
- **endosteum**—a thin membrane that lines the medullary cavity and contains osteoblasts and osteoclasts.

Feeding the long bones

Within compact bone are **haversian systems**. (See *Haversian diversion.*) The haversian systems are made up of the following structures:

- **lamellae**—thin layers of ground substance
- **lacunae**—small hollow spaces that contain osteocytes
- **canaliculi**—small canals
- **haversian canals**—central canals that contain blood and lymph vessels, nerves and, sometimes, marrow.

Blood reaches bone by arterioles in haversian canals; by vessels in Volkmann's canals, which connect one haversian canal to another and to the outer bone; and by vessels in the bone ends and within the marrow. (See *Two views of a long bone*, page 54.)

Beyond the dictionary

Haversian diversion

The **haversian systems** were named in honor of the 17th century British doctor and anatomist Clopton Havers, who discovered them.

Anatomically speaking

Two views of a long bone

Here's a look at a long bone from interior and cross-section views.

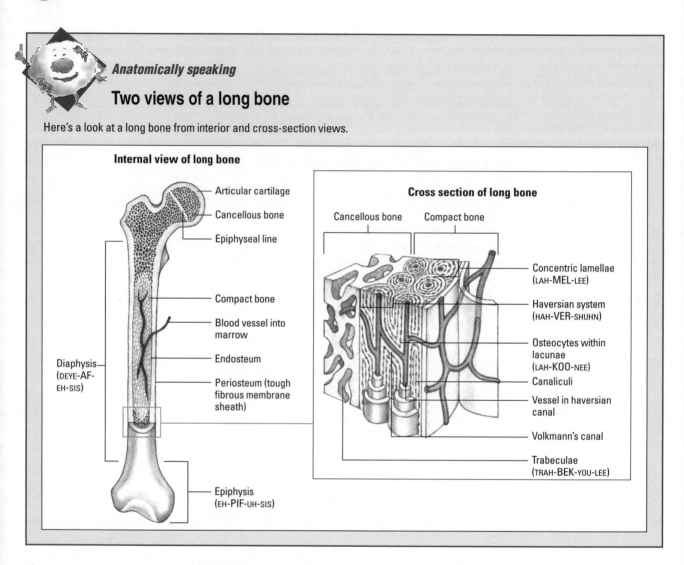

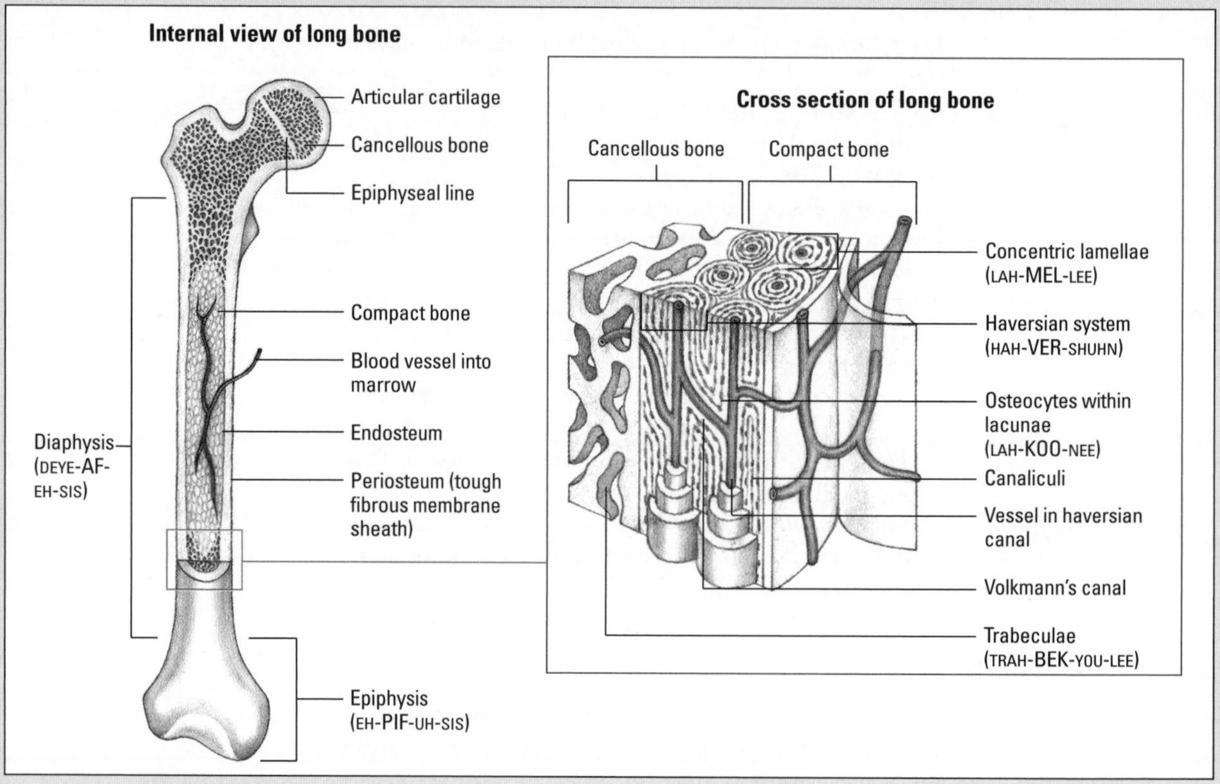
Internal view of long bone
Articular cartilage
Cancellous bone
Epiphyseal line
Compact bone
Blood vessel into marrow
Endosteum
Periosteum (tough fibrous membrane sheath)
Diaphysis (DEYE-AF-EH-SIS)
Epiphysis (EH-PIF-UH-SIS)
Cross section of long bone
Cancellous bone
Compact bone
Concentric lamellae (LAH-MEL-LEE)
Haversian system (HAH-VER-SHUHN)
Osteocytes within lacunae (LAH-KOO-NEE)
Canaliculi
Vessel in haversian canal
Volkmann's canal
Trabeculae (TRAH-BEK-YOU-LEE)

To marrow, and to marrow, and to marrow...

In a child's body, nearly all the bones contain **red bone marrow.** In an adult, red bone marrow is found in the femur, ribs, vertebrae, and the ends of the humerus in the upper arm. Red bone marrow performs **hematopoiesis,** making new RBCs for the body.

Bone growth and resorption

Bones grow both in length and in thickness. At the epiphyses, they grow longer; at the diaphyses, they grow in diameter through the activity of osteoblasts in the perios-

Beyond the dictionary

Bone up on *osteo-* and *oss-*

Osteon, Greek for *bone,* provides a key word-forming root for medical terms relating to bones, ***oste-*** or ***osteo-***. **Osteoblast** is a compound of ***osteo-*** and ***-blast;*** the latter is another common medical root derived from a Greek word that means a *bud* or a *shoot of a developing organism.* An **osteoblast** is thus *a cell that buds forth new bone tissue.* The Greek word ***clast,*** on the other hand, means *to break* or *fragment.* Therefore, an **osteoclast** is *a cell that breaks down bone.*

The Romans had a name for it

Another very common root for forming words is the Latin word ***os,*** or ***oss-,*** also meaning *bone.* This root is contained in words like **ossify,** meaning *to change* or *to become bone,* and **ossification,** *the process of becoming bone.*

teum. A hormone secreted by the anterior lobe of the pituitary gland controls bone growth. (See *Bone up on* osteo- *and* oss-.)

As osteoblasts add new tissue to the outside of a bone, large phagocytic cells called **osteoclasts** eat away bony tissue in the medullary cavity to keep the bone from becoming too thick. A healthy bone is constantly broken down, resorbed, and repaired long after it stops growing in size. During adulthood, bone formation (or **ossification**) and bone **resorption** balance one another so that each bone remains a constant size. During childhood and adolescence, ossification is faster than resorption and bones grow larger.

Cartilage

Bones and joints need support as well as shock absorption. **Cartilage** is a dense connective tissue that has these capabilities. It consists of fibers embedded in a strong, gel-like substance. Unlike rigid bone, cartilage has the flexibility of firm plastic.

Cartilage supports and shapes various structures, such as the auditory canal and the intervertebral disks. It also cushions and absorbs shock. Cartilage has no blood or nerve supply.

Types of cartilage

Cartilage may be fibrous, hyaline, or elastic:

• **Fibrous cartilage** forms at the meniscus and the intervertebral disks.
• **Hyaline cartilage** covers articular bone surfaces (where one or more bones meet at a joint), connects the ribs and sternum, and appears in the trachea, bronchi, and nasal septum.
• **Elastic cartilage** is located in the auditory canal, external ear, and epiglottis.

Bone movement

Bones are rigid structures that can't bend without being damaged, so individual bones move at joint sites, or **articulations.** Every bone in the body except the hyoid bone, which anchors the tongue, is connected to another bone by flexible connective tissue.

Classifying joints

Joints can be classified by the type of movement they allow and by their structure.

How does it move?

The three classes of joints identified by the range of movement they allow are:
• **synarthrosis**—immovable
• **amphiarthrosis**—slightly movable
• **diarthrosis**—freely movable.

Our joints are jumpin'! It must be that diarthrosis.

What is it made of?

By structure, a joint may be classified as fibrous, cartilaginous, or synovial. In **fibrous joints,** the articular surfaces of the two bones are bound closely by fibrous connective tissue and little movement is possible. The cranial sutures are examples of fibrous joints.

In **cartilaginous joints,** cartilage connects one bone to another; these joints allow slight movement. An example is the symphysis pubis (the junction of the pelvic bones).

Body surfaces in the **synovial joints** are covered by articular cartilage and joined by **ligaments** (dense, strong, flexible bands of fibrous connective tissue that bind bones to other bones) lined with synovial membrane. Freely movable, synovial joints include most joints of the arms and legs. Synovial joints also include an **articular capsule**—a saclike envelope, whose outer layer is lined with a vascular synovial membrane. This membrane contains synovial fluid—a viscid fluid, produced by the synovial membrane that lubricates the joint.

Small **bursae** (singular: **bursa**) are synovial fluid sacs located at friction points of all types of joints as well as between tendons, ligaments, and bones. Bursae cushion these structures and decrease stress on adjacent ones. (See *The bag for bones.*)

Beyond the dictionary

The bag for bones

You may notice that the word **bursa** sounds a bit like the word **purse.** That's more than a coincidence. Both words come from the Latin word ***bursa,*** which means *a small bag or sac.*

In the body, bursae are sacs of synovial fluid that cushion skeletal structures, such as tendons, ligaments, and bones.

Synovial subdivisions—joints to live in

Based on their structure and the type of movement, synovial joints fall into various subdivisions:

- **Gliding joints,** such as the wrists and ankles, allow adjacent bone surfaces to move against one another.
- **Hinge joints,** such as the elbows and knees, permit movement in only one direction.
- **Pivot joints,** also called **rotary joints** or **trochoid joints,** allow a movable bone to pivot around a stationary bone. The neck and elbows contain pivot joints.

Knuckleheads

- **Condylar,** or **knuckle joints,** contain an oval head of one bone that fits into a shallow depression in a second bone. The union between the radius (arm bone) and the carpal bones of the hand is an example of a condylar joint.
- **Saddle joints** resemble condylar joints but allow greater freedom of movement. The only saddle joints in the body are the carpometacarpal joints of the thumb.
- **Ball-and-socket joints (spheroid joints)** get their name from the way their bones connect—the spherical head of one bone fits into a socket of another bone. The hip and shoulder joints are the only ball-and-socket joints in the body.

Physical examination terms

When a patient seeks medical help for a skeletal problem, it's usually because of a physical mishap. Here are some terms related to examination of the skeletal system that you'll need to know:

- **angular**—at an angle
- **circular**—circlelike or round

- **crepitus**—a cracking noise or the sensation that's commonly felt when the hand is placed over a fracture site and the broken bone ends are moved
- **posture**—the position of the limbs or the body as a whole
- **range of motion**—the total degree of motion or joint movement
- **symmetry**—equality of two sides of the body.

Movement and range of motion

Common terms used to describe movement and range of motion in joints include:

- **abduction**—moving away from the midline
- **adduction**—moving toward the midline
- **circumduction**—moving in a circular manner
- **extension**—straightening or increasing the joint angle
- **flexion**—bending or decreasing the joint angle
- **pronation**—turning downward
- **internal rotation**—turning toward midline
- **external rotation**—turning away from midline
- **supination**—turning upward.

Remembering what arthralgia is can be easy when you break it apart: ***arthr-*** is the root for *joint;* ***-algia*** is the suffix for *pain.*
SNAP

Common complaints

Patients with joint injuries usually complain of pain, swelling, or stiffness, and they may have noticeable deformities. A deformity can also occur with a bone fracture, which causes sharp pain when the patient moves the affected area.

Common terms used to describe patient complaints include:

- **arthralgia**—pain in a joint
- **arthredema**—joint swelling
- **arthropyosis**—pus formation in a joint cavity
- **bursitis**—inflammation of a bursa, the fluid-filled sac that prevents friction within a joint
- **chondralgia**—pain originating in the cartilage
- **chondritis**—inflammation of the cartilage
- **chondromalacia**—abnormal softening of the cartilage
- **coxitis**—inflammation of the hip joint
- **epiphysitis**—inflammation of the epiphysis of a bone
- **hemarthrosis**—blood in a joint cavity

- **hydrarthrosis**—accumulation of watery fluid in a joint cavity
- **kyphosis**—the Greek word for *hunchback*, an abnormally increased convexity in the curvature of the thoracic spine
- **lordosis**—forward curvature of the lumbar spine; also known as **sway back**
- **lumbago**—pain in the lower back (lumbar) region
- **ostealgia**—bone pain
- **osteitis**—inflammation of bone
- **osteochondritis**—inflammation of bone and cartilage
- **osteolysis**—degeneration of bone from calcium loss.

Diagnostic tests

Tests to determine bone and joint diseases or injuries include blood tests, aspiration tests, and radiologic tests.

Blood tests

Several blood tests help determine bone and joint disorders:

- **Alkaline phosphatase (ALP)** is an enzyme produced by the bones and liver. Because blood concentrations of ALP rise with increased activity of bone cells, high ALP levels help diagnose bone disorders.
- **Erythrocyte sedimentation rate (ESR)** is the rate at which RBCs settle in a tube of unclotted blood. An elevated ESR indicates inflammation.
- **Rheumatoid factor** is a blood test used to distinguish rheumatoid arthritis from other disorders.
- **Serum calcium** measures the amount of calcium in the blood. Abnormally high levels are present with Paget's disease and other diseases of the bone.

Aspiration tests

Aspiration tests use fluid withdrawn by a suction device, usually a needle:

- In **arthrocentesis**, a joint is surgically punctured with a needle to aspirate synovial fluid for analysis or to remove accumulated fluid. (See *Simplifying* arthrocentesis.)

Beyond the dictionary

Simplifying *arthrocentesis*

Arthrocentesis becomes a simple compound word when its components are understood. ***Arthro-*** comes from the Greek word ***arthron,*** which means *joint*, and ***-centesis*** derives from the Greek word ***kentesis,*** which means *puncture*. So **arthrocentesis** must be *a joint puncture.*

• In **bone marrow aspiration,** a needle is forced through the outer cortex of a flat bone—such as the sternum or iliac crest—and bone marrow is aspirated for analysis.
• In **lumbar puncture,** a needle is inserted into the subarachnoid space surrounding the spinal cord to remove a sample of cerebrospinal fluid.

Radiologic tests

• **Bone X-ray,** the simplest radiologic procedure, is used to examine a bone for disease or fracture.
• A **computed tomography (CT) scan,** or **computerized tomography scan,** is a series of X-ray photographs that represent cross-sectional images of the bone. These images are translated by a computer and displayed on an oscilloscope. (See *Cat's tale.*)
• **Arthrography** employs contrast dye to observe the interior of a joint, such as the knee, shoulder, ankle, or elbow. Dye is injected into the joint space, and a CT scan records images of the joint.
• **Bone densitometry** is a noninvasive technique in which X-rays are used to measure bone mineral density and identify the risk of osteoporosis. The results are analyzed by computer to determine bone mineral status.
• A **bone scan** helps detect bony metastasis, benign disease, fractures, avascular necrosis, and infection. After I.V. administration of a radioactive material, a counter detects the gamma rays, indicating areas of increased uptake, suggesting an abnormality.
• **Myelography** is a radiographic examination of the spinal cord following injection of a contrast medium.

The real world

Cat's tale

You may also hear a **CT scan** referred to as a **CAT scan,** which is short for *computed axial tomography.*

Procedures

• **Arthroscopy** is also used to observe the interior of a joint—most commonly the knee. A fiberoptic viewing tube is inserted directly into the joint, allowing a doctor to examine its interior.
• A **bone marrow biopsy** removes a piece of bone containing intact marrow.
• **Magnetic resonance imaging** uses an electromagnetic field and radio waves to transfer visual images of soft tissue, such as tendons, to a computer screen.

Disorders

Disorders of the skeletal system include fractures, dislocations, herniations, cancer, and other diseases.

Fractures and other injuries

Fractures, traumatic injuries or breaks in bone tissue, most commonly occur in the long bones of the arms and legs. They can occur in all age-groups in any portion of the skeletal system. Fractures can be caused by direct injury or can occur spontaneously when bone is weakened by disease; the latter is called a **pathologic fracture.** **Closed** (simple) **fracture** is seen when the broken bone doesn't protrude through the skin. **Open** (compound) **fracture** occurs when the bone breaks through the skin, causing tissue damage.

Fracture features

Fractures can be classified according to the bone fragment position or by the fracture line:

- **Colles' fracture**—a fracture of the radius at the lower end of the wrist in which the bone fragment is displaced backward
- **linear fracture**—a fracture that runs along the long axis of a bone
- **comminuted fracture**—a bone is broken into two or more fragments
- **greenstick fracture**—involves a break in only one part of the bone thickness
- **transverse fracture**—the fracture line is perpendicular to a bone's long axis
- **spiral fracture**—the fracture line goes around, or spirals, the bone.

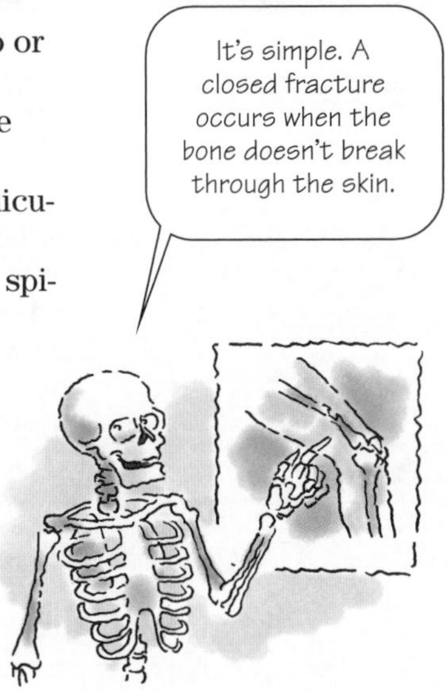
It's simple. A closed fracture occurs when the bone doesn't break through the skin.

Bone away from home

A **dislocation** is the displacement of a bone from its normal position within the joint. It can occur at birth, called a **congenital dislocation,** or may be caused by a disease or trauma. With a dislocation, joint tissue is torn and stretched, possibly rupturing blood vessels. **Subluxation,** partial dislocation that separates the joint's movable surfaces, occurs most commonly in the shoulder, hip, and knee.

Don't play this disk

Herniated disk, a ruptured area in the cartilage that cushions the intervertebral disks of the spinal column, is a painful condition. The soft, central cartilage balloons out from the disk and puts pressure on the nerve roots. Herniation can happen suddenly with lifting or twisting or may result from degenerative joint disease and other chronic conditions.

Don't be callous about bunions

Here are some other injuries related to the skeletal system that you may encounter:

- **Bunions** are localized areas of swelling that occur on the foot near the joint of the big toe. They're caused by inflammation and fibrosis of the bursae.
- **Calluses** are hard bone formations that may occur at the site of bone fractures.

Diseases

Some of the most common diseases of the skeletal system and terms to describe skeletal disorders are presented here:

- **Ankylosing spondylitis** is a slow, progressive inflammatory disease of the spine, the **sacroiliac** joint, and the larger joints of the extremities (hips, knees, and shoulders) that leads to a fibrous or bony ankylosis (immobility) and deformity.
- **Osteoarthritis,** also known as **degenerative arthritis,** affects the joints of the hand, knee, hip, and vertebrae. It's a major cause of disability.
- **Osteomalacia** is softening of the bones that's characterized by inadequate mineralization of newly formed bone matrix due to vitamin D deficiency; it's the adult form of rickets.
- **Osteomyelitis** is an inflammation of the bone, bone marrow, and surrounding soft tissue that's caused by **pyogenic** (pus-producing) bacteria.
- **Osteoporosis** is a disorder in which bone mass is reduced, leading to enhanced bone fragility and an increased fracture risk.

Oh my! Osteomyelitis is an inflammation of the bone, bone marrow, or soft tissue that's caused by bacteria.

• **Rickets** is a condition of abnormal bone growth in children caused by insufficient vitamin D, calcium, and phosphorus.
• **Rheumatoid arthritis** is a chronic autoimmune disorder that affects the synovial membranes. Painful inflammation of the joints may lead to crippling deformities and affect many organ systems.
• **Scurvy** is a condition caused by lack of vitamin C in the diet, which results in abnormal bones and teeth.

Bone tumors

Bone tumors can be **benign** (noncancerous) or **malignant** (cancerous). Here are some tumor types:
• **Osteochondroma** is a common tumor that causes **projections** (spurs) at the end of long bones, especially the knees, ankles, hips, shoulders, and elbows. (See *Tumor term.*)
• **Osteosarcoma** is a fast-growing malignant tumor of skeletal tissue with a high mortality rate. Common sites of involvement are the tibia, femur, and humerus. This tumor commonly metastasizes to the lungs.
• **Chondrosarcoma** is a large, slow-growing malignant tumor that affects the hyaline cartilage. It occurs most often in the femur, spine, pelvis, ribs, or scapulae.

Beyond the dictionary

Tumor term

The word for a bone tumor begins with the common root ***osteo-***, meaning *bone.* ***Chondr-*** is a root meaning *cartilage,* and ***-oma*** is a suffix meaning *tumor.* **Osteochondroma** is thus *a tumor of the bone and cartilage.*

Treatments

Noninvasive treatment for bone and joint injuries includes:
• a **splint,** which is a removable appliance that immobilizes, restrains, and supports the injured or displaced body part
• a **cast,** which is a rigid dressing that's placed around an injured body part to support, immobilize, and protect it and promote healing
• a **closed reduction,** which is a manual alignment of a fracture and may precede the application of a cast
• **traction,** which uses a system of weights and pulleys to immobilize and relieve pressure on a fractured bone to maintain proper position and to facilitate healing.

Bones, bones—a fixation on bones

Some fractures require **internal fixation** devices, such as pins, plates, screws, wires, and surgical cement, to stabilize the bone fragments. An **open reduction with internal fixation** is a surgical procedure that allows the surgeon to directly align the fractured bone and apply internal fixation devices. (See *Let's reduce that reduction.*)

The real world

Let's reduce that reduction

In the real world, you may hear people refer to open reduction with internal fixation as an "ORIF."

Cut to the bone

These terms relate to invasive treatment of joints and bones:

- **Arthrectomy** is the excision of a joint.
- In **arthrodesis,** a bone graft (typically from the patient's iliac crest) is used to fuse joint surfaces; it's called **spondylosyndesis** when this procedure is applied to the vertebrae. (See *Spelling out* spondylosyndesis.)
- **Arthroplasty** surgically reconstructs a joint.
- **Bone marrow transplant** involves I.V. administration of marrow aspirated from the donor's bones to a recipient.
- In **chemonucleolysis,** a drug is injected into a herniated disk that dissolves the **nucleus pulposus,** the pulpy, semifluid center of the disk.
- **Costectomy** is the surgical excision of a rib.
- **Diskectomy** is the excision of an intervertebral disk.
- In **hip replacement,** a diseased hip joint is replaced with a **prosthesis** (artificial substitute for a missing body part).
- **Laminectomy** is the surgical excision of the lamina.
- **Laminotomy** is the transection of a vertebral lamina.
- **Ostectomy** is the excision of a bone or part of a bone.
- **Osteotomy** is an incision or transection of a bone.
- A **sternotomy** is a cut made through the sternum.

Beyond the dictionary

Spelling out *spondylosyndesis*

Spondylo- comes from the Greek word ***spondylos,*** which means *vertebra;* ***syndesis*** is the Greek word that means *binding together.* Therefore, **spondylosyndesis** is the *binding together of the spine,* or *spinal fusion.*

systole
parietal

Vocabulary builders

At a crossroads

Completing this crossword puzzle will help you bone up on your medical vocabulary. Good Luck!

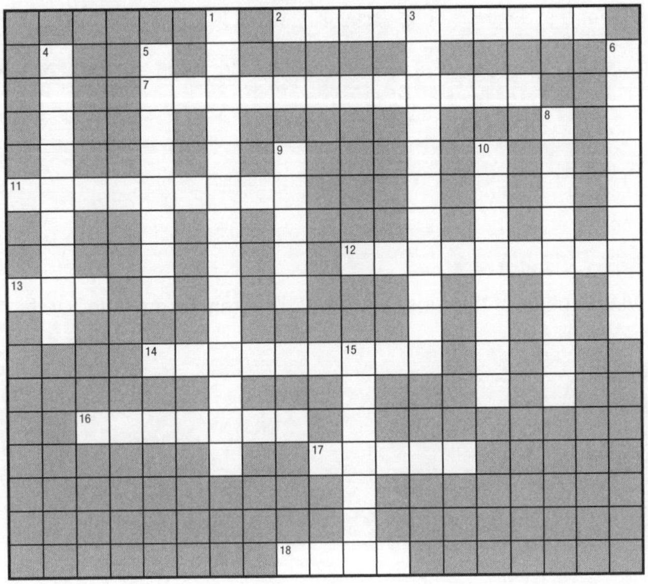

Across

2. Bone's membrane
7. Another name for a joint
11. Dense connective tissue
12. Collarbones
13. Color of marrow that makes blood cells
14. Ends of a long bone
16. Mineral found in bones
17. Bag of synovial fluid
18. Rigid dressing on an extremity

Down

1. Degenerative joint disease
3. Immature bone cells
4. Fingers and toes
5. Jaw bone
6. Main shaft of a long bone
8. Bone cavity
9. Upper leg bone
10. Two bones at top of the head
15. Immovable joints

Answers are on page 68.

Finish line

The root ***osteo-,*** meaning *bone,* forms many words related to bone disorders and diseases. Complete the sentences below by filling in each blank with the appropriate word that begins with ***osteo-.***

1. Osteo______________ is a disorder in which bone mass is reduced.
2. A generalized infection of the bone marrow is called osteo______________.
3. A term used to describe the cutting of a bone is osteo______________.
4. A cell that destroys bone tissue is an osteo______________.
5. Osteo____________ is a common tumor that causes spurs at the end of long bones.

Match game

Match each of the musculoskeletal system terms below with its definition.

Terms

1. Sternum
2. Tibia
3. Hematopoiesis
4. Coccyx
5. Epiphyses
6. Humerus
7. Femur
8. Osteochondritis
9. Phalanges
10. Mandible

Definitions

A. Production of red blood cells in the bone marrow

B. Jaw bone

C. Tailbone

D. Flat, sword-shaped bone that's attached to the collarbones

E. Upper arm bone

F. Finger or toe bones

G. The largest and strongest of the lower leg bones

H. The longest and heaviest bone in the body

I. Bulbous ends of long bones that provide a large surface for muscle attachment and give stability to joints

J. Inflammation of bone and cartilage

Answers are on page 68.

Talking in circles

Use the clues below to fill in the blanks with the appropriate word. Then unscramble the circled letters to find the answer to the question posed below.

1. ___ ___ ◯ ___ ___ ◯ ___
2. ___ ___ ◯ ___ ___ ___
3. ◯ ___ ___ ___ ___ ◯
4. ___ ___ ___ ___ ◯ ___ ___
5. ◯ ___ ___ ___ ◯ ___ ___ ___ ◯ ___ ___
6. ___ ___ ◯ ◯ ___ ___ ___ ___ ___ ___

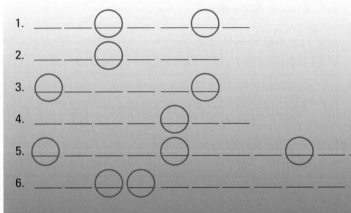

1. This is the suture that connects the frontal bone with the parietal bones.
2. This is the cartilage that attaches the sternum to the ribs.
3. This is what the lower arm bone on the thumb side is called.
4. This is the type of joint in the wrists and ankles.
5. This is the term for displacement of a bone from its normal position.
6. This is the term for joint swelling.

Our bones really move freely in this joint. What makes this possible?

Answers are on page 68.

Answers

At a crossroads

						1 O		2 P	E	R	I	3 O	S	T	E	U	M	
	4 P			5 M		S						S						6 D
	H			7 A	R	T	I	C	U	L	A	T	I	O	N			I
	A			N		E						E				8 M		A
	L			D		O		9 F				O		10 P		E		P
11 C	A	R	T	I	L	A	G	E				B		A		D		H
	N			B		R		M				L		R		U		Y
	G			L		T		U		12 C	L	A	V	I	C	L	E	S
13 R	E	D		E		H		R				S		E		L		I
	S					R						T		T		A		S
				14 E	P	I	P	H	Y	15 S	E	S		A		R		
						T				U				L		Y		
		16 C	A	L	C	I	U	M		T								
						S			17 B	U	R	S	A					
										R								
										E								
								18 C	A	S	T							

Finish line

1. Porosis; 2. Myelitis; 3. Tomy; 4. Clast; 5. Chondroma

Match game

1. D; 2. G; 3. A; 4. C; 5. I; 6. E; 7. H; 8. J; 9. F; 10. B

Talking in circles

1. Coronal; 2. Costal; 3. Radius; 4. Gliding; 5. Dislocation; 6. Arthredema
Answer to puzzle—Diarthrosis

4

Muscular system

Just the facts

In this chapter, you'll learn:

- terminology related to the structure and function of the muscular system
- terminology needed for physical examination of the muscular system
- tests that help diagnose muscular disorders
- disorders of the muscular system and their treatments.

Muscle structure and function

A key to learning terminology related to the muscular system is knowing the medical prefix for muscle, ***my(o)-***, from the Greek word for muscle, ***mys.*** Combined with other words, this prefix forms such terms as **myology** (the study of muscles), **myocardium** (heart muscle), and **myositis** (inflammation of voluntary muscle tissues). (See *A close look at* myocardium and *Pronouncing key muscular system terms*, page 70.)

More than just heavy lifting

Muscles have three functions:

1. They support the body.
2. They permit movement.
3. They produce body heat.

They're also an integral part of internal organs, such as the heart, lungs, uterus, and intestines.

Beyond the dictionary

A close look at *myocardium*

The Greek word for *muscle* is ***myos,*** and ***cardiac*** is the Greek word for *heart.* Therefore, **myocardium** means *heart muscle.*

Pump up your pronunciation

Pronouncing key muscular system terms

Below is a list of key terms, along with the correct way to pronounce them.

Aspartate aminotransferase	AHS-PAR-TAYT AH-MEE-NOH-TRANS-FUHR-RAYS
Buccinator	BUHK-SUH-NAY-TUHR
Creatine kinase	KREE-UH-TEEN KEYE-NAYS
Dystonia	DIS-TOH-NEE-UH
Epimysium	EP-UH-MISS-EE-UHM
Fasciorrhaphy	FASH-EE-OR -EH-FEE
Gastrocnemius	GAS-TROK-NEE-MEE-UHS
Leiomyosarcoma	LEYE-OH-MEYE-OH-SAR-KOH-MUH
Myasthenia gravis	MEYE-AHS-THEE-NEE-UH GRAH-VUHS
Myokinesimeter	MEYE-OH-KIN-UH-SIM-UH-TER
Myositis purulenta	MEYE-OH-SEYE-TIS PER-UH-LENT-UH
Sarcolemma	SAR-KOH-LEM-UH
Torticollis	TOR-TUH-KOL-LIS
Trapezius	TRAH-PEE-ZEE-UHS

Our bodies have about 600 muscles—not all of them are as easy to identify as my biceps brachii!

Tissue issue

The three major types of muscle in the human body are classified by the tissue they contain:

- **Skeletal** muscles are **voluntary** (controlled by will) muscles that attach to the skeleton and consist of **striated** (in thin bands) tissue. They move body parts and the body as a whole, maintain posture, and implement voluntary and reflex movements. Skeletal muscles also generate body heat. (See *A close look at skeletal muscles.*)
- **Visceral** muscles are **involuntary** (not controlled by will) muscles that contain smooth-muscle tissue. They're found in such organs as the stomach and intestines. (See *Gut reaction.*)

Beyond the dictionary

Gut reaction

The word **visceral** is derived from the Latin word ***viscera,*** meaning *internal organs.* **Visceral** also means *intensely emotional* or *instinctive.* Think of a "gut reaction."

Anatomically speaking

A close look at skeletal muscles

Each muscle is classified by the movement it permits. For example, flexors permit the bending of joints, or flexion; abductors permit shortening so that joints can be straightened, or abducted. The illustrations below show some of the body's major muscles.

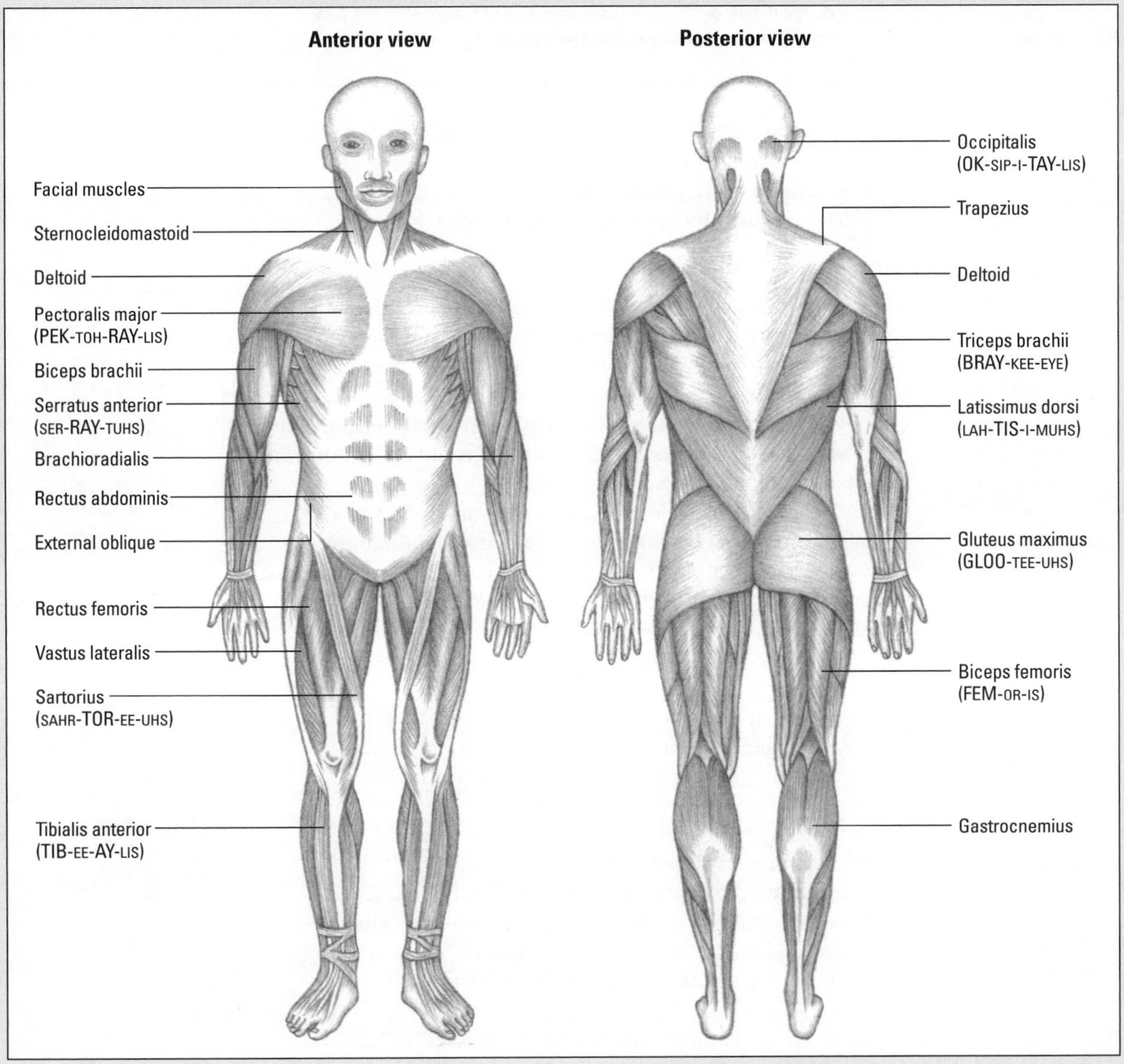
Anterior view
Posterior view
Facial muscles
Sternocleidomastoid
Deltoid
Pectoralis major (PEK-toh-RAY-lis)
Biceps brachii
Serratus anterior (ser-RAY-tuhs)
Brachioradialis
Rectus abdominis
External oblique
Rectus femoris
Vastus lateralis
Sartorius (sahr-TOR-ee-uhs)
Tibialis anterior (TIB-ee-AY-lis)
Occipitalis (OK-sip-i-TAY-lis)
Trapezius
Deltoid
Triceps brachii (BRAY-kee-eye)
Latissimus dorsi (lah-TIS-i-muhs)
Gluteus maximus (GLOO-tee-uhs)
Biceps femoris (FEM-or-is)
Gastrocnemius

Beyond the dictionary

Origins of *sarcolemma* and *sarcoplasm*

A muscle fiber's plasma membrane is called a **sarcolemma,** and its cytoplasm is called **sarcoplasm.** In Latin, ***sarco*** means *flesh.* Both **sarcolemma** and **sarcoplasm** share this Latin root.

- **Cardiac** muscle is made up of involuntary, striated tissue. It's controlled by the autonomic nervous system and specialized **neuromuscular** (meaning both nerve and muscle) tissue located within the right atrium.

The muscles' makeup

Muscle tissue cells perform specialized activities and vary greatly in size and length. Because they're usually long and slender with a threadlike shape, muscle cells are called **fibers.**

Connective tissue holds muscle fibers together. Bundles of muscle fibers are enclosed by a fibrous membrane sheath called **fascia.**

Although muscle cells have the same parts as other cells, several of their structures have special names. A muscle fiber's plasma membrane is called a **sarcolemma** and its cytoplasm is called **sarcoplasm.** (See *Origins of* sarcolemma *and* sarcoplasm.)

The word **ligament** comes from the Latin ***ligare,*** which means *to tie or bind*—and that is exactly what ligaments do to your bones.

The ties that bind us

Tendons are bands of fibrous connective tissue that attach muscles to the **periosteum,** a fibrous membrane that covers the bone. Tendons enable bones to move when skeletal muscles contract, creating energy through the release of the enzyme **adenosine triphosphate** from the cells.

Ligaments are dense, strong, flexible bands of fibrous connective tissue that bind bones to other bones. Ligaments in the skeletal muscle system connect the **articular** (relating to a joint) ends of bones. They provide stability and can either limit or facilitate movement. Deeper inside the body, ligaments support the organs.

Most skeletal muscles are attached to bones either directly or indirectly. In a direct attachment, the **epimysium** (fibrous sheath around a muscle) of the muscle fuses to the **periosteum** of the bone. In an indirect attachment, the fascia extends past the muscle as a tendon or **aponeurosis** (deeply set fascia), which in turn attaches to the bone. In the human body, indirect attachments outnumber direct attachments.

Putting it in motion

Muscles depend on one another for movement; a muscle rarely acts on its own. **Prime movers** are muscles that actively produce a movement. **Antagonists** are muscles that oppose the prime movers and relax as the prime movers contract. **Synergists** contract along with the prime movers and help execute the movement or provide stability.

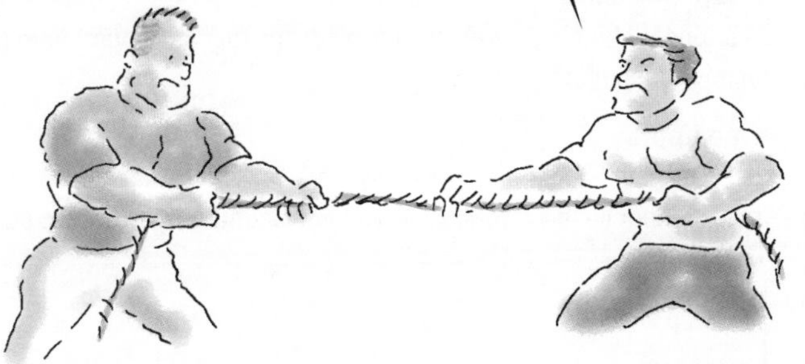
Remember: An **antagonist** is one who opposes another...

During contraction, one of the bones to which the muscle is attached stays stationary while the other is pulled in the opposite direction. The point where the muscle attaches to the stationary bone is called the **origin;** the point where it attaches to the more moveable bone, the **insertion.** The origin usually lies on the **proximal** (nearest to) end of the bone; the insertion, on the **distal** (farthest away) end.

...and **synergy** means working together.

Key muscles

The name of a skeletal muscle may come from its location, action, size, shape, attachment points, number of divisions, or direction of fibers. (See *Muscle structure*, page 74.)

Anatomically speaking

Muscle structure

Each muscle contains cell groups called *muscle fibers* that extend the length of the muscle. A sheath of connective tissues—called the **perimysium**—binds the fibers into a bundle, or **fasciculus.**

A strong sheath

A stronger sheath, the **epimysium,** binds the fasciculi together to form the fleshy part of the muscle. Beyond the muscle, the epimysium becomes a tendon.

Fine fibers

Each muscle fiber is surrounded by a plasma membrane called the **sarcolemma.** Within the **sarcoplasm** (or cytoplasm) of the muscle fiber lie tiny myofibrils. Arranged lengthwise, myofibrils contain still finer fibers, called *thick fibers* and *thin fibers.*

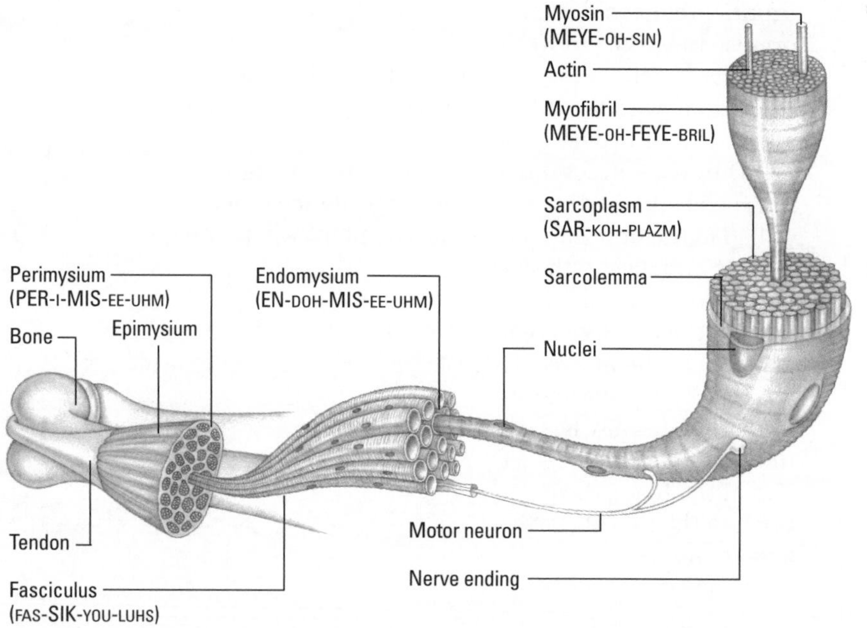
Myosin (MEYE-OH-SIN)
Actin
Myofibril (MEYE-OH-FEYE-BRIL)
Sarcoplasm (SAR-KOH-PLAZM)
Sarcolemma
Nuclei
Perimysium (PER-I-MIS-EE-UHM)
Endomysium (EN-DOH-MIS-EE-UHM)
Bone
Epimysium
Tendon
Fasciculus (FAS-SIK-YOU-LUHS)
Motor neuron
Nerve ending

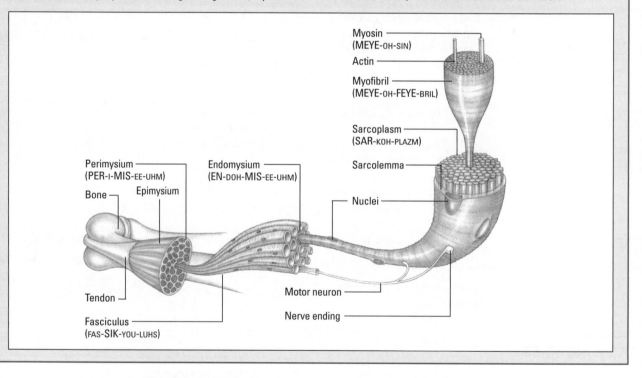

Scalp muscles

The top of the head contains no muscles but has a broad, flat tendon called the **epicranial aponeurosis** that connects to three nearby muscle groups. (See *Dissecting* epicranial aponeurosis.)

- The **occipitofrontal group** houses both the **occipitalis** muscle, which pulls the scalp backward, and the **frontalis** muscle, which pulls it forward. Raising the eyebrows and wrinkling the forehead use the frontalis muscle.
- The **temporoparietal group** includes the **temporalis** muscle, which tightens the scalp and moves the ears forward.
- The **auricular group** contains three muscles (the **anterior, superior,** and **posterior**), which move the ear forward, upward, and backward.

Facial muscles

Facial expressions, such as a smile, frown, or look of surprise, depend on specialized muscles.

Smile later, buccinator

The **buccinator** muscle, also called the **trumpeter** muscle, compresses the cheeks for smiling or blowing (***bucca*** means *cheek* in Latin). The **corrugator supercilii** draws the eyebrows together in a frown (***corrugatus*** means *wrinkled*, as in a corrugated box). When the eyes widen in surprise, the **orbicularis oculi** (***orbit*** means *around* and **ocul** means *eye*) moves the eyelids.

Chew on this

The **masseters** are the chewing muscles (***masticate*** means *chew*), and the **pterygoids** open and close the mouth. The prefix ***pteryx-*** means *wing* and describes the shape of these muscles. (See *Saying* pterygoid *isn't p-terribly difficult*, page 76.)

Neck and shoulder muscles

Sternocleidomastoid muscles are paired muscles on either side of the neck that allow the head to move. This name combines the muscles' origins in the **sternum** and **clavicle** with their insertion point in the **mastoid process** of the temporal bone.

No shrugging it off

The **trapezius** muscle on the back of the neck raises and lowers (shrugging) the shoulders. Arms can be crossed

Beyond the dictionary

Dissecting *epicranial aponeurosis*

Epicranial aponeurosis looks intimidating until you break it down. In Greek, ***epi*** means *upon,* ***kranion*** means *skull,* ***apo*** means *away,* and ***neuron*** means *tendon.* Epicranial aponeurosis is a fibrous membrane that covers the **cranium,** or skull, between the occipital and frontal muscles of the scalp.

Arrgh! When you see my cheeks (or **buccae,** in Latin) go up in a smile, you know I'm using my buccinator muscles!

> *Beyond the dictionary*
>
> **Saying *pterygoid* isn't p-terribly difficult**
>
> English doesn't have a sound for the consonant cluster ***pt*** at the beginning of a word. **Pterygoid** is derived from the Greek word for *wing*, ***pteryx.*** When ***pt*** is pronounced in English, the ***p*** is simply silent, as it is when you say the name of the "winged" dinosaur, the pterodactyl. Therefore, **pterygoid** is pronounced TEHR-IH-GOYD.

when the **pectoralis major** muscle adducts and flexes the upper arm.

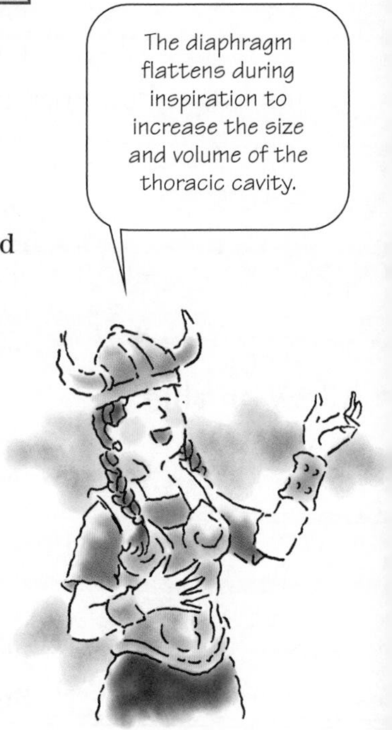
The diaphragm flattens during inspiration to increase the size and volume of the thoracic cavity.

Thorax muscles

The **diaphragm,** a dome-shaped muscle located in the chest, flattens during inspiration to increase the size and volume of the thoracic cavity. This allows air to enter the lungs.

Now for a little ribbing

The **external intercostal** (***costa*** means *rib* in Latin) muscles lift the ribs during breathing, and the **internal intercostals** lower them. The use of these muscles is most noticeable when a person is out of breath.

Abdominal muscles

Muscles in the abdominal cavity form three layers, the **external oblique** (the outermost), the **internal oblique** (the middle), and the **transversus abdominus** (the innermost), with fibers running in different directions.

A muscular girdle

The three layers form a strong "girdle" of muscle that protects and supports the internal organs. These muscles contract during childbirth, defecation, coughing, and sneezing. The **rectus abdominis** muscle runs down the midline of the abdomen and helps flex the spinal column as well as support the abdomen.

The prefix **brachi-** comes from the Latin word that means *arm*, **brachium,** from which we also get the word **embrace!**

Arm and hand muscles

Several important muscles contribute to the movement of the arms and hands:

- **triceps brachii,** which extends the lower arm
- **brachialis,** which flexes the lower arm
- **biceps brachii,** which flexes the lower arm and **supinates** (turns upward) it along with the hand
- **pronator teres,** which flexes and pronates (rotates the forearm so that the palm of the hand faces downward) the lower arm.

It's all in the wrist

Many small muscles work together to flex and extend the wrists, hands, and fingers. Here are a few examples:

- **Flexor** muscles bend the fingers.
- **Lumbrical** muscles allow fine movements of the hands.
- The **flexor carpiradalis** and the **flexor carpiulnaris** both flex and adduct the wrist joints.

Pelvic floor muscles

A muscular "floor" called the **perineum** supports the pelvic organs and protects the diamond-shaped pelvic opening. The perineum occupies the space between the anus and vagina in females and the anus and scrotum in males.

The **levator ani** muscle and the **ischiococcygeus** and **sacrococcygeus** muscles support the pelvic organs and assist with childbirth and defecation. (See *How do I say* coccygeus?, page 78.) The **sphincter ani** muscle keeps the anus closed.

Thigh and upper leg muscles

Three groups of muscles affect movement in the thigh and upper leg area.

The first group includes those that cross the front of the hip:

- The **internal obturator** laterally rotates the thigh and extends and abducts the thigh when it's flexed.

Pump up your pronunciation

How do I say *coccygeus?*

Coccygeus is pronounced COCK-SIHJ-EE-UHS. It's derived from ***coccyx,*** the Greek name for the *cuckoo,* whose bill was thought to have a similar shape to the small bone (henceforth termed the **coccyx**) at the base of the spinal cord in the human body.

The quadratus femoris flexes and extends the leg, in addition to laterally rotating the thigh.

- The **external obturator,** along with both the **superior** and **inferior gemellus,** laterally rotates the thigh as well.
- The **piriformis** laterally abducts, rotates, and extends the thigh.
- The **quadratus femoris** flexes and extends the leg in addition to laterally rotating the thigh.

Bringing up the rear

The second group consists of the **gluteals** (from the Greek word ***gloutos,*** which means *buttocks*). The **gluteus minimus** and **medius** abduct and rotate the thigh while the **gluteus maximus** extends and rotates the thigh.

Adduction is the function

The third group, the **adductors,** includes the powerful **longus, brevis,** and **magnus** muscles, which draw back the thigh after abduction. The **gracilis** flexes and adducts the leg and also adducts the thigh.

Lower leg muscles

Two groups of muscles move the lower leg. The first, the **quadriceps femoris,** includes the **vastus lateralis, medialis,** and **intermedius**—all of which work to extend the leg—and the **rectus femoris,** which flexes the thigh and extends the leg. (See *Quads.*)

The second group of muscles passes behind the thigh, and their tendons form the **hamstrings,** from which the group takes its name. The **semimembranosus**

The real world

Quads

While working out in the gym, you often hear the word **quads** applied to the thigh muscles as a whole. In medical terminology, it's important to know the four muscles that make up the **quadriceps femoris**—the **rectus femoris, vastus lateralis, vastus medialis,** and **vastus intermedius.**

and **semitendinosus** extend the thigh, and the **biceps femoris** helps to both extend the thigh and flex the leg.

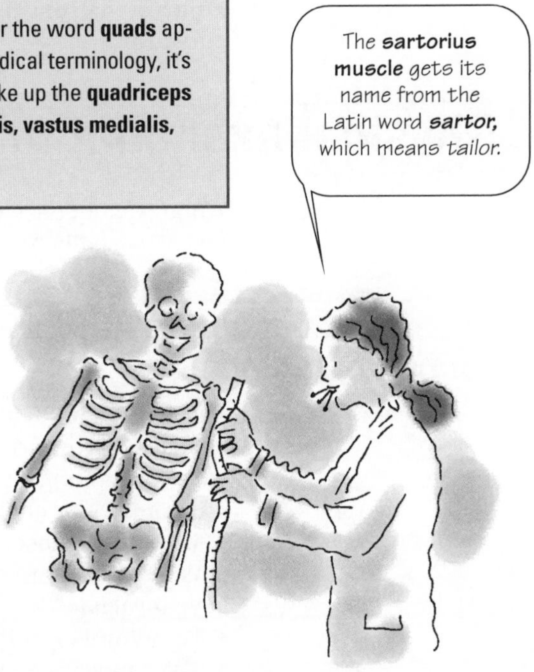
The **sartorius muscle** gets its name from the Latin word ***sartor,*** which means *tailor.*

Tailor made

Other lower leg muscles include the **gastrocnemius** and the **sartorius.** The gastrocnemius flexes the leg and extends the foot. It's commonly called the **calf muscle** (the **Achilles tendon** attaches to this muscle). The sartorius flexes and adducts the leg into the "tailor" position.

Foot muscles

Extrinsic foot muscles are located in the leg but pull on tendons that move bones in the ankle and foot. These muscles allow **dorsiflexion** (upward turning of the foot or toes), **plantar flexion** (movement toward the toes), **inversion** (turning inward movement), and **eversion** (turning outward movement) of the foot.

Intrinsic foot muscles are located within the foot and produce flexion, extension, abduction, and adduction of the toes. The most important muscles of the foot include:

- **soleus,** which extends and rotates the foot (the Latin word for *sun* is ***sol;*** just as the sun causes the earth to rotate, this muscle causes the foot to rotate)
- **tibialis anterior,** which elevates and flexes the foot

• **tibialis posterior,** which extends the foot and turns it inward
• **peroneus longus,** which extends and abducts the foot and turns it outward
• **peroneus brevis,** which extends and abducts the foot
• **peroneus tertius,** which flexes the foot and turns it outward.

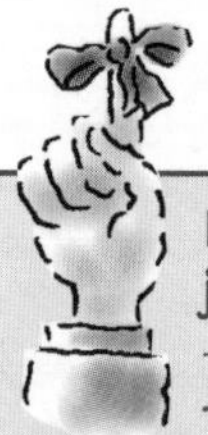

Memory jogger

The acronym **TIPS** will keep you on your toes and help you remember the muscles of the foot:

TIbialis anterior and posterior

Peroneus longus, brevis, and tertius

Soleus.

Physical examination terms

When a patient seeks medical help for a muscular problem, it's usually because of a physical mishap or a chronic ache.

Common complaints

The term **myopathy** refers to any disease of the skeletal muscles. Below are other terms you may need to know when examining a patient with a myopathic condition or other muscular complaints:
• **Myalgia** is muscle pain or tenderness. For instance, an athlete with a patient with a sore pitching shoulder might have myalgia.
• **Myoclonus** is a spasm of a muscle.
• **Myotasis** is a continual stretching of a muscle, commonly referred to as a **pulled muscle.**
• **Myotonia** is chronic muscle contraction or irritability. Myotonia may be confirmed if there's isometric **contraction**—the muscle length remains the same as the tension on it increases.
• **Tenalgia** is a pain in the tendon, such as tennis elbow.
• **Tetany** is hyperexcitability of nerves and muscles, which results from lessened concentration of extracellular ionized calcium.
• A **tic** is a small muscle spasm.

The suffix -algia comes from the Greek and means pain. So tenalgia means pain in the tendon. I could tell you that!

Common observations

Below are some terms that are useful while performing a physical examination:
• **Myelomalacia** is muscle softening, which may indicate **myoatrophy** (muscle wasting) or **myonecrosis** (death of muscle tissue fibers).
• **Myosclerosis** is muscle hardening.

Action reaction

- **Myobradia** is the term used to describe the slow reaction of a muscle to prodding. It may be caused by tissue wasting or death.
- **Myospasm** is the term used to describe muscle convulsions that occur with prodding. It may signal an inflammation of the voluntary muscle tissue, or **myositis.**

Diagnostic tests

Three types of samples—blood, urine, and tissue—may be taken to diagnose muscle disorders. Scanners and other equipment are commonly necessary as well. Below are some of the terms, tests, and tools that may be used.

Physical tests

Three tests are commonly used to assess a patient for carpal tunnel syndrome.

Tingle is the signal

Tinel's sign—a tingling over the median nerve on light percussion—is seen in cases of carpal tunnel syndrome.

Flex test

Phalen's maneuver is used to reproduce the symptoms of carpal tunnel syndrome. In this test, the patient extends his forearms horizontally while completely flexing the wrists for 1 minute. If the patient experiences tingling, numbness, or pain, carpal tunnel syndrome may be present.

If Phalen's maneuver produces pain, carpal tunnel syndrome is present.

Compression impression

A **compression test** can be used to support a diagnosis of carpal tunnel syndrome. A blood pressure cuff is placed on the forearm and inflated above the patient's systolic blood pressure for 1 to 2 minutes. If carpal tunnel syndrome is present, this intervention produces paresthesia along the distribution of the median nerve.

Blood tests

Enzyme levels or the presence of acids in the bloodstream can help diagnose muscular disease. Blood tests are named after the enzyme or acid they're designed to detect:

- Elevated levels of **alanine aminotransferase,** a skeletal enzyme, may indicate muscle tissue damage.
- Elevated levels of **aspartate aminotransferase,** another skeletal muscle enzyme, may indicate muscle damage from muscle trauma or muscular dystrophy.
- **Creatine kinase,** an isoenzyme found in both skeletal and cardiac muscle, may indicate damage from muscle trauma, I.M. injections, myocardial infarction, or muscular dystrophy.

The presence of myoglobin in a urine sample indicates extensive muscle damage.

Urine tests

A **myoglobin** urine test is used to detect the presence of myoglobin in urine. Myoglobin is normally found in the heart and skeletal muscle and, when found in the urine, indicates extensive muscle damage.

Muscle biopsy

In **muscle biopsy,** a needle or incision biopsy is used to extract a specimen of muscle tissue for examination. This microscopic evaluation of muscle tissue samples is commonly required for an accurate diagnosis of muscular disorders.

Tools of the trade

An accurate "image" of the myopathy, which is possible with the use of various types of equipment, may aid in diagnosis.

The equipment

In **computed tomography scanning,** multiple X-ray beams pass through the body at different angles, striking radiation detectors that produce electrical impulses. A computer converts the impulses into digital information that detects tumors in muscle tissue. (See *CAT scan.*)

The real world

CAT scan

The **computed tomography scan** was originally known as the **computerized axial tomography scan**. That's why in practice you'll still hear this test referred to as a **CAT scan.**

An **electromyogram** records the electrical activity of skeletal muscles through surface or needle electrodes. It's used to diagnose neuromuscular disorders and pinpoint motor nerve lesions.

In **magnetic resonance imaging,** a powerful magnetic field and radiofrequency energy are used to produce images based on the hydrogen content of body tissues. Also called **nuclear magnetic resonance,** it's used to diagnose muscle disease.

A **myokinesimeter** measures the muscular contractions that result from stimulating the muscles with electrical current.

Disorders

A wide range of factors, including trauma, heredity, autoimmunity, and the normal aging process, can lead to muscle disorders. This section covers terms associated with muscular disorders.

Muscle conditions

Below are terms for common muscle conditions:

- **Atrophy** is the wasting of muscle.
- **Contractures,** the abnormal flexion and fixation of joints, are typically caused by muscle atrophy and may be permanent.
- **Footdrop** is the inability to maintain the foot in a normal, flexed position (dragging of the foot). This complication is commonly associated with trauma or paralysis.
- A **shin splint** is a strain of the long flexor muscle of the toes that's caused by strenuous athletic activity.
- **Spastic paralysis** is the involuntary contraction of a muscle with an associated loss of function.
- A **sprain** is a complete or incomplete tear in the supporting ligaments surrounding a joint.
- A **strain** is an injury to a muscle or tendinous attachment.

Tumors and lesions

Below are terms for muscle tumors and lesions:

- A **fibroid tumor,** or **leiomyoma,** is a **benign** (noncancerous) tumor found in smooth muscle. It's most common in the uterus.
- A **leiomyosarcoma** is a malignant tumor of smooth muscle that's usually found in the uterus.
- A **myoblastoma** is a benign lesion of soft tissue.
- A **myofibroma** is a benign tumor containing muscular and fibrous tissue.
- A **myosarcoma** is a malignant tumor derived from muscle tissue.
- A **rhabdomyoma** is a benign tumor of striated muscle.
- A **rhabdomyosarcoma** is a highly malignant tumor that originates from striated muscle cells.

Infection and inflammation

Listed here are terms for muscular infection and inflammation:

Epicondylitis anyone?

- **Bursitis** is a painful inflammation of one or more of the **bursae,** closed sacs that cushion muscles and tendons over bony prominences such as the knee.
- **Dermatomyositis** is a connective tissue disease that's marked by itching and skin inflammation in addition to tenderness and weakness of muscles.
- **Epicondylitis,** also known as **tennis elbow,** is an inflammation of tendons in the forearm at their attachment to the humerus.
- **Fasciitis** is inflammation of the fasciae.
- **Myocellulitis** is inflammation of the cellular tissue within a muscle.
- **Myofibrosis** is an overgrowth of fibrous tissue that replaces muscle tissue.
- **Myositis purulenta** is any bacterial infection of the muscle tissue that may result in pus formation and, ultimately, gangrene.
- **Tendinitis,** a painful inflammation of tendons and their muscle attachments to bone, is commonly caused by trauma, congenital defects, or rheumatic diseases. (See *Understanding the suffix* -itis.)

Beyond the dictionary

Understanding the suffix *-itis*

The suffix ***-itis*** is derived from Greek and means *the inflammation of.* Anyone who has suffered the burning pain of **tendinitis** (inflammation of the tendons and their attachments to the bone) can confirm the accuracy of this suffix.

People who do a lot of typing commonly suffer from carpal tunnel syndrome.

Syndromes and diseases

Below are terms for muscular syndromes and diseases:

- An **Achilles tendon contracture** is a shortening of the Achilles tendon. It can cause pain and reduced dorsiflexion.
- **Carpal tunnel syndrome** is a painful disorder of the wrist and hand that results from rapid, repetitive flexion and extension of the wrist.
- **Dupuytren's contracture** is a progressive, painless contracture of the palmar fasciae. It causes the last two fingers to contract toward the palm. (See *Dupuytren's contracture,* page 86.)
- **Fibromyalgia syndrome,** the cause of which is unknown, is a chronic disorder that produces pain in the muscles, bones, or joints.
- **Muscular dystrophy** is a group of degenerative genetic diseases characterized by weakness and progressive atrophy of skeletal muscles, with no evidence of involvement of the nervous system.
- **Myasthenia gravis** is an abnormal weakness and fatigability, especially in the muscles of the throat and face. It results from a defect in the conduction of nerve impulses at the myoneural junction.
- **Torticollis** is a neck deformity in which the neck muscles are spastic and shortened, causing the head to bend toward the affected side and the chin to rotate toward the unaffected side.

Treatments

Rest is commonly all that's needed to treat muscle conditions. Other common options include immobilizing the muscle with a **sling** (a bandage that supports an injured body part), **splint** (an orthopedic appliance that immobilizes and supports an injured body part), or **cast** (a rigid dressing that's placed around an extremity); undergoing physical therapy; applying cold or hot **compresses** (wet or dry cloths); and medicating with prescription drugs.

Douse the flame

Drug therapy includes nonsteroidal anti-inflammatory drugs to decrease inflammation, muscle relaxants to combat spasticity and relax muscles, and corticosteroids to combat inflammation.

Drain the pain

When inflammation is the problem, as in such conditions as tendinitis and bursitis, fluid is sometimes removed from the joint with a hollow needle. The term for this procedure is **aspiration.**

Free at last

When a muscle compresses a nerve, as in carpal tunnel syndrome, surgery may be required if more conservative treatments fail. In carpal tunnel syndrome, **neurolysis,** the freeing of the nerve fibers, is used to remove the entire carpal tunnel ligament so there's more space for the median nerve to pass through the carpal tunnel.

Heat wave

Short-wave diathermy, in which a current is used to generate heat within the muscle, is used to control pain and decrease muscle spasm.

Rub-out

Massage is the methodical use of manipulation, pressure, friction, and kneading to promote circulation, relieve pain, and reduce tension. Massage is used for patients who have restricted movement.

Beyond the dictionary

Dupuytren's contracture

Guillaume Dupuytren (DOO-PWEE-TRAH) (1777-1835) was a French surgeon and clinical teacher. He became intrigued by a peculiar form of **contracture** (the permanent contraction of a muscle) that caused the fingers to curl in the hand. After dissection, he discovered the problem was centered in the palmar fasciae.

systole
parietal

Vocabulary builders

At a crossroads

Here's a little crossword puzzle to help pump up your mental muscle. Good luck!

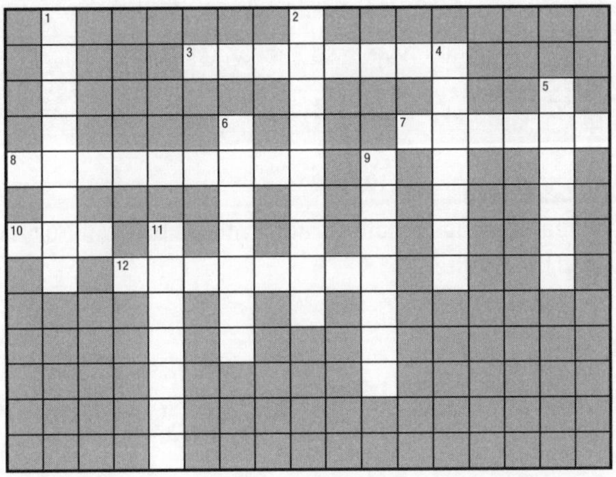

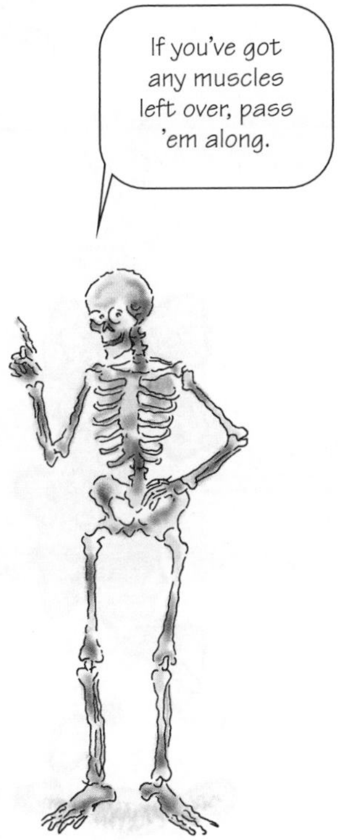
If you've got any muscles left over, pass 'em along.

Across

3. Floor of the pelvis
7. Fibrous membrane sheath
8. Critical for breathing
10. A muscle twitch
12. Muscles composed of thin bands

Down

1. Inflamed bursae
2. Responsible for attaching bones to each other
4. Muscle pain or tenderness
5. Muscle cell groups
6. Adjective for heart muscles
9. Attaches muscles to the periosteum
11. Reduction in the size of muscles

Answers are on page 90.

Finish line

The suffix ***-itis*** comes from the Greek and means *the inflammation of.* Fill in the blanks below to form the correct muscle disorder.

1. Painful inflammation of tendons is called _______________ itis.
2. Painful inflammation of one or more bursae is called _______________ itis.
3. Inflammation of the fasciae is called _______________ itis.
4. Inflammation of cellular tissue within a muscle is called _______________ itis.
5. Inflammation of connective tissue and weakness of muscle is called _______________ itis.

O see, can you say?

Sound out each group of pictures and symbols below to reveal a term that was reviewed in the chapter.

1.

+ E +

2.

+ TROK +
+ MEE + UHS

3.

+ SUH +
+ TUMR

4.

+ O + M
+ O + SAR + KOH +

Answers are on page 90.

Talking in circles

Use the clues below to fill in the blanks with the appropriate word. Then unscramble the circled letters to find the answer to the question posed below.

1. __ __ (◯) __ __ __ __ __ __
2. __ __ __ __ __ __ __ __ (◯)
3. __ __ __ __ __ (◯) __ __ __
4. __ __ __ __ __ __ __ (◯) __ __
5. __ __ __ __ (◯) __ __ __ __
6. __ (◯) __ __ __ __

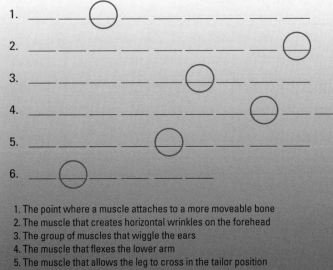

1. The point where a muscle attaches to a more moveable bone
2. The muscle that creates horizontal wrinkles on the forehead
3. The group of muscles that wiggle the ears
4. The muscle that flexes the lower arm
5. The muscle that allows the leg to cross in the tailor position
6. A paroxysmal muscle spasm

Playing in the sun is reminding me of the muscle that makes the foot rotate. Do you know which muscle I mean?

Answers are on page 90.

Answers

At a crossroads

	1 B							2 L								
	U				3 P	E	R	I	N	E	U	4 M				
	R							G				Y			5 F	
	S					6 C		A			7 F	A	S	C	I	A
8 D	I	A	P	H	R	A	G	M		9 T		L			B	
	T				R			E		E		G			E	
10 T	I	C		11 A		D		N		N		I			R	
	S		12 S	T	R	I	A	T	E	D		A			S	
				R		A		S		O						
				O		C				N						
				P						S						
				H												
				Y												

Finish line

1. Tendin; 2. Burs; 3. Fasci; 4. Myocellul; 5. Dermatomyos

O see, can you say?

1. Trapezius; 2. Gastrocnemius; 3. Buccinator; 4. Leiomyosarcoma

Talking in circles

1. Insertion; 2. Frontalis; 3. Auricular;
4. Brachialis; 5. Sartorius; 6. Tetany
Answer to puzzle—Soleus

Let's mosey on out of the muscular system and into the integumentary system!

5

Integumentary system

Just the facts

In this chapter, you'll learn:

- terminology related to the structure and function of the integumentary system
- terminology needed for physical examination of the integumentary system
- tests that help diagnose disorders of the integumentary system
- disorders of the integumentary system and their treatments.

Skin structure and function

The largest body system, the integumentary system includes the skin, or **integument** (from the Latin word ***integumentum,*** which means *covering*), and its appendages—hair, nails, and certain glands. It covers an area that measures 10¾ to 21½ ft^2 and accounts for about 15% of body weight. (See *Pronouncing key integumentary system terms*, page 92.)

Dermatology, the study of skin, comes from the Greek words ***derma,*** which means skin, and ***logos,*** which means science.

Skin layers

Two distinct layers of skin, the **epidermis** and **dermis,** lie above a third layer of **subcutaneous fat.**

On the face of it

The outermost layer, the **epidermis,** varies in thickness from less than 0.1 mm on the eyelids to more than 1 mm on the palms and soles. It's composed of **avascular** (without a direct blood supply),

Pump up your pronunciation

Pronouncing key integumentary system terms

Below is a list of key terms, along with the correct way to pronounce them.

Aphthous stomatitis	AF-THUHS STOH-MUH-TEYE-TIS
Ecchymosis	EK-EE-MO-SIS
Eczema	EK-ZEH-MUH
Erythema	ER-EH-THEE-MUH
Onychomycosis	ON-EH-KOH-MEYE-KOH-SIS
Petechia	PEH-TEE-KEE-UH
Phthirus pubis	THEYE-RUHS PYOU-BIS
Rosacea	ROH-ZAY-SHEE-UH
Sebaceous	SEE-BAY-SHUHS
Subcutaneous	SUHB-KYOU-TAY-NEE-UHS
Telangiectasis	TEL-AN-JEE-EK-TAY-SIS
Verrucae	VEH-ROO-KEE
Vitiligo	VIT-IH-LEYE-GOH

squamous tissue that's **stratified** (arranged in multiple layers). (See *Squamous tissue revealed.*)

The **stratum corneum,** the outermost part of the epidermis, consists of cellular membranes and **keratin,** a protein. Langerhans' cells are interspersed among the keratinized cells below the stratum corneum. Epidermal cells are usually shed from the surface as **epidermal dust.**

Stratum basale, also called the **basal** or **base layer,** produces new cells to replace superficial keratinized cells that are continuously shed or worn away. It also contains specialized skin cells called **melanocytes** that protect the skin by producing and dispersing **melanin** to surrounding epithelial cells. Melanin is a brown pigment

The word **stratum** comes from the Latin ***sternere,*** which means to spread out.

Anatomically speaking

Close-up view of the skin

The illustration below can help you visualize the major components of the skin.

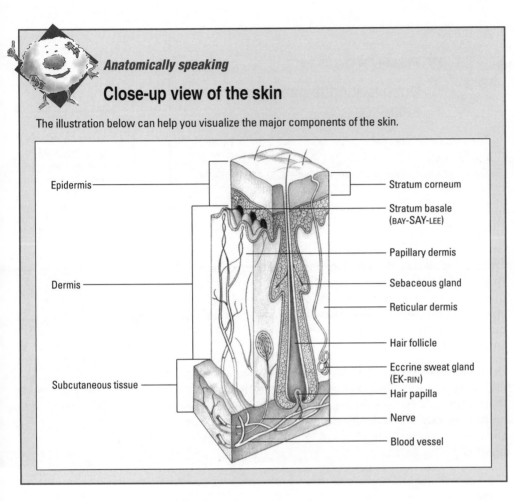

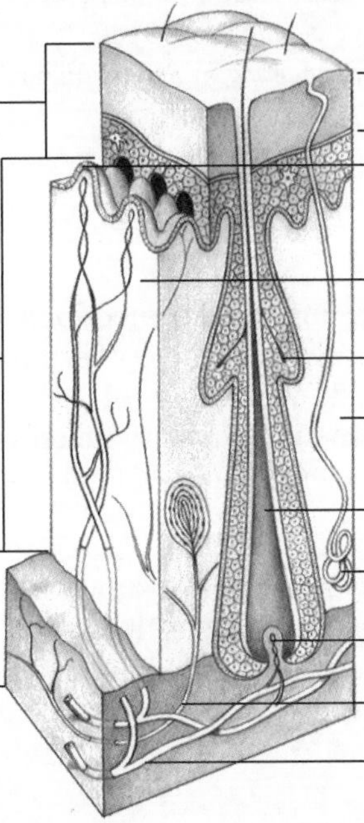
Epidermis
Dermis
Subcutaneous tissue
Stratum corneum
Stratum basale
(BAY-SAY-LEE)
Papillary dermis
Sebaceous gland
Reticular dermis
Hair follicle
Eccrine sweat gland
(EK-RIN)
Hair papilla
Nerve
Blood vessel

Beyond the dictionary

Squamous tissue revealed

Squamous is derived from the Latin term for the scale of a fish or serpent, ***squama.*** It's used in anatomy to describe thin, flat platelike or scalelike structures—in this case, squamous tissue.

that helps filter ultraviolet light. (See *Close-up view of the skin.*)

Digging beneath the surface

The skin's second layer, the **dermis,** also called the **corium,** is an elastic system that contains and supports blood vessels, lymphatic vessels, nerves, and epidermal appendages.

Most of the dermis is made up of extracellular material called **matrix.** Matrix contains connective tissue fibers, including **collagen,** a protein that gives strength to the dermis; **elastin,** which makes the skin pliable; and **reticular fibers,** which bind the collagen and elastin fibers together. These fibers are produced by **dermal fibroblasts,** spindle-shaped connective tissue cells.

> ***Beyond the dictionary***
>
> **Uncovering the panniculus adiposus**
>
> The **panniculus adiposus** is a specialized skin layer that's primarily composed of fat cells. In fact, ***panniculus*** is a Latin term that means *a small piece of cloth or covering,* or *a layer.* **Adipose** means *fat.*

Put the emphasis on the **p.** The **p**apillary dermis has **p**rojections that **p**ush into and nourish the epidermal cells above it.

The dermis has two layers:

- The **papillary dermis** has fingerlike projections (papillae) that nourish epidermal cells. The epidermis lies over these papillae and bulges downward to fill the spaces. A collagenous membrane known as the **basement membrane** separates the epidermis and dermis and holds them together.
- The **reticular dermis** covers a layer of subcutaneous tissue, the **adipose** or **panniculus adiposus,** that's primarily composed of fat cells. In addition to insulating the body, the reticular dermis provides energy and absorbs mechanical shock. (See *Uncovering the panniculus adiposus.*)

Epidermal appendages

Numerous epidermal appendages occur throughout the skin. They include the hair, nails, **sebaceous glands,** and two types of sweat glands—**eccrine** and **apocrine.**

Hair

Hairs are long, slender shafts composed of keratin. At the expanded lower end of each hair is a bulb or root. On its undersurface, the root is indented by a **hair papilla,** a cluster of connective tissue and blood vessels.

A hair-raising experience

Each hair lies within an epithelial-lined sheath called a **hair follicle.** A bundle of smooth-muscle fibers, the **ar-**

rector pili, extends through the dermis and attaches to the base of the follicle. When these muscles contract, hair stands on end.

Nails

Situated over the distal surface of the end of each finger and toe, nails are specialized types of keratin. The **nail plate,** surrounded on three sides by the **nail folds** (or **cuticles**), lies on the **nail bed.** The nail plate is formed by the **nail matrix,** which extends proximally about ¼″ (5 mm) beneath the nail fold.

Under the keratin moon

The distal portion of the matrix shows through the nail as a pale crescent-moon-shaped area, called the **lunula.** The translucent nail plate distal to the lunula exposes the nail bed. The **vascular bed** imparts the characteristic pink appearance under the nails. (See *Lunar expedition.*)

The sebaceous glands

Sebaceous glands occur on all parts of the skin except the palms and soles. They are most prominent on the scalp, face, upper torso, and genitalia.

Nature's conditioner

Sebaceous glands produce **sebum,** an oily, lipid substance that helps protect hair and skin. Sebaceous glands secrete sebum into hair follicles via the sebaceous ducts. Sebum then exits through the hair follicles' openings to reach the skin's surface.

The sweat glands

Widely distributed throughout the body, **eccrine glands** produce an odorless, watery fluid with a sodium concentration equal to that of plasma. A duct (pore) from the coiled secretory portion passes through the dermis and epidermis, opening onto the skin surface.

Located chiefly in the axillary and anogenital areas, the **apocrine glands** have a coiled secretory portion that lies deeper in the dermis than that of the eccrine glands. Ducts connect the apocrine glands to the upper portions of the hair follicles.

Beyond the dictionary

Lunar expedition

The **lunula** gets its name from its crescent-moon shape. ***Luna*** is the Latin word for *moon* and the suffix ***-ula*** indicates *small.* Another word that shares this root is **lunacy**—literally, *moon-sickness.*

A puddle under pressure

Eccrine glands in the palms and soles secrete fluid, mainly in response to emotional stress. The other three million eccrine glands respond primarily to thermal stress, effectively regulating temperature.

Apocrine glands begin to function at puberty. They have no known biological function but may be involved with sexual olfactory messages. As bacteria decompose the fluids that these glands produce, body odor occurs.

Beyond the dictionary

Calling Doctor Langerhans

Many medical terms are named after the doctors who first brought attention to them.

Paul Langerhans (1847-1888), a German doctor, anatomist, and pathologist, is best known for his research on clusters of pancreatic cells, now known as the **islets of Langerhans.** However, he also identified **Langerhans' cells,** which are specialized cells in the skin that help enhance the body's immune system.

Function

The integumentary system performs many vital functions, including protection of inner body structures, sensory perception, and regulation of body temperature and blood pressure.

More than just a pretty face

The top layer of the skin protects the body against traumatic injury, noxious chemicals, and bacterial and microorganismal invasion. **Langerhans' cells,** specialized cells in this layer, enhance the body's immune response by helping process antigens that enter the skin. (See *Calling Doctor Langerhans.*)

Keeping you in touch

Sensory nerve fibers originate in the nerve roots along the spine and terminate in segmental areas of the skin known as **dermatomes.** These nerve fibers carry impulses from the skin to the central nervous system.

Memory jogger

To remember the functions of the skin, think **PPR:**

Perception (sensory)

Protection (of the body)

Regulation (of body temperature and blood pressure).

An all-weather covering

Abundant nerves, blood vessels, and eccrine glands within the skin's deeper layer aid **thermoregulation,** or control of body temperature. When the skin is too cold, blood vessels constrict, leading to a decrease in blood flow through the skin and conservation of body heat.

When the skin is too hot, small arteries in the second skin layer dilate, increasing blood flow and reducing body heat. If this doesn't adequately lower temperature, the eccrine glands act to increase sweat production, and subsequent evaporation cools the skin.

Pressure cooker

Dermal blood vessels also aid regulation of systemic blood pressure through vasoconstriction.

Other odd jobs

When stimulated by ultraviolet light, the skin synthesizes vitamin D_3 (cholecalciferol). It also excretes sweat through the sweat glands. Sweat contains water, electrolytes, urea, and lactic acid.

Physical examination terms

The skin can provide useful information about the body's overall condition. Below are terms associated with a complete skin examination.

Skin color

Decreased hemoglobin level and oxygen in the blood cause changes in skin color. Skin color also responds to changes in the quality and amount of blood circulating through superficial blood vessels.

Cyanosis is Greek to me no longer. **Cyan-** comes from the Greek word **kuanos**, meaning dark blue.

Blue in the face

Cyanosis is a bluish skin color that's caused by an excess of oxygen-starved hemoglobin molecules in the blood. Pale skin is called **pallor,** and pale, cyanotic skin around the lips is known as **circumoral pallor.**

Seeing red

Ecchymosis is a reddish purple skin discoloration that's caused by hemorrhages in the dermal or intradermal spaces. **Erythema** refers to redness or inflammation of the skin resulting from congestion of the superficial capillaries.

Purpura is purple-red or brown-red discoloration on the skin due to hemorrhage in the tissues. Small (pinpoint) discolored areas are called **petechiae,** whereas large ones are called **ecchymoses.**

Feeling yellow—not mellow

Yellowing of the skin, known as **jaundice,** is caused by elevated bilirubin levels.

Carotenemia is a yellow-orange skin discoloration that's caused by excess levels of **carotene** in the bloodstream.

Carotene is an enzyme that's also found in carrots. When a person has **carotenemia,** an excess of carotene in the bloodstream, he turns orange like a carrot.

Skin turgor

Turgor is a condition of normal tension in the skin and reflects the skin's elasticity.

Keeping its shape

Turgor is assessed by gently grasping and pulling up a fold of skin. Normal skin returns to its flat shape within 3 seconds. Abnormal (slow) turgor may be a sign of dehydration or connective tissue disorders. (See Turgor *and its Latin root.*)

Lesions

Allergens, weather, injury, and various diseases can produce **lesions,** or abnormal changes in the skin. Types of lesions include wounds, sores, tumors, and rashes.

First signs of trouble

Primary lesions are the first lesions of an onsetting disease. Below are examples:

- A **bulla** is a fluid-filled lesion, also called a **blister** or **bleb.**
- A **cyst** is a semisolid encapsulated mass that extends deep into the dermis.
- A **macule** is a flat, pigmented area that's less than ⅜″ in diameter; a **freckle** is an example of a macule.
- A **papule** is a firm, raised lesion up to ¼″ in diameter that may be the same color as the skin or may be pigmented.
- A **plaque** is a flat, raised patch on the skin.
- A **pustule** is a lesion that contains pus, which gives it a yellow-white color.
- A **tumor** is an elevated solid lesion larger than ¾″ that extends into the dermal and subcutaneous layers.

Beyond the dictionary

Turgor and its Latin root

Turgid and **turgor** come from the Latin word ***turgidus,*** which means *swollen.* However, **turgor** refers to the normal tension of the skin, or the lack of excessive swelling.

• A **vesicle** is a raised, fluid-filled lesion that's less than ¼″ in diameter. Chickenpox produces vesicles.
• A **wheal** is a raised, firm lesion with intense, usually temporary, swelling around the area. **Urticaria,** or hives, are a type of wheal.

Urtica is the Latin word for the nettle plant. **Urticaria,** or hives, are temporary lesions that are similar to the ones you get when you accidentally rub up against a nettle.

As if that wasn't bad enough

A **secondary lesion** results when changes occur in a primary lesion. Below are examples:
• **Atrophy** is thinning of the skin surface that may be caused by a disorder or aging.
• **Crust** is dried **exudate** (drainage) covering an eroded or weeping area of skin.
• An **erosion** is a lesion that's caused by loss of the epidermis.
• **Excoriation** is a linearly scratched or abraded area.
• **Fissures** are linear cracks in the skin that extend into the dermal layer. Chapped skin causes fissures.
• A **keloid** is a hypertrophied scar.
• **Lichenification** is characterized by thick, roughened skin with exaggerated skin lines.
• **Scales** are thin, dry flakes of shedding skin.
• **Scars** are fibrous tissue caused by trauma, deep inflammation, or a surgical incision.
• An **ulcer** is an epidermal and dermal destruction that may extend into the subcutaneous tissue.

Diagnostic tests

Many skin conditions are diagnosed on sight, but several studies are used to diagnose skin disorders and systemic problems.

Allergy testing

The **patch test** identifies allergies to such substances as dust, mold, and foods. During this test, paper or gauze that has been saturated with a possible **allergen** (a substance capable of producing an allergic reaction) is applied to the skin. The test result is positive if redness or swelling develops.

Scratching the surface

Another method for detecting allergies is the **scratch test.** This test involves inserting small amounts of possible allergens into scratches on the skin surface and watching for a sensitivity reaction.

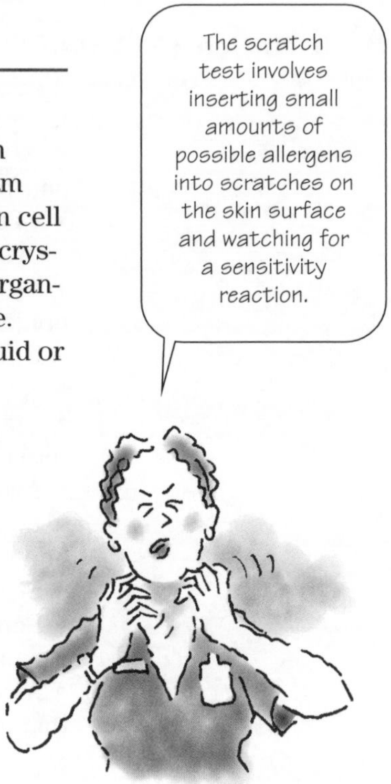
The scratch test involves inserting small amounts of possible allergens into scratches on the skin surface and watching for a sensitivity reaction.

Cultures

Gram stains rapidly provide diagnostic information about which organism is causing an infection. A Gram stain separates bacteria into two categories based on cell wall composition. **Gram-positive** organisms retain crystal violet stain after decoloration. **Gram-negative** organisms lose the violet stain but stain red with safranine.

The **Tzanck test** requires smearing vesicular fluid or drainage from an ulcer on a glass slide, then staining the slide with several chemicals. Herpes virus infection is confirmed by examining the fluid under a microscope. (See *How do I say* Tzanck?)

A sensitive matter

A **culture** is used to isolate and identify an infectious agent. In a culture, a sample of tissue or fluid is placed in a jellylike medium that provides nutrients for microorganisms. If an organism is present, it may multiply rapidly or may take several weeks to grow.

A **sensitivity** test determines the drug that will best treat an infection. Drugs are added to a cultured sample to see which ones kill the offending organism.

Pump up your pronunciation

How do I say *Tzanck?*

Named after Arnault Tzanck (1886-1954), a Russian dermatologist who worked in Paris, the **Tzanck test** requires smearing vesicular fluid or drainage from an ulcer on a glass slide, then staining the slide with several chemicals. The ***t*** sound in **Tzanck** is silent as is the ***t*** sound in **tsar.** Therefore, **Tzanck** is pronounced ZANK.

Biopsies and smear tests

A **biopsy** is the removal of tissue for microscopic examination. Below are types of biopsies used for skin disorders:

- A **skin biopsy** is used to test a small piece of tissue from a lesion suspected of malignancy or other disorder.
- In a **shave biopsy,** the lesion is shaved above the skin line, leaving the lower layers of dermis intact.
- In a **punch biopsy,** an oval plug is removed from the center of a lesion.
- An **excision biopsy** may be used to remove an entire lesion, if it's small enough.

A smear campaign

A somewhat less invasive method than biopsy is the **smear test,** in which cells are spread on a slide and studied under a microscope. In the **buccal smear** test, cells are scraped from the inner surface of the cheek to detect hereditary abnormalities.

Tools of the trade

During **phototesting,** small areas of skin are exposed to ultraviolet light to detect photosensitivity (acute sensitivity to light). A **Wood's light** is an ultraviolet light that's used to diagnose **tinea capitis.** Hairs infected by this fungus appear fluorescent under a Wood's light.

Disorders

Skin forms a barrier against the environment and also reflects problems within the body, so it's an easy target for infection, injury, and infestation.

Bacterial infections

Below are some common bacterial infections:

- **Impetigo** is a contagious, superficial skin infection that's usually caused by *Staphylococcus aureus.* Impetigo lesions start as macules, then develop into vesicles that become pustular with a honey-colored crust. When the vesicle breaks, a thick yellow crust forms from the exudate.

- **Cellulitis** is an inflammation of subcutaneous and dermal tissues caused by a bacterial infection. It often appears around a break in the skin, such as an insect bite or a puncture wound. The affected area is red, swollen, and warm. Fever, chills, headache, and tiredness commonly accompany cellulitis.
- **Folliculitis** is a bacterial infection of the hair follicles that's usually caused by *S. aureus.* A **furuncle,** or **boil,** begins deep in the hair follicles. When a boil spreads to surrounding tissue and produces a cluster of furuncles, it's called a **carbuncle.**
- A **stye** is an abscess in the eyelash follicle that's caused by a staphylococcal infection.

Carbuncle means a *small live coal* in Latin. The burning and glowing of hot coals is an apt image for a carbuncle, which is a cluster of angry, painful boils.

Viral infections

Two common manifestations of viral infections are the sores associated with different types of **herpes** and **warts.**

A not-so-simple(x) infection

The word **herpes,** often used as a singular word, actually refers to a variety of viruses. Below are some common types of herpes:

- **Herpes simplex virus type 1** causes painful cold sores and fever blisters on the skin and mucous membranes. After initial infection, patients are susceptible to recurrent bouts with the virus. Outbreaks are accompanied by burning pain, swelling, redness, and fatigue.
- **Herpes simplex virus type 2,** also known as **genital herpes,** produces lesions in the genital area. Patients complain of flulike signs and symptoms, including headache, fatigue, muscle pain, fever, and loss of appetite. Both herpes simplex types 1 and 2 are caused by contact with an infected lesion.
- **Herpes zoster,** also known as **shingles,** is caused by **varicella-zoster,** the chickenpox virus. Lesions called **spinal ganglia** appear along spinal nerve fibers outside the central nervous system. The virus is dormant until the patient's resistance is low, then a row of vesicular skin lesions erupts along a spinal nerve pathway, accom-

panied by severe pain, fever, and weakness. (See *A creeping virus.*)

As common as a toad

Verrucae (warts) are common, harmless infections of the skin and mucous membranes. They're caused by the human **papillomavirus** and can be transmitted by direct contact. Diagnosed by their appearance, warts are divided into the following categories:

- **common** (also called **verruca vulgaris**)—rough, elevated wart appearing most commonly on extremities, especially hands and fingers
- **filiform**—stalklike, horny projection commonly occurring around the face and neck
- **flat**—multiple groupings of up to several hundred slightly raised lesions with smooth, flat, or slightly rounded tops
- **genital** (also called **condyloma acuminatum**)—sexually transmitted infection appearing on the penis, scrotum, vulva, and anus
- **periungual**—rough wart appearing around the edges of fingernails and toenails
- **plantar**—appearing as a singular lesion or in large clusters, primarily at pressure points of the feet, with lesions that are slightly elevated or flat.

Beyond the dictionary

A creeping virus

Hippocrates used the term ***herpes,*** the Greek word for *creeping,* to describe a spreading cutaneous infection. Galen later revived the term during the 2nd century and diagnosed three types of the infection. Until the 18th century, the term was used for a number of conditions, including varieties of eczema and psoriasis. Around this time, English doctor Robert Willan restricted its use to the definition used today.

Parasitic infections

Pediculosis results from the infestation of bloodsucking lice. These lice feed on human blood and lay their eggs, or **nits,** in body hair or clothing fibers. When a louse bites, it injects a toxin into the skin that produces mild irritation and a reddened spot. Repeated bites can lead to serious inflammation. Three types of lice attack humans:

- ***Pediculus humanus capitis,*** or head louse
- ***Pediculus humanus corporis,*** or body louse
- ***Phthirus pubis,*** or pubic louse (see *Crabs*, page 104).

The nesting instinct

Scabies, another common parasitic infection, is caused by a female mite that penetrates and burrows into the skin. Under the skin, the mite lays eggs that mature and rise to the surface. A scabies infestation produces intense itching and secondary infections from the excoriation caused by scratching. Wavy, brown, threadlike lines appear on the hands, arms, body folds, and genitals.

> **The real world**
>
> ### Crabs
>
> In nonmedical settings, you'll often hear pubic lice called **crabs.** This makes sense figuratively because pubic lice move in a crablike manner. Thus, the term **crabs** has become common slang for cases of sexually transmitted pubic lice.

Fungal infections

Dermatophytosis is the general name for a fungal infection. Mushrooms, molds, and yeasts are common **fungi** (plural of **fungus**). Fungi are present in the air, soil, and water, but only a few species of fungi cause disease.

One of the most common fungal disorders is **tinea,** or **ringworm.** Each type of tinea is named according to the body part it affects:

- **Tinea barbae** affects the bearded area of the face and neck. This infection produces raised areas that have marked crusting.
- **Tinea capitis** is characterized by small, spreading papules on the scalp that cause patchy hair loss with scaling.
- **Tinea corporis** affects the body and produces lesions with a ring-shaped appearance.
- **Tinea cruris,** commonly called **jock itch,** produces red, raised itchy lesions on the groin and surrounding areas.
- **Tinea pedis** is also called **athlete's foot.** This infection causes scaling and maceration between the toes, severe itching, and pain.
- **Tinea unguium,** also called **onychomycosis,** usually starts at the tip of one or more toenails and produces gradual thickening, discoloration, and crumbling of the nail.

Remember to break down seemingly difficult words such as **dermatophytosis.** In Greek, ***derma*** means *skin,* ***phyto*** means *plant,* and ***osis*** means *disease.*

The red on a baby's bottom

Candidiasis, also called **moniliasis,** is a mild, superficial fungal infection of the skin, nails, or mucous membranes. The patient develops a scaly, reddened papular rash with severe itching and burning. This fungus is often the culprit in diaper rash and vaginal infections. It's diagnosed through skin scrapings.

The white on another set of cheeks

Thrush is a fungal infection of the oral mucous membranes caused by *Candida albicans.* This infection develops most commonly in patients whose defenses are weakened by illness, malnutrition, infection, or prolonged treatment with antibiotics. White patches develop on a red, moist, inflamed surface inside the mouth, usually the inner cheeks. Thrush is accompanied by pain and fever.

Inflammatory disorders

Different types of dermatitis make up the most common inflammatory skin disorders.

Dermatitis

Superficial skin infections are known as **dermatitis.** Dermatitis can be caused by numerous things, including drugs, plants, chemicals, and food.

Hands off!

Contact dermatitis occurs when direct contact with an irritant causes the epidermis to become inflamed and damaged. Touching such substances as poison ivy, poison oak, detergents, and industrial chemicals can lead to pain, burning, itching, and swelling—signs and symptoms of dermatitis.

Other types of dermatitis include:

- **atopic dermatitis**—a chronic inflammatory response. **Atopic** refers to a tendency to develop allergies, and **dermatitis** is an inflammation of the skin. The most common symptoms are dry, itchy (pruritic) skin and rashes on the face, inside the elbows, on the hands and feet, and behind the knees. Atopic dermatitis is often called **eczema**.
- **exfoliative dermatitis**—a severe chronic inflammation characterized by peeling of the skin
- **localized dermatitis**—a superficial inflammation characterized by redness and widespread erythema and scaling
- **nummular dermatitis**—a chronic form of dermatitis characterized by coin-shaped, pruritic, crusted scales
- **seborrheic dermatitis**—an acute or subacute skin disease that primarily affects the scalp and face and is characterized by dry or moist greasy scales and yellowish crusts
- **stasis dermatitis**—fragility with fibrous changes of the skin that are accompanied by tan pigmentation,

patchy redness, and petechiae; typically caused by swelling from impaired venous circulation.

To pronounce **psoriasis**, think of the word "sore." The *p* is silent.

Other inflammatory disorders

Here are some other inflammatory skin disorders, including allergies.

Don't eat that!

Angioedema is characterized by urticaria and edema that occur as an allergic reaction, usually to a certain food. It occurs in the subcutaneous tissues of isolated areas, such as the eyelids, hands, feet, tongue, larynx, GI tract, or lips.

Silvery scales

Psoriasis is a chronic skin disorder, commonly with unknown causes, that's characterized by periods of remission and worsening. Psoriasis usually starts between ages 25 and 30. Lesions appear as reddened papules and plaques covered with silvery scales; they vary widely in severity and location.

Skin tumors

Most skin tumors are **benign** (noncancerous), but they can be a starting point for skin cancer.

An **angioma** is formed by a group of blood vessels that dilate and form a tumorlike mass. A port-wine birthmark is a typical angioma. **Spider angiomas,** also called **telangiectases,** are made up of tiny, dilated veins that spread outward with a spiderlike appearance. (See *Caught in a web.*)

Beyond the dictionary

Caught in a web

The word **telangiectases** derives from Greek. ***Tela*** is the Greek term for *weblike,* ***angi-*** is a Greek affix for *vessels,* and ***ectasia*** is the Greek word for *distended.* Put them all together and you have a good description of **telangiectases**—distended weblike veins.

Not so benign...

Basal cell carcinoma is a type of skin cancer arising in the basal cell layer of the epidermis. Commonly found on the face and upper trunk, these tumors are painless and may go unnoticed by the patient.

Squamous cell carcinoma, another form of skin cancer, begins in the epidermis and produces a firm, **nodular** (knotlike) lesion covered with a crust or a central ulceration.

...and malignant

In **malignant melanoma,** cancer arises from the **melanocytes** (pigment cells) of the skin and its underlying structures. There are three types of malignant melanoma, which are categorized by location and description:

- **Superficial spreading melanoma** arises from an area of chronic irritation and is characterized by irregular colors and margins.
- **Nodular melanoma** grows vertically, invading the dermis and metastasizing early.
- **Lentigo maligna melanoma** arises from a lentigo maligna on an exposed skin surface and features a large lesion with scattered black nodules.

Cutaneous ulcers

An **ulcer** is an open sore. Ulcers on the skin are usually caused by a lack of circulation to a vulnerable area. Ulcers may be **superficial,** caused by local skin irritation, or **deep,** originating in the underlying tissue.

Under pressure

Pressure ulcers are localized areas of cellular death that occur most commonly in the skin and subcutaneous tissue over bony prominences. Increased pressure impairs circulation.

Not in a good flow

Stasis ulcers are caused by chronic **venous stasis** (poor blood flow) due to inefficient or obstructed veins. Prolonged standing in one position and obesity are predisposing factors for stasis ulcers.

Remember, **ulcer** comes from the Latin word ***ulcus,*** which means *sore.*

Burns and cold injury

The skin is an effective protective covering. It can, however, be severely damaged when it comes in contact with excessive heat or cold.

Too hot

A burn is an injury to tissue caused by contact with dry heat (fire), moist heat (steam),

Assessing burns

Assessing a burn means determining the depth of skin and tissue damage. It's traditional to describe burn depth by degrees, although most burns are a combination of different degrees and thickness.

First-degree, or superficial, burn
In a first-degree burn, damage is limited to the epidermis, causing redness and pain. The skin is dry, with no blisters or drainage. A sunburn is a type of first-degree burn.

Second-degree, or partial-thickness, burn
In a second-degree burn, the epidermis and part of the dermis are damaged, producing blisters and mild-to-moderate edema and pain. Large, moist blisters may occur, and the skin is mottled with dull white, tan, pink, or cherry-red areas. Spilling a hot cup of coffee on the skin could produce a second-degree burn.

Third-degree, or full-thickness, burn
In a third-degree burn, the dermis and epidermis are damaged. No blisters appear, but white, brown, or black leathery tissue and thrombosed vessels are visible. Little or no pain accompanies this burn because the nerves are damaged. The skin doesn't blanche with pressure. Contact with hot liquids, flames, chemical, or electricity may cause a third-degree burn.

Fourth-degree burn
In a fourth-degree burn, damage extends through deeply charred subcutaneous tissue to muscle and bone.

electricity, chemicals, lightning, or radiation. Categorized according to depth, burns are referred to as **superficial, partial-thickness,** or **full-thickness.** When named according to severity, burns are called **first, second, third,** or **fourth degree.** (See *Assessing burns.*)

Too cold

Cold injury, or **frostbite,** results from overexposure to cold air or water. Upon returning to a warm place, a person with superficial frostbite experiences burning, tingling, numbness, swelling, and a mottled, blue-gray skin color. Deep frostbite causes pain, blisters, tissue death, and gangrene. The skin appears white until it thaws and then appears purplish blue.

Chilblain is a combination of the English word ***chill*** and the Old English word for sore, ***blain.***

Other skin disorders

Here are some other common skin disorders:
- **acne**—an inflammatory skin eruption caused by plugged sebaceous glands, resulting in papules and pustules
- **albinism**—an inherited condition of defective melanin production, causing lack of pigmentation to the skin
- **alopecia**—hair loss
- **aphthous stomatitis (canker sores)**—recurring ulcers on the mucous membrane of the mouth, with small, white lesions

• **chigger**—the larvae of a mite, which attach to the host's skin, causing severe itching and dermatitis
• **chilblain**—redness, burning, and swelling of the skin caused by exposure to cold, damp conditions
• **nevus**—a benign birthmark
• **rosacea**—a chronic skin disease that causes dilated and inflamed surface blood vessels and reddening of the nose and adjoining areas; commonly is accompanied by acne **(acne rosacea)**
• **vitiligo**—irregularly shaped patches of lighter or white skin caused by the loss of pigment-producing cells.

Treatments

Treating skin disorders is an example of hands-on health care. Most medicines are applied **topically** (to the affected area only). Surgery is typically performed with only a local anesthetic, and monitoring depends mostly on simple observation.

Drug therapy

Drugs used to treat skin disorders include **local anti-infectives** to treat infection, **topical corticosteroids** to reduce inflammation, **protectants** to prevent skin breakdown, **keratolytics** to loosen thickened layers of skin, **astringents** to shrink tissues, and **emollients** and **demulcents** to soothe the skin.

Laser surgery

The word **laser** stands for "light amplification by the stimulated emission of radiation." The highly focused and intense light of **lasers** is used to treat many types of skin lesions. Performed on an outpatient basis, laser surgery typically spares normal tissue (with the exception of carbon dioxide [CO_2] lasers), promotes healing, and helps prevent postsurgical infection.

Set your lasers on...

Three types of lasers are used in dermatology:
• The blue-green light of **argon lasers** is absorbed by the red pigment in hemoglobin. It coagulates small blood vessels and treats superficial vascular lesions.

• The CO_2 **laser** emits an invisible beam in the far-infrared wavelength; water absorbs this wavelength and converts it to heat energy. This laser helps treat warts and malignancies.
• The **tunable dye laser** is also absorbed by hemoglobin and has successfully treated port-wine stains.

I don't know why I'm crying. **Cryosurgery** may sound complicated but it's often just liquid nitrogen applied to the skin with a cotton-tipped applicator.

Other surgery

Cryosurgery causes epidermal-dermal separation above the basement membranes, which prevents scarring. In this common dermatologic procedure, the application of extreme cold leads to tissue destruction. It can be performed simply by applying liquid nitrogen to the skin with a cotton-tipped applicator or may involve a complex cryosurgical unit.

Mohs' micrograph surgery involves excising (cutting out) the smallest possible amount of cancerous tissue in a step-by-step manner to determine whether all cancer cells have been removed. This procedure helps prevent cancer recurrence by removing all malignant tissue.

No more childhood scars

Dermabrasion is the removal of superficial scars on the skin using revolving wire brushes or sandpaper. Dermabrasion is typically used to reduce facial scars caused by acne.

Skin grafts

Skin grafts cover defects caused by burns, trauma, or surgery. They're used when primary closure of the skin isn't possible or cosmetically acceptable, when the defect is on a weight-bearing surface, when primary closure would interfere with functioning, and when a skin tumor is **excised**.

Types of skin grafts include:
• **split-thickness grafts,** which consist of the epidermis and a small portion of dermis
• **full-thickness grafts,** which include all of the dermis as well as the epidermis
• **composite grafts,** which also include underlying tissues, such as muscle, cartilage, and bone.

The gift of the graft

An **autologous graft,** or **autograft** (***auto-*** means *self*), is taken from the patient's own body and is the most successful type of skin graft. A graft from a genetically similar person, such as a twin, is an **isologous** graft, or **isograft** (***iso-*** means *alike*).

Patching it up

Biological dressings function like skin grafts to ease pain and prevent infection and fluid loss. However, they're only temporary; eventually the body rejects them. If the underlying wound hasn't healed, these dressings must be replaced with an autologous graft.

There are four types of biological dressings:

- **Homografts (allografts),** which are harvested from cadavers, are rejected in 7 to 10 days. They're used to debride wounds, protect new tissue growth, serve as test grafts before skin grafting, and temporarily cover burns. (***Allo*** is Greek for *deviating from normal* and ***homo*** refers to *human beings.*)
- **Heterografts (xenografts),** grafts harvested from animals (usually pigs), are also rejected after 7 to 10 days. They're used for the same purposes as homografts and are also used to cover exposed tendons and burns that are only slightly contaminated.
- **Amnion,** made from the amnion and chorion membranes (fetal membranes), is used to protect burns and temporarily cover new tissue while awaiting an autograft.
- **Biosynthetic grafts,** which are woven from manmade fibers, are used to cover donor graft sites, protect wounds awaiting autografts, and cover meshed autografts.

Debridement is borrowed from the French and means *to unbridle.* Originally a medical term, it was first used to describe the cutting of constricting bands—similar to a horse's bridle.

Debridement

Debridement is the use of mechanical, chemical, or surgical techniques to remove **necrotic** (dead) tissue from a wound. Although it can be extremely painful, debridement is necessary to prevent infection and promote healing of burns and skin ulcers.

There are three types of debridement:

- **Chemical debridement** involves special wound-cleaning beads or topical medications, which absorb drainage and debris from a wound. These agents also absorb bacteria, reducing the risk of infection.
- **Mechanical debridement** may involve dressings, irrigation, **hydrotherapy** (whirlpool baths), or bedside removal of necrotic tissue. During bedside debridement, dead tissue is scraped off or cut away with a scalpel or scissors.
- **Surgical debridement** requires anesthesia and is usually reserved for burn patients or those with extremely deep or large ulcers.

Therapeutic baths

Also known as **balneotherapy,** baths are used to treat many skin conditions, including psoriasis, eczema, exfoliative dermatitis, and bullous diseases that cause blisters.

The four types of baths commonly used are **antibacterial, colloidal, emollient,** and **tar.** In addition to promoting relaxation, these baths permit treatment of large areas. Therapeutic baths are limited to 30 minutes because they can cause dry skin, itching, scaling, and fissures. (See *The baths.*)

The baths

There are four types of therapeutic baths:

- **Antibacterial baths** are used to treat infected eczema, dirty ulcerations, and furunculosis. Acetic acid, hexachlorophene, potassium permanganate, and povidone iodine are commonly used.
- **Colloidal baths** relieve itching and soothe irritated skin. They're indicated for any irritating or oozing skin condition, such as atopic eczema. Oatmeal, starch, and baking soda are used for colloidal baths.
- In **emollient baths,** bath oils and mineral oil are used to clean and hydrate the skin. They're helpful for any dry skin condition.
- In **tar baths,** special bath oils are used with tar or coal tar concentrate to treat scaly skin disorders. This bath loosens scales and relieves itching.

Phototherapy

Used to treat skin conditions such as psoriasis by exposure to ultraviolet radiation, **phototherapy** slows the growth of epidermal cells, most likely by inhibiting the synthesis of deoxyribonucleic acid. Two different ultraviolet light wavelengths are used: ultraviolet A (UVA) is the component of sunlight that tans skin and ultraviolet B is the component that causes sunburn.

Light plus drugs equals...

Photochemotherapy is a treatment in which a drug called **psoralen** is given to the patient to make his skin more sensitive to UVA light. The combination of psoralen with UVA is also known as **PUVA therapy.**

systole
parietal

Vocabulary builders

At a crossroads

Hopefully, this is a crossword puzzle that won't get under your skin. Good luck!

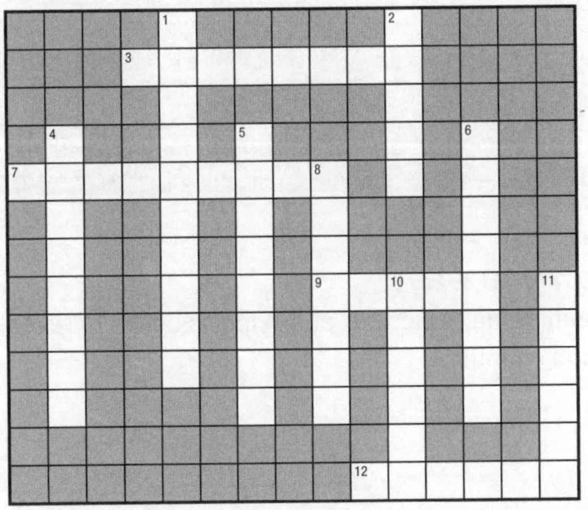

Get ready to toughen up! These puzzles are pretty difficult.

Across

3. An excess of this enzyme turns the skin yellow-orange
7. The outermost layer of skin
9. A fluid-filled lesion
12. Word that describes pale skin

Down

1. The specialized cells in the skin layer that enhance the immune system are named after this doctor
2. The Greek word for *skin*
4. Glands that begin to function at puberty
5. A contagious, superficial skin infection
6. A protein that gives strength to the dermis
8. Caused by female mites
10. Crescent-moon-shaped area on the nail
11. Condition of normal tension in the skin

Answers are on page 116.

Finish line

One of the most common fungal disorders is tinea. Each specific type of tinea is named according to the body part it affects. Fill in the blanks to complete each type of this fungal disorder.

1. Tinea ______________ affects the bearded area of the face and neck.
2. Tinea ______________ produces raised itchy lesions in the groin area.
3. Tinea ______________ is also called *athlete's foot.*
4. Tinea ______________ usually starts at the tip of one or more of the toenails.
5. Tinea ______________ affects the body.
6. Tinea ______________ is characterized by small papules on the scalp.

O see, can you say?

Sound out each group of pictures and symbols below to reveal a term that was reviewed in the chapter.

1.

+
+ SHUHS

2.

VEH +
+

3.

PEH +
+
+ UH

Answers are on page 116.

Talking in circles

Use the clues below to fill in the blanks with the appropriate word. Then unscramble the circled letters to find the answer to the question posed below.

1. ___ ___ ___ ___ (___) ___ ___ ___ ___ ___
2. ___ ___ (___) ___ ___ ___ ___ ___
3. ___ ___ (___) ___ ___ ___ ___ ___ ___ ___ ___
4. ___ (___) ___ ___ ___ ___ ___ ___
5. ___ ___ ___ (___) ___ ___ ___ ___ ___

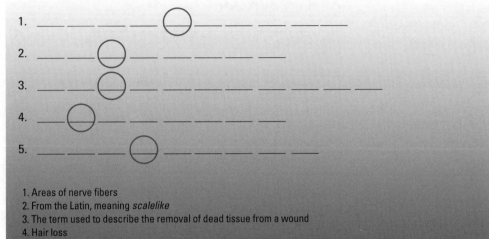

1. Areas of nerve fibers
2. From the Latin, meaning *scalelike*
3. The term used to describe the removal of dead tissue from a wound
4. Hair loss
5. A word from the English word for *chill* and the Old English word for *sore*

You're working at a "blistering" pace. What skin lesion are you likely to get?

Answers are on page 116.

Answers

At a crossroads

				1 L						2 D				
			3 C	A	R	O	T	E	N	E				
				N						R				
	4 A			G		5 I				M		6 C		
7 E	P	I	D	E	R	M	I	8 S		A		O		
	O			R		P		C				L		
	C			H		E		A				L		
	R			A		T		9 B	U	10 L	L	A		11 T
	I			N		I		I		U		G		U
	N			S		G		E		N		E		R
	E					O		S		U		N		G
										L				O
									12 P	A	L	L	O	R

Finish line

1. Barbae; 2. Cruris; 3. Pedis; 4. Unguium; 5. Corporis; 6. Capitis

O see, can you say?

1. Sebaceous; 2. Verrucae; 3. Petechia

Talking in circles

1. Dermatomes; 2. Squamous; 3. Debridement; 4. Alopecia; 5. Chilblain
Answer to puzzle—Bulla

Good goin.' Let's move on to the cardiovascular system without skipping a beat.

6

Cardiovascular system

Just the facts

In this chapter, you'll learn:

- terminology related to the structure and function of the cardiovascular system
- terminology needed for physical examination of the cardiovascular system
- tests that help diagnose cardiovascular disorders
- disorders of the cardiovascular system and their treatments.

Heart structure and function

A key to learning terminology related to the cardiovascular system is knowing the medical word for *heart:* it's the Latin word ***cardium,*** which is borrowed from the Greek word ***kardia.*** Cardium is often combined with other words in the forms ***cardi*** or ***cardio.*** Some examples include *cardiology*, *electrocardiogram*, and *tachycardia.* (See Cardiac *versus* heart and *Pronouncing key cardiovascular system terms*, page 118.)

The heart's protector

The heart is protected by a thin sac called the **pericardium.** ***Peri-*** is a Greek prefix that means *around.* The pericardium has an inner, or **visceral,** layer that forms the **epicardium** and an outer, or **parietal,** layer.

A three-layered heart

The heart wall is composed of three layers. The outer layer is the **epicardium.** ***Epi-*** is a Greek prefix that means *on.* The **myocardium** is the heart muscle itself,

Beyond the dictionary

Cardiac versus heart

The word **cardiac** is nearly as familiar to most English-speaking people as the word **heart.** Because Greek and Latin were the primary languages of universities up until the 1900s, terms from those languages were adopted for scientific use. Some of those terms, like **cardiac,** have migrated into ordinary English speech as well.

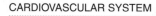

Pump up your pronunciation

Pronouncing key cardiovascular system terms

Below is a list of key terms, along with the correct ways to pronounce them.

Aneurysm	AN-YOU-RIZM
Angina	AN-JEYE-NUH
Arrhythmia	AH-RITH-MEE-UH
Arteriosclerosis	AR-TEER-EE-OH-SKLER-OH-SIS
Coarctation	KOH-ARK-TAY-SHUHN
Defibrillation	DEE-FIB-RUH-LAY-SHUHN
Diuretic	DEYE-YUH-REH-TIK
Electrophysiologic	E-LEK-TROH-FIZZ-EE-OH-LOJ-IK
Ischemia	IS-KEE-MEE-UH
Paroxysmal atrial tachycardia	PAR-OK-SIZZ-MUHL AY-TREE-UHL TAK-EH-KAR-DEE-UH
Pericardiocentesis	PER-UH-KAR-DEE-OH-SEN-TEE-SIS
Prinzmetal angina	PRINTS-MET-UHL AN-JEYE-NUH
Sphygmomanometer	SFIG-MOH-MAHN-OM-UH-TER
Thrombophlebitis	THROM-BOH-FLEH-BEYE-TIS

and the **endocardium** is the innermost layer, which lines the heart's chambers and covers its valves. ***Endo-*** is a Greek prefix that means *within.*

Welcome to my chambers

The heart consists of four chambers. Each of the two upper chambers is called an **atrium** (plural: **atria**). The atria are thin-walled chambers that serve as reservoirs for blood. Each atrium is connected by its own valve to a chamber below it. The two lower chambers are called **ventricles** (also called **ventriculi**). The ventricles have thick walls and are responsible for pumping blood throughout the body. (See *Why the atria are called* atria.)

Beyond the dictionary

Why the atria are called *atria*

It's fitting that the upper chambers of the heart are called **atria** because, in a Roman house, the atrium was an entrance where a person was greeted before moving into other rooms. The atria are the first chambers in the heart to receive blood before it empties into the ventricles and is pumped throughout the body.

And those ventricles? The word **ventricle** derives from the Latin word ***ventriculus,*** which means *little stomach* and refers to any small cavity of the body. There are two ventricles in the heart and four in the brain.

Pump up your pronunciation

How do I say *vena cava?*

In the term **vena cava,** the first word looks like the word **vein,** and that's exactly what it means. It's pronounced VEE-NAH. The second word is pronounced with a long first ***a*** and a short final ***a*** sound, CAY-VAH. The plural **venae cavae,** pronounced VEE-NAY KAH-VAY, refers to both veins.

Blood's path

Blood is carried into the heart through several major vessels, all of which empty into either the **superior vena cava** or **inferior vena cava** (plural: **venae cavae**). The superior vena cava carries blood from the upper body to the right atrium; it's called **superior** because that means *near the top*. **Inferior** means *situated below*, and the inferior vena cava carries blood from the lower body to the right atrium. (See *How do I say* vena cava?)

Through the pulmonary artery and into the lungs

Blood in the right atrium empties into the right ventricle mostly by gravity. When the ventricle contracts, the blood is ejected into the **pulmonary artery** (called such because ***pulmon*** is the Latin word for *lung*). The blood is pushed through the pulmonary arteries to the lungs.

The final trip

From the lungs, blood travels to the left atrium through the **pulmonary veins.** The left atrium empties blood into the left ventricle. The left ventricle pumps the blood into the **aorta** and, from there, it travels throughout the body. (See *Why call it the* aorta?)

The heart's valves

The heart contains two **atrioventricular (AV)** valves (the tricuspid and mitral) and two **semilunar** valves (the pulmonic and aortic). The **tricuspid** valve separates the right atrium from the right ventricle. It has three flaps or cusps.

The **pulmonic** valve separates the right ventricle from the pulmonary artery.

Beyond the dictionary

Why call it the *aorta?*

Aorta means *that which is hung.* Because of the arching curve in the aorta as it exits the heart and its subsequent descent into the body, it looks something like a modern clothes hanger. Apparently, Aristotle had a similar notion; he was the first to apply the name to this artery.

Anatomically speaking

Inside the heart

This illustration shows a cross-sectional view of the structures and blood flow of the heart and major blood vessels.

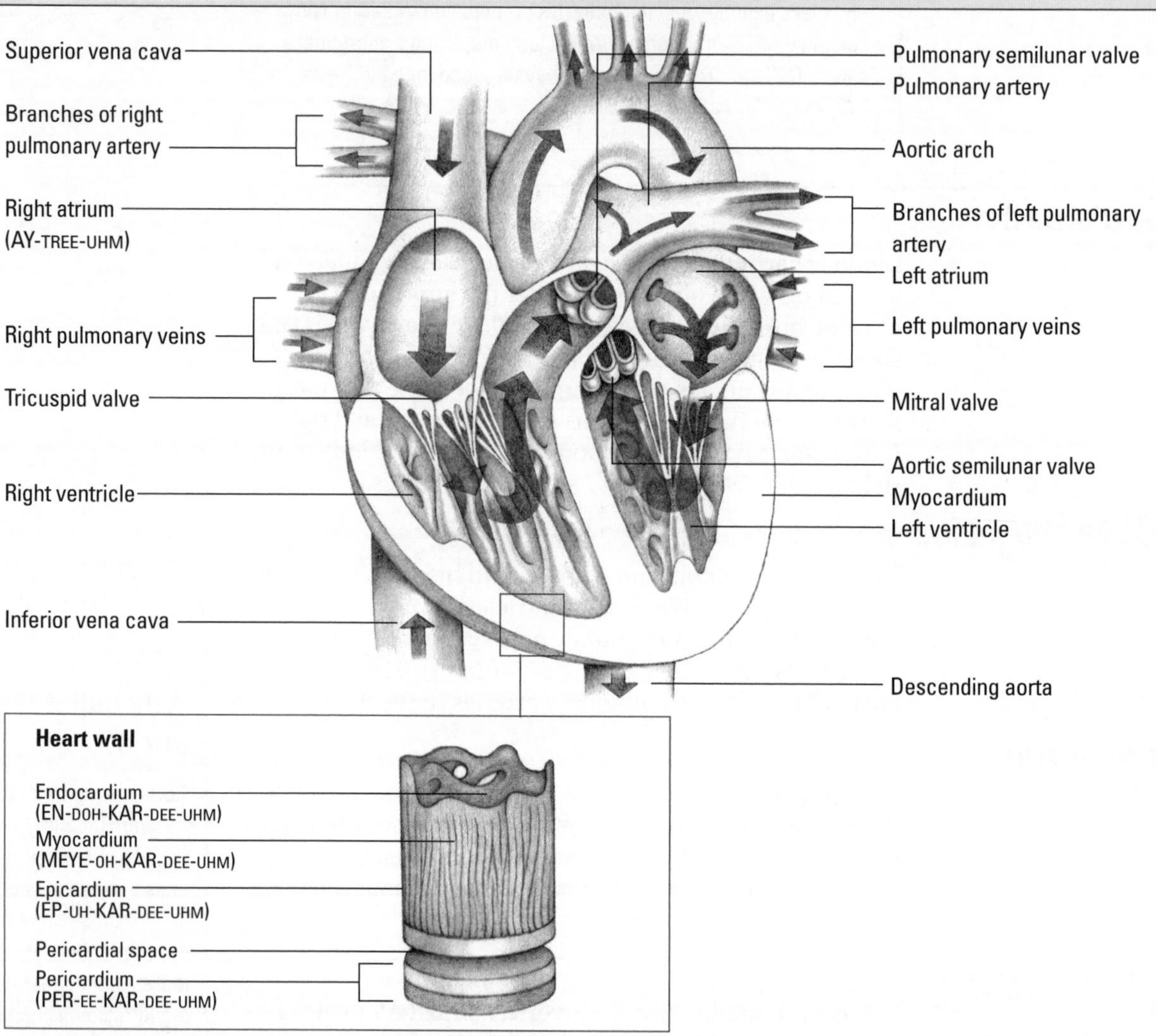

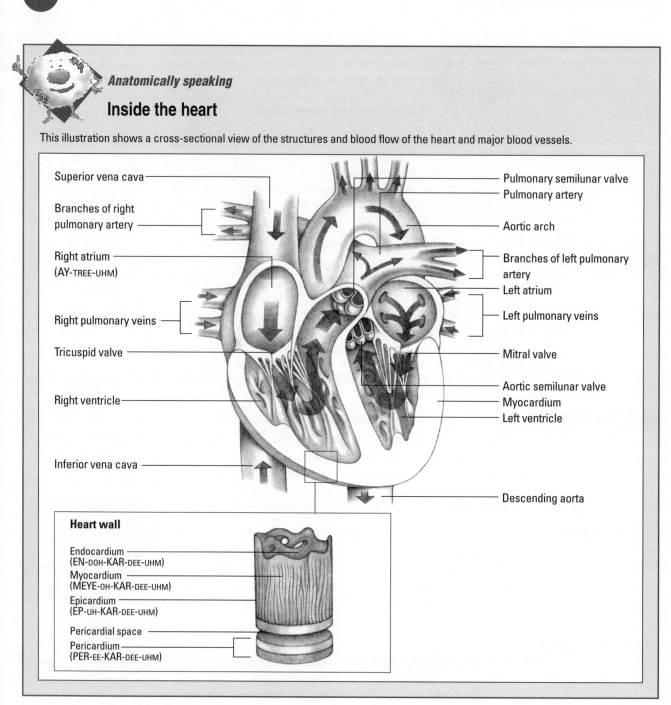

Superior vena cava
Branches of right pulmonary artery
Right atrium (AY-TREE-UHM)
Right pulmonary veins
Tricuspid valve
Right ventricle
Inferior vena cava
Pulmonary semilunar valve
Pulmonary artery
Aortic arch
Branches of left pulmonary artery
Left atrium
Left pulmonary veins
Mitral valve
Aortic semilunar valve
Myocardium
Left ventricle
Descending aorta
Heart wall
Endocardium (EN-DOH-KAR-DEE-UHM)
Myocardium (MEYE-OH-KAR-DEE-UHM)
Epicardium (EP-UH-KAR-DEE-UHM)
Pericardial space
Pericardium (PER-EE-KAR-DEE-UHM)

The **mitral** valve separates the left atrium from the left ventricle. It has two flaps or cusps and is also known as the **bicuspid** valve. (See *Inside the heart.*)

The heart's rhythm

Contractions of the heart occur in a rhythm—the cardiac cycle—and are regulated by impulses that normally begin at the **sinoatrial (SA) node,** the heart's pacemaker. The impulses are conducted from there through the **AV node,** down through the **AV bundle,** or the **bundle of His** (pronounced HIHS), and through the **Purkinje fibers,** where the impulse stimulates ventricular contraction. (See *What's a Purkinje?*)

The mitral valve looks like a bishop's miter—hence the name **mitral valve.**

For every opposite action

The autonomic nervous system has two divisions that have opposite actions on the heart. The **parasympathetic** division acts on the SA and AV nodes. This division slows heart rate, reduces impulse conduction, and dilates coronary arteries.

The **sympathetic** division also acts on the SA and AV nodes but with an opposite effect. This division increases heart rate and impulse conduction and constricts and dilates the coronary arteries.

Cardiac cycle

No discussion of heart functions would be complete without an explanation of the **cardiac cycle,** the period from the beginning of one heartbeat to the beginning of the next. During this cycle, electrical and mechanical events must occur in the proper sequence and to the proper degree to provide adequate blood flow to all body parts. (See *Cardiac conduction route*, page 122.)

The two phases

The cardiac cycle has two phases: systole and diastole. **Systole** is the period when the ventricles contract and send blood on an outward journey to the aorta or the pulmonary artery. **Diastole** is when the heart relaxes and fills with blood. During diastole, the mitral and tricuspid valves are open, and the aortic and pulmonic valves are closed. (See *Systole and diastole*, page 122.)

Diastole—passive then active

Diastole consists of two parts, **ventricular filling** and **atrial contraction.** During the first part of diastole, 70%

Beyond the dictionary

What's a Purkinje?

The Purkinje (PUHR-KIN-JEE) fibers are microscopic muscles first distinguished from ordinary heart muscle tissue by the Czech physiologist Jan Purkinje (1787-1869), who also originated the analysis and classification of fingerprints.

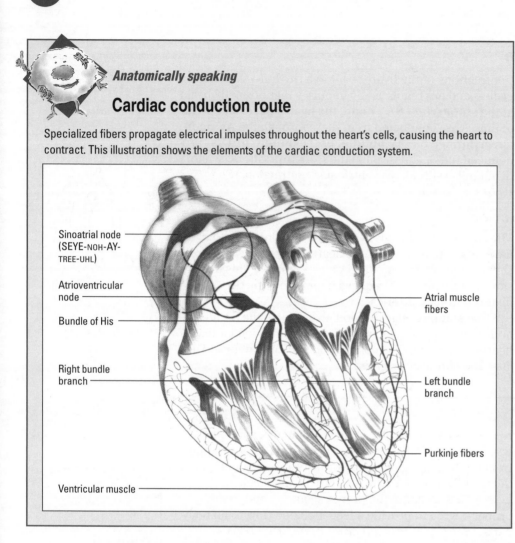

Anatomically speaking

Cardiac conduction route

Specialized fibers propagate electrical impulses throughout the heart's cells, causing the heart to contract. This illustration shows the elements of the cardiac conduction system.

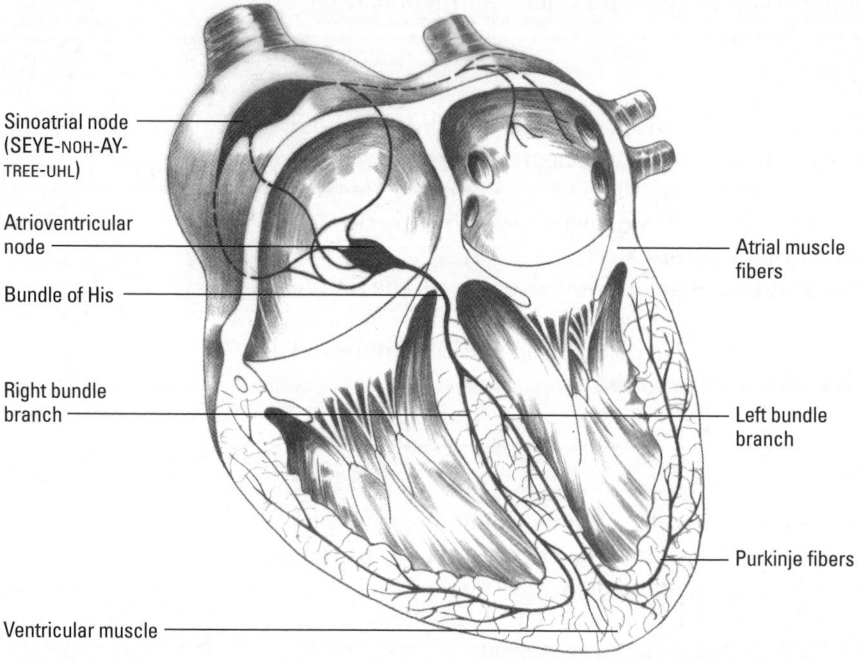
Sinoatrial node (SEYE-NOH-AY-TREE-UHL)
Atrioventricular node
Bundle of His
Right bundle branch
Ventricular muscle
Atrial muscle fibers
Left bundle branch
Purkinje fibers

of the blood in the atria drains into the ventricles as a result of gravity, a passive action.

The active period of diastole, atrial contraction (also called **atrial kick**), accounts for the remaining 30% of blood that passes into the ventricles. Diastole is also the period in which the heart muscle receives its own supply of blood, which is transported there by the **coronary arteries.**

Lub...

Systole is the period of ventricular contraction. As pressure within the ventricles rises, the mitral and tricuspid

(Text continues on page 123.)

Beyond the dictionary

Systole and diastole

Systole (pronounced SIS-TOH-LEE) and ***diastole*** (pronounced DEYE-AH-STOH-LEE) have the same Greek root, ***stole,*** which means *to send.*

Apart or together?
The prefixes are the keys to these words. The prefix ***dia-*** means *apart;* and ***sy-,*** a contraction of ***syn-,*** means *together.* If you think about the relaxation of the muscle and the walls moving apart, you'll remember **diastole.** If you think about the interior wall of the ventricles contracting, coming closer together, you'll remember **systole.**

Incredibly Easy miniguide: The heart

A key to learning terminology related to the cardiovascular system is knowing the medical word for *heart*.
Medical terminology Made Incredibly Easy
The Latin word ***cardium***, which is borrowed from the Greek word ***kardia,*** is the medical word for *heart*.
Medical Terminology Made Incredibly Easy
Latin
Cardium is commonly combined with other words in the forms ***cardi*** or ***cardio.*** Some examples include **cardiology, pericardium, electrocardiogram,** and **tachycardia.**
ium
logy
Cardio
ia

Incredibly Easy miniguide: The heart

Within the heart lie four chambers (two atria and two ventricles). A system of blood vessels carries blood to and from the heart.

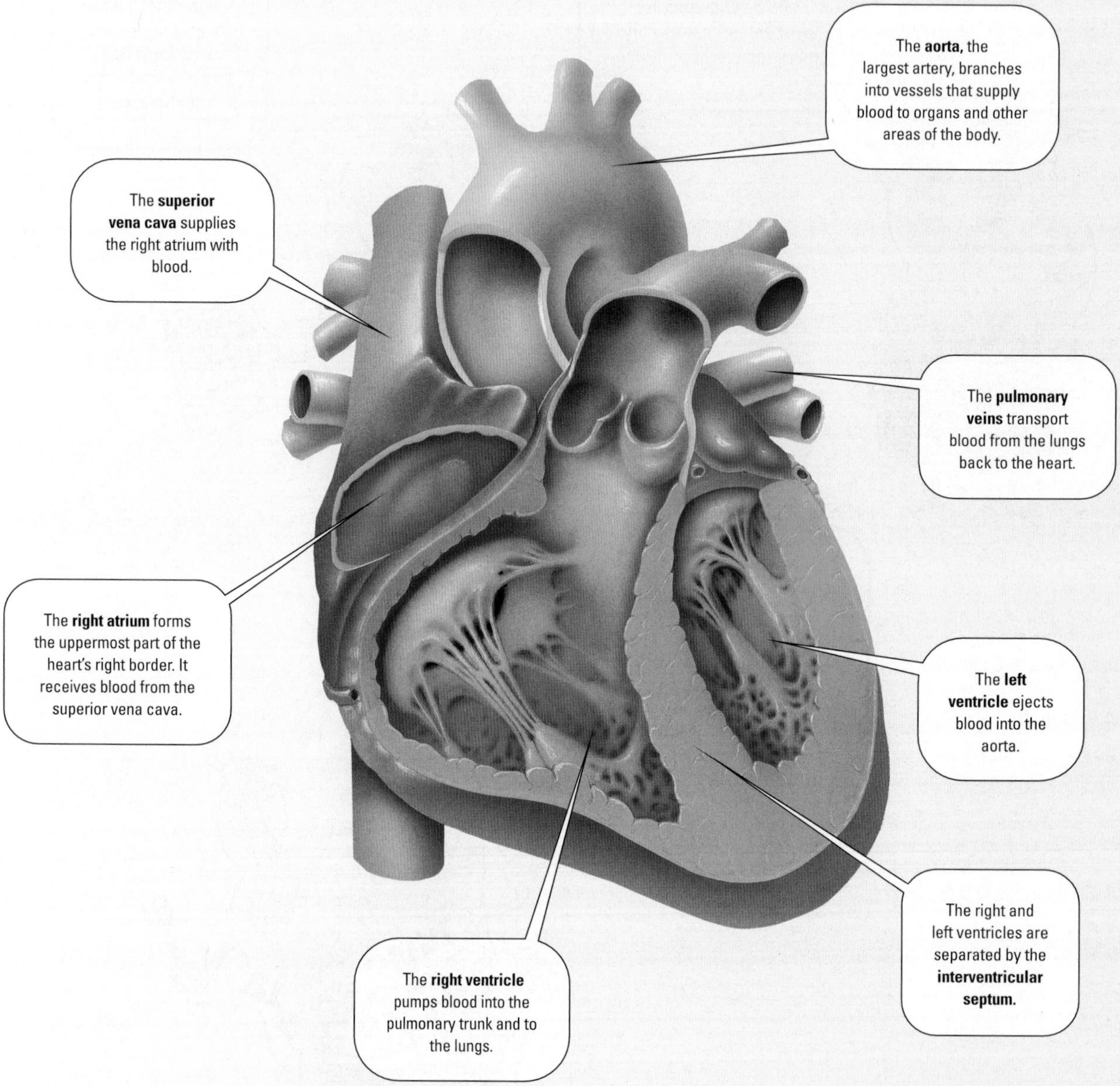
The **aorta,** the largest artery, branches into vessels that supply blood to organs and other areas of the body.
The **superior vena cava** supplies the right atrium with blood.
The **pulmonary veins** transport blood from the lungs back to the heart.
The **right atrium** forms the uppermost part of the heart's right border. It receives blood from the superior vena cava.
The **left ventricle** ejects blood into the aorta.
The right and left ventricles are separated by the **interventricular septum.**
The **right ventricle** pumps blood into the pulmonary trunk and to the lungs.

Incredibly Easy miniguide: The heart

The semilunar valves of the heart have three cusps that are shaped like half-moons. The two atrioventricular valves separate the atria from the ventricles.

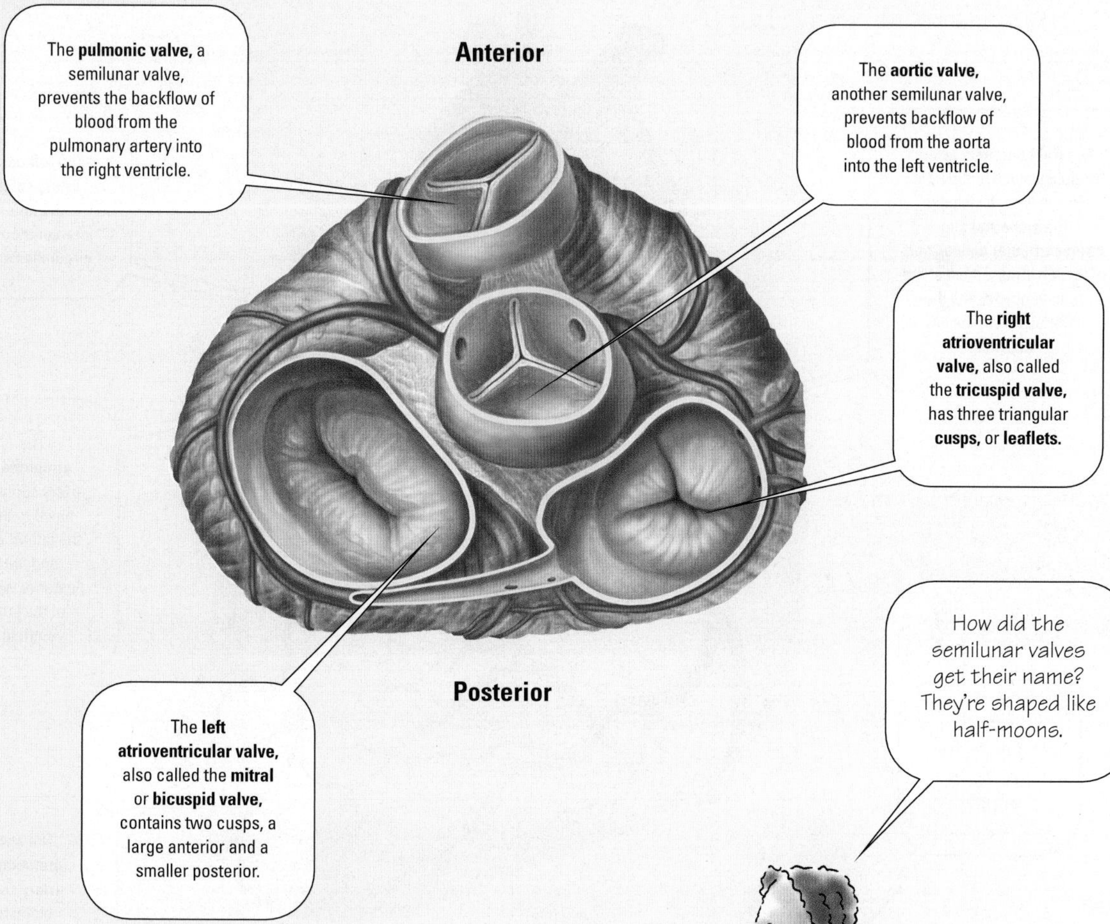
Anterior
The **pulmonic valve,** a semilunar valve, prevents the backflow of blood from the pulmonary artery into the right ventricle.
The **aortic valve,** another semilunar valve, prevents backflow of blood from the aorta into the left ventricle.
The **right atrioventricular valve,** also called the **tricuspid valve,** has three triangular **cusps,** or **leaflets.**
Posterior
The **left atrioventricular valve,** also called the **mitral** or **bicuspid valve,** contains two cusps, a large anterior and a smaller posterior.

How did the semilunar valves get their name? They're shaped like half-moons.

Incredibly Easy miniguide: The heart

The heart relies on the coronary arteries and their branches for its supply of oxygenated blood.

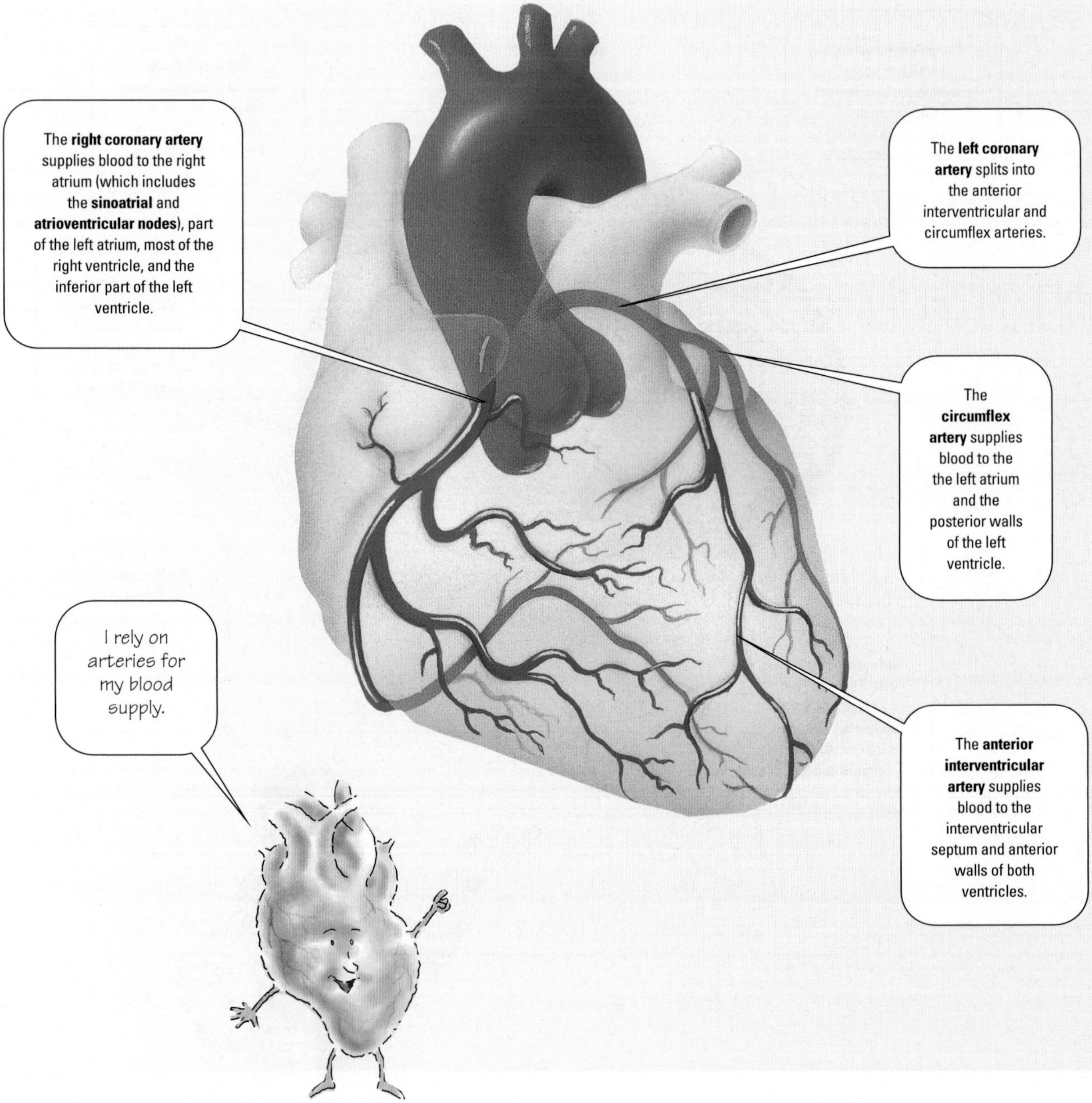

The **right coronary artery** supplies blood to the right atrium (which includes the **sinoatrial** and **atrioventricular nodes**), part of the left atrium, most of the right ventricle, and the inferior part of the left ventricle.
The **left coronary artery** splits into the anterior interventricular and circumflex arteries.
The **circumflex artery** supplies blood to the the left atrium and the posterior walls of the left ventricle.
The **anterior interventricular artery** supplies blood to the interventricular septum and anterior walls of both ventricles.
I rely on arteries for my blood supply.

valves snap closed. This closure leads to the first heart sound, S_1 (the ***lub*** of ***lub-dub***).

When the pressure in the ventricles rises above the pressure in the aorta and pulmonary artery, the aortic and pulmonic valves open. Blood then surges from the ventricles into the pulmonary artery to the lungs and into the aorta to the rest of the body.

Coronary **arteries** got their name because they encircle the heart like a crown. The word **coronary** comes from the Greek **koron,** which means *crown.*

...then *dub*

At the end of ventricular contraction, pressure in the ventricles drops below the pressure in the aorta and the pulmonary artery. That pressure difference forces blood to back up toward the ventricles and causes the aortic and pulmonic valves to snap shut, which produces the second heart sound, S_2 (the ***dub*** of ***lub-dub***). As the valves shut, the atria fill with blood in preparation for the next period of diastolic filling, and the cycle begins again.

Pumping it out

Cardiac output refers to the amount of blood pumped out by the heart in 1 minute and is determined by the **stroke volume,** the amount of blood ejected with each heartbeat multiplied by the number of beats per minute. Stroke volume, in turn, depends on three factors:

- **Contractility** refers to the ability of the myocardium to contract normally.
- **Preload** is the stretching of muscle fibers in the ventricles. This stretching results from the volume of blood in the ventricles at the end of diastole. The more muscles stretch, the more forcefully they contract during systole.
- **Afterload** refers to the pressure the ventricular muscles must generate to overcome the higher pressure in the aorta.

Vascular network

The peripheral vascular system consists of a network of arteries, arterioles, capillaries, venules, and veins.

Keep air in there

Artery comes from the Greek words ***aer,*** which means *air,* and ***terein,*** which means *to keep,* because the ancients believed that arteries contained air. Arteries carry blood away from the heart. Nearly all arteries carry oxygen-rich blood from the heart to the rest of the body. The only exception is the pulmonary artery, which carries oxygen-depleted blood to the lungs.

Smaller and smaller

The exchange of fluid, nutrients, and metabolic wastes between blood and cells occurs in the **capillaries.** Capillaries are connected to arteries and veins through intermediary vessels called **arterioles** and **venules,** respectively. (See *Call it a capillary.*)

You're so vein

Veins carry blood toward the heart. Nearly all veins carry oxygen-depleted blood. The sole exception to this is the pulmonary vein, which carries oxygen-rich blood from the lungs to the heart.

> **Beyond the dictionary**
>
> **Call it a capillary**
>
> ***Capillary*** is a Latin word that means *hairlike.* It refers to the minute size of these vessels.

Physical examination terms

This section introduces terms associated with examination of the heart and abnormalities an examination might reveal.

Vital signs

The physiologic condition of a patient is reflected in his vital signs. The vital signs that are directly related to the cardiovascular system are pulse and blood pressure.

Stay on the beat

A patient's **pulse** is the expansion and contraction of an artery in a regular, rhythmic pattern; this happens when the left ventricle of the heart ejects blood into the aorta as it contracts, causing waves of pressure.

We thrive on pressure

A person's **blood pressure** is maintained by the complex interaction of the homeostatic mechanisms of the body and is influenced by the volume of blood, the lumen of the arteries and arterioles, and the force of the cardiac contraction.

When you take a blood pressure, you're measuring the pressure exerted by the circulating volume of blood on the walls of the arteries, the veins, and the chambers of the heart.

Systole and diastole again

A typical blood pressure reading consists of systolic blood pressure and diastolic blood pressure; pulse pressure is a third measurement that depends on the other two pressures. Here's a description of each:

- **Systolic blood pressure** is the blood pressure caused by the contraction phase, or systole, of the left ventricle of the heart. It's the top number given in a blood pressure measurement. For example, the systolic blood pressure in a measurement of 120/80 mm Hg is 120.
- **Diastolic blood pressure** is the pressure during the heart's relaxation phase, or diastole. It's the bottom number given in a blood pressure measurement. For example, the diastolic blood pressure in a measurement of 120/80 mm Hg is 80.
- **Pulse pressure** is the numerical difference between the systolic and diastolic blood pressures. For example, if the patient's blood pressure reading is 120/80 mm Hg, his pulse pressure is 40 mm Hg.

Sphygmoma-
...what? Oh, it's just a jazzed-up name for a blood pressure cuff.

Tools of the trade

To take a blood pressure, you use a **sphygmomanometer,** an instrument that consists of an inflatable cuff, an inflatable bulb, and a gauge, which is designed to measure arterial blood pressure.

You also listen to the sound of flowing blood with a **stethoscope.** The word **stethoscope** comes from the Greek words ***stethos,*** which means *chest,* and **skopein,** which means *to examine.* A stethoscope is an instrument used for auscultation of respiratory, cardiac, intestinal, uterine, fetal, arterial, and venous sounds; it consists of two earpieces that are connected by flexible tubing to a diaphragm, which is placed against the patient's body.

What you hear

In determining blood pressure, you should listen for **Korotkoff sounds,** which are typically the first faint sounds heard as the pressure in the cuff is released and blood begins to flow and the last sound heard before silence as blood flows. These two points correspond to the systolic and diastolic pressures, respectively.

Abnormalities in the physical examination

Auscultation may reveal a **murmur,** a soft blowing or fluttering sound of cardiac or vascular origin, or a **bruit,** an abnormal sound heard over arteries that indicates turbulent blood flow. (See *What's all the bruit about?*)

Pump up your pronunciation

What's all the bruit about?

It's easy to mispronounce **bruit** because it's a French word. It means *noise, din,* or *racket.* It's pronounced BROOEE; the ***t*** sound is dropped.

Color matters, too

Other signs of cardiovascular problems include **cyanosis,** a bluish discoloration of the skin and mucous membranes that results from an excessive amount of deoxygenated hemoglobin in the blood or a structural defect in the hemoglobin molecule. The word **cyanosis** comes from the Greek word ***cyanos,*** which means *dark blue.* You may also encounter patients with **pallor.** Pallor is a fancy term for paleness, or a decrease or absence of color in the skin.

Too much liquid

The examination can also reveal **edema,** the accumulation of abnormal amounts of fluid in the intercellular tissues, pericardial sac, pleural cavity, peritoneal cavity, or joint capsules. Any of these conditions may be accompanied by **diaphoresis,** profuse perspiration associated with an elevated body temperature, physical exertion, heat exposure, and mental or emotional stress. (See *Edema! That's just swell!*)

Too much pain

Angina, also called **angina pectoris,** is chest pain that lasts several minutes and results from an inadequate supply of oxygen and blood flow to the heart muscle.

Beyond the dictionary

Edema! That's just swell!

The word **edema** is a recent borrowing from Greek. It means *swelling.*

Diagnostic tests

No single test can help diagnose cardiovascular disease. Therefore, your patient will undergo more than one—

sometimes several—tests if a cardiovascular disease or disorder is suspected. These tests are described here.

Blood tests

Three important blood tests may be used to help diagnose cardiovascular problems.

Clotting by the clock

Activated partial thromboplastin time, the test to measure the time required for formation of a fibrin clot, requires a blood sample to evaluate all the clotting factors (except platelets) of the intrinsic pathway.

Any damage here?

The **cardiac enzyme** test is used to determine if cardiac tissue has been damaged. Normally present in high concentrations within the heart muscle, cardiac enzymes are released into the bloodstream from their normal intracellular area during cardiac trauma and create an elevation of the serum cardiac enzyme levels. Elevated levels of the enzyme creatine kinase (CK) and the isoenzyme CK-MB over a 72-hour period usually confirm a myocardial infarction (MI).

Did I have an MI?

In the **cardiac troponin** test, a blood sample is used to measure the cardiac protein called **troponin.** This is the most precise way to diagnose an MI.

I know I'm good-looking, but a little contrast medium and an X-ray *really* show me off!

Radiologic tests

Here are some terms for common radiologic tests:
- **Cardiac catheterization** is a diagnostic procedure in which a catheter is inserted into a large artery or vein (usually in an arm or the groin) and then threaded through the vessel to the patient's heart. After injection of a radiopaque contrast medium, X-rays are taken to detect heart anomalies.
- **Angiocardiography** creates an X-ray of the heart and great vessels after injection of contrast medium into a blood vessel or one of the heart chambers. (See *Angiocardiography*, page 128.)

- **Angiography** produces an X-ray of the blood vessels after injection of a radiopaque contrast medium.

Let's see what's going on in there

A **radionuclide scan** is a test that helps to measure heart function and damage. During this test, a mildly radioactive material is injected into the patient's bloodstream. Computer-generated pictures are used to locate the radioactive element in the heart.

Running hot and cold

The **thallium stress test** helps diagnose coronary artery disease. For this test, the patient is given a thallium isotope I.V. after a treadmill stress test. The isotope doesn't collect in areas of poor blood flow and damaged cells, so these areas show up as "cold spots" on a scanner.

Beyond the dictionary

Angiocardiography

The word **angiocardiography** looks overwhelming but it becomes easier if you break it down. ***Angio-*** comes from the Greek word for *vessel,* ***cardi-*** means *heart,* and ***-graphy*** comes from the Greek word ***graphein,*** which means *to write.*

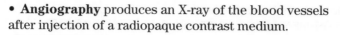

Other invasive tests

Electrophysiologic studies are invasive tests that help diagnose conduction system disease and serious heart rhythm disturbances. The **cardiologist** (heart specialist) induces a rhythm disturbance by using different medications or procedures. After identifying the source of the rhythm disturbance, the cardiologist either administers medications to terminate the disturbance or eliminates the abnormal pathway in the heart by treatment with high-frequency waves.

Beyond the dictionary

Two troublesome terms

Pericardiocentesis and **transesophageal** look like hard words, but they're easy to understand if broken apart.

Around the heart + puncture

Pericardiocentesis comes from the Greek word ***kentesis,*** which means *to puncture.* The prefix ***peri-*** means *around,* and the root ***cardio-*** means *heart.* Put it all together and you have the meaning—*a procedure that requires puncturing the sac around the heart.*

Through the esophagus

The first part of **transesophageal, *trans-*,** means *through;* therefore, **transesophageal** means *through the esophagus.* Transesophageal echocardiography is an echocardiogram performed through the esophagus.

Pericardiocentesis is a surgical procedure in which the pericardium cavity is punctured for the aspiration of fluid from the pericardial sac. This procedure can be performed for both diagnosis and treatment of some cardiac disorders.

Transesophageal echocardiography is a technique in which a probe is passed through the mouth and down the esophagus to study the structure and motion of the heart using an echo obtained from beams of ultrasonic waves directed through the esophagus. (See *Two troublesome terms.*)

Noninvasive tests

An **electrocardiogram** (ECG) is a graphic record that's produced by an electrocardiograph and shows variations in electrical potential, as detected at the body surface, resulting from excitation of the heart muscle. An ECG displays a wave that represents phases of the cardiac cycle. (See *Electrocardiogram.*)

In a normal rhythm, the P wave is the first wave seen in the cardiac cycle. Atrial depolarization is represented on the ECG by the P wave. After atrial depolarization, electrical activity is absent for a brief period. This is known as the PR interval.

Next, ventricular depolarization is represented on the ECG by a waveform configuration known as the QRS complex. After ventricular activation, ventricular repolarization begins. The ST segment represents the actual recovery or repolarization of the ventricular muscle. The T wave represents the actual recovery.

Let me sound you out

Transthoracic echocardiography is a diagnostic technique that's used to study the structure and motion of the heart by the echo obtained from beams of ultrasonic waves directed through the chest wall. (See *Did you hear an echo?*)

Beyond the dictionary

Electrocardiogram

The prefix ***electro-*** comes from the Greek word ***elektron,*** which refers to the semiprecious stone amber. (Rubbing amber produces an electric charge.) **Cardiogram** comes from the Latin word ***cardium,*** which means *heart,* and the Greek term ***gramma,*** which means *mark.*

The real world

Did you hear an echo?

In practice, you'll commonly hear **echocardiography** referred to as an **echo.** You'll also hear **cardiac catheterization** referred to as **cath.** For example, you might hear someone say, "Mrs. Heartman is scheduled for her **echo** today."

Disorders

Some cardiovascular problems occur suddenly and without warning, whereas others are long-term problems. Either way, when the heart is sick, the entire body is affected. Many types of injury or illness cause problems for the heart, resulting in serious cardiac complications. (See *Cardiac complications.*)

Types of cardiac disorders include:
- cardiac arrhythmias
- congenital heart defects
- degenerative disorders
- inflammatory heart disease
- vascular disorders
- valvular heart disease.

Cardiac arrhythmias

Arrhythmia means the lack of normal heart rhythm (indicated by the prefix ***a-***). A more accurate term to describe what are commonly referred to as arrhythmias is **dysrhythmia,** which means an abnormality in rhythm. However, these terms are used interchangeably.

There are a number of different arrhythmias:
- **Atrial flutter** is an arrhythmia in which atrial rhythm is regular, but the rate is 250 to 400 beats/minute. The flutter waves that result have a sawtooth appearance. The ventricular rate is variable.

Cardiac complications

Here's a list of cardiac complications you may encounter:
- **Cardiac arrest** is when the heart stops abruptly with an absence of blood pressure or pulse.
- In **cardiac tamponade,** blood or fluid fills the pericardial space and presses against the heart, compressing the heart chambers and obstructing venous return to the heart.
- **Cardiogenic shock,** also called *pump failure,* results when more than 40% of the heart muscle is damaged by a myocardial infarction. As a result, the heart can't pump effectively and body tissues don't receive the necessary amounts of oxygen and nutrients.
- **Hypotension** refers to blood pressure that's below normal values.
- **Hypovolemic shock** occurs when reduced intravascular blood volume causes circulatory dysfunction and inadequate blood flow to tissues.
- **Pulmonary edema** is an accumulation of excess fluid in the lungs.
- **Ventricular aneurysm** is an outpouching of the ventricular wall that's most commonly seen in the left ventricle.

- **Bradycardia** is a slow heartbeat, usually less than 60 beats/minute.
- **Fibrillation** refers to an uncoordinated, irregular contraction of the heart muscle, which may originate in the atria (atrial fibrillation) or in the ventricles (ventricular fibrillation). If left untreated, ventricular fibrillation can result in cardiac arrest.
- **Heart block** describes an impaired conduction of the heart's electrical impulses at the AV node, which commonly leads to a slow heartbeat.
- **Paroxysmal atrial tachycardia** is an arrhythmia in which the atrial and ventricular rates are regular and exceed 160 beats/minute. This arrhythmia is typically characterized by a sudden onset and termination.
- **Premature atrial contraction** is an arrhythmia characterized by premature abnormal-looking P waves that differ in configuration from normal P waves followed by normal QRS complexes.
- In **premature ventricular contraction (PVC),** the QRS complex is premature, wide, and distorted. PVCs occur singly, in pairs, or in larger groups and alternate with normal beats. They may originate from one or more sites in the ventricles.
- **Tachycardia** refers to a resting heartbeat greater than 100 beats/minute.
- **Ventricular tachycardia** is a potentially deadly arrhythmia in which QRS complexes are wide and bizarre and originate in the ventricles.

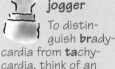

Memory jogger

To distinguish **bra**dycardia from **ta**chycardia, think of an airplane either **bra**king (slowing down) or **ta**king off (speeding up) on the runway.

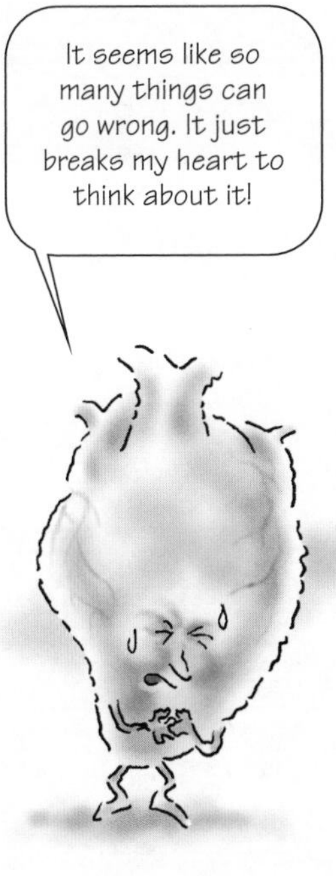
It seems like so many things can go wrong. It just breaks my heart to think about it!

Congenital heart defects

Congenital means *present at birth.* Infants with congenital heart problems have structural defects of the heart or its blood vessels. The term **blue baby** describes cyanosis that's caused by several of these congenital defects:

- **Atrial septal defect** is an opening between the two atria. Because left atrial pressure is slightly higher than right atrial pressure, blood shunts from left to right. This shunting causes an overload on the right side of the heart, which enlarges to accommodate the increased volume.
- **Coarctation of the aorta** is narrowing of the **lumen** (opening of the aorta), which results in high pressure above and low pressure below the stricture.

• **Patent ductus arteriosus** occurs when the **ductus arteriosus,** a passage between the aorta and pulmonary artery that normally closes at birth, remains open, sending oxygenated blood back through the lungs.
• The **Tetralogy of Fallot** got its name because it involves four (hence ***tetra-***) major defects of the heart and great vessels and was first described by the French doctor Etienne Fallot (1850-1911).
• In **ventricular septal defect,** an opening between the two ventricles allows blood to shunt between them. Depending on the anomaly's size, spontaneous closure may occur (if small); if closure doesn't occur, right- and left-sided heart failure and cyanosis occur.

Degenerative heart conditions

Degenerative heart disease is a progressive deterioration of heart structures, tissue, and function. Some forms of degenerative heart disease are listed here:
• **Coronary artery disease** (**CAD**) occurs when the arteries that serve the heart are obstructed or narrowed. The most common cause of CAD is **atherosclerosis** (deposits of plaque inside the arteries). In addition to slowing blood flow, atherosclerosis damages and deforms the muscular arterial walls, increasing the risk of aneurysm. (See *Atherosclerosis: The hard facts.*)
• In **dilated cardiomyopathy,** the heart dilates and takes on a round shape as a result of extensively damaged heart muscle fibers.
• **Heart failure** develops when the heart can't effectively pump blood and becomes congested with extra fluid.
• **Hypertension** refers to blood pressure that's above normal values, typically greater than 140/90 mm Hg (or 130/80 mm Hg in patients with diabetes or chronic kidney failure). A patient with a systolic blood pressure of 120 to 139 and a diastolic pressure of 80 to 89 is considered **prehypertensive.**
• **Hypertrophic cardiomyopathy** is a primary disease of cardiac muscle that's characterized by disproportionate thickening of the interventricular septum and ventricular walls.
• In an **MI,** commonly called a **heart attack,** reduced blood flow through one of the coronary arteries results in myocardial **ischemia** (lack of blood supply) and **necrosis** (tissue death).

Beyond the dictionary

Atherosclerosis: The hard facts

Breaking apart the word **atherosclerosis** is easy. The Greek word ***athere*** means *soft, fatty,* and *gruel-like,* and ***scler-*** means *hard.* Put them together and these terms accurately describe the material deposited on the inner lining of an artery that causes atherosclerosis.

• **Restrictive cardiomyopathy** is characterized by restricted ventricular filling (the result of left ventricular hypertrophy) and endocardial fibrosis.

Inflammation can be pretty serious business.

Inflammatory heart disease

Types of heart inflammation, caused by injury or tissue destruction, are described below:

• **Endocarditis** is a bacterial or fungal infection of the heart valves or endocardium.

• **Myocarditis** is an inflammation of the heart muscle that can be acute or long term.

• **Pericarditis** is an inflammation of the pericardium, the protective sac that encloses the heart. In **constrictive** pericarditis, the pericardium thickens and constricts the heart's ability to pump, causing heart failure.

• **Rheumatic fever** is a childhood disease caused by streptococcal bacteria.

Vascular disorders

The following terms are associated with disorders of the vascular system:

• **Arterial occlusive disease** is caused by obstruction of the lumen of the arteries, causing **ischemia** (decreased blood flow and tissue hypoxia), most commonly to the legs and feet.

• **Raynaud's disease** is an arteriospastic disease characterized by episodic vasospasm in the arteries or arterioles that's precipitated by cold or stress.

• **Thrombophlebitis** is an acute condition characterized by inflammation and thrombus formation. Thrombophlebitis may occur in deep (intramuscular) or superficial (subcutaneous) veins. Deep vein thrombophlebitis can affect small veins, such as the soleal venus sinuses, or large veins such as the venae cavae.

Weak walls

An **aneurysm** (a weakening of the walls of a vessel) occurs most commonly in the aorta but can happen in any vessel and can take a number of different forms:

• **Abdominal aortic aneurysm,** an abnormal dilation in the arterial wall, most commonly occurs in the aorta below the renal arteries and above the iliac branches.

• **Aortic dissection** is usually caused by high blood pressure that forces the layers of the aortic walls to separate, creating a false lumen. Acute aortic dissection is characterized by sharp, tearing pain in the chest or back.
• **Thoracic aortic aneurysm** is an abnormal widening of the ascending, transcending, or descending part of the aorta above the diaphragm.

Aneurysms may be **saccular** (unilateral pouchlike bulge with a narrow neck), **fusiform** (spindle-shaped bulge encompassing the entire diameter of the vessel), or **false** (a pulsating hematoma resulting from trauma and often mistaken for an abdominal aneurysm).

Valvular disorders

When a valve fails, several different disorders can result, including stenosis and cardiac insufficiency.

The thick of it

Stenosis, a thickening of valvular tissue that results in narrow valve openings, can occur as one of three types:
• **Aortic stenosis,** or narrowing of the aortic valve, creates elevated pressure in the left ventricle.
• **Mitral stenosis,** or narrowing of the mitral valve, obstructs blood flow from the left atrium to the left ventricle, causing enlargement of the left atrium as a form of compensation.
• **Tricuspid stenosis** obstructs blood flow from the right atrium to the right ventricle, causing the right atrium to enlarge.

Valves can be tricky!

Insufficient funds

Four types of **coronary insufficiency,** the incomplete closure of a valve, may also result:
• **Aortic insufficiency** occurs when blood leaks back into the left ventricle during the diastolic phase of the heartbeat, when the ventricles rest. The left ventricle enlarges and fluid builds up in the left atrium and the pulmonary system, leading to left-sided heart failure and pulmonary edema.
• **Mitral valve insufficiency** occurs when blood from the left ventricle flows back into the left atrium, causing the left atrium and ventricle to enlarge as compensation for the heart's decreased efficiency.

• **Pulmonary valve insufficiency** allows blood from the pulmonary artery to flow back into the right ventricle during diastole.
• In **tricuspid insufficiency,** blood flows back into the right atrium as the ventricles contract during systole. This reduces blood flow to the lungs and the left side of the heart and also decreases cardiac output.

Treatments

Cardiovascular disorders can be treated with drug therapy and surgery. Here's a list of treatments and surgical interventions.

Drug therapy

These drugs may be used alone or in combination to treat cardiovascular disorders:
• **Adrenergics** help treat serious hypotension.
• **Angiotensin-converting enzyme inhibitors** are used to treat hypertension and heart failure. They're also used to prevent future heart attcks.
• **Antianginal** drugs treat or prevent cardiac pain.
• **Antiarrhythmics** can prevent or treat arrhythmias.
• **Antihypertensives** reduce cardiac output or decrease peripheral vascular resistance to lower blood pressure.
• **Beta-adrenergic blockers** are used to treat hypertension, angina, and heart failure.
• **Calcium channel blockers** lower blood pressure and reduce the workload of the heart.
• **Cardiac glycosides** are used to manage heart failure and certain types of arrhythmias.
• **Diuretics** treat edema and hypertension by reducing circulating fluid volume.
• **Thrombolytic therapy** is used to dissolve clots.

Surgery

Here are some common surgical procedures used to correct functional or structural heart problems:
• **Ablation** is a procedure in which small, selected areas of the heart are destroyed to treat refractive tachycardia.

• **Cardiac conduction surgery** is done to treat atrial and ventricular tachycardias that can't be controlled by drug therapy or pacing.
• **Coronary artery bypass graft (CABG)** surgery restores circulation when occluded coronary arteries prevent normal blood flow to the heart muscle. Occluded arteries are replaced with segments (grafts) from other vessels, most commonly the saphenous veins in the leg. This can also be accomplished using a less invasive procedure called **minimally invasive surgery.** (See Cabbage *is slang for CABG.*)
• **Heart transplantation** is a complex and controversial procedure that involves replacing a diseased heart with the healthy heart of a brain-dead donor.

The real world

Cabbage is slang for CABG

You may hear **coronary artery bypass surgery** referred to as **cabbage. Cabbage** is slang for CABG, the abbreviation for coronary artery bypass graft. A **triple cabbage** is a three-vessel bypass procedure.

Other treatments

• **Advanced cardiac life support** involves the recognition and treatment of acute cardiac emergencies, such as cardiac arrest, MI, and lethal arrhythmias.
• **Cardiopulmonary resuscitation** is a basic life support procedure performed on victims with cardiac arrest.
• In **defibrillation,** an electric shock is used to terminate tachyarrhythmias.
• An **implantable cardioverter-defibrillator** is an implanted device that senses an arrhythmia and delivers an electric shock to the myocardium, terminating the arrhythmia.
• In **intra-aortic balloon counterpulsation,** used to temporarily reduce the left ventricle's workload, an inflatable balloon is inserted into the patient's aorta. A pump inflates the balloon while the ventricle rests and deflates it at the start of each ventricular contraction. The inflated balloon forces blood into the major arteries and reduces the heart's workload during contraction.
• During **laser-enhanced angioplasty,** a doctor threads a laser-containing catheter into the diseased artery. Rapid laser pulses destroy the occlusion, and balloon angioplasty is performed later.
• **Pacemakers** use electrical impulses to regulate cardiac rhythm. Pacemakers can be permanent, transvenous, or transcutaneous.
• **Percutaneous transluminal coronary angioplasty (PTCA)** is a nonsurgical alternative to CABG surgery.

Beyond the dictionary

Profiling PTCA

The term **percutaneous transluminal coronary angioplasty** is abbreviated **PTCA**.

First half

The first component of the term, ***per-***, means *through* and ***cutaneous*** means *the skin*—so *through the skin.* The prefix ***trans-*** means *through;* ***luminal*** refers to *a blood vessel.*

Second half

Coronary refers to the two arteries and their branches that stem from the aorta, which supply the heart tissue with blood. ***Angio-*** also means *blood vessel* and ***plasty*** is a suffix that means *the repair of.*

All together

So PTCA really means *repair of a coronary blood vessel by way of the skin and another blood vessel.*

During this procedure, a guide catheter is threaded into the coronary artery and positioned at the site of an stenosis or occlusion. A doctor then inserts a small balloon catheter through the guide catheter and positions the balloon inside the stenosis or occlusion. When the balloon is inflated, the coronary artery dilates and blood flow improves. (See *Profiling PTCA.*)

- In some cases, a **stent** (tube or coil) is placed inside the artery to support it and prevent reocclusion.
- **Synchronized cardioversion** delivers an electric charge to the myocardium at the peak of the R wave on the ECG. This electrical charge stops the arrhythmia and allows the SA node to resume control.
- **Valve replacement surgery** is used to replace faulty valves in patients with severe symptoms who don't respond to more conservative approaches. Both mechanical and biological prosthetic valves are commonly used.
- A **ventricular assist device** is a temporary, life-sustaining treatment that diverts systemic blood flow from a diseased ventricle into a centrifugal pump.

There sure are a lot of ways to get me back in the game.

systole
parietal

Vocabulary builders

At a crossroads

Here's a puzzle that's sure to tug at your heartstrings. Good luck!

This type of exercise is hard work but mental exercise can be pretty tough, too!

Across

5. Return blood to the heart
7. Smallest blood vessels
9. Hardening of the arteries
10. Thin sac that protects the heart
12. Rapid heartbeat
13. Chest pain
14. Blue-colored skin
15. Lower chamber of the heart
16. Carry blood away from the heart
17. Upper chamber of the heart

Down

1. Lining of the heart's chambers
2. High blood pressure
3. Slow heartbeat
4. Word for *abnormal paleness*
6. When the heart contracts
8. Deviation from normal rhythm
11. Heart muscle

Answers are on page 142.

Finish line

The Latin word ***cardium,*** which means *heart,* appears in almost all medical terminology relating to that structure. Fill in each of the blanks below with the prefix, suffix, or root that finishes the heart-related term.

1. A heart doctor is a cardi ______________
2. A patient with ______________ cardia has a slow heartbeat.
3. Another name for the condition of an enlarged heart is cardio ______________
4. Inflammation of the heart muscles due to infection is called card ______________
5. The ______________ cardio ______________ is a device for recording the electrical activity of the myocardium.

O see, can you say?

Sound out each group of pictures and symbols below to reveal a term that was reviewed in the chapter.

1.

D + yuh + reh +

2.

Throm + + fleh + b + tis

3.

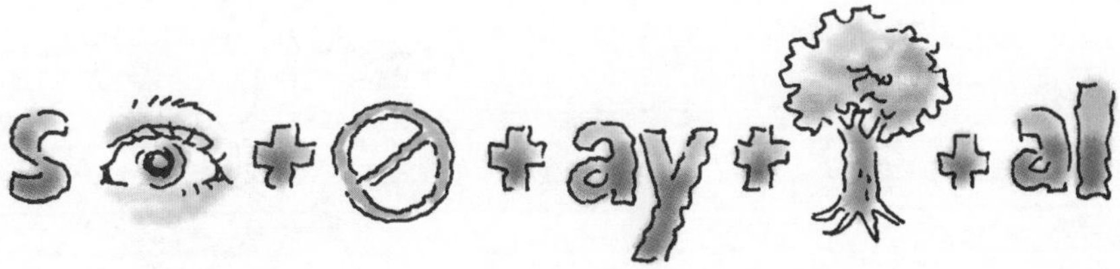
s + + ay + + al

Answers are on page 142.

Match game

Match the choices below to the appropriate answers.

Clues

1. Add the prefix that means rapid to the correct form of the root **cardium.** ________

2. Add the prefix that means *around* and the affix that means *to puncture* to the correct form of the root **cardium.** ________

3. Add the prefix that means *muscle* to the correct form of the root **cardium.** ________

4. Add the suffix that refers to the *lungs* to the correct form of the root **cardium.** ________

5. Add the prefix that means *within* to the correct form of the root **cardium.** ________

6. Add the prefix that means *on* to the correct form of the root **cardium.** ________

7. Add the prefix that means *vessel* and the suffix that means *to write* to the correct form of the root **cardium.** ________

Choices

A. Pericardiocentesis

B. Tachycardia

C. Cardiopulmonary

D. Myocardial

E. Epicardium

F. Angiocardiography

G. Endocardium

Add muscle to cardium? You've got it!

Answers are on page 142.

Talking in circles

Use the clues below to fill in the blanks with the appropriate word. Then unscramble the circled letters to find the answer to the question posed below.

1. (◯) ___ ___ ___ (◯) ___ ___ ___ ___ ___ ___ ___
2. ___ ___ ___ ___ ___ ___ (◯) ___ (◯)
3. (◯) ___ ___ ___ ___ ___ ___ ___
4. ___ ___ ___ (◯) ___ (◯) ___ ___
5. ___ ___ ___ ___ (◯) ___

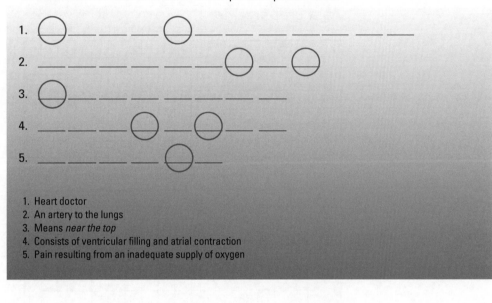

1. Heart doctor
2. An artery to the lungs
3. Means *near the top*
4. Consists of ventricular filling and atrial contraction
5. Pain resulting from an inadequate supply of oxygen

What's it called when a person has the "blues?"

Answers are on page 142.

Answers

At a crossroads

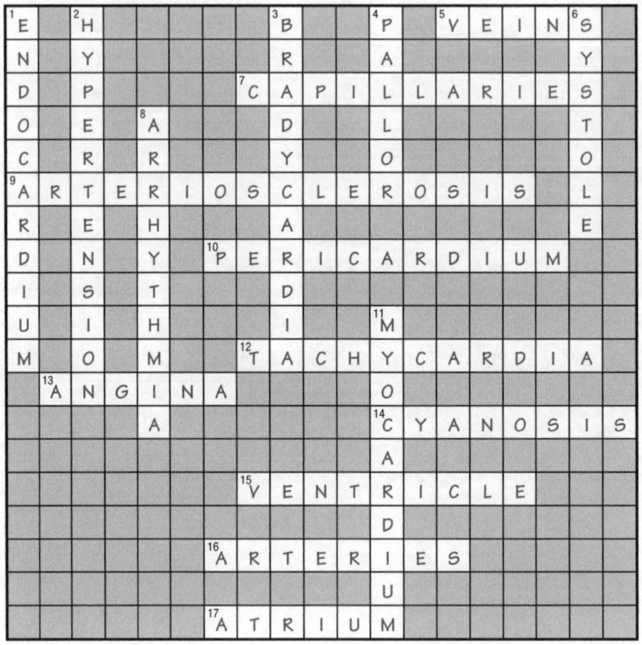

Finish line

1. Ologist; 2. Brady; 3. Megaly; 4. Itis; 5. Electro, graph

O see, can you say?

1. Diuretic; 2. Thrombophlebitis; 3. Sinoatrial

Match game

1. B; 2. A; 3. D; 4. C; 5. G; 6. E; 7. F

Talking in circles

1. Cardiologist; 2. Pulmonary; 3. Superior; 4. Diastole; 5. Angina
Answer to puzzle—Cyanosis

WOW! That wasn't easy!

7

Respiratory system

Just the facts

In this chapter, you'll learn:

- terminology related to the structure and function of the respiratory system
- terminology needed for physical examination of the respiratory system
- tests that help diagnose respiratory disorders
- common respiratory system disorders and their treatments.

Respiratory structure and function

The **respiratory system** consists of the upper and lower respiratory tracts and the thoracic cage. In addition to maintaining the exchange of oxygen (O_2) and carbon dioxide (CO_2) in the lungs and tissues, the respiratory system helps regulate the body's acid-base balance. (See *Pronouncing key respiratory system terms*, page 144.)

Upper respiratory tract

The **upper respiratory tract** consists primarily of the nose, mouth, nasopharynx, oropharynx, laryngopharynx, and larynx. Besides warming and humidifying inhaled air, these structures enable taste, smell, and the chewing and swallowing of food. (See *Structures of the respiratory system*, page 145.)

Nose

Air enters the respiratory tract through the mouth and **nares** (nostrils). In the nares, small hairs filter out dust

Pump up your pronunciation

Pronouncing key respiratory system terms

Below is a list of key terms related to the respiratory system, along with the correct ways to pronounce them.

Alveoli	AL-VEE-OH-LEYE
Atelectasis	AHT-UH-LEHK-TAY-SIS
Bronchioles	BRONG-KEE-OHLZ
Conchae	KON-KEE
Cor pulmonale	KOR-PULL-MAH-NAL-LEE
Oropharynx	OR-OH-FAR-INKS
Sarcoidosis	SAHR-KOY-DOH-SIS

and large foreign particles. Air then passes into the two **nasal passages,** which are separated by the **septum. Cartilage** forms the anterior walls of the nasal passages.

Humidifiers

Bony structures, **conchae** (singular: **concha**), form the posterior walls of the nasal passages. The conchae warm and humidify air before it passes into the **pharynx** (plural: **pharynges**) or **throat,** which serves as a passageway for the digestive and respiratory tracts.

Pharynx

The pharynx consists of three sections:

- The **nasopharynx** extends from the posterior nares to the soft palate.
- The **oropharynx** extends from the soft palate to the upper portion of the epiglottis.
- The **laryngopharynx** extends to the esophagus and larynx. (See *The three pharynges.*)

Beyond the dictionary

The three pharynges

Notice that the words for the three parts of the pharynx are all connected by the common root ***pharynx,*** which is Greek for *throat.* **Nasopharynx** uses the word for *nose,* ***naso,*** and the root ***pharynx*** to describe the upper portion of the pharynx. **Oropharynx** uses the Latin word for *mouth,* ***or,*** from which we also get *orifice.* **Laryngopharynx** adds **laryngo,** a form of **larynx** that's used when it's combined with another word.

Anatomically speaking

Structures of the respiratory system

This illustration shows the structures of the respiratory system, which include the organs responsible for external respiration.

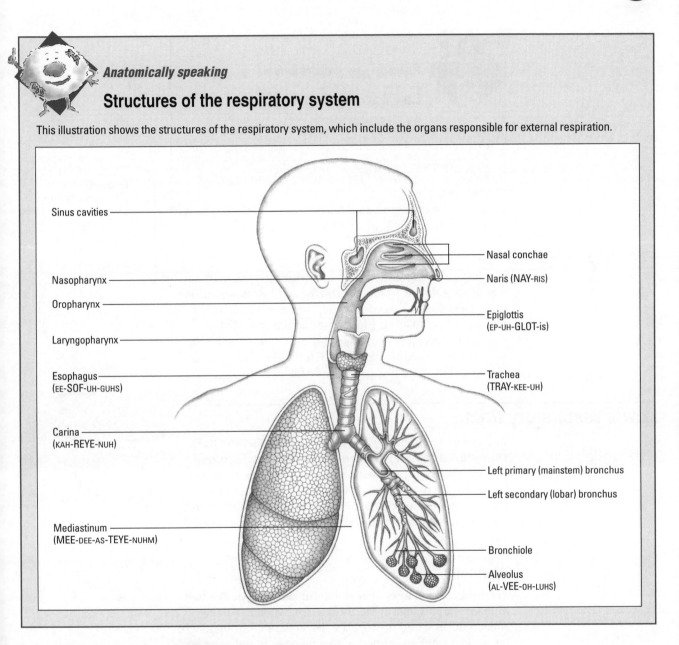

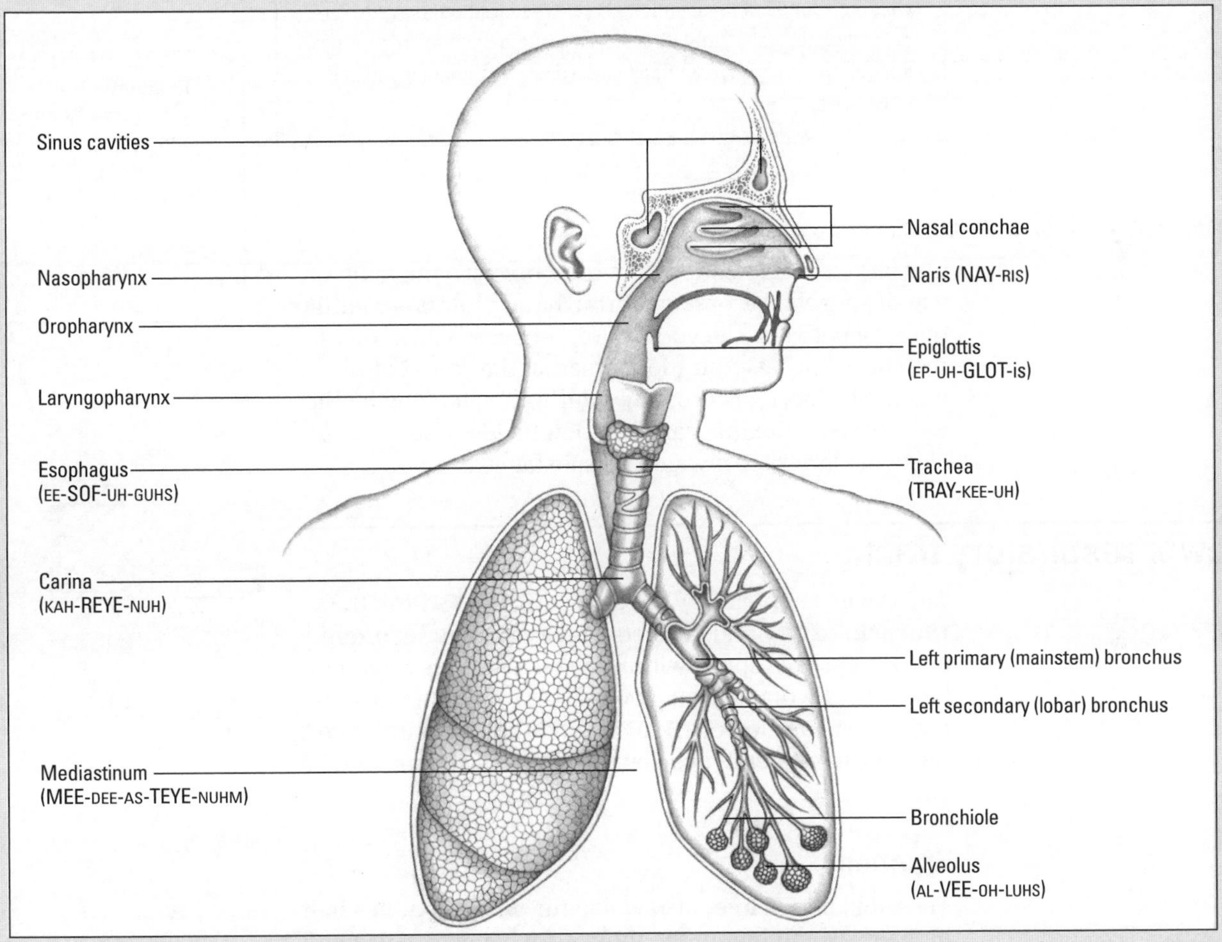
Sinus cavities
Nasal conchae
Nasopharynx
Naris (NAY-RIS)
Oropharynx
Epiglottis
(EP-UH-GLOT-is)
Laryngopharynx
Esophagus
(EE-SOF-UH-GUHS)
Trachea
(TRAY-KEE-UH)
Carina
(KAH-REYE-NUH)
Left primary (mainstem) bronchus
Left secondary (lobar) bronchus
Mediastinum
(MEE-DEE-AS-TEYE-NUHM)
Bronchiole
Alveolus
(AL-VEE-OH-LUHS)

Larynx

The **larynx,** which contains the **vocal cords,** connects the pharynx with the trachea. (See *Learn to say* larynx, page 146.)

Pump up your pronunciation

Learn to say *larynx*

It's likely you'll hear **larynx** (LAHR-INKS) pronounced LAHR-NIKS, with the sounds of the L and the N reversed. Although this reversal of sounds, called **metathesis,** is a common mix-up in all languages, you may save yourself some embarrassment if you say LAHR-INKS.

Speaking of the voice box

The larynx is also called the **voice box.** It's the main organ of speech. Air passing through the **glottis**—a slitlike opening between the vocal cords—causes vibration of the cords during expiration, creating the sound of the voice. The larynx is protected during swallowing by the **epiglottis,** a flexible cartilage that bends reflexively to close the larynx to swallowed substances.

Epiglottis...let's see. The prefix ***epi-*** comes from Greek, meaning *upon.* ***Glottis*** comes from the Greek word ***glossa,*** which means *tongue.*

Lower respiratory tract

The **lower respiratory tract** is contained within the **thoracic cavity** and consists of the **trachea, bronchi,** and **lungs.** This space within the chest wall is bounded below by the diaphragm, above by the scalene muscles and fasciae of the neck, and around the circumference by the ribs, intercostal muscles, vertebrae, sternum, and ligaments.

Trachea

The tubular **trachea,** also called the **windpipe,** lies half in the neck and half in the thorax. C-shaped cartilage rings reinforce and protect the trachea, preventing its collapse. The trachea is lined with a mucous membrane covered with small hairlike projections called **cilia.** The cilia continuously sweep foreign material out of the breathing passages toward the mouth.

Bronchi

The trachea branches at the **carina** (also known as the **tracheal bifurcation**) into two smaller airways, the left and right **mainstem bronchi** (primary bronchi). (See *Careening with the carina.*)

The right mainstem bronchus—shorter, wider, and more vertical than the left—supplies air to the right lung; the left mainstem bronchus delivers air to the left lung.

A way in

The mainstem bronchi—along with blood vessels, nerves, and lymphatics—enter the **pleural cavity** (the space between the visceral and parietal pleurae) at the hilum. Located behind the heart, the **hilum** is a slit on the lungs' medial surface where nerves, lymphatic ducts, and blood vessels enter and leave the lungs. In the lung, the mainstem bronchi divide into five **lobar bronchi** (secondary bronchi), so called because they enter into the **lobes** of the lung, one for each of the three lobes of the right lung and two for the left.

First branches, now twigs

The lobar bronchi divide into smaller and smaller branches, until they become **bronchioles.** Each bronchiole branches into a **lobule.** The lobule includes **terminal bronchioles** and the **acinus**—the chief respiratory unit for gas exchange. (See *Looking at a lobule*, page 148.)

Beyond the dictionary

Careening with the carina

It's more accurate to say the *carina of the trachea* because a **carina** (KAH-REYE-NAH) can be any keel-shaped or ridge-shaped anatomic part. The word derives from Latin, meaning *hull* or *keel of a ship,* and was pronounced KAH-REE-NAH. This is still the word **carina's** secondary pronunciation, and it's the pronunciation for the verb ***careen,*** which is also derived from **carina.**

Looking at a lobule

As illustrated below, each lobule contains terminal bronchioles and the acinus, which consists of respiratory bronchioles and alveolar sacs.

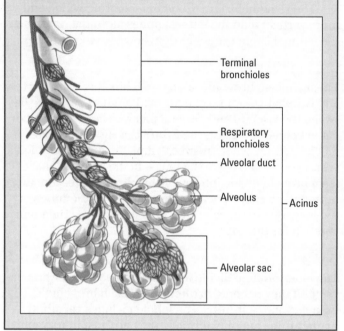

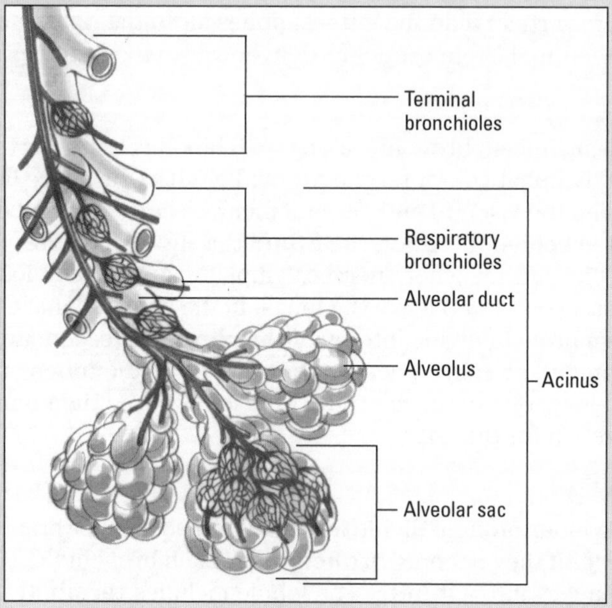
Terminal bronchioles
Respiratory bronchioles
Alveolar duct
Alveolus
Acinus
Alveolar sac

Ducts and sacs

Within the acinus, terminal bronchioles branch into yet smaller **respiratory bronchioles.** The respiratory bronchioles feed directly into alveoli at sites along their walls. The respiratory bronchioles eventually become **alveolar ducts,** which terminate in clusters of capillary-swathed alveoli called **alveolar sacs.**

Fruit of the vine

The walls of the ducts contain **alveoli** (singular: **alveolus**), grapelike clusters where O_2 is exchanged for CO_2.

Capillary network

Surrounded by networks of tiny blood vessels called **capillaries,** alveoli have thin walls through which gas exchange occurs. The average pair of lungs has about 300 million alveoli.

Lungs

The cone-shaped lungs differ slightly from one another. The right lung is shorter, broader, and larger than the left. The right lung has three lobes and handles 55% of gas exchange. The left lung has only two lobes; it shares the left side of the thoracic cavity with the heart. Each lung's concave base rests on the **diaphragm.** The **apex** (extreme top) of each lung extends about ⅓″ (1 cm) above the first rib. (See *Studying the lungs.*)

> ***Beyond the dictionary***
>
> **Studying the lungs**
>
> **Pulmonology,** which comes from the Latin word ***pulmo,*** meaning *lung,* and the suffix ***-ology,*** meaning *the study of,* is the science that studies the lungs.

Remember the membrane

The **pleura** is the membrane that totally encloses the lungs. It's composed of a visceral layer and parietal layer. The **visceral pleura** hugs the entire lung surface, including the areas between the lobes. The **parietal pleura** extends from the roots of the lungs and covers the sides of the pericardium to the chest wall and backward to the spine.

Fluid space

The **pleural cavity**—the tiny area between the visceral and parietal pleural layers—contains a thin film of **serous fluid.** This fluid has two functions:

1. It lubricates the pleural surfaces so that they slide smoothly against each other during respiration.

2. It creates a bond between the layers that causes the lungs to move within the chest wall during breathing.

In the middle

The **mediastinum** (the space between the lungs) contains the

- heart and pericardium
- thoracic aorta
- pulmonary artery and veins
- venae cavae and azygos veins
- thymus, lymph nodes, and lymphatic vessels
- trachea, esophagus, and thoracic duct
- vagus, cardiac, and phrenic nerves.

See the space between my lobes? It's called the **mediastinum.**

Thoracic cage

Several structures support and protect the lungs and aid in respiration. Composed of bone and cartilage, the **tho-**

racic cage supports and protects the lungs and permits them to expand and contract. The anterior portion of the thoracic cage consists of the **manubrium, sternum, xiphoid process,** and 10 pairs of **ribs.** The posterior portion of the thoracic cage consists of the **vertebral column,** the same 10 pairs of ribs, and 2 pairs of floating ribs.

Respiration

Effective respiration consists of a gas exchange in the lungs, called **external respiration,** and a gas exchange in the tissues, called **internal respiration.** External respiration occurs through three processes:

- **diffusion**—gas movement through a semipermeable membrane from an area of greater concentration to one of lesser concentration (internal respiration occurs only through diffusion)
- **pulmonary perfusion**—blood flow from the right side of the heart, through the pulmonary circulation, and into the left side of the heart
- **ventilation**—gas distribution into and out of the pulmonary airways.

Air supply

Adequate ventilation depends on the proper working of the nervous, musculoskeletal, and respiratory systems to accomplish the necessary changes in lung pressure. (See *Ventilation and perfusion.*)

Adequate ventilation depends on the proper working of the nervous, musculoskeletal, and respiratory systems.

At the base

The most important muscle for respiration is the **diaphragm,** a dome-shaped organ composed of muscle and membrane that separates the thoracic and abdominal cavities. During inspiration, the diaphragm moves down and expands the volume of the thoracic cavity; during expiration, it moves up, reducing the volume.

Respiration chemistry

The body depends on a delicate balance between acids and bases to sustain life. The lungs help maintain this bal-

Now I get it!

Ventilation and perfusion

Effective gas exchange depends on a stable relationship between ventilation and perfusion. You'll see this called the **$\dot{V}/\dot{Q}$ ratio.** A **$\dot{V}/\dot{Q}$ mismatch** accounts for many respiratory disorders and can affect all body systems. The following types of mismatch can occur.

Need more oxygen

Inadequate ventilation, also called a **shunt,** occurs when pulmonary circulation is adequate but not enough oxygen (O_2) is available in the lungs. As a result, a portion of the blood flowing through the pulmonary capillaries doesn't receive O_2. Perfusion without ventilation usually results from airway obstruction, particularly that caused by acute diseases, such as atelectasis and pneumonia, which produce a low $\dot{V}/\dot{Q}$ ratio.

Need more blood

Inadequate perfusion, also called **dead-space ventilation,** produces a high $\dot{V}/\dot{Q}$ ratio. Ventilation is normal, but blood flow in the pulmonary capillaries isn't adequate. Narrowed capillaries, decreased cardiac output, and pulmonary emboli (blood clots) commonly cause this condition.

Need both!

Inadequate ventilation and perfusion, also referred to as a **silent unit,** describes a lack of O_2 in the lungs (ventilation) and in the pulmonary circulation (perfusion). When entire sections of the lung become "silent," the body compensates by delivering blood flow to better ventilated lung areas. Chronic alveolar collapse and pulmonary emboli can create silent units.

Please don't shunt me out!

ance by altering the rate and depth of respiration in response to changes in blood pH.

Acids and bases

To understand acid-base balance, you need to know three important terms:

- **acids,** which are substances that dissociate (become *fragmented,* or *separate*) in solution, releasing hydrogen ions (carbonic acid is an example of an acid found in the body)

- **bases,** such as bicarbonate, which are substances that dissociate to yield hydroxide ions in aqueous solutions
- **pH,** which represents the relative concentration of hydrogen ions in a solution compared to the hydrogen ion concentration of a standard solution (normally, blood pH level measures 7.35 to 7.45).

A solution with more base than acid contains fewer hydrogen ions, resulting in a higher pH. A solution that contains more acid than base has more hydrogen ions, resulting in a lower pH.

Think of it this way. More base elevates the pH.

Staying in balance

A deviation in pH level can compromise essential body functions, including electrolyte balance, the activity of critical enzymes, muscle contraction, and basic cellular function. The body normally maintains a pH level within a narrow range by carefully balancing acidic and alkaline elements. When one aspect of that balancing act breaks down, the body can't maintain a healthy pH level as easily, and problems arise.

Regulating method

The lungs use **hyperventilation** (increased ventilation) or **hypoventilation** (decreased ventilation) to regulate blood levels of CO_2, a gas that combines with water to form **carbonic acid.** Increased carbonic acid levels lead to a decrease in pH level.

Eliminate CO_2, increase pH

Chemoreceptors in the brain sense pH changes and vary the rate and depth of breathing to compensate. Breathing faster or more deeply eliminates more CO_2 from the lungs. The more CO_2 is expelled, the less carbonic acid is made and, as a result, the pH level rises. (See *CO_2 and hyperventilation.*)

Increase CO_2, reduce pH

The body normalizes such a change in pH by slowing the rate or decreasing the depth of breathing, thus reducing CO_2 excretion. CO_2 and pH move in opposite directions. If pH rises, CO_2 falls, and vice versa.

CO_2 and hyperventilation

When a patient's respiratory rate increases, carbon dioxide (CO_2) is "blown off" and the CO_2 level drops.

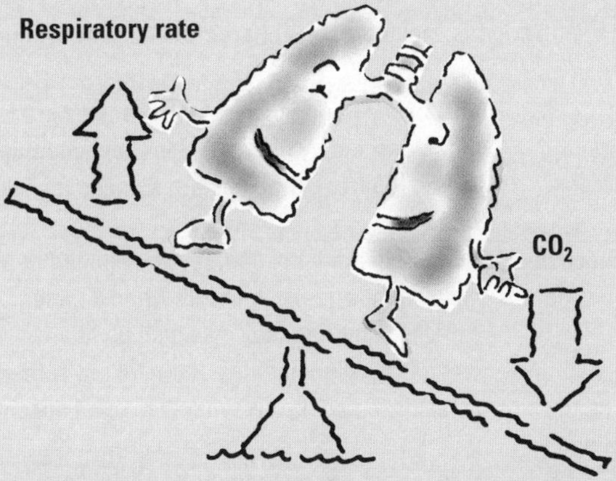
Respiratory rate
CO_2

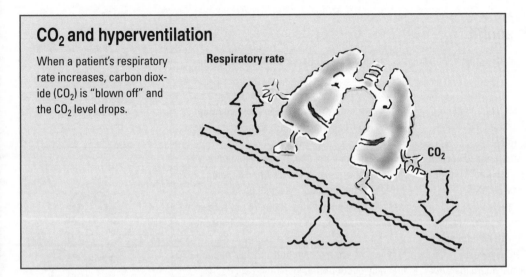

Physical examination terms

Examining a patient's respiratory status requires observation, palpation, and the ability to identify breath sounds. (See *Name that breath sound*, page 154.) Before you can perform a complete physical examination you need to understand these essential respiratory terms:

- **anoxia**—absence or near absence of O_2 in inhaled air, body tissues, or arterial blood
- **auscultation**—assessment step; listening, either directly or with a stethoscope, for sounds within the body
- **bronchospasm**—sudden, forceful, involuntary contraction of the smooth muscle of the bronchi, causing narrowing and obstruction of the airway
- **chest retraction**—visible depression of soft tissues of the chest between and around the cartilaginous and bony ribs, occurring with increased inspiratory effort
- **clubbing**—enlargement of the soft tissues of the distal phalanges that occurs in children with congenital heart disease and in older children and adults with long-standing pulmonary disease
- **cyanosis**—bluish discoloration of the skin and mucous membranes resulting from an excessive amount of deoxygenated hemoglobin in the blood
- **dyspnea**—shortness of breath, difficulty breathing, or labored breathing

Name that breath sound

Listed below are normal and abnormal breath sounds, including their characteristics and where they're heard.

Normal sounds

Normal breath sounds reflect air movement through the tracheobronchial tree. Normal breath sounds are described below:

- **Tracheal** breath sounds are harsh, discontinuous sounds heard over the trachea. They occur when a patient inhales or exhales.
- **Bronchial** breath sounds are loud, high-pitched sounds normally heard below the trachea at the manubrium. They're discontinuous and loudest when the patient exhales.
- **Vesicular** breath sounds are heard in front of the chest, on both sides, and in back. They're longer and louder during inspiration than expiration and can be heard in the peripheral lung fields.
- **Bronchovesicular** breath sounds can be auscultated over the mainstem bronchi and between the shoulder blades. They have a soft, medium-pitched, breezy sound. They're lower-pitched than bronchial sounds, but higher-pitched than vesicular sounds.

Abnormal sounds

Abnormal breath sounds, also called **adventitious sounds,** help diagnose many respiratory disorders.

- **Crackles** are crackling sounds, like hairs being rubbed together, usually heard first over the lung bases during inspiration. Crackles are further classified by pitch as **high (fine), medium,** or **low (coarse).** Crackles are sometimes called **rales.**
- **Rhonchi** are loud, coarse, low-pitched bubbling sounds heard primarily when a patient exhales, although they may also be heard when the patient inhales. Rhonchi are sometimes called **sonorous wheezes.** You'll auscultate rhonchi over the central airways.
- **Wheezes** are high-pitched, musical sounds that may occur during inspiration but occur predominantly during expiration. Wheezes are heard over the large bronchi.
- **Pleural friction rubs** are coarse, low-pitched abnormal breath sounds heard at the anterolateral chest wall (in front, near the ribs) during inspiration and expiration. A friction rub sounds like pieces of sandpaper being rubbed together.
- **Grunting** respirations refer to a coarse, grunting noise heard during expiration.
- **Stridor** is a crowing sound heard during inspiration that is caused by air whistling as it passes through swollen upper airways.
- **Decreased breath sounds** describes abnormally diminished sounds in areas of the lung.
- **Absent breath sounds** refers to a lack of sound over areas of the lungs that normally have breath sounds.

Abnormal breath sounds are also called **adventitious** sounds. It may help you to think of the word **adventure,** because these sounds are out of the ordinary.

The real world

Three-pillow orthopnea

You may hear the term **three-pillow orthopnea** used to describe a patient's sleeping habits. This means the patient requires three pillows to breathe comfortably while sleeping.

- **expectoration**—ejection of mucus from the trachea and lungs by coughing and spitting
- **expiration**—act of exhaling air
- **hemoptysis**—coughing or spitting up blood
- **inspiration**—act of inhaling air
- **orthopnea**—discomfort in breathing except in an upright position (see *Three-pillow orthopnea*)
- **palpation**—assessment step; feeling the body surface with the hand

(Text continues on page 155.)

Incredibly Easy miniguide: The lungs

The lower respiratory tract, which is contained within the thoracic cavity, consists of the trachea, bronchi, and lungs. The diaphragm is a dome-shaped organ that plays a vital part in respiration.

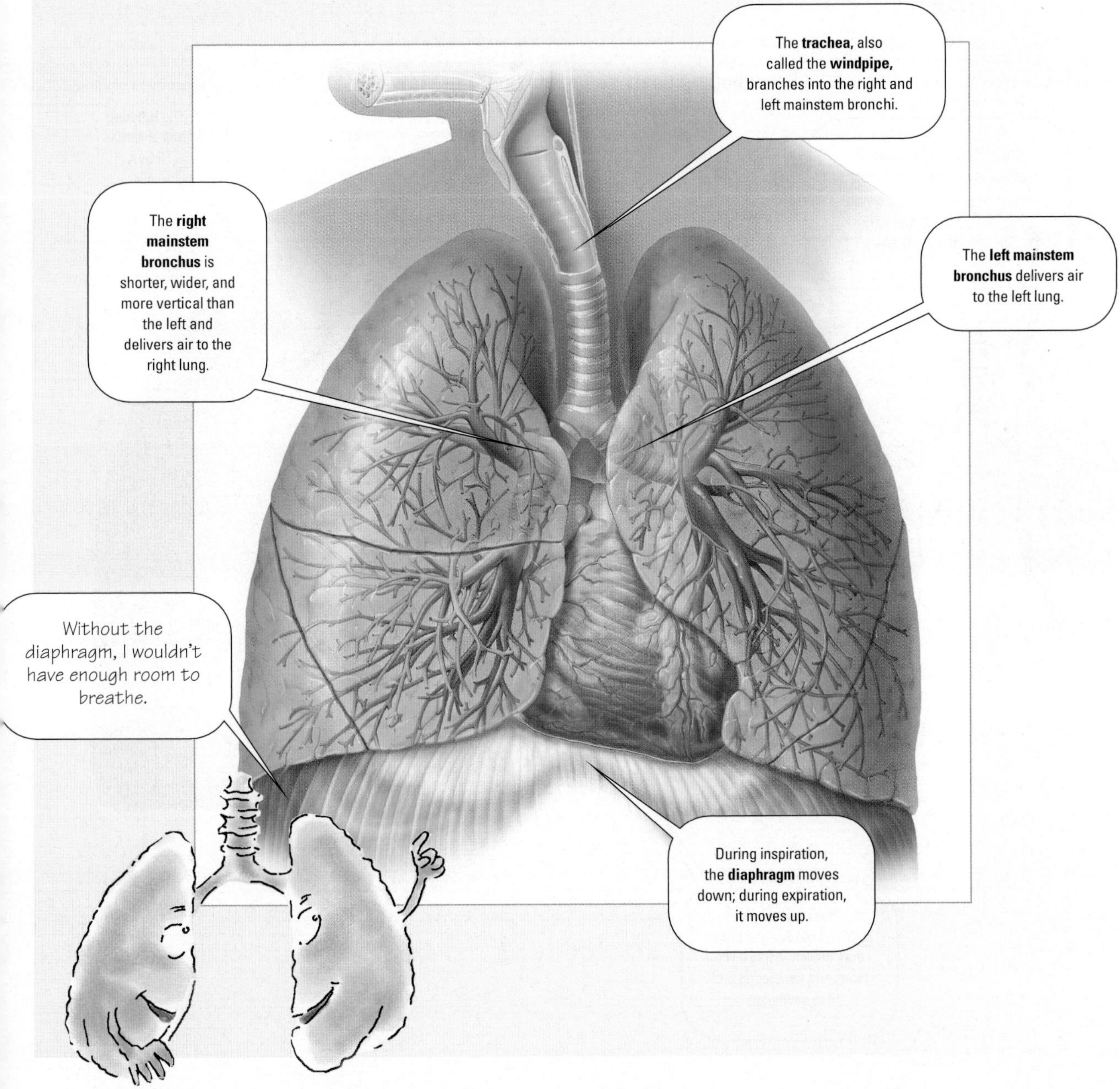
The **trachea,** also called the **windpipe,** branches into the right and left mainstem bronchi.
The **right mainstem bronchus** is shorter, wider, and more vertical than the left and delivers air to the right lung.
The **left mainstem bronchus** delivers air to the left lung.
Without the diaphragm, I wouldn't have enough room to breathe.
During inspiration, the **diaphragm** moves down; during expiration, it moves up.

Incredibly Easy miniguide: The lungs

The right lung is separated into the superior, middle, and inferior lobes by the horizontal and oblique fissures. The left lung is separated into the upper and lower lobes by the oblique fissure. A cavity between the lobes (cardiac notch) accommodates the heart.

Bronchopulmonary segments (anterior view)

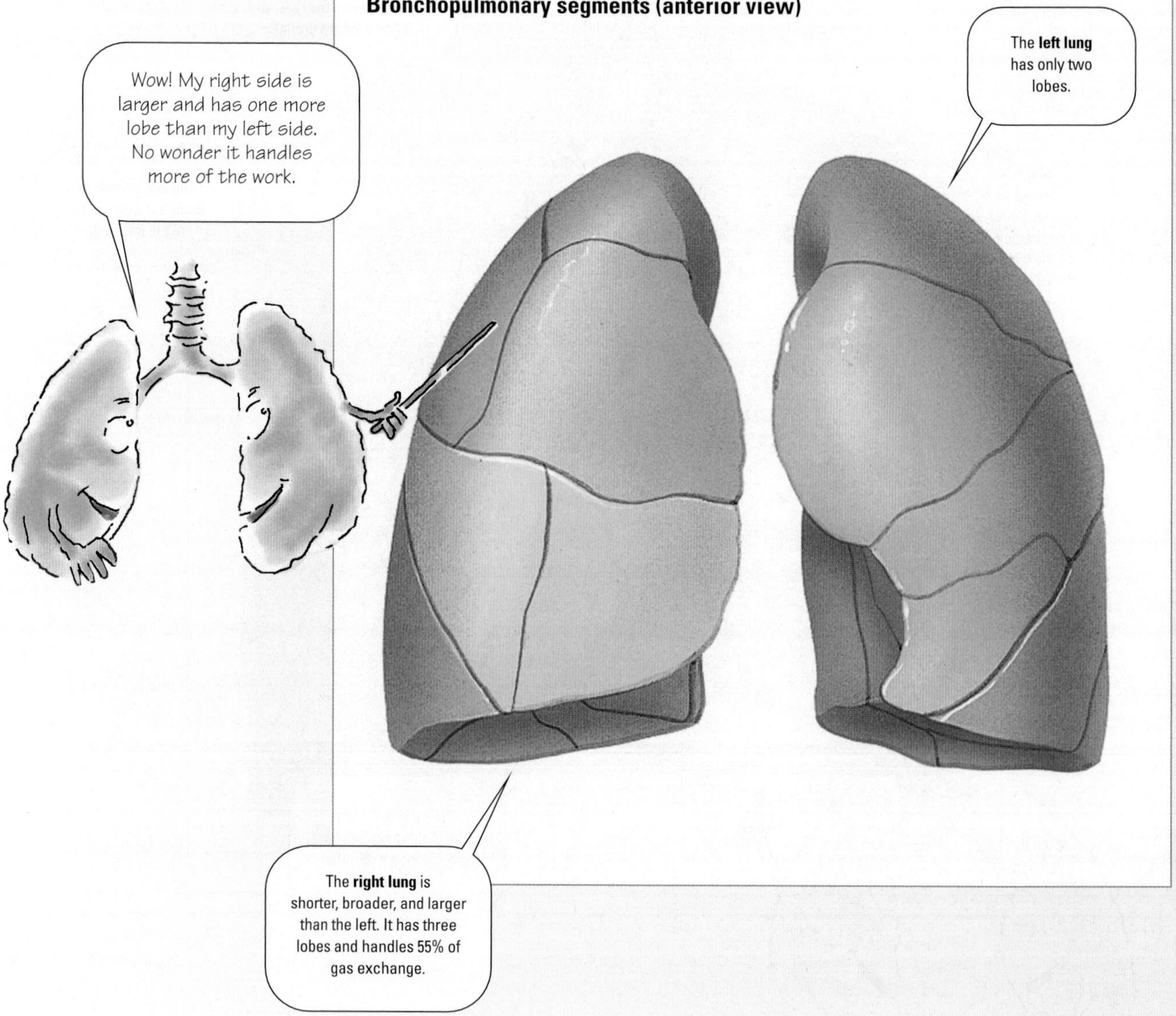
Wow! My right side is larger and has one more lobe than my left side. No wonder it handles more of the work.
The **left lung** has only two lobes.
The **right lung** is shorter, broader, and larger than the left. It has three lobes and handles 55% of gas exchange.

Incredibly Easy miniguide: The lungs

The lungs in a typical adult contain about 300 million alveoli, which are surrounded by an extensive network of capillaries.

Intrapulmonary airway

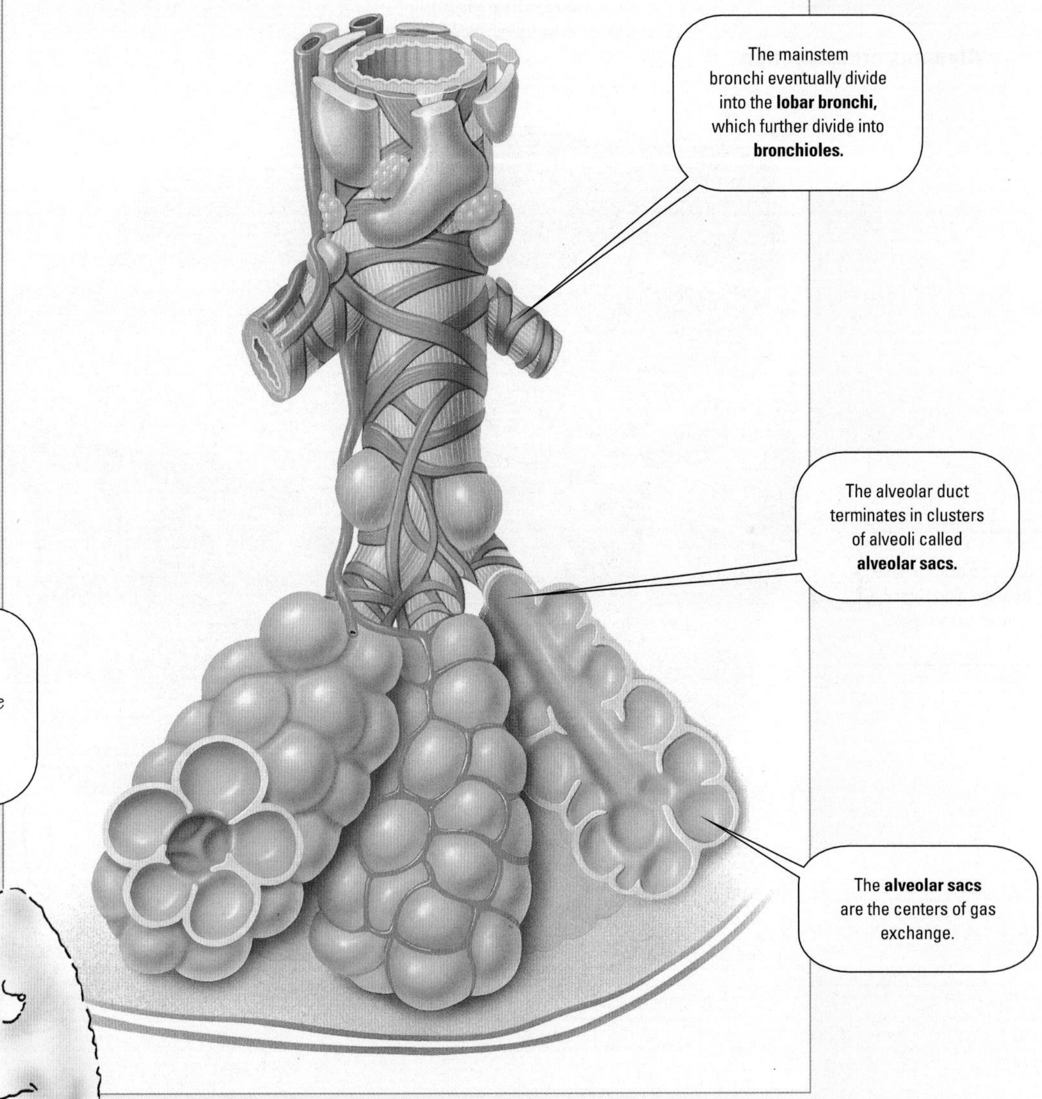
The mainstem bronchi eventually divide into the **lobar bronchi,** which further divide into **bronchioles.**
The alveolar duct terminates in clusters of alveoli called **alveolar sacs.**
The **alveolar sacs** are the centers of gas exchange.

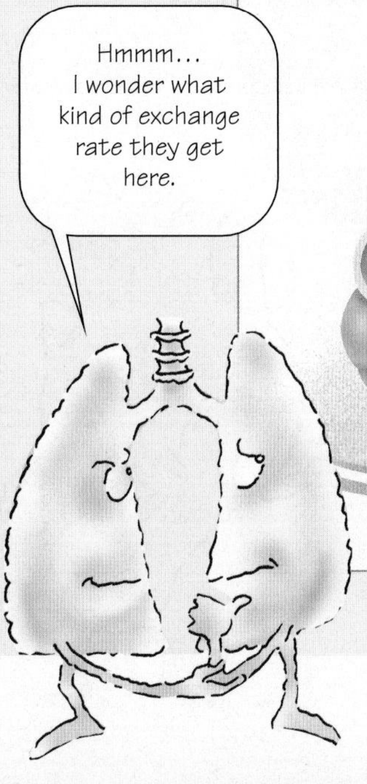
Hmmm… I wonder what kind of exchange rate they get here.

Incredibly Easy miniguide: The lungs

Oxygen (O2) and carbon dioxide (CO2) diffusion among the alveoli, blood, and tissues depends on the concentrations and pressures of these gases.

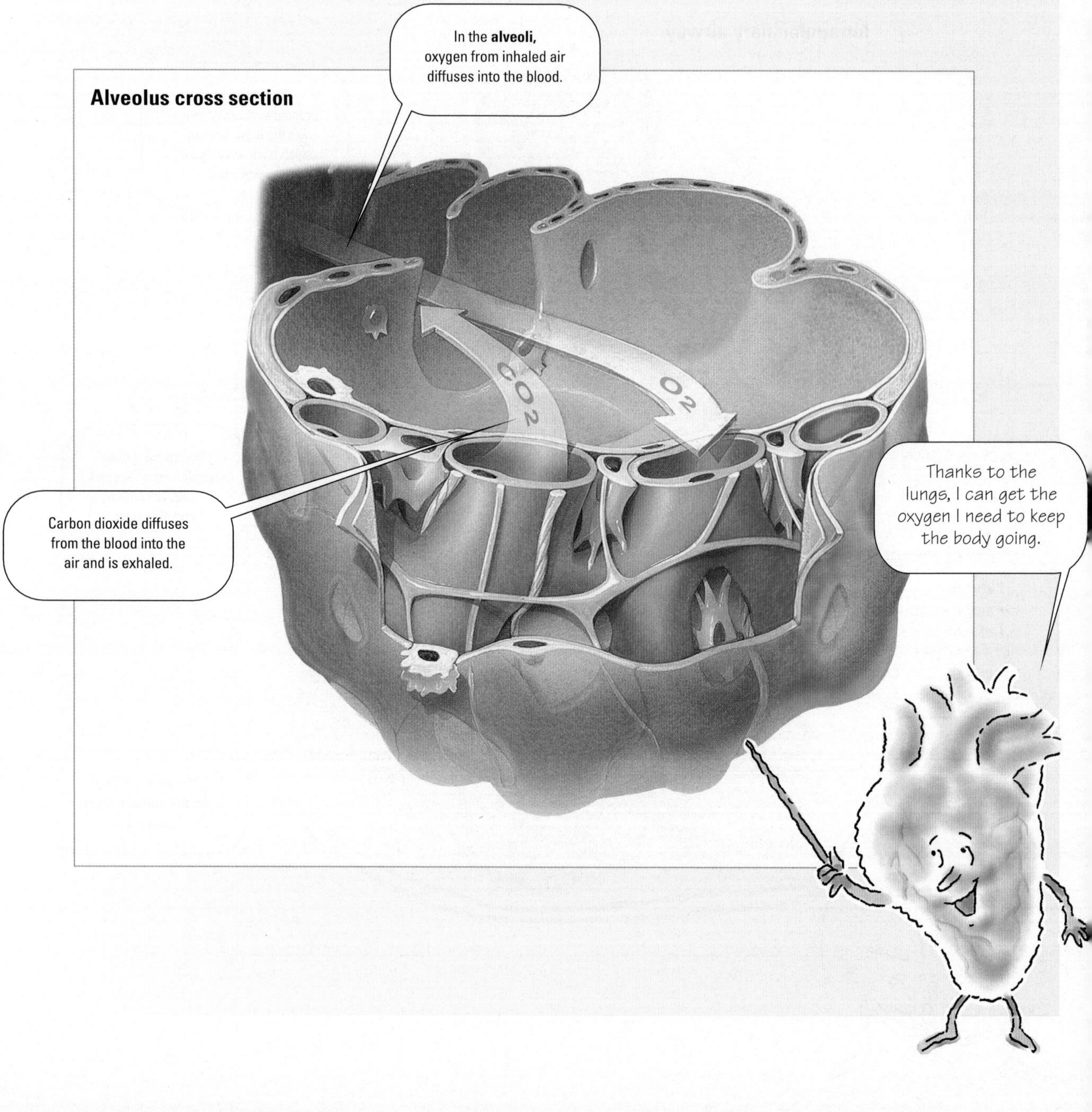
Alveolus cross section
In the **alveoli,** oxygen from inhaled air diffuses into the blood.
CO_2
O_2
Carbon dioxide diffuses from the blood into the air and is exhaled.
Thanks to the lungs, I can get the oxygen I need to keep the body going.

• **percussion**—assessment step; striking a part of the body with short, sharp blows of the fingers to detect changes in sound or mobilize lung secretions
• **respiratory rate**—number of breaths per minute
• **shunting**—condition in which blood moves from the venous circulation to the arterial circulation without participating in gas exchange, leading to hypoxemia
• **subcutaneous crepitus**—soft, popping sound produced by palpation or stroking of the skin; caused by bubbles of air or other gases such as CO_2 trapped in the subcutaneous tissue; may occur with pneumothorax
• **tactile fremitus**—vibration in the chest wall that may be felt when a hand is applied to the thorax while the patient is speaking.

Beyond the dictionary

Cheyne-Stokes

Cheyne-Stokes respirations were named after John Cheyne, a Scottish doctor, and William Stokes, an Irish doctor.

Respiratory patterns

The following terms describe different respiratory patterns:
• **apnea**—absence of breathing (may be periodic)
• **apneustic breathing**—prolonged, gasping inspirations followed by extremely short, inefficient expirations
• **Biot's respirations**—irregular periods of apnea alternating with periods of four or five breaths having the same depth
• **bradypnea**—unusually slow, regular respirations
• **Cheyne-Stokes respirations**—alternating periods of apnea and deep, rapid breathing (see *Cheyne-Stokes*)
• **eupnea**—normal respiratory rate and rhythm
• **Kussmaul's respirations**—faster and deeper respirations than normal, without pauses
• **tachypnea**—abnormally rapid respiratory rate.

Diagnostic tests

Below are the names of some diagnostic tests for the respiratory system and its associated disorders.

Ventilation tests

Ventilation tests, also called **pulmonary function tests,** include a series of measurements that evaluate the lungs' ventilatory function:

- **diffusing capacity for carbon monoxide (DLCO)**—amount of carbon monoxide diffused per minute across the alveolar membrane
- **expiratory reserve volume (ERV)**—volume of air that can be exhaled after normal expiration is completed
- **forced expiratory volume (FEV)**—volume of air expired in the first, second, and third seconds of the forced vital capacity test
- **forced vital capacity (FVC)**—volume of air that can be exhaled after maximum inspiration
- **functional residual capacity (FRC)**—volume of air remaining in the lungs after normal expiration
- **inspiratory capacity (IC)**—volume of air that can be inhaled after normal expiration
- **inspiratory reserve volume (IRV)**—maximum volume of air that can be inspired after normal inspiration is complete
- **maximum voluntary ventilation (MVV)**—the greatest volume of air breathed per unit of time
- **minute volume (V_E)**—volume of air breathed per minute, calculated from the tidal volume
- **residual volume (RV)**—volume of air that is *always* in the lungs and can't be exhaled (must be measured indirectly)
- **tidal volume (V_T)**—volume of air inhaled or exhaled during normal breathing
- **total lung capacity (TLC)**—volume of the lungs at peak inspiration
- **vital capacity (VC)**—maximum volume of air that can be exhaled after maximum inspiration.

Radiologic tests

I could paint you a picture but radiologic tests help you get a good look at me.

Radiologic tests, which use X-rays or electromagnetic waves to create images of interior structures, can be used to diagnose respiratory problems:

- **Chest radiography,** commonly known as **chest X-ray,** creates an image of the thorax to reveal abnormalities.
- **Magnetic resonance imaging (MRI)** is a procedure in which the patient is placed in a magnetic field into which a radiofrequency beam is introduced. Resulting energy changes are measured and computed, generating images on a monitor. Cross-sectional images of the anatomy can be viewed in multiple planes.

• **Pulmonary angiography,** also called **pulmonary arteriography,** is the radiographic examination of the pulmonary circulation after injection of a radiopaque contrast dye into the pulmonary artery or one of its branches.
• **Thoracic computed tomography (CT) scan** provides cross-sectional views of the chest by passing an X-ray beam from a computerized scanner through the body at different angles. CT scanning may be done with or without an injected contrast dye.
• **Ventilation-perfusion scan** combines two procedures to evaluate the lungs' ventilation and perfusion. The ventilation scan is performed after the patient inhales a mixture of air and radioactive gas that delineates areas of the lung ventilated during respiration. The perfusion scan produces an image of pulmonary blood flow after I.V. injection of a radioactive dye.

Other tests

Here are other tests used to diagnose respiratory system disorders:
• **Arterial blood gas measurement** provides levels of O_2 and CO_2 in arterial blood to evaluate acid-base balance and to assess and monitor a patient's ventilation and oxygenation status. (See *What a gas!* and *What arterial blood gases reveal*, page 158.)
• **Bronchoscopy** allows visual inspection of the tracheobronchial tree. (See *Understanding bronchoscopy*, page 158.)
• **Culture and sensitivity tests** help identify the causative organism in bacterial, viral, or fungal infections.
• **Pulse oximetry** is a continuous noninvasive study of arterial blood oxygen saturation using a probe or clip attached to a sensor site.
• **Sputum analysis** is the examination of a sample of expectorated material from the patient's lungs.
• In **thoracentesis**, a needle is used to puncture the chest and aspirate fluid from the parietal cavity for diagnostic or therapeutic purposes.

The real world

What a gas!

In practice, you'll commonly hear **arterial blood gases** referred to as *ABGs, blood gases,* or simply *gases*—as in "Let's draw some gases."

Understanding bronchoscopy

In **bronchoscopy,** a bronchoscope is used to examine the bronchi. This procedure is also used to obtain specimens or to remove foreign bodies.

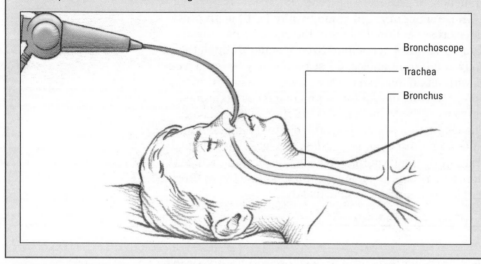

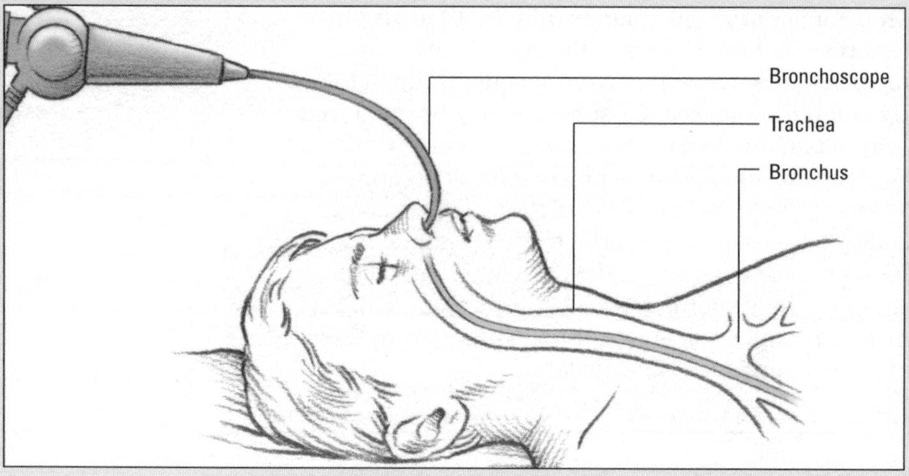
Bronchoscope
Trachea
Bronchus

What arterial blood gases reveal

Arterial blood gas analysis helps to diagnose the following disorders:

- **respiratory acidosis,** or excess carbon dioxide (CO_2) retention, which is typically caused by hypoventilation
- **respiratory alkalosis,** which occurs when too much CO_2 is excreted (hyperventilation is the primary cause)
- **metabolic acidosis,** which reflects elevated acid levels and may be caused by loss of bicarbonate, excess acid production, or a combination of both
- **metabolic alkalosis,** which reflects elevated bicarbonate levels, decreased acid levels, or both (prolonged vomiting and loss of potassium can deplete the body's acid stores; overuse of alkaline medications such as antacids can produce elevated bicarbonate levels).

Disorders

The respiratory system is such a complex network that many things can go wrong. Here's is a list of major respiratory disorders:

- **Acute bronchitis** is an inflammation of the bronchi accompanied by mucus production and subsequent obstruction of airflow. Infectious agents, such as influenza virus, streptococci, pneumococci, staphylococci, and *Haemophilus* organisms, can cause acute bronchitis.
- **Acute respiratory failure (ARF)** is caused by the cardiac and pulmonary systems inadequately exchanging O_2 and CO_2 in the lungs.
- **Acute respiratory distress syndrome (ARDS)** is a form of pulmonary edema that can quickly lead to acute respiratory failure.
- **Asbestosis** is caused by prolonged inhalation of asbestos fibers, which become encased in the bronchioles and alveolar walls in a proteinlike sheath.
- **Atelectasis** is the collapse of lung tissue or incomplete expansion of a lung caused by the absence of air in a por-

tion of the lung or the entire lung. (See *Expanding on atelectasis.*)

- **Bronchiectasis** is a condition marked by chronic abnormal dilation of bronchi and destruction of bronchial walls.
- **Chronic obstructive pulmonary disease (COPD)** refers to a group of long-term pulmonary disorders marked by resistance to air flow (hence the term **obstructive**). Types of COPD include:

  – **asthma**—episodic airway obstruction caused by bronchospasm, increased mucus secretion, and mucosal edema; may be either **extrinsic (atopic),** a reaction to specific external allergens, or **intrinsic,** a reaction to internal, nonallergenic factors

  – **chronic bronchitis**—characterized by excessive mucus production with productive cough lasting at least 3 months per year for 2 successive years; usually caused by prolonged exposure to bronchial irritants such as smoking, secondhand smoke, air pollution, dust, and toxic fumes

  – **emphysema**—abnormal, permanent enlargement of the acini that's accompanied by destruction of the alveolar walls. It occurs when alveolar gas is trapped and gas exchange is compromised.
- **Cor pulmonale** is a heart condition in which hypertension of the pulmonary circulation leads to enlargement of the right ventricle.
- **Croup** is a severe inflammation and obstruction of the upper airway that usually follows an upper respiratory tract infection. It's a childhood disease characterized by a sharp barklike cough.
- **Cystic fibrosis** is a multisystem genetic disorder, a defect of the exocrine glands, causing tenacious mucus in the lungs.
- **Empyema** is a form of pleural effusion in which the fluid in the pleural space contains pus.
- **Epiglottiditis** is an acute inflammation of the epiglottis that tends to cause airway obstruction.
- **Hemothorax** is a collection of blood in the pleural cavity.
- **Hypoxemia** is a deficiency of O_2 in the arterial blood but isn't as severe as anoxia.
- **Hypoxia** is a deficiency of O_2 at a cellular level.

Beyond the dictionary

Expanding on atelectasis

Atelectasis derives from the Greek terms ***ateles,*** meaning *imperfect,* and ***ektasis,*** meaning *expansion.* It refers to the collapse of lung tissue or incomplete expansion of a lung.

• **Legionnaires' disease** is an acute, noncommunicable bronchopneumonia caused by an airborne bacillus.
• **Lung abscess** is a lung infection accompanied by pus accumulation and tissue destruction.
• **Pleural effusion** is accumulation of fluid in the interstitial and air spaces of the lung.
• **Pleurisy** is an inflammation of the pleurae characterized by dyspnea and stabbing pain, leading to restriction of breathing.
• **Pneumonia** is an acute infection of lung parenchyma commonly impairing gas exchange.
• **Pneumothorax** is a collection of air in the pleural cavity that leads to partial or complete lung collapse. (See *Pneuma: A breath of air.*) Different types of pneumothorax include:
– **closed pneumothorax**—condition in which air enters the pleural space from within the lungs
– **open pneumothorax**—condition in which atmospheric air flows directly into the pleural cavity
– **tension pneumothorax**—condition in which air in the pleural space compresses the thoracic organs, possibly causing **mediastinal shift** of organs and blood vessels, thus reducing blood flow to and from the heart.
• **Pulmonary edema** is a common complication of cardiac disorders in which extravascular fluid accumulates in the lung tissues and alveoli.
• **Pulmonary embolism** occurs when a clot or foreign substance lodges in a pulmonary artery.
• **Pulmonary fibrosis** is scar tissue formation in the connective tissue of the lungs.
• **Pulmonary hypertension** is any condition that increases resistance to blood flow in the pulmonary vessels. The most common cause is COPD.
• **Pulmonary infarction** occurs when lung tissue is denied blood flow and dies.
• **Respiratory distress syndrome,** also called **hyaline membrane disease,** is the most common cause of neonatal mortality. In respiratory distress syndrome, the premature infant develops widespread alveolar collapse.
• **Sarcoidosis** is a multisystem, granulomatous disorder that characteristically produces enlarged lymph nodes, pulmonary infiltration, and skeletal, liver, eye, or skin lesions.

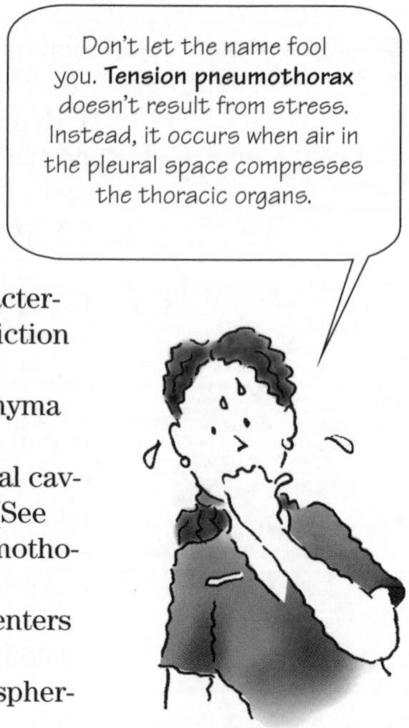
Don't let the name fool you. **Tension pneumothorax** doesn't result from stress. Instead, it occurs when air in the pleural space compresses the thoracic organs.

Beyond the dictionary

Pneuma: A breath of air

In English, the ***Pn-*** combination always indicates a word of Greek origin, and the ***p*** isn't pronounced. ***Pneuma,*** the Greek word for *breath, spirit,* or *wind,* has given rise to a number of words. In medical terminology it means *air* or *lung.* ***Thorax*** is a Greek word that means *chest.* It makes sense then that a **pneumothorax** is a collection of air in the chest.

- **Silicosis** is a progressive disease characterized by nodular lesions that commonly progress to fibrosis.
- **Sudden infant death syndrome (SIDS),** also known as **crib death,** is the unexplained sudden death of a healthy infant (younger than 1 year) during sleep. Although the cause is unknown, placing the infant on his back to sleep has been shown to significantly decrease the incidence of SIDS.
- **Tuberculosis** is an infectious disease in which pulmonary infiltrates accumulate in the lungs, cavities develop, and masses of granulated tissue form. It may also infect other body organs and tissues.

Treatments

In this section, you'll learn the devices, surgical interventions, and other treatments used to improve oxygenation.

Tools of the trade

These are names of medical devices used to treat respiratory disorders:

- **bronchoscope**—used therapeutically to remove foreign bodies and tenacious secretions from the trachea and bronchi and to visualize the tissues
- **chest tube**—a tube inserted through a thoracostomy into the pleural space and used to remove blood, fluid, or air in cases of hemothorax, pleural effusion, pneumothorax, or acute empyema
- **endotracheal (ET) tube**—a flexible catheter inserted into the trachea via the mouth or nose and used to deliver O_2 into the lungs and maintain a patent airway
- **nasal cannula**—small tubes that deliver a variable, low-flow O_2 supply through the nasal passages (see *A look at a nasal cannula*)
- **nebulizer**—a device that delivers a fine spray for inhalation of moisture or drug therapy
- **resuscitation bag**—an inflatable device that can be attached to a facemask or directly to an ET or tracheostomy tube that's designed to manually deliver O_2 or room air into the lungs
- **stethoscope**—an instrument used for auscultation of respiratory, cardiac, arterial, and venous sounds consist-

A look at a nasal cannula

A *nasal cannula* delivers a low-flow oxygen supply to the nasal passages through small, plastic tubes, as shown in the illustration below.

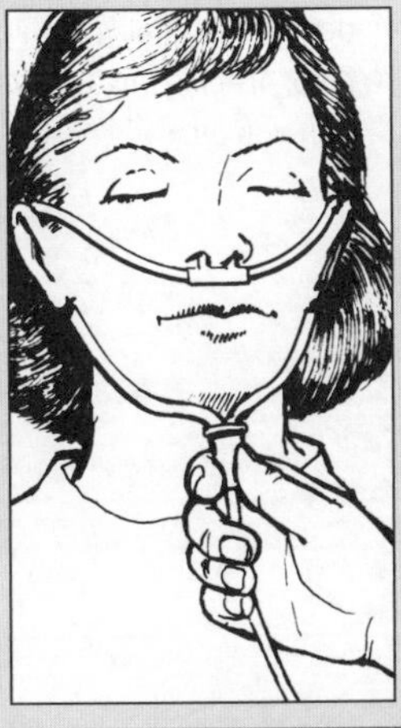

A look at a tracheostomy tube

A *tracheostomy tube* is used to relieve upper airway obstruction and to aid breathing. The tube can be made of plastic or metal and comes in three varieties: uncuffed, cuffed, and fenestrated. A plastic-cuffed tracheostomy tube is shown here.

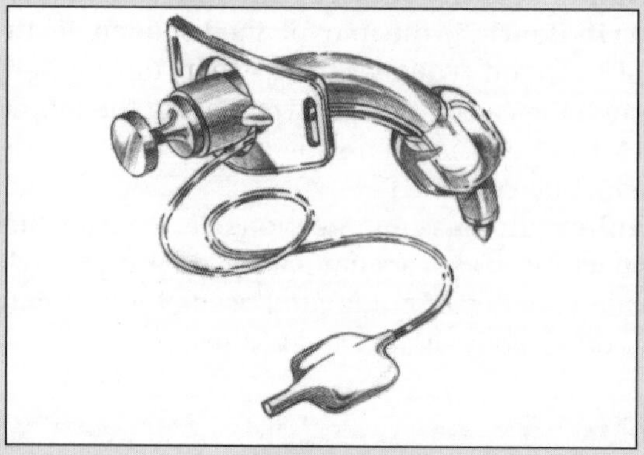

ing of two earpieces connected by flexible tubing to a diaphragm, which is placed against the patient's body
- **tracheostomy tube**—a tube inserted into the surgical opening through the neck into the trachea, which is used to relieve upper airway obstruction and aid breathing; may be used with a mechanical ventilator (see *A look at a tracheostomy tube*)
- **Venturi mask**—a device designed to deliver a high-flow, precise O_2 mixture (see *A look at a Venturi mask*).

A look at a Venturi mask

A *Venturi mask* is a device designed to deliver a high-flow, precise mixture of oxygen and air.

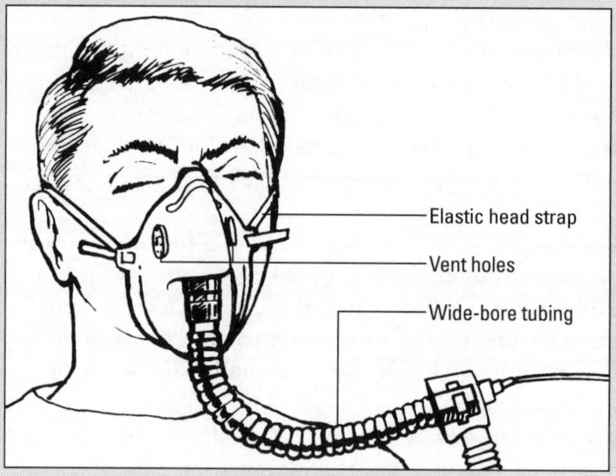
Elastic head strap
Vent holes
Wide-bore tubing

Surgery

Here are the names of surgical procedures used to treat respiratory disorders:

- **pneumonectomy**—surgical removal of the lung
- **thoracentesis**—a needle puncture of the chest performed to drain fluid from the parietal cavity; it may be performed at the bedside or as an outpatient procedure
- **thoracostomy**—the surgical creation of an opening in the chest wall for the purpose of drainage
- **thoracotomy**—a surgical incision in the chest wall made to excise a lung or portions of it; thoracotomy can be further classified in three ways:
  - **lobectomy**—the surgical excision of a lobe of a lung
  - **segmental resection**—surgical removal of one or more of the lung's segments (removes more functional tissue than a lobectomy)
  - **wedge resection**—the surgical removal of a triangular section of lung tissue
- **tracheotomy**—a surgical opening in the trachea that provides an airway for intubated patients who need prolonged mechanical ventilation; also used to help remove lung secretions and bypass upper airway obstruction.

Ventilation therapies

Ventilation therapy moves air in and out of a patient's lungs, but it doesn't ensure adequate gas exchange.

Manual ventilation

In **manual ventilation**, a handheld resuscitation bag is used to deliver room air or O_2 to the lungs of a patient who can't breathe spontaneously. (See *Vent 'em, bag 'em.*)

Mechanical ventilation

Mechanical ventilators may supply negative or positive pressure. Negative pressure on the chest and lungs expands them during inspiration and is used to treat neuromuscular disorders. Positive pressure, the most commonly used mechanical ventilation system, is used to treat respiratory disorders.

The real world

Vent 'em, bag 'em

The handheld resuscitation bag is commonly referred to as an **Ambu bag.** You may hear people refer to the process of using this device as *bagging the patient.* For example, "Disconnect him from the ventilator and bag him." If a patient requires a mechanical ventilator to assist with breathing, you may hear people say that the patient is *on a vent.*

Be positive

The **positive-pressure system** exerts positive pressure on the airway to inflate alveoli during inspiration. The inspiratory cycles of these ventilators may vary in volume, pressure, or time. There are three inspiratory cycle types:
- **Pressure-cycled** ventilation provides a continuous flow of O_2 until a preset pressure is reached.
- **Time-cycled** ventilation provides flow for a preset amount of time.
- **Volume-cycled** ventilation delivers a preset volume of air.

In the mode

Ventilation is provided through several ventilator modes:
- **Control mode** completely controls the patient's respiration, delivering a set tidal volume at a prescribed rate.
- **Assist mode** allows the patient to initiate a breath and receive a tidal volume from the machine.
- **Assist-control mode** allows the patient to initiate breathing, but a backup control delivers a preset number of breaths at a set volume.
- **Continuous positive-airway pressure (CPAP)** maintains positive pressure in the airways throughout the entire respiratory cycle.
- In the **positive end-expiratory pressure (PEEP) mode**, positive pressure is applied during expiration.
- **Pressure support ventilation** augments the patient's spontaneous breath with a preset pressure. It doesn't provide the entire volume. The rate isn't set by the machine; it's set by the patient's spontaneous efforts.
- In **synchronized intermittent mandatory ventilation (SIMV),** a machine delivers a set number of specific-volume breaths. The patient can breathe on his own between SIMV breaths at volumes that differ from those on the machine. SIMV is commonly used as a weaning tool, conditioning the patient's respiratory muscles.

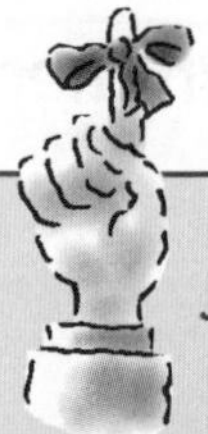

Memory jogger

In this case, mad is good! To remember the essentials of drug therapy for respiratory disorders, think **"ME MAD"**:

Methylxanthine agents

Expectorants

Mucolytics

Antitussives

Decongestants

Drug therapy

Drug therapy for respiratory disorders includes:
- **antitussives** to suppress cough
- **decongestants** to relieve swelling in nasal passages
- **expectorants,** which liquefy secretions to help remove mucus

• **methylxanthine agents** to relax bronchial smooth muscle in patients with asthma and to stimulate respiratory drive in patients with bronchitis, emphysema, and apnea
• **mucolytics** to enhance mucus removal.

Other therapies

Here are other therapies to treat respiratory disorders:
• **Aerosol treatments** deliver drugs by way of a nebulizer, which turns liquid into a spray the patient breathes.
• **Deep breathing** loosens secretions and opens airways.
• **Oxygen therapy** is delivered by a nasal cannula, catheter, mask, or transtracheal catheter; it prevents hypoxemia and eases the patient's breathing.
• **Postural drainage** uses gravity to help move secretions from the lungs and bronchi into the trachea to be coughed up.
• **Percussion** involves cupping hands and fingers together and clapping them alternately over the patient's lung fields to loosen secretions for expectoration.
• An **ultrasonic nebulizer** mobilizes thick secretions and promotes a productive cough.

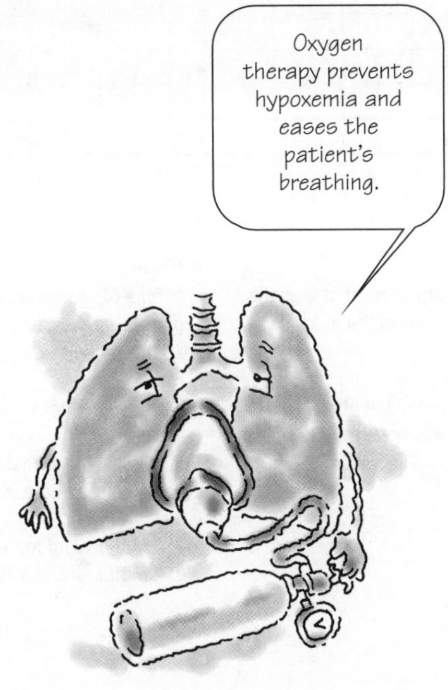
Oxygen therapy prevents hypoxemia and eases the patient's breathing.

systole

Vocabulary builders

At a crossroads

Completing this crossword puzzle will help you breathe more easily about respiratory system terms. Good luck!

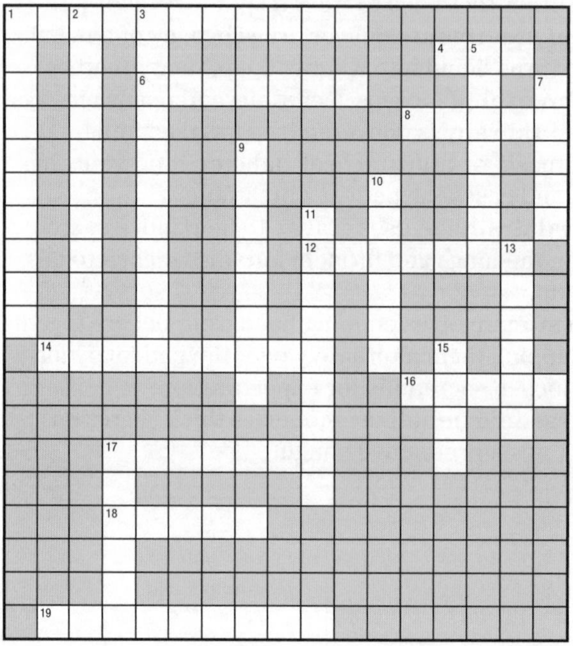

No need to hyperventilate. This is just a game.

Across

1. Space between the lungs
4. Acronym for volume of air that can be exhaled after maximum inspiration
6. Another word for **windpipe**
8. Absence of breathing
12. Deficiency of O_2 at a cellular level
14. Surgical excision of a lung lobe
16. Slit on the lungs' medial surface
17. Bony structures that form the posterior walls of the nasal passages
18. The lung that's shorter, broader, and larger than the other
19. Unusually slow, regular respirations

Down

1. Type of ventilation that uses a positive-pressure system
2. Most important muscle for respiration
3. Drug type that acts to suppress cough
5. Eponym for a mask designed to deliver a high-flow, precise O_2 mixture
7. Another word for **nostrils**
9. Another word for **larynx**
10. The respiratory system structure that separates the nasal passages
11. Plural form of **pharynx**
13. Chief respiratory unit for gas exchange
15. Eponym for respirations characterized by irregular periods of apnea alternating with four or five breaths of the same depth
17. Another word for **tracheal bifurcation**

Answers are on page 170.

Match game

When assessing a patient's respiratory system, it's important to know the terms for different breath sounds. Match the description of each breath sound below to its name.

Clues

Normal sounds

1. Loud, high-pitched sounds that are heard at the manubrium and are loudest on expiration ____

2. Sounds heard in the lung's periphery, in front of the chest, on both sides, and in back that are longer and louder during inspiration than expiration ____

3. Soft, medium-pitched, breezy sounds that are lower pitched than bronchial sounds but higher pitched than vesicular sounds ____

Abnormal sounds

4. Sounds like hairs being rubbed together, usually heard first over the lung bases ____

5. Loud, coarse, low-pitched bubbling sounds heard primarily during expiration ____

6. High-pitched, musical sounds that may occur during both inspiration and expiration but predominantly during expiration ____

7. Coarse, low-pitched sounds heard at the anterolateral chest wall (in front, near the ribs) during inspiration and expiration that sound like pieces of sandpaper being rubbed together ____

8. Crowing sound heard during inspiration, caused by air whistling as it passes through swollen upper airways ____

9. Abnormally diminished breath sounds in areas of the lung ____

10. Lack of sound over areas of the lungs that normally have breath sounds ____

Choices

A. Absent

B. Bronchial

C. Bronchovesicular

D. Crackles

E. Decreased

F. Pleural friction rubs

G. Rhonchi

H. Stridor

I. Vesicular

J. Wheezes

Answers are on page 170.

Talking in circles

Use the clues below to fill in the blanks with the appropriate word. Then unscramble the circled letters to find the answer to the question posed below.

1. ___ ___ ___ (◯) ___ ___
2. ___ ___ ___ ___ ___ ___ ___ ___ ___ ___ ___ (◯)
3. ___ ___ ___ (◯) ___
4. ___ ___ (◯) ___ ___
5. ___ (◯) ___ ___ ___ ___ ___

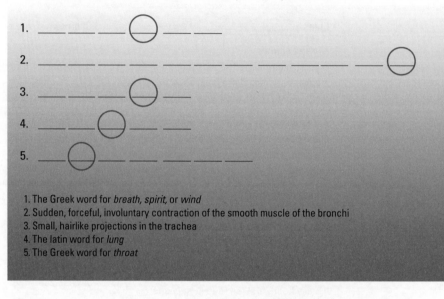

1. The Greek word for *breath, spirit,* or *wind*
2. Sudden, forceful, involuntary contraction of the smooth muscle of the bronchi
3. Small, hairlike projections in the trachea
4. The latin word for *lung*
5. The Greek word for *throat*

You probably enter a house through a door, but my friends—the lungs—admit my blood vessels and the mainstem bronchi through what structure?

Answers are on page 170.

O see, can you say?

Sound out each group of pictures and symbols below to reveal a term that was reviewed in the chapter.

1.

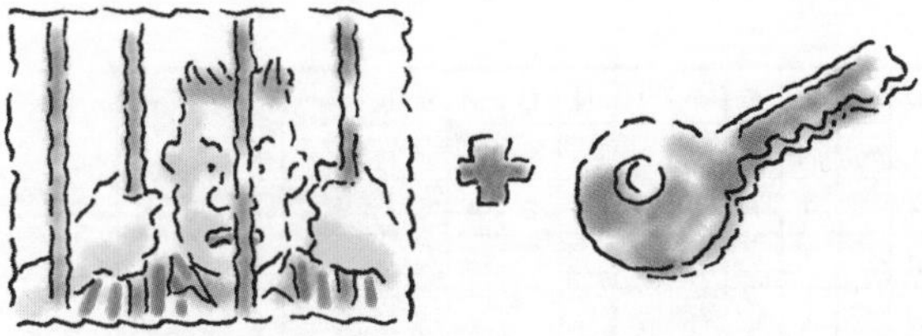

2.

+ + uh

3.

al + V + + L

4.

kah + r + nuh

5.

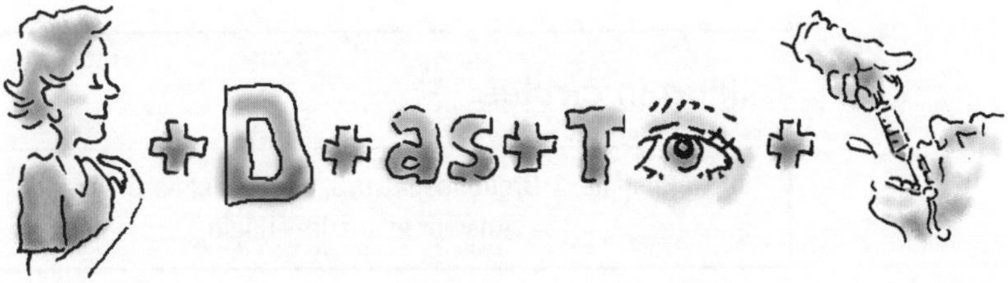
+ D + as + T +

Answers are on page 170.

Answers

At a crossroads

[1]M	E	[2]D	I	[3]A	S	T	I	N	U	M						
E		I		N									[4]F	[5]V	C	
C		A		[6]T	R	A	C	H	E	A				E		[7]N
H		P		I								[8]A	P	N	E	A
A		H		T			[9]V							T		R
N		R		U			O				[10]S			R		E
I		A		S			I		[11]P		E			U		S
C		G		S			C		[12]H	Y	P	O	X	I	[13]A	
A		M		I			E		A		T				C	
L				V			B		R		U				I	
	[14]L	O	B	E	C	T	O	M	Y		M		[15]B		N	
							X		N			[16]H	I	L	U	M
									G				O		S	
			[17]C	O	N	C	H	A	E				T			
			A						S							
			[18]R	I	G	H	T									
			I													
			N													
	[19]B	R	A	D	Y	P	N	E	A							

Match game

1. B; 2. I; 3. C; 4. D; 5. G; 6. J; 7. F; 8. H; 9. E; 10. A

Talking in circles

1. Pneuma; 2. Bronchospasm; 3. Cilia; 4. Pulmo; 5. Pharynx
Answer to puzzle—Hilum

O see, can you say?

1. Conchae; 2. Trachea; 3. Alveoli; 4. Carina; 5. Mediastinum

8

Gastrointestinal system

Just the facts

In this chapter, you'll learn:

- terminology related to the structure and function of the GI system
- terminology needed for physical examination of the GI system
- tests that help diagnose GI disorders
- common GI disorders and their treatments.

GI structure and function

This chapter introduces terms associated with the GI system, the system responsible for digestion and elimination. The first part of the word **gastrointestinal,** *gastro-*, is a Greek word that means *stomach;* it's used in many medical terms. The second part of the word refers, of course, to the intestines. But the GI system includes more than just the stomach and the intestines. (See *Pronouncing key GI system terms*, page 172.)

Let's see. ***Gastro*** *means stomach;* ***entero*** means *intestine;* and ***-ology*** means study. Seems simple—**gastroenterology** is *the study of the stomach and intestines.*

Two parts

The GI system has two major components:
• **alimentary canal** (also called the **GI tract**)—the mouth, pharynx, esophagus, stomach, intestines, rectum, and anus
• **accessory GI organs**—the liver, gallbladder, biliary duct system, and pancreas.

Two functions

Together, the alimentary canal and the accessory organs serve two major functions:

Pump up your pronunciation

Pronouncing key GI system terms

Below is a list of key terms related to the GI system, along with the correct ways to pronounce them

Anastomosis	UH-NAS-TUH-MOH-SIS
Cachexia	KUH-KEK-SEE-UH
Cholangiogram	KOH-LAN-JEE-OH-GRAM
Diverticulosis	DEYE-VER-TIK-YOO-LOH-SIS
Gastroenteritis	GAS-TROH-EN-TER-EYE-TIS
Submandibular	SUHB-MAN-DIHB-YOU-LUHR
Tunica adventitia	TOO-NIK-UH AD-VEN-TI-SHUH

- **digestion**—the breakdown of food and fluid into simple chemicals that can be absorbed into the bloodstream and transported throughout the body
- **elimination**—the expulsion of waste products from the body through excretion of feces.

The breakdown of food begins in the **oral cavity**—that's the mouth.

Alimentary canal

Here are the terms and descriptions of structures of the alimentary canal.

Mouth

Also called the **buccal cavity** or **oral cavity,** the mouth is bounded by the lips, cheeks, **palate** (the roof of the mouth), and tongue. It also contains the teeth. The mouth initiates the mechanical breakdown of food. Ducts connect the mouth with three major pairs of **salivary glands,** which secrete **saliva** to moisten food during chewing and convert starch into maltose. The three pairs are:

- **parotid**—located at the side of the face in front of and below the external ear
- **submandibular**—located, as the name indicates, beneath the **mandible,** or lower jaw

Anatomically speaking

Structures of the GI system

The GI system includes the alimentary canal (the pharynx, esophagus, stomach, and small and large intestines) and the accessory organs (the liver, biliary duct system, and pancreas). These structures are shown below.

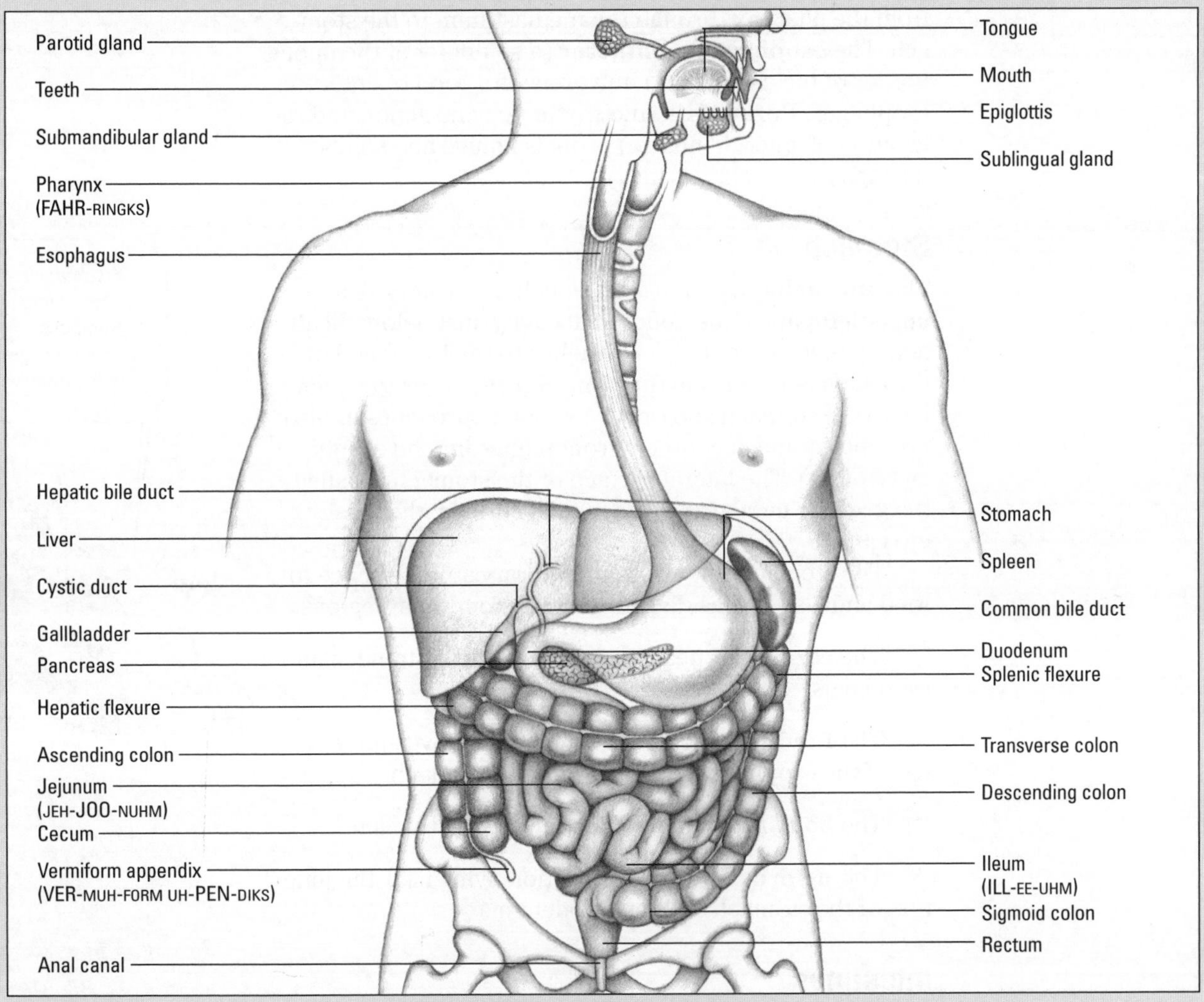
Parotid gland
Teeth
Submandibular gland
Pharynx
(FAHR-RINGKS)
Esophagus
Hepatic bile duct
Liver
Cystic duct
Gallbladder
Pancreas
Hepatic flexure
Ascending colon
Jejunum
(JEH-JOO-NUHM)
Cecum
Vermiform appendix
(VER-MUH-FORM UH-PEN-DIKS)
Anal canal
Tongue
Mouth
Epiglottis
Sublingual gland
Stomach
Spleen
Common bile duct
Duodenum
Splenic flexure
Transverse colon
Descending colon
Ileum
(ILL-EE-UHM)
Sigmoid colon
Rectum

- **sublingual**—located, as the name indicates, under the tongue. (See *Structures of the GI system.*)

Pharynx

The **pharynx,** or throat, a cavity extending from the base of the skull to the esophagus, aids swallowing by grasping food and propelling it toward the esophagus.

Esophagus

The **esophagus** is a hollow, muscular tube that extends from the pharynx through the mediastinum to the stomach. The **esophageal sphincter** (a sphincter at the upper border of the esophagus) must relax for food to enter the esophagus. **Peristalsis** (the rhythmic contraction and relaxation of smooth muscle) propels liquids and solids through the esophagus into the stomach.

Stomach

The **stomach** is a collapsible, pouchlike structure in the upper left part of the abdominal cavity, just below the diaphragm. Its upper border attaches to the lower end of the esophagus. The **cardiac sphincter** guards the opening to the stomach and opens as food approaches. It also prevents stomach contents from reentering the esophagus (reflux). The lateral surface of the stomach is called the **greater curvature;** the medial surface, the **lesser curvature**.

Stomach's the name. Temporary food storage is my game.

The stomach serves as a temporary storage space for food and also begins digestion. It has four main regions:

1. The **cardia** lies near the junction of the stomach and esophagus.
2. The **fundus** is the enlarged portion above and to the left of the esophageal opening into the stomach.
3. The **body** is the middle portion of the stomach.
4. The **pylorus** is the lower portion, lying near the junction of the stomach and the duodenum.

Intestines

After mixing food with gastric secretions, the stomach breaks it down into **chyme,** a semifluid substance, and then moves the gastric contents into the intestines, which consist of the small intestine and the large intestine.

Small but really lo-o-o-o-n-n-g

Although it's called "small," the narrow tube called the **small intestine** is actually about 20′ (6.1 m) long and is composed of three major divisions:

- The **duodenum** is the most superior division and most active in digestion.
- The **jejunum** is the middle portion.
- The **ileum** is the most inferior portion.

The small intestine completes food digestion. Food molecules are absorbed through its wall into the circulatory system, from which they're delivered to body cells.

Now LARGE

The **large intestine** extends from the **ileocecal valve** (the valve between the ileum of the small intestine and the first segment of the large intestine) to the **anus.** The large intestine absorbs water, secretes mucus, and eliminates digestive wastes. It has six segments:

- The **cecum,** a saclike structure, makes up the first few inches of the large intestine, beginning just below the ileocecal valve.
- The **ascending colon** rises on the right posterior abdominal wall, then turns sharply under the liver at the hepatic flexure.
- The **transverse colon,** situated above the small intestine, passes horizontally across the abdomen and below the liver, stomach, and spleen. At the left splenic flexure it turns downward.
- The **descending colon** starts near the spleen and extends down the left side of the abdomen into the pelvic cavity.
- The **sigmoid colon** descends through the pelvic cavity, where it becomes the rectum. (See Sigmoid *has an "S" shape.*)
- The **rectum,** the last few inches of the large intestine, terminates at the **anus.**

Inner lining

The wall of the GI tract consists of several layers. The innermost layer, the **mucosa** (also called the **tunica mucosa**), consists of epithelial and surface cells and loose connective tissue. The **submucosa** (also called the **tunica submucosa**) encircles the mucosa. It's composed of loose connective tissue, blood and lymphatic vessels, and a nerve network.

Memory jogger

No pussy-footing around this tip. To remember the structures of the large intestine, think "**CAT DESIRE**":

Cecum

Ascending colon

Transverse colon

DEscending colon

SIgmoid colon

Rectum.

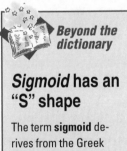

Beyond the dictionary

Sigmoid has an "S" shape

The term **sigmoid** derives from the Greek word ***sigma,*** the name of the eighteenth letter of the Greek alphabet. In Greek, the letter is represented like this: ς, a kind of truncated ***s,*** which pretty closely resembles the shape of the sigmoid colon.

Around the submucosa lies the **tunica muscularis,** which is composed of skeletal muscle in the mouth, pharynx, and upper esophagus and longitudinal and circular smooth muscle fibers elsewhere in the tract.

Outer covering

The **visceral peritoneum** is the GI tract's outer covering. In the esophagus and rectum, it's also called the **tunica adventitia;** elsewhere in the GI tract, it's called the **tunica serosa.**

The visceral peritoneum covers most of the abdominal organs and lays next to an identical layer, the **parietal peritoneum,** that lines the abdominal cavity.

Vital accessories

Accessory organs—the liver, the biliary duct system, and pancreas—contribute hormones, enzymes, and bile, which are vital to digestion. They deliver their secretions to the duodenum through the **hepatopancreatic ampulla,** also called the **ampulla of Vater** (named after Abraham Vater, a German anatomist). (See *The little jug*.)

The entry of bile and pancreatic juice is controlled by a muscular valve called the **hepatopancreatic sphincter,** or **Oddi's sphincter** (named after Ruggero Oddi, an Italian doctor).

Liver and lobule

The **liver's** digestive function is to produce bile for export to the duodenum. The **liver's** functional unit, the **lobule,** consists of a plate of hepatic cells, or **hepatocytes,** that encircle a central vein and radiate outward.

Caps off to sinusoids

Separating the hepatocyte plates from each other are **sinusoids,** the liver's capillary system.

Toxic clean up

Kupffer's cells, which line the sinusoids, remove bacteria and toxins that have entered the blood through the intestinal capillaries. (Kupffer's cells are named after Karl Wilhelm von Kupffer, a German anatomist.)

Beyond the dictionary

The little jug

Who could resist breaking down **hepatopancreatic ampulla?**

Easy ones first

Hepato- comes from the Greek word for the liver, ***hepatikos.*** **Pancreatic** originated from the Latin term ***pancreaticus,*** which means *pertaining to the pancreas.*

Now for the hard part

Ampulla is a Latin term that means *little jug* or, in medical terms, a flasklike dilation of a tubular structure.

All together now

When these terms are put together, they describe a structure in which the ducts that deliver bile and pancreatic juice from the liver **(hepato)** and pancreas **(pancreatic)** unite at a flasklike **(ampulla)** junction called the **hepatopancreatic ampulla.**

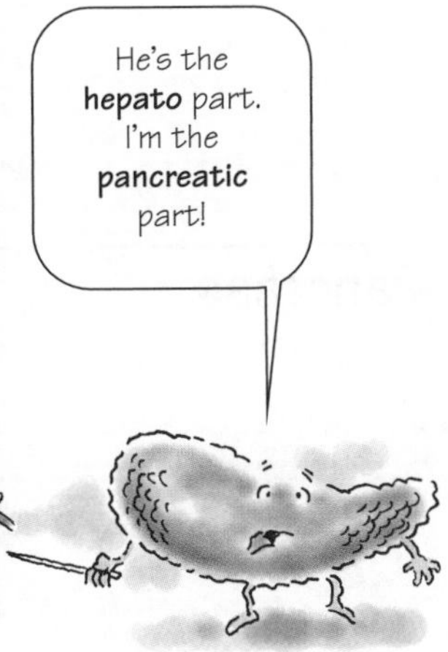
He's the **hepato** part. I'm the **pancreatic** part!

Ducts

Bile, recycled from bile salts in the blood, leaves through biliary ducts that merge into the right and left hepatic ducts to form the **common hepatic duct.** This duct joins the **cystic duct** from the gallbladder to form the **common bile duct,** which leads to the duodenum.

I'm very proud of my three ducts.
Common Hepatic Duct
Cystic Duct
Common Bile Duct

Bully for bile

A yellow-greenish liquid composed of water, cholesterol, bile salts, electrolytes, and phospholipids, **bile** breaks down fats and neutralizes gastric secretions in chyme. Bile prevents jaundice by assisting with excretion of **conjugated bilirubin,** an end product of normal hemoglobin breakdown.

Gallbladder

The **gallbladder** is a pear-shaped organ that's nestled under the liver and joined to the larger organ by the cystic duct. The gallbladder's job is to store and concentrate bile produced by the liver. (See *Why not bilebladder?*)

Of all the gall!

When stimulated by a hormone called **cholecystokinin,** the gallbladder contracts, the hepatopancreatic ampulla relaxes, and bile is released into the common bile duct for delivery to the duodenum. (See *Bile, bladder, and protein.*)

> ***Beyond the dictionary***
>
> **Why not bilebladder?**
>
> We might just as well call the gallbladder a **bilebladder** because the two words, **gall** and **bile,** refer to the same thing. **Gall** appears in Old English as early as the year 825 in a translation of the Psalms. The word **gall** actually refers to the yellowish color of bile. The word **bile,** on the other hand, is a relatively recent borrowing from Latin by way of French; this word doesn't show up in English until the 17th century.

Pancreas

The **pancreas** lies behind the stomach, with its head and neck extending into the curve of the duodenum and its tail lying against the spleen. The pancreas contains two cell types:

- **endocrine cells,** from which hormones are secreted into the blood
- **exocrine cells,** from which enzymes are secreted through ducts to the digestive system.

In the islets of Langerhans

The pancreas's endocrine function involves the **islets of Langerhans,** named for Paul Langerhans (1847-1888), the German doctor who discovered them. These microscopic structures—over 1 million of them—are scattered throughout the pancreas and house two cell types:

- **alpha cells,** which secrete **glucagon,** a hormone that stimulates the breakdown of glycogen to glucose in the liver—a process referred to as **glycogenolysis**
- **beta cells,** which secrete **insulin** to promote carbohydrate metabolism.

Physical examination terms

Before you can perform a complete examination of the GI tract, you need to understand the associated terminology:

- **Aaron's sign**, named for American physician Charles Aaron (1866-1951), refers to pain in the chest or abdominal area that's elicited by applying gentle but steadily increasing pressure over McBurney's point (2″ [5.1 cm] below the right anterior superior spine of the ilium, on a line between that spine and the umbilicus). A positive sign indicates appendicitis.

- **Abdominal distention** refers to increased abdominal girth—the result of increased intra-abdominal pressure forcing the abdominal wall outward.
- **Anorexia** is a loss of appetite.
- **Ascites** refers to the abnormal accumulation of serous fluid in the peritoneal cavity.
- **Auscultation** is an assessment method; it means to listen carefully, usually with a stethoscope.
- **Ballottement,** lightly tapping or bouncing fingertips against the abdominal wall, elicits abdominal muscle resistance or guarding.
- **Bowel sounds** are auscultated with a stethoscope and provide information about **bowel motility** (movement) and the underlying vessels and organs. Normally, air and fluid moving through the bowel create soft, bubbling sounds, which are often mixed with soft clicks and gurgles, that occur every 5 to 15 seconds. Bowel sounds are described using the following terms:
  – **absent bowel sounds,** when no bowel sounds are heard
  – **borborygmi,** the familiar "growling stomach" of a hungry patient
  – **hyperactive,** which describes rapid, high-pitched, loud gurgling sounds
  – **hypoactive,** which occur at a rate no greater than one per minute.
- **Cachexia** is a profound state of overall ill health and malnutrition characterized by weakness and emaciation.
- **Colic** is acute abdominal pain.
- **Constipation** refers to a decreased passage of stools. A constipated stool is characteristically hard and dry.
- **Cullen's sign** refers to irregular, bluish hemorrhagic patches on the skin around the umbilicus and occasionally around abdominal scars. Cullen's sign indicates massive hemorrhage.
- **Diarrhea** is rapid movement of fecal material through the intestines that causes poor absorption of water and nutrients. Diarrhea stools are watery and frequent.
- **Dyspepsia** is gastric discomfort, such as fullness, heartburn, bloating, and nausea, that occurs after eating.
- **Dysphagia** is difficult or painful swallowing.
- **Emesis,** from Greek, is an expulsion of the stomach contents by vomiting.

Beyond the dictionary

Bile, bladder, and protein

Cholecystokinin is easy to dissect:
Chole- is Greek for bile.
Cysto- comes from the Greek word ***kystis,*** meaning *bladder.*
Kinin is a general term for plasma proteins—like this hormone.

Borborygmi is the familiar "growling stomach" of a hungry patient.

- **Epigastrium** refers to the upper and middle regions of the abdomen.
- **Fecal impaction** is an accumulation of hardened feces in the rectum or sigmoid colon that can't be evacuated.
- **Fecal incontinence** refers to an inability to prevent the discharge of feces.
- **Flatulence** refers to a sensation of gaseous abdominal fullness.
- **Grey Turner's sign** is characterized by a bruiselike discoloration of the skin of the flanks that appears 6 to 24 hours after the onset of retroperitoneal hemorrhage in acute pancreatitis.
- **Guarding** is moving away or flinching when a tender area of the abdomen is touched.
- **Heartburn,** also referred to as **pyrosis,** is a burning sensation in the esophagus or below the sternum in the region of the heart.
- **Hematemesis** is vomiting blood.
- **Hematochezia** is fresh, bright red blood passed from the rectum.
- **Hemoperitoneum** refers to a leakage of blood into the peritoneal cavity.
- **Hepatomegaly** is an enlarged liver.
- **Hypogastrium** is the lowest, middle abdominal region.
- **Ileus** is a mechanical intestinal obstruction.
- **Jaundice** is a yellow appearance of the skin, mucous membranes, and sclerae of the eyes, resulting from elevated serum bilirubin levels.
- **Meconium** is the substance that fills the entire intestine before birth. A neonate's first stool is called a **meconium stool.**
- **Melena** is black, tarry stools—a common sign of upper GI bleeding.
- **Murphy's sign** refers to pain on deep inspiration that occurs when an inflamed gallbladder is palpated by pressing the fingers under the rib cage. Hepatitis may also produce a positive Murphy's sign.
- **Nausea** is an unpleasant feeling that typically precedes vomiting.
- **Occult blood** is an amount of blood so small that it can be seen or detected only by a chemical test or microscopic examination.
- **Odynophagia** is painful swallowing.
- **Pica** refers to the craving and ingestion of normally inedible substances, such as plaster, charcoal, clay, wool, ashes, paint, and dirt.

Occult blood refers to minute amounts of blood that can be seen or detected only by a chemical test or microscopic examination.

- **Polyphagia** is consuming abnormally large amounts of food.
- **Polydipsia** is chronic, excessive thirst.
- **Rebound tenderness,** also referred to as **Blumberg's sign,** is pain that occurs when a hand pressing on the abdomen is suddenly released.
- **Rectal tenesmus** is a spasmodic contraction of the anal sphincter with a persistent urge to defecate and involuntary, ineffective straining. This occurs in inflammatory bowel disorders, such as ulcerative colitis and Crohn's disease, and in rectal tumors.
- **Regurgitation** is the backflowing or return of food and fluids into the mouth without nausea or belching.
- **Rigidity** describes a stiff abdominal wall, sometimes called a *boardlike abdomen.*
- **Rovsing's sign,** named after the Copenhagen surgeon Niels Rovsing (1862-1927), who first described this symptom, occurs in acute appendicitis. Pressure on the left lower quadrant of the abdomen will cause pain in the right lower quadrant.
- **Steatorrhea** is excessive fat in the feces that floats and is frothy and foul-smelling.
- **Tympany** is a clear, hollow, drumlike sound heard when palpating the abdomen.
- **Vomiting** is forcibly expelling the contents of the stomach through the mouth. Vomiting can be described as:
  - **cyclic** (recurring attacks of vomiting)
  - **dry** (attempt to vomit without emesis)
  - **projectile** (ejected with great force).

Diagnostic tests

This section covers diagnostic tests used to identify GI disorders.

Blood tests

Serum studies of enzymes, proteins, and formed elements are used to investigate disorders involving the liver, pancreas, gallbladder, and intestinal tract. You'll see the following tests ordered most often:

- The **alkaline phosphatase test** measures the enzyme activity of several alkaline phosphatase isoenzymes found in the liver, bone, kidneys, intestines, and biliary system.

- The *Helicobacter pylori* **antibodies test** checks for the presence of *H. pylori*, which are associated with chronic gastritis and idiopathic chronic duodenal ulceration.
- The **serum amylase test** measures the level of the pancreatic enzyme alpha-amylase, which is active in the digestion of starch and glycogen. Amylase is released with pancreatic damage.
- The **serum bilirubin test** measures serum levels of bilirubin, the main pigment in bile and the major product of hemoglobin breakdown.
- The **serum lipase test** measures the amount of lipase in the blood; large amounts indicate pancreatic damage.
- The **total cholesterol test** measures the circulating levels of free cholesterol and cholesterol esters.

The different serum tests examine the levels of substances in the blood. For example, a serum bilirubin test measures bilirubin level.

Radiologic and imaging tests

Tests that use X-rays, electromagnetic waves, and sound waves to create images of internal structures of the GI system and its function include:

- **Abdominal X-ray,** also called a **flat plate** (or **flat and erect plates**) **of the abdomen,** helps visualize the position, size, and structure of abdominal contents.
- **Barium enema** is the radiographic examination of the large intestine after rectal instillation of barium, a radiopaque contrast medium.
- **Barium swallow** is the radiographic examination of the throat and esophagus after ingestion of a radiopaque contrast medium.
- **Cholangiogram** is an X-ray of the gallbladder and biliary duct system that's obtained by injecting a radiopaque contrast medium.
- **Computerized tomography (CT) scan** translates the action of multiple X-ray beams into three-dimensional images.
- **Contrast radiography** is a general term that describes several procedures that use a radiopaque contrast medium to accentuate differences among densities of fat, air, soft tissue, and bone.
- **Endoscopic retrograde cholangiopancreatography (ERCP)** is a radiographic examination of the pancreatic

ducts and hepatobiliary tree after injection of a contrast medium into the **duodenal papilla** (small nipplelike elevation). This test is done by use of an **endoscope** guided by the use of fluoroscopy. (See *I'd rather say* ERCP.)

- **Esophagogastroduodenoscopy (EGD)** allows visual examination of the esophagus, stomach, and duodenum using a fiberoptic endoscope.
- **Liver-spleen scan** uses a gamma-ray camera to record the distribution of radioactivity within the liver and spleen after injection of a radioactive colloid.
- **Magnetic resonance cholangiopancreatography** is used in much the same way as ERCP but isn't as invasive. It creates images using electromagnetic waves and helps to visualize the biliary structures, bile ducts, pancreatic ducts, and gallbladder.
- **Magnetic resonance imaging (MRI)** creates images by computer analysis of electromagnetic waves directed into the tissues.
- In **percutaneous transhepatic cholangiography** a radiopaque contrast medium is introduced through a catheter inserted through the skin into the liver to allow examination of the biliary system.
- **Ultrasonography** creates images of deep structures of the body by computer analysis of ultrasonic (high-frequency sound) waves directed into and reflected from tissues.
- **Upper GI and small bowel series** involves the fluoroscopic examination of the esophagus, stomach, and small intestine after the patient ingests a contrast medium.

Beyond the dictionary

I'd rather say *ERCP*

Endoscopic retrograde cholangiopancreatography (ERCP) is a real mouthful, but this word is easy to dissect: **Endoscopic** refers to the optical instrument used in the procedure. **Retrograde** means *moving against the usual flow* and refers to dye injected the wrong way in the ampulla of Vater. **Cholangio-** refers to the biliary tract, **pancrea-** means *pancreas*, and **-graphy** is a recording. Therefore, ERCP is a recording of the function of the biliary tract and pancreas.

Other tests

Other tests used to diagnose abnormalities of the GI system include:

- **Basal gastric secretion test** measures basal acid secretion during fasting by aspirating stomach contents through a nasogastric (NG) tube.
- **Breath hydrogen analysis** is a simple method of detecting lactose intolerance.
- **Colonoscopy** is an endoscopic examination of the colon.
- **Endoscopy** is a visual inspection of a body cavity using an optical instrument called an endoscope.
- **Esophageal acidity test** evaluates the competence of the lower esophageal sphincter—the major barrier to re-

Here's a little tune I like to call "Getting to know me."

flux—by measuring the pH within the esophagus with an electrode that is attached to a special catheter.

- **Fecal lipids test** is used to detect excessive excretion of lipids in patients with signs of malabsorption.
- **Gastric acid stimulation test** measures the secretion of gastric acid for 1 hour after subcutaneous injection of a drug that stimulates gastric acid output.
- **Gastric emptying study** is used to diagnose impaired gastric motility.
- **Laparoscopy** is an endoscopic examination of the interior of the peritoneal cavity.
- **Manometry** is the use of water-filled catheters connected to pressure transducers in different parts of the GI system to evaluate contractility.
- **Percutaneous liver biopsy** involves aspiration of a core of liver tissue for analysis.
- **Peritoneal fluid analysis** examines a specimen of peritoneal fluid obtained by paracentesis for appearance, red blood cell and white blood cell counts, cytologic studies, microbiologic studies for bacteria and fungi, and determinations of protein, glucose, amylase, ammonia, and alkaline phosphatase levels.
- **Sigmoidoscopy** is an endoscopic examination of the sigmoid colon.
- **Stool culture** is a bacteriologic examination of feces.
- **Urine bilirubin test** detects abnormally high urine concentrations of direct bilirubin, possibly indicating liver disease.
- **Urine urobilinogen test** detects impaired liver function by measuring urine levels of urobilinogen, which results from the reduction of bilirubin by intestinal bacteria.

Sigmoidoscopy is an endoscopic examination of the sigmoid colon.

Disorders

Here are descriptions of disorders of the organs of the GI system.

Mouth and esophagus

The following are important terms used to describe disorders of the upper alimentary canal:

- **Achalasia** is an esophageal motility disorder resulting from neural dysfunction and lower esophageal sphincter dysfunction.

• **Cleft lip** and **cleft palate** are developmental anomalies present at birth. These congenital disabilities typically require surgical repair.
• **Esophageal atresia** refers to a closed esophagus.
• **Esophageal diverticula** are hollowed outpouchings in the esophageal wall.
• **Esophageal stricture** is a narrowing of the esophagus.
• **Esophageal varices** are enlarged, torturous veins in the lower esophagus that are caused by portal hypertension.
• **Erythroplakia** is a red, velvelty mucosal lesion on the surface of the oral mucosa.
• **Esophagitis** is the inflammation of the mucous membrane that lines the esophagus.
• **Gastroesophageal reflux** refers to the backflow of gastric or duodenal contents into the esophagus. Severe reflux disease is called **gastroesophageal reflux disease (GERD).**
• **Gingivitis** is an inflammation of the gums.
• **Glossitis** is an inflammation of the tongue.
• **Hiatal hernia** is the protrusion of the stomach through a structural defect in the diaphragm at the esophageal opening.
• **Kaposi's sarcoma** is a cancer associated with acquired immunodeficiency syndrome. Lesions occur in the skin, lymph nodes, and viscera.
• **Leukoplakia** are firmly attached white patches on the oral mucosa.
• **Mallory-Weiss syndrome** refers to lacerations in the mucous membrane at the esophagogastric junction that result in massive bleeding. The syndrome is typically preceded by vomiting.
• **Periodontitis** refers to progression of gingivitis involving an inflammation of the oral mucosa.
• **Pyloric stenosis** is an obstruction of the pyloric sphincter caused by hypertrophy of the sphincter muscle. It's most commonly seen in boys between ages 1 and 6 months.
• **Stomatitis** is an inflammation of the mouth.
• **Tracheoesophageal fistula** is an abnormal connection between the trachea and the esophagus.
• **Vincent's stomatitis,** also known as **trench mouth,** is a severe form of gingivitis that causes necrosis and ulceration of the gums.

Esophageal atresia means the esophagus is closed.
NO ENTRY

Stomach and intestines

Here are terms that relate to diseases and abnormalities of the stomach and intestines:

• **Ascites** is the accumulation of fluid in the peritoneal cavity.

• **Celiac disease** is a chronic disease in which an individual can't tolerate foods containing gluten (usually found in wheat, rye, barley, and oats).

• **Crohn's disease** is a chronic inflammatory bowel disease that usually involves the proximal portion of the colon and, less commonly, the terminal ileum. It's named after the American surgeon Burrill Crohn (1884-1983), who first described it in 1932.

• **Curling ulcer** is a stress ulcer of the duodenum that results from burn injuries.

• **Cushing ulcer** is a stress ulcer of the duodenum associated with severe head trauma or brain surgery.

• **Diverticular disease** refers to bulging pouches **(diverticula)** in the GI wall—typically in the sigmoid colon—that push the mucosal lining through the surrounding muscle. (See *A diversion on diverticulum.*) Diverticular disease has two clinical forms:

– **Diverticulitis** is the inflammation of one or more diverticula.

– **Diverticulosis** is the presence of diverticula without accompanying inflammation.

• **Gastritis** refers to inflammation of the stomach and stomach lining.

• **Gastroenteritis** is inflammation of the lining of the stomach and intestines that accompanies numerous GI disorders.

• **Hirschsprung's disease,** also called **congenital megacolon,** is a congenital disorder of the large intestine characterized by the absence or marked reduction of nerve cells in the colorectal wall, which results in impaired intestinal motility and constipation.

• **Inactive colon** is a state of chronic constipation that, if left untreated, may lead to fecal impaction.

• **Inguinal hernia** is protrusion of the large or small intestine, omentum, or bladder into the inguinal canal resulting from weakened abdominal muscles, traumatic injury, or aging. The hernia is:

– **reducible** if it can be moved back into place easily

– **incarcerated** if it can't be reduced

Curling ulcer gets its name from an English surgeon, Thomas Curling, who lived from 1811 to 1888 and was the first person to describe this condition.

– **strangulated** if a portion of the herniated intestine becomes twisted or swollen so that blood flow is impaired.

- **Intestinal obstruction** occurs when the **lumen** (opening) of the bowel is partly or fully blocked. Obstruction is classified as mechanical or nonmechanical:
  – **Mechanical obstruction** results from foreign bodies or compression of the bowel wall.
  – **Nonmechanical obstruction** results from physiologic disturbances, such as paralytic ileus, electrolyte imbalance, and blood clots that cause ischemia of the mesenteric vessels.
- **Intussusception** refers to a telescoping of a portion of bowel into an adjacent distal portion.
- **Irritable bowel syndrome** is a condition characterized by diarrhea, resulting from increased bowel motility, alternating with constipation.
- **Lactose intolerance** is the inability to digest milk sugar.
- **Necrotizing enterocolitis** is an inflammatory disease characterized by diffuse or patchy intestinal necrosis and is accompanied by infection in about one-third of cases. It mostly affects premature infants.
- **Paralytic ileus** is a physiologic form of intestinal obstruction that usually develops in the small bowel after abdominal surgery.
- **Peptic ulcer** is a disruption in the gastric or duodenal lining that occurs when normal defense mechanisms are overwhelmed or impaired by acid or pepsin. An acute form of peptic ulcer is called a **stress ulcer.**
- **Peritonitis** is an acute or chronic inflammation of the **peritoneum** (the membrane that lines the abdominal cavity and covers visceral organs).
- **Pseudomembranous enterocolitis** is an acute inflammation and **necrosis** (tissue death) of the small and large intestines, usually affecting only the mucosa.
- **Ulcerative colitis** is a chronic, inflammatory disease that affects the mucosa of the colon and produces edema and ulcerations. It typically begins in the rectum and sigmoid colon and may extend upward into the entire colon. It rarely affects the small intestine.
- **Volvulus** is a twisting of intestine at least 180 degrees on its mesentery, resulting in blood vessel compression and ischemia.

Beyond the dictionary

A diversion on diverticulum

A **diverticulum** is, in fact, a *diversion.* The small pouches divert contents of the GI tract; this action gives the structures their name.

Got milk? Not if you're lactose intolerant, you don't.
Fat-free

Anus and rectum

Disorders of the anus and rectum include:

- **Anal fissure** is a laceration or crack in the lining of the anus.
- **Anorectal abscess** is a localized collection of pus due to inflammation of the soft tissue near the rectum or anus.
- **Anorectal fistula** is an abnormal opening in the anal skin that may communicate with the rectum. Inflammation caused by an anorectal abscess may cause the fistula to form.
- **Anorectal stenosis** is narrowing of the anorectal sphincter.
- **Anorectal stricture** occurs when the anorectal lumen size decreases.
- **Hemorrhoids** are varicosities in the veins of the rectum or anus that result in swelling and pain.
- **Pilonidal cyst** is a hair-containing dermoid cyst that forms in the midline gluteal fold.
- **Proctitis** is an acute or chronic inflammation of the rectal mucosa.
- **Pruritus ani** is perianal itching, irritation, or superficial burning.
- **Rectal polyps** are masses of tissue that rise above the mucosal membrane and protrude into the GI tract.
- **Rectal prolapse** is the circumferential protrusion of one or more layers of the mucous membrane through the anus.

Proctitis is an acute or chronic inflammation of the rectal mucosa.

Accessory organs

Disorders of the appendix, liver, gallbladder, and pancreas include:

- **Appendicitis** is an inflammation of the vermiform appendix due to an obstruction.
- **Cholecystitis** is acute or chronic inflammation of the gallbladder, typically caused by gallstones.
- **Cholelithiasis** is the presence of gallstones in the gallbladder. (See *Lithos = stone.*)
- **Choledocholithiasis** occurs when gallstones pass from the gallbladder and lodge in the common bile duct, causing complete or partial obstruction.

• **Cirrhosis** refers to a chronic, degenerative liver disease in which the lobes are covered with fibrous tissue, the liver parenchyma degenerates, and the lobules are infiltrated with fat.
• **Fatty liver,** also known as **steatosis,** is the accumulation of triglycerides and other fats in liver cells.
• **Hepatic coma** is a neurologic syndrome that develops as a complication of hepatic encephalopathy.
• **Hepatic encephalopathy** is a degenerative brain condition caused by advanced liver disease.
• **Hepatitis** occurs in two forms, nonviral and viral:
– **Nonviral hepatitis** is usually caused by exposure to toxins or drugs.
– **Viral hepatitis** is an acute inflammation of the liver marked by liver-cell destruction, necrosis, and **autolysis** (destruction of tissue by enzymes).

Assessment findings are similar for the different types of hepatitis. The six forms of viral hepatitis are:
– **type A,** which is spread by direct contact through the oral-fecal route
– **type B,** which is transmitted by contaminated serum through blood transfusion, needles, I.V. drug use, and direct contact with body fluids
– **type C,** which is spread through needle sticks, blood transfusion, and I.V. drug use
– **type D,** which is found only in patients with acute or chronic episodes of hepatitis B and requires the presence of hepatitis B surface antigen (hepatitis D is rare, except among I.V. drug users)
– **type E,** which is transmitted by the oral-fecal and water-borne routes, much like type A (because this virus is inconsistently shed in the feces, detection is difficult)
– **type G,** which is transmitted by parenteral and sexual means, has been discovered most recently.
• **Hepatocellular carcinoma (hepatocarcinoma)** is cancer of the liver.
• **Pancreatitis** is an acute or chronic inflammation of the pancreas.
• **Portal hypertension** is increased pressure in the portal vein as a result of obstruction of blood flow through the liver.
• **Wilson's disease** is a rare inherited metabolic disorder characterized by excessive copper retention in the liver, brain, kidneys, and corneas. These deposits of copper eventually lead to hepatic failure.

Beyond the dictionary

Lithos = stone

Cholecystitis is a combination of Greek terms: ***chole*** means *bile*; ***cyst*** means *bladder,* and ***-itis*** means *inflammation.* So it makes sense that cholecystitis is *inflammation of the gallbladder.*

Now take it one step further. ***Lithos*** is the Greek term for *stone,* so it makes sense that **cholelithiasis** is the term for *gallstones.*

Many words associated with me begin with **hepa-,** from the Greek word for *liver.*

Treatments

Here are terms identifying surgical procedures and other treatments to correct GI disorders.

GI tubes

Here are terms related to GI tubes used to treat patients with GI disorders:

- **Gastric lavage** is irrigation or washing of the stomach with sterile water or saline solution using an NG tube.
- **Gavage** is feeding a patient through a stomach tube.
- **Intestinal decompression** removes fluids and gas from the intestine by the insertion of one of several types of tubes:
  – The **Miller-Abbott tube** is a double-lumen tube in which one lumen contains a weighted balloon to ease passage and the other lumen facilitates drainage.
  – The **Harris tube,** used for gastric and intestinal decompression, is a mercury-weighted single-lumen tube that's inserted through the nose and carried through the digestive tract by gravity.
  – The **Cantor tube,** used to relieve obstruction in the small intestine, is a double-lumen nasoenteric tube. One lumen is used to inflate the distal balloon with air; the other, to instill mercury to weight the tube. The tube also allows for aspiration of intestinal contents.
- **Nasogastric intubation** is insertion of a tube into the stomach through the nose.
- **Sengstaken-Blakemore intubation** is insertion of a triple-lumen catheter used to stop hemorrhaging from esophageal varices. Two lumens end in balloons; one is inflated in the stomach to hold the catheter in place and compress the vessels around the cardia, and the other is inflated in the esophagus to exert pressure against varices in the wall of the esophagus. The third lumen is used to **aspirate** (withdraw) stomach contents.

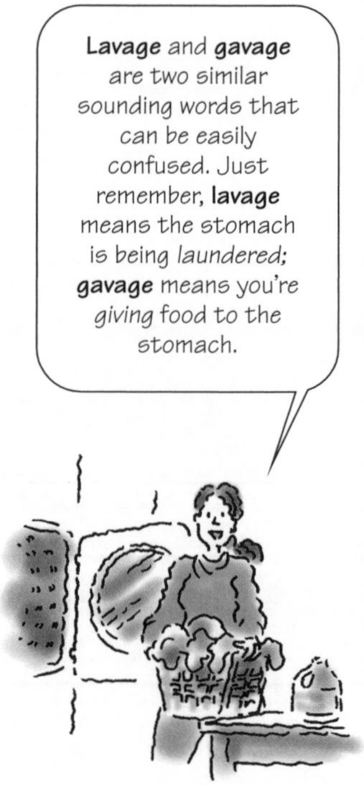
Lavage and **gavage** are two similar sounding words that can be easily confused. Just remember, **lavage** means the stomach is being *laundered;* **gavage** means you're *giving* food to the stomach.

Pharyngeal and esophageal surgeries

Surgical procedures performed on the esophagus include:

- **cricopharyngeal myotomy**—a partial or total incision of the cricopharyngeal muscle that relieves diverticula or severe cricopharyngeal muscle spasm

- **esophagectomy**—removal of part of the esophagus.
- **esophagogastrectomy**—removal of all or part of the stomach and esophagus
- **esophagogastrostomy**—removal of a portion of the esophagus then connecting the remaining healthy portion to the stomach
- **esophagojejunostomy**—attachment of the jejunum to the esophagus to provide a bypass for food for patients with esophageal stricture.

Remember, the suffix ***-ectomy*** means *removal of*, and the suffix ***-ostomy*** means *creation of an opening.*

Gastric and abdominal surgeries

Surgical procedures on the stomach are explained below:

- **Antrectomy** is the removal of the **antrum,** the lower part of the stomach, which produces gastric acid.
- **Billroth I** is a partial removal of the distal portion of the stomach; the remaining stomach is connected to the duodenum.
- **Billroth II** is a surgical excision of a portion of the stomach with connection of the remaining portion to the jejunum.
- **Gastric bypass surgery (Roux-en-y)** is a weight-loss (bariatric) procedure in which a small pouch is created at the top of the stomach and a bypass is created to a portion of the small intestine.
- **Gastrostomy** is the creation of a hole into the stomach through the abdominal wall to insert an feeding tube.
- **Laparotomy** is a surgical opening of the abdomen. (See *Gastric lingo.*)
- **Pyloroplasty** is surgical enlargement of the pylorus to improve drainage of gastric contents into the small bowel.
- **Total gastrectomy** is removal of the entire stomach.

The Austrian surgeon Christian Albert Theodore Billroth gave his name to two surgeries. Both involve removing a portion of the stomach. I'll keep all my portions, thank you.

Bowel surgery

Listed below are important surgical terms concerning the small intestine, large intestine, and colon:

- **Abdominal perineal resection** is a procedure in which a colostomy is created and the distal sigmoid colon, rectum, and anus are removed.
- **Anastomosis** is a surgical procedure in which two blood vessels, ducts, or other tubelike structures are joined to allow the flow of substances between them.

- **Colectomy** is excision of a portion of the colon.
- **Hemicolectomy** is the removal of one-half or less of the colon.
- **Hemorrhoidectomy** is the surgical excision of a hemorrhoid.
- **Ileostomy** is the creation of an opening between the ileum and the abdominal wall through which fecal matter is expelled.
- An **ostomy** is an artificial opening or stoma created in the GI or urinary canal or in the trachea.

Colostomy

A **colostomy,** bowel surgery that creates an opening between the colon and the abdominal wall through which feces are expelled, may be created in different portions of the intestine and structured several ways.

Different locations

Named according to their location in the colon, colostomies can be:

- **ascending**—located on the ascending portion of the colon
- **transverse**—located on the transverse portion of the colon
- **descending**—located on the descending portion of the colon
- **sigmoid**—located on the sigmoid colon.

Different structures

These are the main types of colostomy construction:

- A **double-barrel colostomy** creates two separate stomas—usually temporarily—on the abdominal wall. The proximal stoma is the functioning end and is continuous with the upper GI tract. The distal stoma, also referred to as a **mucous fistula,** opens into the nonfunctioning section of the colon that's continuous with the rectum.
- An **end colostomy** creates a single stoma on the abdomen created from the end of the colon, which is brought out through an opening in the abdominal wall.
- A **loop colostomy** involves bringing a loop of bowel through an incision in the abdominal wall.

The real world

Gastric lingo

Let's run another lap
In practice, people commonly refer to an **exploratory laparotomy** as an *exploratory lap* or *ex-lap.* So you might hear someone say, "We need to take this patient for an exploratory lap."

NG tube
Rarely will you hear someone refer to a **nasogastric tube** by its full name. In practice, it's simply referred to as an *NG tube.*

Liver surgery

Important terms concerning liver surgery are listed below:

- **Hepatic lobectomy** is removal of a lobe of the liver.
- **Liver resection** is removal of a portion of the diseased or damaged liver tissue.
- **Liver transplant** is reserved for patients with a life-threatening liver disorder that doesn't respond to other treatment.
- **Partial hepatectomy** is excision of a portion of the liver.
- **Transjugular intrahepatic portosystemic shunt** is a procedure in which the radiologist cannulates (creates a tunnel) in the right internal jugular vein and then inserts a metallic, flexible stent into a new pathway created by balloon dilation of the tissue between the hepatic and portal veins in the liver. This artificial shunt creates a new pathway for blood flow and reduces portal hypertension.

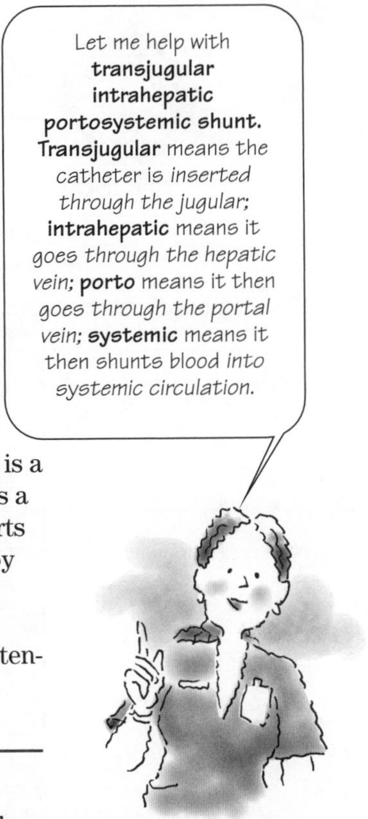
Let me help with **transjugular intrahepatic portosystemic shunt.** **Transjugular** means the catheter is inserted through the jugular; **intrahepatic** means it goes through the hepatic vein; **porto** means it then goes through the portal vein; **systemic** means it then shunts blood into systemic circulation.

Gallbladder and appendix surgery

Surgical procedures performed on the gallbladder and appendix are explained below:

- **Appendectomy** is the removal of the vermiform appendix.
- **Cholecystectomy** is removal of the gallbladder. (See *Open chole.*)
- **Cholecystoduodenostomy** is anastomosis of the gallbladder and duodenum.
- **Choledochojejunostomy** is anastomosis of the common bile duct to the jejunum of the small intestine.

The real world

Open chole

You may hear a conventional **cholecystectomy** be referred to as an *open chole,* pronounced KOH-LEE. This means an open abdominal incision was required to remove the gallbladder, as opposed to **laparoscopic surgery,** which doesn't require an abdominal incision.

systole

Vocabulary builders

At a crossroads

Completing this crossword puzzle will help you digest GI system terms. Good luck!

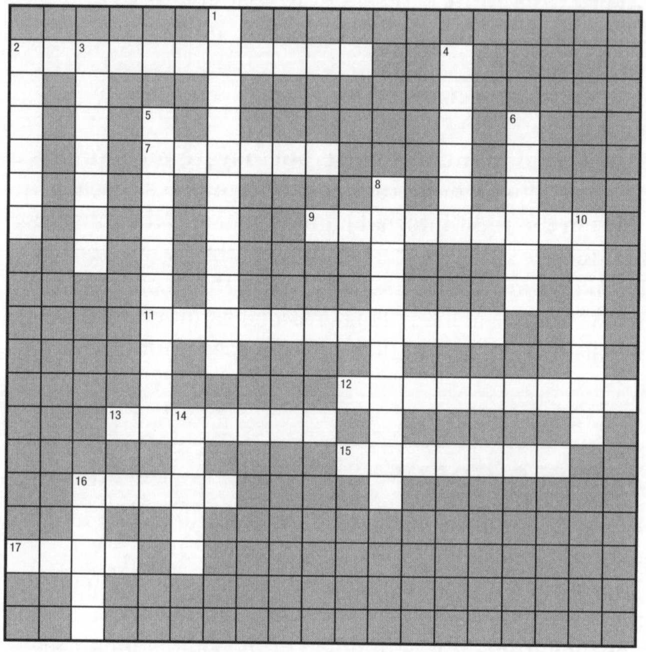

Eating helps me think.

Across

2. Rhythmic contraction and relaxation of smooth muscle in the alimentary canal
7. Liver's functional unit
9. Inflammation of the tongue
11. Another name for **Vincent's stomatitis** (two words)
12. Difficult or painful swallowing
13. Clear, hollow, drumlike sound heard on abdominal palpation
15. Greek word that means *little jug*
16. Saclike structure that makes up the first few inches of the large intestine
17. Yellow-green liquid that breaks down fats and neutralizes gastric secretions

Down

1. Pear-shaped organ nestled under the liver
2. Roof of the mouth
3. Eponym for diagnostic sign of appendicitis
4. Enlarged portion of the stomach above and to the left of the esophageal opening
5. Canal also called the **GI tract**
6. Root from Greek that means *stomach*
8. Growling sound in the stomach that indicates hunger
10. Part of the colon named after a Greek letter
14. Also called the **buccal cavity**
16. Acute abdominal pain

Answers are on page 196.

Match game

Eponyms can be confusing. There are lots of eponyms for GI structures, disorders, and tests. See if you can match each person to their discovery.

Clues	Choices
1. ________ sphincter	A. Karl Wilhelm von Kupffer, German anatomist
2. Ampulla of _______	B. Paul Langerhans, German doctor
3. _______ cells	C. Ruggero Oddi, Italian doctor
4. Islets of _______	D. Charles Aaron, American physician
5. _______'s disease	E. Abraham Vater, German anatomist
6. ________'s sign	F. Burnil Crohn, American surgeon

O see, can you say?

Sound out each group of pictures and symbols below to reveal a term that was reviewed in the chapter.

1.

2+
HI NICK
+uh
NEW... IMPROVED
+
+ i-shuh

2.

+
+dihb-u-luhr

3.

koh-lan-g-
-
GI

Answers are on page 196.

Answers

At a crossroads

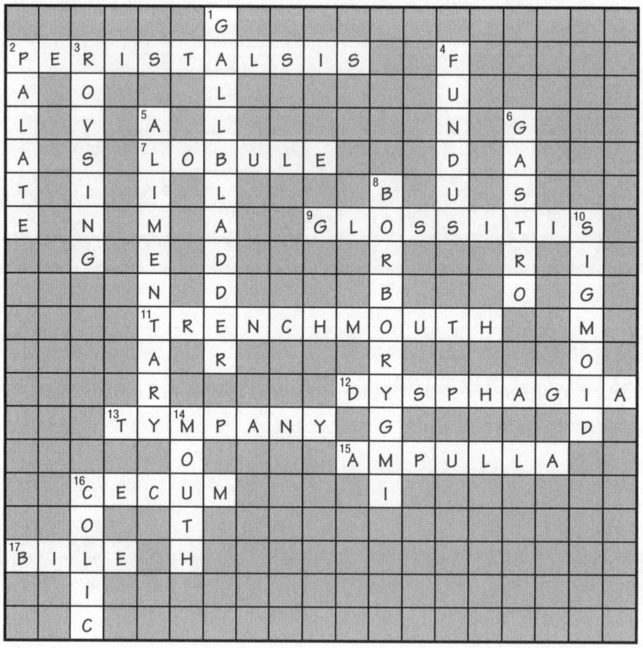

1 GALLBLADDER
2 PERISTALSIS
2 PALATE
3 ROVSING
4 FUNDUS
5 ALIMENTARY
6 GASTRO
7 LOBULE
8 BORBORYGMI
9 GLOSSITIS
10 SIGMOID
11 TRENCHMOUTH
12 DYSPHAGIA
13 TYMPANY
14 MOUTH
15 AMPULLA
16 CECUM
16 COLIC
17 BILE

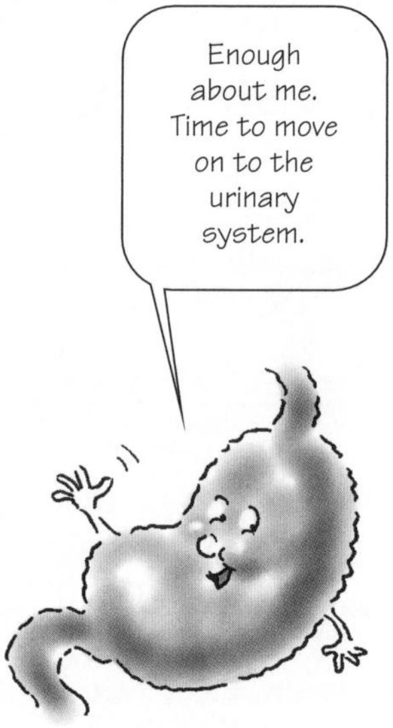

Enough about me. Time to move on to the urinary system.

Match game

1. C; 2. E; 3. A; 4. B; 5. F; 6, D

O see, can you say?

1. Tunica adventitia; 2. Submandibular; 3. Cholangiogram

9

Urinary system

Just the facts

In this chapter, you'll learn:

- terminology related to the structure and function of the urinary system
- terminology needed for physical examination of the urinary system
- tests that help diagnose urinary system disorders
- common urinary system disorders and their treatments.

Urinary structure and function

The **urinary tract** is the body's water treatment plant. It filters the blood and collects and expels the resulting liquid waste products as urine. To help you understand many of the terms relating to this waste control system, three key root words deserve special attention.

In the key of pee

The first key root is the syllable ***ur-*** or its other forms, ***urin-*** or ***uro-***. This term derives from the Greek verb ***ourein,*** which means *to urinate.* Appropriately, the study of the urinary system is called **urology.**

Two keys to the kidneys

The second and third key terms refer to the kidneys. The second is the adjective **renal.** This word derives from ***ren,*** the Latin word for *kidney.* The kidneys are the filter of our bodies' water treatment plant and perform a number of other vital functions, including:

- regulating acid-base balance

Pump up your pronunciation

Pronouncing key urinary system terms

Below is a list of key terms related to the urinary system, along with the correct ways to pronounce them.

Azotemia	AZ-OH-TEE-MEE-UH
Creatinine	KREE-AT-IH-NIN
Cystourethroscopy	SIS-TOH-YOU-REE-THROHS-KUH-PEE
Glomerulonephritis	GLAW-MER-YUH-LOH-NEF-REYE-TIS
Nephrotic syndrome	NEH-FROT-IK SIN-DROHM
Prostatitis	PROS-TUH-TEYE-TIS
Pyuria	PYE-YOU-REE-UH

- regulating electrolyte balance
- regulating blood pressure
- aiding in red blood cell (RBC) formation.

The word **renal** can show up in various medical contexts.

A medical subspecialization within urology focuses on just the renal system. The name of this specialization, **nephrology,** employs the Greek word for *kidney,* ***nephros,*** instead of the Latin ***ren. Nephro-,*** or ***nephr-,*** our third key term, is identical in meaning with ***ren,*** and you'll find many words containing these two roots side by side. (See *Pronouncing key urinary system terms.*)

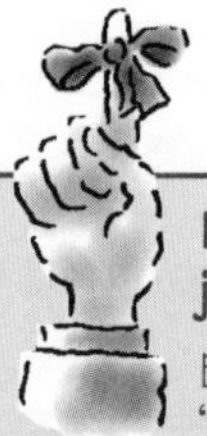

Memory jogger

By thinking **"BARE,"** you'll remember that the kidneys affect four main functions of the body:

Blood pressure

Acid-base balance

Red blood cell formation

Electrolyte balance.

Kidneys

The **kidneys** are bean-shaped, highly vascular organs located at the small of the back on either side of the vertebral column between the 12th thoracic and 3rd lumbar vertebrae. The right kidney, crowded by the liver, is positioned slightly lower than the left. Although each kidney is only about 4″ (10 cm) long, these organs are complicated structures with many functioning units. They receive about 20% of the blood pumped by the heart each minute.

Adrenal gland influence

Atop each kidney lies an **adrenal gland.** These glands affect the renal system by influencing blood pressure and sodium and water retention by the kidneys.

Checking in and checking out

The kidneys receive waste-filled blood from the **renal artery,** a large branch of the abdominal **aorta.** After passing through a complicated network of smaller blood vessels and filtering structures within the kidneys, the filtered blood returns to the circulation by way of the **renal vein,** which empties into the **inferior vena cava,** the major ascending vein of the lower body. (See *Major structures of the kidney,* page 200.)

My three regions

- *The renal cortex* (outer region) contains about 1.25 million renal tubules.
- *The renal medulla* (middle region) functions as my collecting chamber.
- *The renal pelvis* (inner region) receives urine through the major calyces.

A tri-umph of organ-ization

Each kidney has three regions. The **renal cortex,** or outer region, contains blood-filtering mechanisms. The **renal medulla,** or middle region, contains 8 to 12 **renal pyramids,** which are striated wedges composed of tubular structures.

The tapered portion of each pyramid, called the **apex,** empties into a cuplike **calyx** (plural: **calyces**). The calyces channel urine from the renal pyramids into the **renal pelvis,** which is an expansion of the upper end of the ureters.

Getting to know the nephron

The **nephron** is the functional and structural unit of the kidney; each kidney contains about 1.25 million nephrons. The nephron has two main activities:

- selective resorption and secretion of ions
- mechanical filtration of fluids, wastes, electrolytes, and acids and bases.

Glom on the glomerulus

Three processes—**glomerular filtration, tubular reabsorption,** and **tubular secretion**—take place in the nephrons, ultimately leading to urine formation.
Each nephron consists of a long tubular system with a closed, bulbous end called the **glomerular capsule,** or **Bowman's capsule.** Within the capsule are a cluster of capillaries called the **glomerulus** (plural: **glomeruli**). The glomerulus acts as a filter and passes protein-free

Anatomically speaking

Major structures of the kidney

The illustration below shows the structures of the kidney, which plays a major role in the elimination of wastes and excess ions (in urine); blood filtration; acid-base, electrolyte, and blood pressure regulation; and blood cell formation.

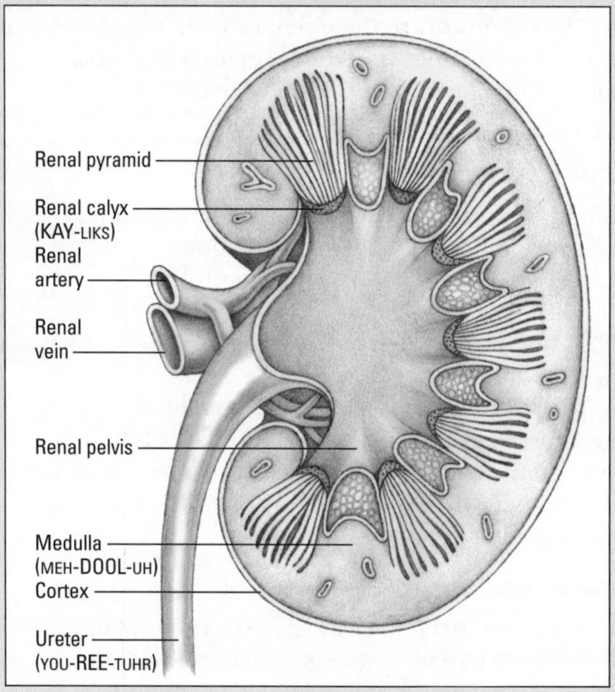
Renal pyramid
Renal calyx (KAY-LIKS)
Renal artery
Renal vein
Renal pelvis
Medulla (MEH-DOOL-UH)
Cortex
Ureter (YOU-REE-TUHR)

and RBC-free filtrate into the tubular system of the nephron. (See *A look at a nephron.*)

A tireless inner tube

This tubular system has three parts through which the filtrate passes in succession:

• The **proximal convoluted tubules,** along with glomeruli, are located in the cortex of the kidney. This part of the nephron has freely permeable cell membranes that allow glucose, amino acids, metabolites, and elec-

Anatomically speaking

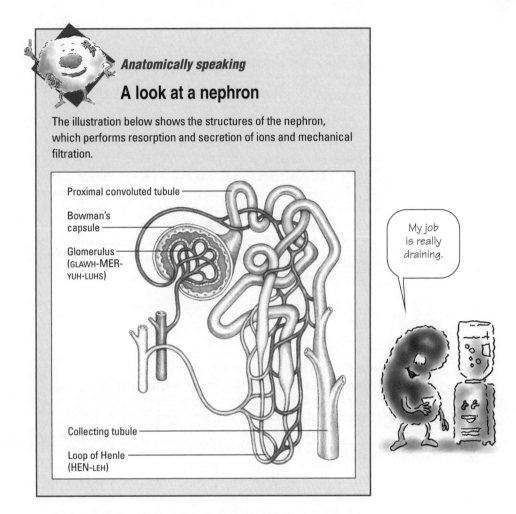

A look at a nephron

The illustration below shows the structures of the nephron, which performs resorption and secretion of ions and mechanical filtration.

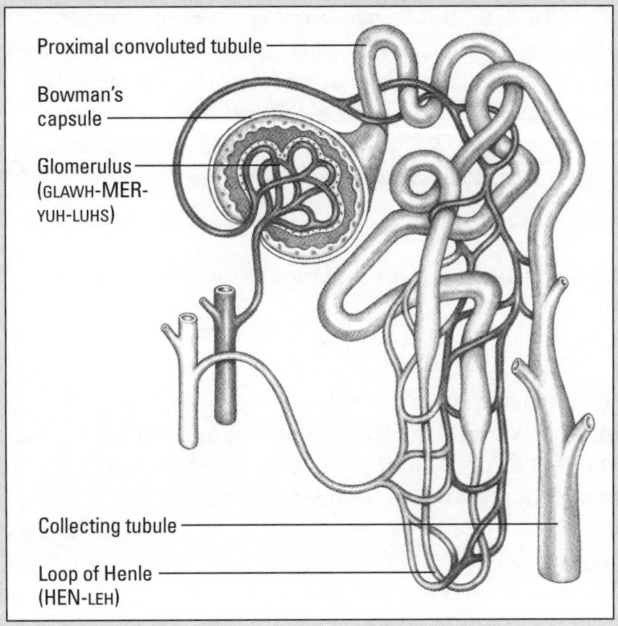
Proximal convoluted tubule
Bowman's capsule
Glomerulus (GLAWH-MER-YUH-LUHS)
Collecting tubule
Loop of Henle (HEN-LEH)

My job is really draining.

trolytes from the filtrate to pass into nearby capillaries and back into the circulatory system.

- The **loop of Henle,** which forms the renal pyramid in the medulla, is a U-shaped continuation of the renal tubule. In the descending loop more water is removed from the filtrate; in the ascending part, sodium and chloride are removed to maintain osmolality.
- The **distal convoluted tubule,** like the proximal tubule, is located in the cortex. In the distal tubule, more sodium and water are removed as potassium and hydrogen ions and ammonia are introduced.

The distal end joins the distal end of other nephrons. Their concentrated filtrate, now urine, flows into larger collecting tubules. These tubules arch back into the

Beyond the dictionary

Two *-in* words

The words **renin** and **angiotensin** both end with the suffix ***-in,*** which derives from Latin and means *of* or *belonging to.*

Ren-* and *angiotens-

As in the word **renal,** the ***ren-*** in **renin** indicates the kidneys; the word literally means *related to the kidneys.* ***Angio-*** derives from Greek and means *blood vessel;* **tens** comes from Latin ***tensum,*** meaning *stretched.* The word **angiotensin** thus means *relating to the stretching (or tension) imposed on blood vessels,* which is measured as blood pressure.

medulla as part of the renal pyramids and empty the urine into the calyces.

It's a hormone thing

Hormones help regulate tubular reabsorption and secretion. For example, **antidiuretic hormone (ADH)** acts in the distal tubule and collecting ducts to increase water reabsorption and urine concentration.

Remember renin

By secreting the enzyme **renin,** the kidneys play a crucial role in regulating sodium retention and, therefore, blood pressure and fluid volume. This regulation takes place mostly through a complicated cascade of events in the **renin-angiotensin system.** (See *Two -*in *words.*)

In the liver, renin converts the substance **angiotensinogen** to **angiotensin I.** Traveling to the lungs, angiotensin I is converted to **angiotensin II,** a potent vasoconstrictor that acts on the adrenal cortex to stimulate the production of the hormone aldosterone.

Retention regulation

Aldosterone affects tubular reabsorption by regulating sodium retention and helping control potassium secretion in the tubules. When serum potassium levels rise, the adrenal cortex responds by increasing aldosterone secretion. Increased aldosterone levels increase sodium and water retention and depress the formation of more renin.

RBC production

Low levels of oxygen in the arterial blood tell the kidneys that the body needs more RBCs to deliver oxygen to the tissues. In response, the kidneys secrete a hormone called **erythropoietin,** which travels to the bone marrow and stimulates increased RBC production.

Get ready for reabsorption!
Okay!

Bladder

Each kidney has a **ureter,** a tube that carries urine by peristalsis from the kidney to the bladder, a hollow, sphere-shaped, muscular organ in the pelvis that stores urine. Urination results from **involuntary** (reflex) and **voluntary** (learned or intentional) processes. When urine fills the bladder, parasympathetic nerve fibers in the bladder wall cause the bladder to contract and the **internal sphincter** to relax.

You can relax now

This parasympathetic response is called the **micturition reflex.** The cerebrum then stimulates voluntary relaxation and contraction of the **external sphincter** of the bladder, causing urine to pass into the urethra for elimination from the body.

Urethra

The **urethra** is a small duct that channels urine outside the body from the bladder. (See *The urinary tract*, page 204.)

Females

In the female, the urethra is embedded in the anterior wall of the vagina behind the **symphysis pubis** (the bony prominence under the pubic hair). The urethra connects the bladder with an external opening called the **urethral meatus,** located anterior to the vaginal opening.

Males

In the male, the urethra passes vertically through the **prostate gland,** then extends through the **urogenital diaphragm** (a triangular ligament) and the **penis.** The male urethra serves as a passageway for semen as well as urine.

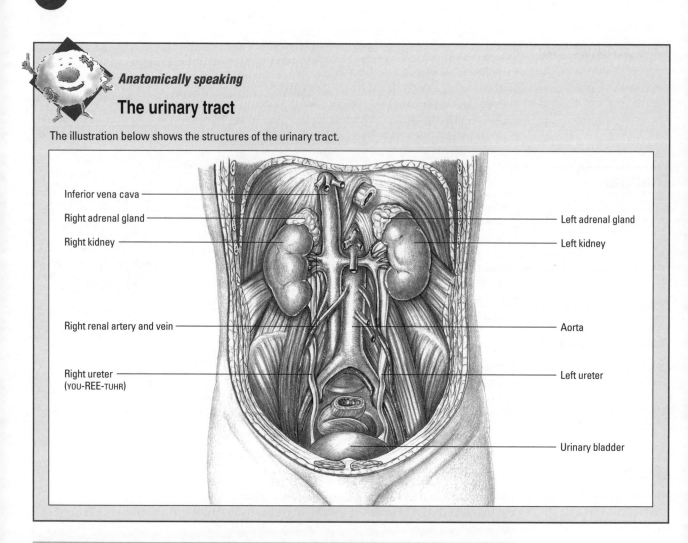

Anatomically speaking

The urinary tract

The illustration below shows the structures of the urinary tract.

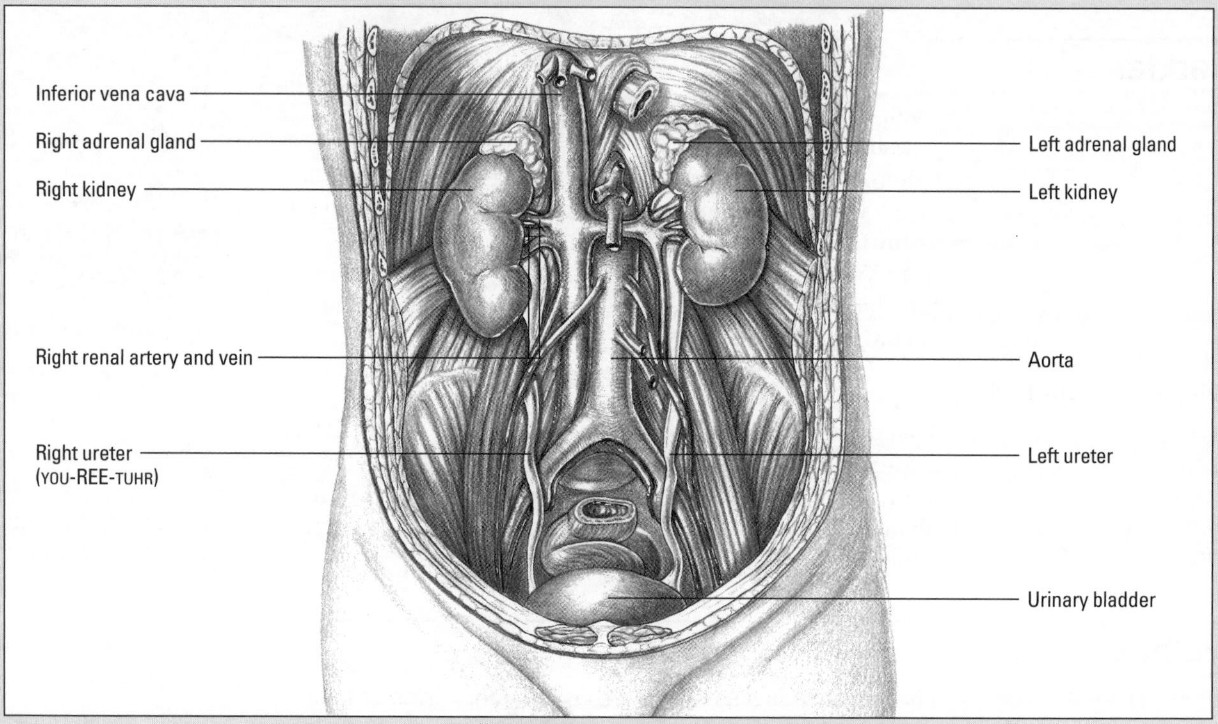
Inferior vena cava
Right adrenal gland
Right kidney
Right renal artery and vein
Right ureter
(YOU-REE-TUHR)
Left adrenal gland
Left kidney
Aorta
Left ureter
Urinary bladder

Physical examination terms

Examining a patient's urinary system requires observation, palpation, and keen interviewing skills. Before you can perform a complete physical examination, you must know these essential urinary system terms:

- **Anuria** is the absence of urine production. Anuria may also refer to absence of urine output (the body produces urine but can't eliminate it).
- **Azotemia,** or **uremia,** refers to accumulation of excess amounts of nitrogenous bodies, particularly **urea,** in the blood.

- **Dysuria** is painful or difficult urination.
- **Enuresis** refers to nighttime urinary incontinence in a girl older than age 5 or boy older than age 6.
- **Glycosuria** is the abnormal presence of glucose in the urine.
- **Hematuria** is the presence of blood in the urine.
- **Nocturia** refers to excessive urination at night.
- **Oliguria** is diminished urine production in relation to fluid intake, usually less than 400 ml in 24 hours.
- **Polyuria** is excessive production of urine.
- **Proteinuria** refers to the presence of protein in the urine.
- **Pyuria** is pus in the urine.
- **Renal colic** is sharp, severe pain occurring in the lower back, radiating forward into the area of the groin caused by kidney stones.
- **Thornton's sign** is severe flank pain resulting from kidney stones.
- **Urinary hesitancy** is difficulty beginning urination and subsequent decreased urine flow.
- **Urinary incontinence** refers to a loss of control over bladder and urethral sphincters, resulting in involuntary leakage of urine.
- **Urinary tenesmus** is persistent, ineffective, painful straining to empty the bladder.
- **Urine retention** is retaining urine in the bladder.

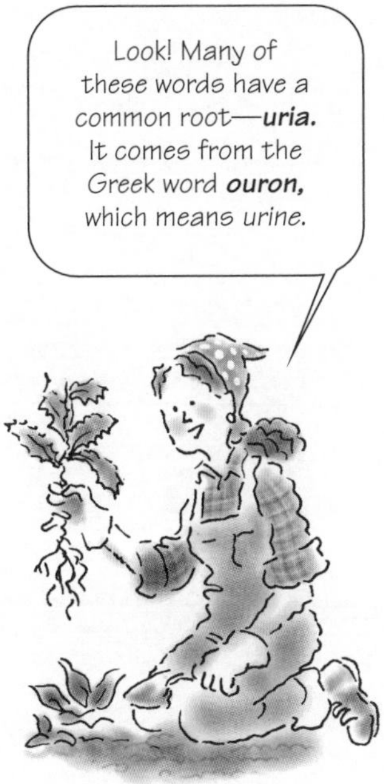
Look! Many of these words have a common root—***uria.*** It comes from the Greek word ***ouron,*** which means urine.

Diagnostic tests

Here are common diagnostic tests for patients with urinary system disorders.

Urine and bladder tests

The following urine and bladder tests provide the most direct assessment of urinary function:

- **Cystometry** assesses the bladder's neuromuscular function, including bladder sensation, capacity, and the presence or absence of detrusor muscle contractions. A **cystometer** is the instrument used to measure the amount, flow, and time of voiding.

- **External sphincter electromyography** evaluates urinary incontinence by measuring electrical activity of the urinary sphincter muscle.
- **24-hour urine specimen** collects urine over a 24-hour period to determine levels of the following:
  - **creatinine,** a nitrogenous waste product produced by working muscle tissue and normally excreted in the urine
  - **protein,** normally absent from urine
  - **uric acid,** an end product of protein metabolism normally excreted in the urine.
- **Urea clearance** measures urine levels of **urea,** the chief end product of protein metabolism. This test measures **glomerular filtration rate (GFR),** but is less reliable than the creatinine clearance.
- **Urinalysis** tests the urine for color, turbidity, specific gravity, pH, protein, glucose, and ketone bodies. This test also examines sediment for blood cells, casts, and crystals.
- **Urine culture** checks for bacterial growth in the urine, which indicates urinary tract infection (urine is normally sterile).
- **Urine myoglobin** detects the presence of **myoglobin,** a red pigment found in the cytoplasm of cardiac and skeletal muscle that is excreted in the urine as a result of muscle injury.
- **Urine osmolality** is the concentration or osmotic pressure of urine expressed in milliosmols per kilogram of water.
- **Uroflowmetry** measures the volume of urine expelled from the urethra in milliliters per second **(urine flow rate)** and also determines the urine flow pattern. Abnormal results can indicate obstruction of the urethra.

The ***glom-*** of **glomerular** derives from the Latin word ***glomus,*** meaning *ball,* and is akin to the Latin ***globus,*** meaning *globe.*

Blood studies

Here are several blood tests used to diagnose urinary disease and evaluate kidney function:

- **Anion gap** is the measurement of the total concentrations of anions and cations in the blood. An increased anion gap is present with renal failure.
- **Blood urea nitrogen** level measures the amount of serum nitrogenous urea. Levels are elevated with kidney failure and dehydration.

- **Calcium and phosphorus levels** indicate the kidney's efficient conversion of vitamin D to a metabolite essential for calcium absorption in the intestines.
- **Chloride tests** measure serum levels of chloride, which helps regulate blood pressure and acid-base balance, and is excreted by the kidneys.
- **Creatinine clearance** assesses the GFR by measuring how well the kidneys remove creatinine from the blood over a 24-hour period. This test is an excellent indicator of renal function because it requires blood and urine specimens.
- **Serum creatinine** measures blood levels of creatinine. Creatinine levels are elevated with renal damage.
- **Serum osmolality** tests the concentration of serum expressed in milliosmols per kilogram of water.
- **Serum potassium levels** measure blood potassium, essential for proper renal functioning.
- **Serum sodium levels** are evaluated in relation to the amount of water in the body. Abnormal ratios may indicate renal disease.
- **Serum uric acid levels** measure uric acid, a normal by-product of metabolism that's excreted by the kidneys. Levels may be abnormally high with gout or impaired renal function. Below-normal levels may indicate problems with renal tubular absorption.

Radiologic and imaging tests

Here are the names of radiologic, tomographic, sonographic, and endoscopic diagnostic procedures:

- **Computerized tomography (CT) scan** generates a three-dimensional, computerized image of the kidneys. This test is useful in detecting kidney stones.
- **Cystourethroscopy** uses an endoscopic instrument to examine the bladder, bladder neck, and urethra. (See *Show me a cystoscope*, page 208.)
- **Excretory urography,** also known as **I.V. pyelography,** injects a radiopaque contrast medium to visualize renal structures, ureter, bladder, and the urethra. (See *IVP in action.*)
- **Kidney-ureter-bladder (KUB) X-ray** is just that, an X-ray of the kidneys, ureter, and bladder.
- **Magnetic resonance imaging (MRI)** creates precise three-dimensional (tomographic) images of tissue by passing magnetic energy through the body.

The real world

IVP in action

In practice, you'll hear **excretory urography** referred to as an **IVP,** an abbreviation for an older name of the test, intravenous pyelography. For example, you might hear someone say, "We need to take the patient for an IVP to check for an obstruction in the ureter."

Show me a cystoscope

This illustration shows a cystoscope being inserted through the male urethra into the bladder. A cystoscope can be used for visual examination of the bladder or to remove tumors.

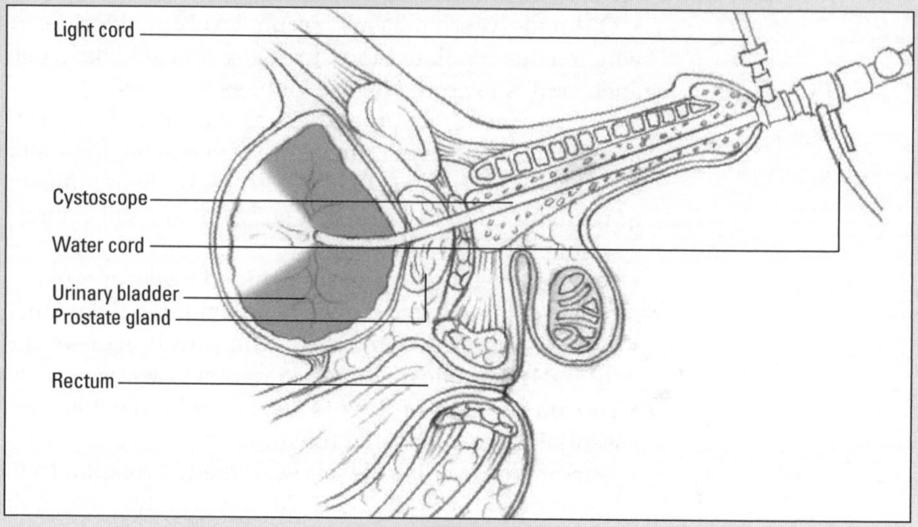
Light cord
Cystoscope
Water cord
Urinary bladder
Prostate gland
Rectum

• **Nephrotomography** creates a tomogram of the kidneys after I.V. injection of a contrast medium.
• **Radionuclide renal scan** requires injecting a **radionuclide** (radioactive material) before **scintigraphy,** which records the relative distribution of radioactivity in the tissues and, therefore, proper functioning of those tissues.
• **Renal angiography** creates X-ray images of renal arterial circulation after the injection of a contrast medium into the aorta and renal arteries.
• **Renal venography** creates X-ray images of the kidneys by injecting a contrast medium into a vein.
• **Retrograde cystography** instills a contrast medium into the bladder, followed by radiographic examination.
• **Ultrasonography** visualizes the urinary system by measuring and recording the reflection of pulses of ultrasonic waves directed into the tissue.
• **Voiding cystourethrography** demonstrates the efficiency of bladder filling and excretion by instilling a contrast medium into the patient's bladder through a urinary catheter. Radiographs are then taken before, during, and after voiding. (See *Cystourethrography.*)

Beyond the dictionary

Cystourethrography

In **cystourethrography** the prefix ***cysto-*** is the Greek word element for *bladder.* ***Urethro*** refers to the urethra and ***-graphy*** is a method of recording. Thus, cystourethrography is a procedure that records (through radiography) bladder and urethra function.

Disorders

This section covers disorders of the urinary system, including varieties of acute renal failure and other disorders.

Acute renal failure

Acute renal failure is the sudden interruption of renal function, caused by obstruction, poor circulation, or kidney disease. Types of this potentially life-threatening condition are classified by the cause of onset:

- **Intrarenal failure,** also called **intrinsic** or **parenchymal renal failure,** results from damage to the kidneys' filtering structures.
- **Postrenal failure** results from obstruction of urine outflow.
- **Prerenal failure** is caused by any condition that reduces blood flow to the kidneys **(hypoperfusion).**

I can't work without a blood supply.

Stages of acute renal failure

Each type of acute renal failure has three distinct phases:

- The **oliguric phase** is marked by decreased urine output (less than 400 ml in 24 hours).
- The **diuretic phase** occurs when the kidneys produce a high volume of urine.
- The **recovery phase** occurs when the cause of diuresis is corrected, azotemia gradually disappears, and the patient begins to improve.

Other disorders

- **Acute poststreptococcal glomerulonephritis** is a relatively common inflammation of the glomeruli after a streptococcal infection of the respiratory tract.
- **Acute pyelonephritis** is a sudden inflammation of the kidney and its pelvis caused by bacteria.
- **Acute tubular necrosis (ATN),** also called **acute tubulointerstitial nephritis,** destroys the tubular segment of the nephron, leading to renal failure and uremia.
- **Alport's syndrome** is a hereditary kidney inflammation in which the patient may have recurrent gross or microscopic hematuria.

• **Benign prostatic hyperplasia** occurs when the prostate gland enlarges enough to compress the urethra, causing urinary obstruction.
• **Chronic glomerulonephritis** is an inflammation of the glomerulus of the kidney characterized by decreased urine production, blood and protein in the urine, and edema.
• **Chronic renal failure** is the typically slow, progressive loss of kidney function and glomerular filtration.
• **Cystitis** refers to inflammation of the bladder, usually caused by an ascending infection.
• **Cystocele** is a herniation of the urinary bladder through the vaginal wall. (See *Cystocele is all Greek.*)
• **Fanconi's syndrome** is a kidney disorder that produces malfunctions of the proximal renal tubules, leading to elevated potassium levels, elevated sodium levels, glucose in the urine and, eventually, rickets and retarded growth and development.
• **Hydronephrosis** refers to a distention of the kidneys by urine that's caused by obstruction of the ureter.
• **Hypospadias** is a condition in which the urethra opening is on the ventral surface of the penis. This condition rarely occurs in females, where the opening occurs within the vagina.
• **Nephrotic syndrome** is a condition marked by proteinuria, low blood albumin levels, and edema.
• **Neurogenic bladder** refers to any dysfunction of the nerves that control the bladder. The patient's bladder becomes spastic or flaccid, and urinary incontinence results.
• **Polycystic kidney disease** is characterized by multiple cysts of the kidney.
• **Prostatitis,** an inflammation of the prostate gland, may be acute or chronic.
• **Renal calculi** are **kidney stones** that form from minerals normally dissolved in the urine, such as calcium or magnesium.
• **Renovascular hypertension** is hypertension that occurs as a result of partial blockage of one or both renal arteries. An excessive release of the enzyme renin occurs, which ultimately produces vasoconstriction and hypertension.

Beyond the dictionary

Cystocele is all Greek

Cystocele is an easy word. **Cysto-** comes from the Greek word ***kystis,*** which means *bladder* or *pouch.* **Cele-** is also derived from a Greek word, ***kele,*** which means *hernia.*

Skipping stones. Great! Having stones inside me. Ouch!

• **Renal infarction** occurs when a thrombus or embolus causes ischemia of a kidney.
• **Renal vein thrombosis** is clotting in the renal vein that results in renal congestion, engorgement and, possibly, infarction.
• **Ureterostenosis** is a ureteral stricture.
• **Urethritis** is inflammation of the urethra.
• **Vesicoureteral reflux** is a condition in which urine flows from the bladder back into the ureters and eventually into the renal pelvis or the parenchyma.

Treatments

Noninvasive procedures, dialysis, and surgeries that treat disorders of the urinary and renal systems are described here.

Lithotripsy

There are two procedures that use a process called **lithotripsy** to reduce the size of renal calculi:
• **Extracorporeal shock-wave lithotripsy (ESWL)** is a noninvasive treatment that breaks up calculi with high-energy shock waves to allow their passage out of the body.
• **Percutaneous ultrasonic lithotripsy** uses an ultrasonic probe inserted through a nephrostomy tube into the renal pelvis. The probe generates ultrahigh-frequency sound waves that shatter calculi and continuous suctioning removes the fragments.

Catheters

Catheters are used in several ways to treat urinary system disorders:
• An **external catheter,** also called a **Texas** or **condom catheter,** is a urine collection device that fits over the penis and resembles a condom.
• An **indwelling urinary catheter** is a urinary catheter with a balloon end designed to remain in the urinary bladder for a prolonged time. (See *Don't fool with my Foley.*)

The real world

Don't fool with my Foley

You may hear an indwelling urinary catheter referred to as a *Foley,* named after Dr. Frederick Foley, the American doctor who designed the device.

• An **intermittent catheterization** is a procedure that drains urine remaining in the bladder after each voiding or as needed for those who can't void.

Dialysis

Dialysis is a technique for removing waste products from the body when the kidneys fail. Several types of dialysis are explained here:

• **Continuous ambulatory peritoneal dialysis (CAPD)** is a form of peritoneal dialysis that allows the patient to continue daily activities.

• **Continuous arteriovenous hemofiltration (CAVH)** filters toxic wastes from the patient's blood and infuses a replacement solution such as lactated Ringer's solution.

• **Continuous arteriovenous ultrafiltration (CAVU)** uses equipment similar to that in CAVH but removes fluid from the patient's blood at a slower rate.

• **Continuous-cycling peritoneal dialysis (CCPD)** uses a machine to perform dialysis at night while the patient sleeps, and the patient performs CAPD in the daytime.

• **Hemodialysis** filters toxic wastes and other impurities directly from the blood of a patient with renal failure. Blood is pumped through a **dialyzing unit** to remove toxins and is then returned to the body.

• **Peritoneal dialysis** removes toxins from the patient's blood by using the peritoneal membrane surrounding the abdominal cavity as a **semipermeable dialyzing membrane.** In this technique, a dialyzing solution **(dialysate)** is instilled through a catheter inserted into the peritoneal cavity. By diffusion, the dialysate draws excessive concentrations of electrolytes and toxins through the peritoneal membrane. Next, excess water is drawn through the membrane. After an appropriate dwelling time, the dialysate is drained, taking toxins and wastes with it.

Dialysis derives from a Greek word meaning *separation.* The medical process separates toxins from the blood.

Surgery

Common surgical procedures to correct urinary system disorders include:

• **Cystectomy** is the partial or total removal of the urinary bladder and surrounding structures. Cystectomy may be partial, simple, or radical:

–A **partial cystectomy,** also called **segmental cystectomy,** involves **resection** (removal) of only cancerous tissue within the bladder. The patient's bladder function is usually preserved.
–A **simple,** or **total, cystectomy** involves resection of the entire bladder, but surrounding structures aren't removed.
–A **radical cystectomy** removes the bladder, prostate, and seminal vesicles in men. The bladder, urethra, uterus, fallopian tubes, ovaries, and a segment of the vaginal wall are removed in women.

I spy two more words derived from the Greek word for bladder: cystectomy and cystotomy!

- **Cystotomy** uses a catheter, which is inserted through the patient's suprapubic area into the bladder to temporarily divert urine away from the urethra and into a closed collection chamber.
- **Kidney transplantation** is one of the most common and successful organ transplant surgeries. This treatment is an alternative to dialysis for patients with end-stage renal disease.
- **Marshall-Marchetti-Krantz operation** helps correct urinary incontinence in female patients by restoring a weakened urinary sphincter.
- **Prostatectomy** is surgical removal of the prostate gland to remove diseased or obstructive tissue and restore urine flow through the urethra. One of four approaches is used:

–**Radical perineal prostatectomy** approaches the prostate through an incision in the perineum between the scrotum and the rectum.
–**Retropubic prostatectomy** uses a low abdominal incision to approach the prostate without opening the patient's bladder.
–**Suprapubic prostatectomy** uses an abdominal approach to open the bladder and remove the prostate gland.
–**Transurethral prostatectomy** approaches the prostate gland through the penis and bladder, using a surgical instrument called a **resectoscope.** The scope has an electric cutting wire to remove tissue. This procedure is also called a **transurethral resection of the prostate (TURP).**

- **Transurethral resection of the bladder (TURB)** is a relatively simple procedure that uses a cystoscope to remove small lesions from the bladder.

Two types of urinary diversion

Cystostomy
A *cystostomy* is a urinary diversion created when a catheter is inserted through the suprapubic area into the bladder. Urine is diverted away from the urethra.

Nephrostomy
A *nephrostomy* is a urinary diversion created when a catheter is inserted through the flank and into the renal pelvis. Urine is diverted away from the bladder.

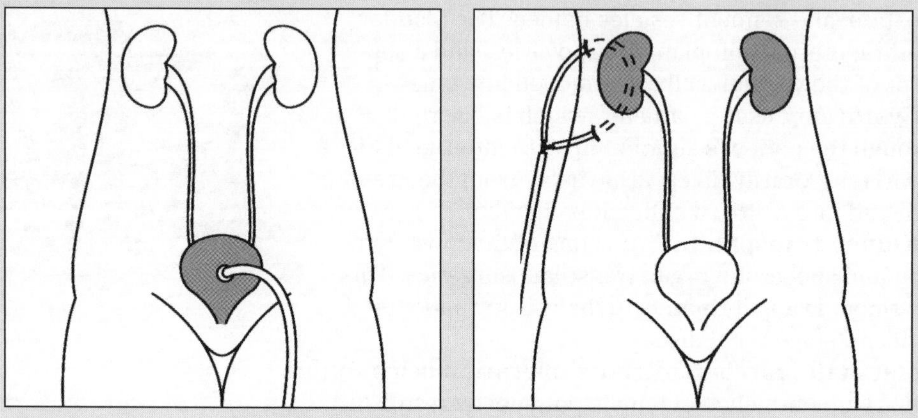

- **Urinary diversion** is a procedure that provides an alternative route for urine excretion when the normal channels are damaged or defective. Several types of urinary diversion surgery are performed. (See *Two types of urinary diversion.*)
  - The **ileal conduit** diverts urine through a segment of the small bowel **(ileum),** which is removed for this purpose. A stoma formed on the abdominal wall continually empties urine into a collection bag.
  - A **continent vesicostomy** allows urine to be diverted to a reservoir constructed from a portion of the bladder wall. A stoma is formed, and accumulated urine can be drained by inserting a catheter into the stoma.
  - In a **ureterostomy,** one or both ureters are dissected from the bladder and brought to the skin surface to form one or two stomas that continuously drain urine.

systole

Vocabulary builders

At a crossroads

Completing this crossword puzzle will help you filter through urinary system terms. Good luck!

Some workout, huh?

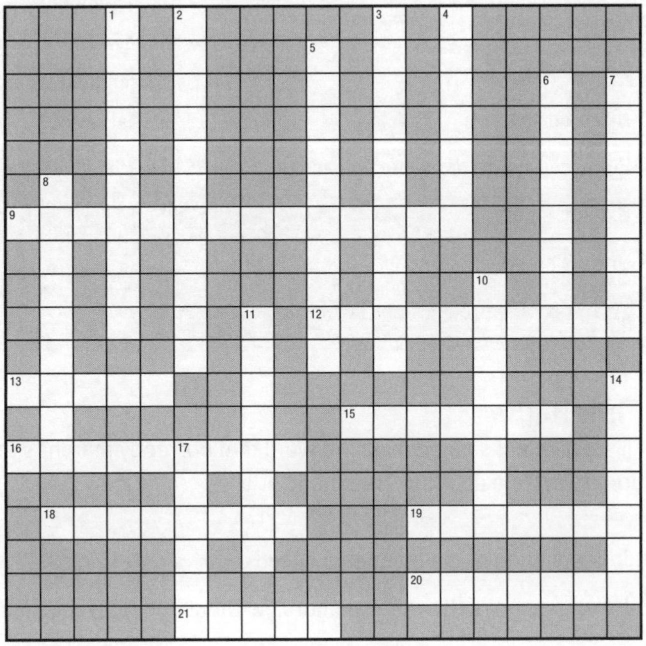

Across

9. Bacterial kidney infection
12. Analysis of urine
13. Artery that brings blood to the kidney
15. Kidney stones
16. Blood in the urine
18. Phase of renal failure when kidneys produce high volume of urine
19. Structure that collects and holds urine
20. Structure through which urine exits the body
21. Hormone involved with blood pressure

Down

1. Study of the renal system
2. Protein in the urine
3. Inflammation of the prostate gland
4. Syndrome resulting from a hereditary kidney inflammation
5. Network of capillaries
6. Striated wedges in the renal medulla
7. Technique for removing waste products when kidneys fail
8. Herniation of the bladder
10. Scant urine output
11. Bladder infection
14. Difficult urination
17. Structure that carries urine from kidney to bladder

Answers are on page 218.

Match the words to their definitions up top, and fill in the blanks down below.

Match game

Match each of the urinary system terms below with its definition.

Clues

1. Catheter that's left in place ____
2. External catheter ____
3. Used for bladder training ____
4. Uses the peritoneal membrane ____
5. Uses blood ____
6. Dialyzing solution ____
7. Surgical removal of the prostate gland ____
8. Bladder surgery ____
9. Ureters brought to the skin surface ____
10. Diverts urine through small bowel ____

Choices

A. Dialysate
B. Ureterostomy
C. Peritoneal dialysis
D. Cystectomy
E. Indwelling catheter
F. Strengthening exercises
G. Ileal conduit
H. Condom catheter
I. Prostatectomy
J. Hemodialysis

Finish line

Fill in the blanks below with the word that correctly matches the definition for each urinary system disorder, treatment, or test.

1. Inflammation of the bladder is called ________.
2. Inflammation of the renal glomeruli without infection is called ______.
3. The severe pain caused by kidney stones is called renal _______ .
4. Kidney stones are also called renal _______.
5. A coagulated, necrotic area in the kidney caused by occlusion of blood vessels is called renal ________.
6. The phase of acute renal failure marked by decreased urine output is the _______ phase.
7. The phase of acute renal failure marked by excess urine output is called the _______ phase.
8. The initials IVP stand for ________.

Answers are on page 218.

O see, can you say?

Sound out each group of pictures and symbols below to reveal a term that was reviewed in the chapter.

1.

+ you-ree-uh

2.

+ + you + ree + Thros + kuh +

3.

kay +

4.

+ Leh

Got it!
SNAP

Answers are on page 218.

Answers

At a crossroads

			1 N		2 P						3 P		4 A					
			E		R				5 G		R		L					
			P		O				L		O		P			6 P		7 D
			H		T				O		S		O			Y		I
			R		E				M		T		R			R		A
	8 C		O		I				E		A		T			A		L
9 P	Y	E	L	O	N	E	O	H	R	I	T	I	S			M		Y
	S		O		U				U		I					I		S
	T		G		R				L		T			10 O		D		I
	O		Y		I		11 C		12 U	R	I	N	A	L	Y	S	I	S
	C				A		Y		S		S			I				
13 R	E	N	A	L			S							G				14 D
	L						T			15 C	A	L	C	U	L	I		Y
16 H	E	M	A	T	17 U	R	I	A						R				S
					R		T							I				U
	18 D	I	U	R	E	T	I	C				19 B	L	A	D	D	E	R
					T		S											I
					E							20 U	R	E	T	H	R	A
					21 R	E	N	I	N									

Match game

1. E; 2. H; 3. F; 4. C; 5. J; 6. A; 7. I; 8. D; 9. B; 10. G

Finish line

1. Cystitis; 2. Glomerulonephritis; 3. Colic; 4. Calculi; 5. Infarction; 6. Oliguric; 7. Diuretic; 8. Intravenous pyelography

O see, can you say?

1. Pyuria; 2. Cystourethroscopy; 3. Calyx; 4. Henle

Incredibly Easy miniguide: The kidney

The kidney is a bean-shaped organ. The right kidney may be lower than the left because the liver crowds it in the abdominal cavity.

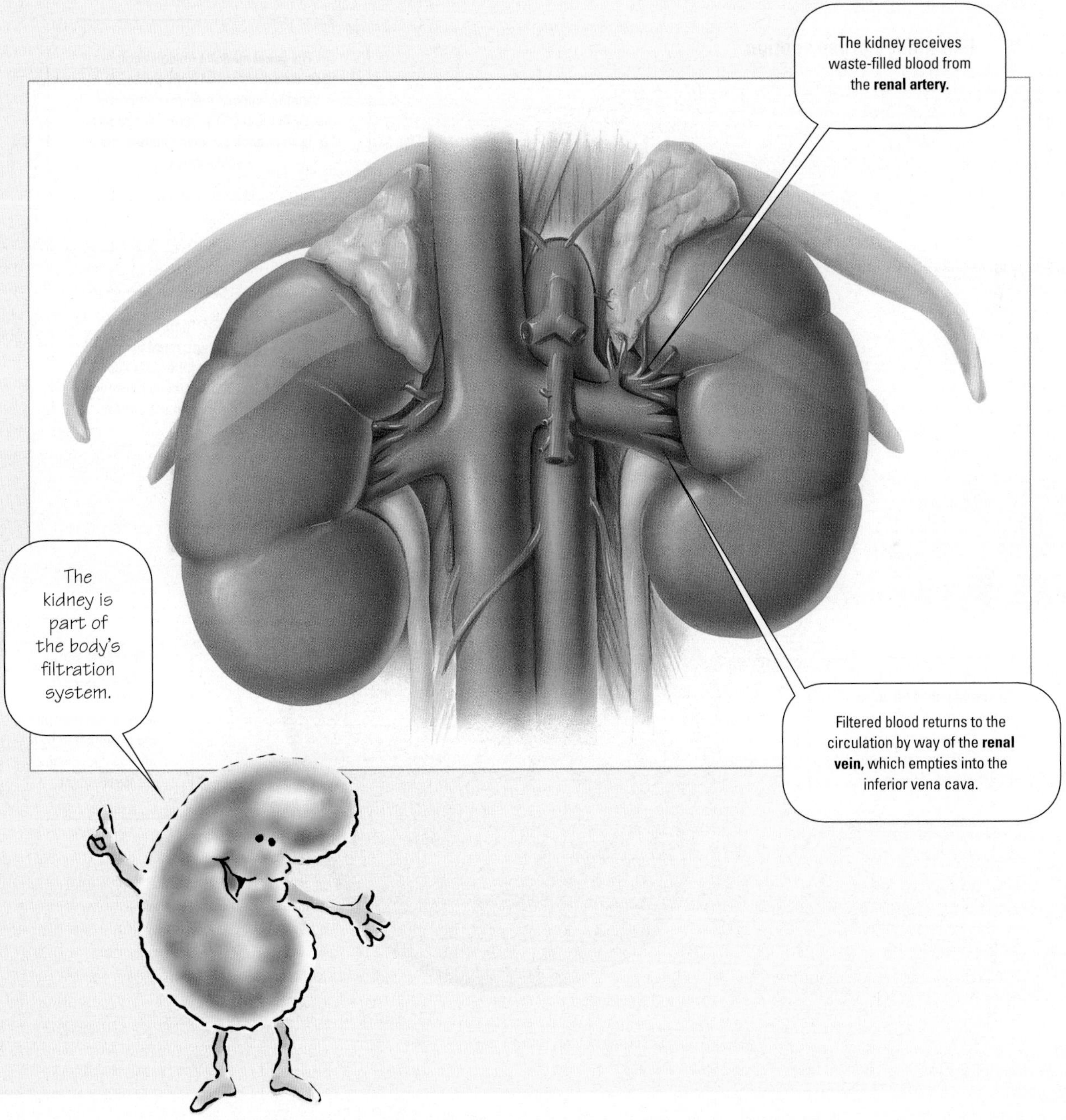
The kidney receives waste-filled blood from the **renal artery.**
The kidney is part of the body's filtration system.
Filtered blood returns to the circulation by way of the **renal vein,** which empties into the inferior vena cava.

Incredibly Easy miniguide: The kidney

Each kidney has three regions: the renal cortex, the renal medulla, and the renal pyramids.

Left kidney cross section

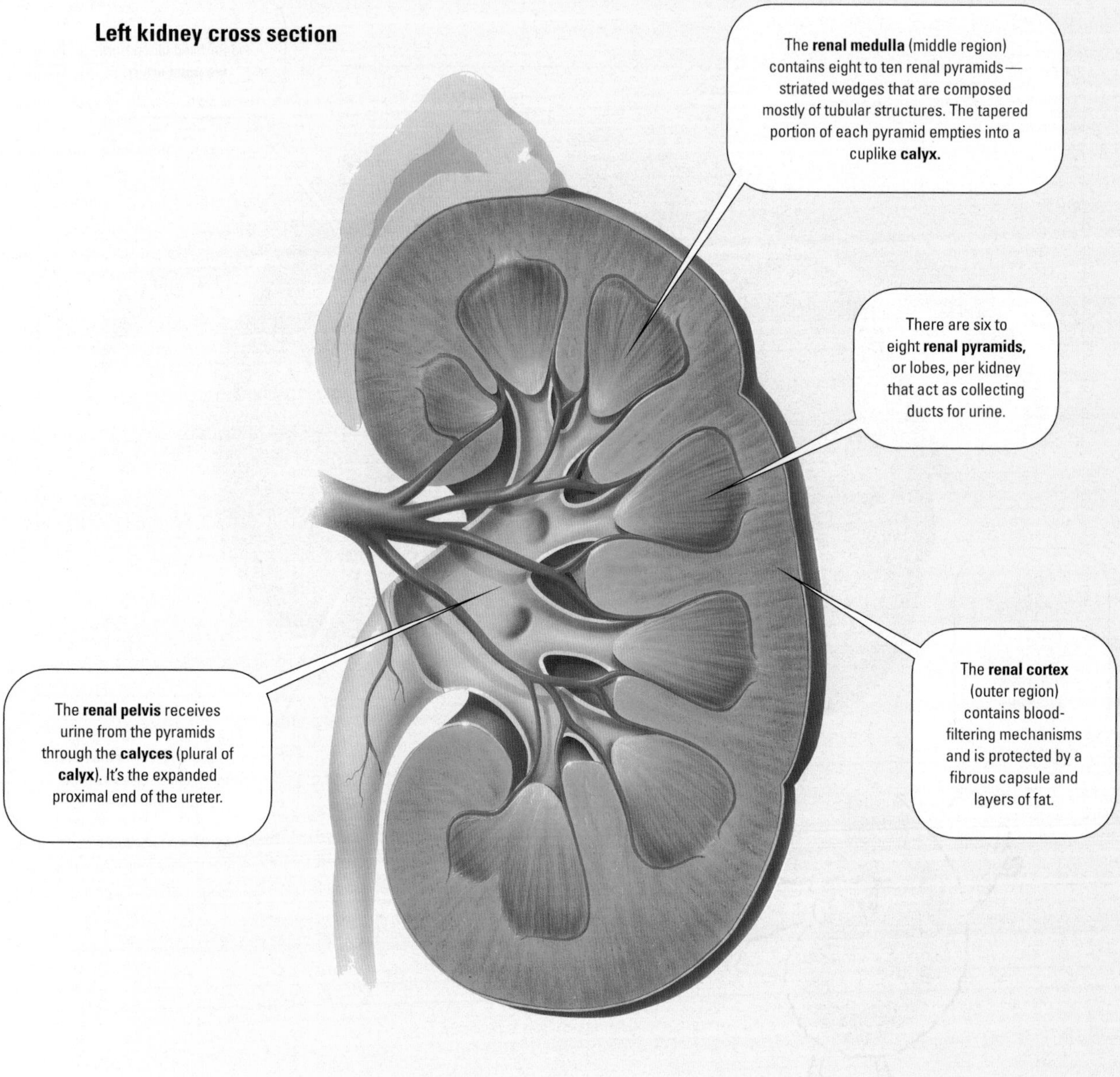
The **renal medulla** (middle region) contains eight to ten renal pyramids—striated wedges that are composed mostly of tubular structures. The tapered portion of each pyramid empties into a cuplike **calyx.**
There are six to eight **renal pyramids,** or lobes, per kidney that act as collecting ducts for urine.
The **renal cortex** (outer region) contains blood-filtering mechanisms and is protected by a fibrous capsule and layers of fat.
The **renal pelvis** receives urine from the pyramids through the **calyces** (plural of **calyx**). It's the expanded proximal end of the ureter.

Incredibly Easy miniguide: The kidney

The nephron is the functional and structural unit of the kidney. It's responsible for selective reabsorption of ions and the mechanical filtration of fluids, wastes, electrolytes, and acids and bases.

The nephron

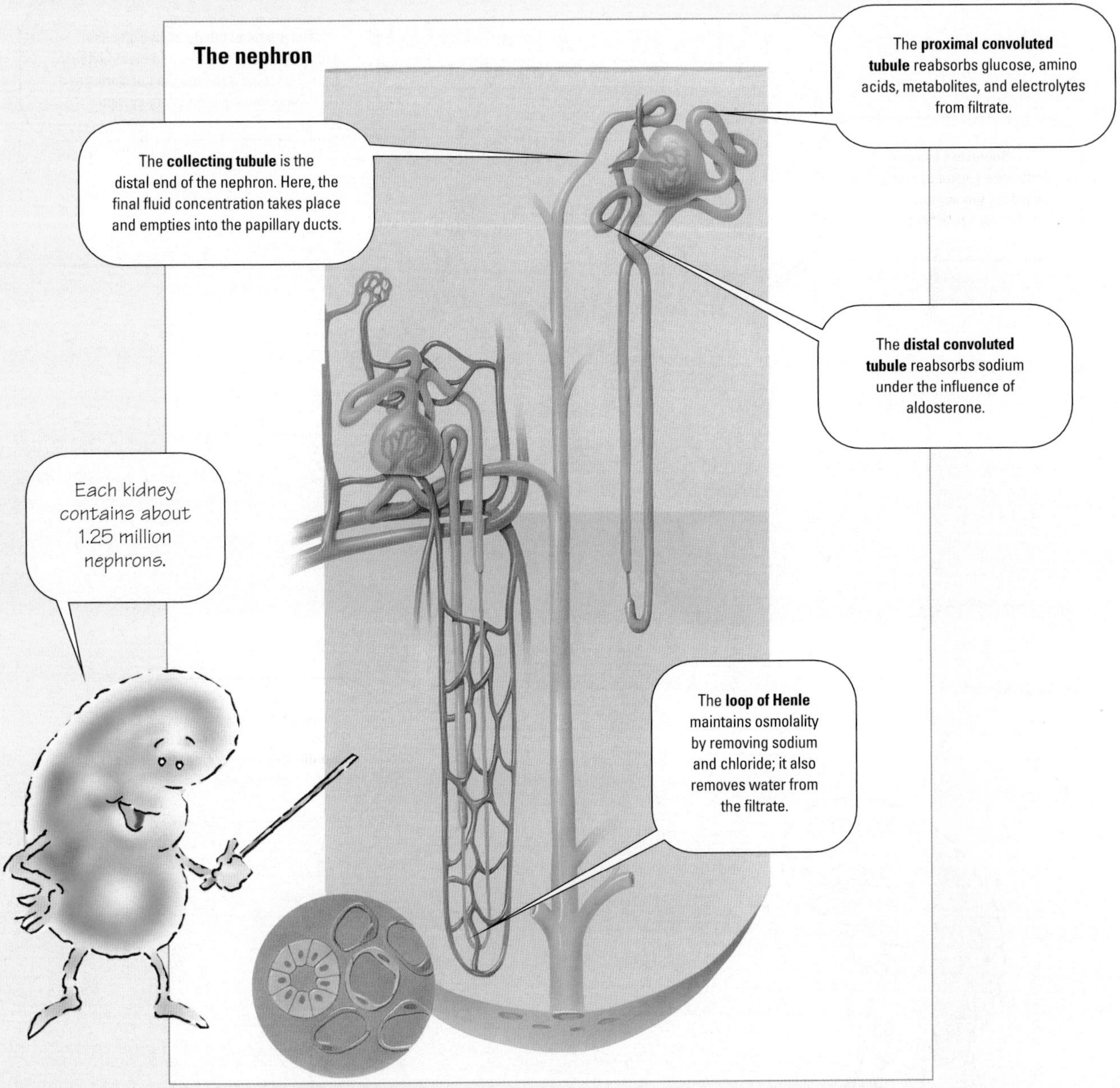
The **proximal convoluted tubule** reabsorbs glucose, amino acids, metabolites, and electrolytes from filtrate.
The **collecting tubule** is the distal end of the nephron. Here, the final fluid concentration takes place and empties into the papillary ducts.
The **distal convoluted tubule** reabsorbs sodium under the influence of aldosterone.
Each kidney contains about 1.25 million nephrons.
The **loop of Henle** maintains osmolality by removing sodium and chloride; it also removes water from the filtrate.

Incredibly Easy miniguide: The kidney

The enclosed end of the nephron is called Bowman's capsule.

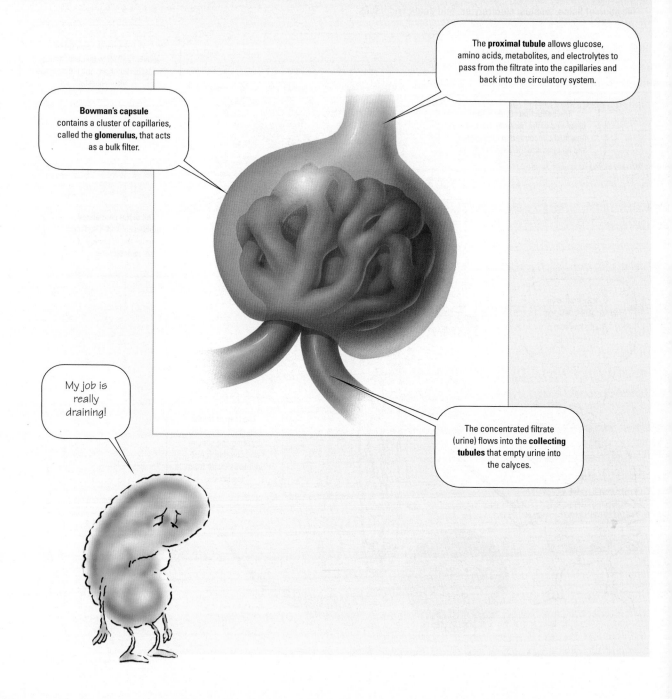

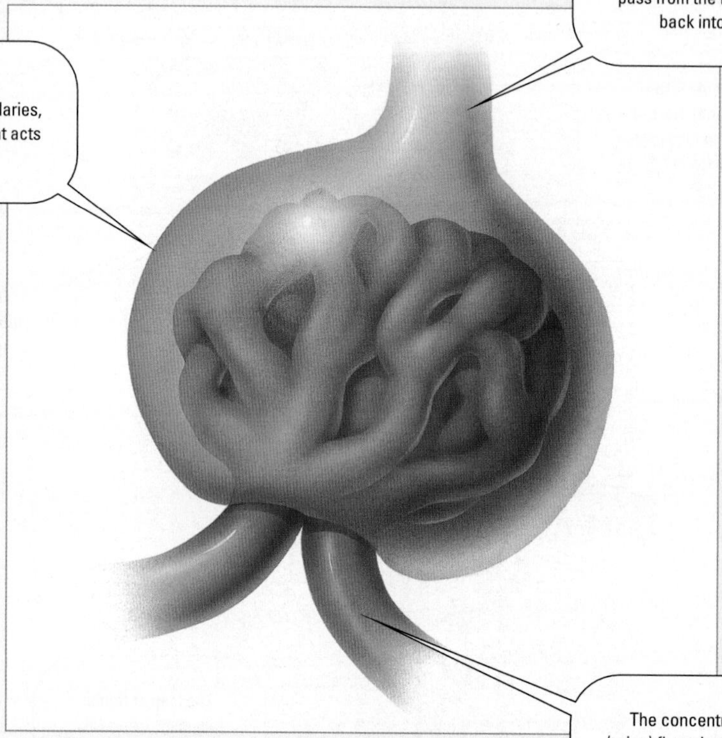
The **proximal tubule** allows glucose, amino acids, metabolites, and electrolytes to pass from the filtrate into the capillaries and back into the circulatory system.
Bowman's capsule contains a cluster of capillaries, called the **glomerulus,** that acts as a bulk filter.
The concentrated filtrate (urine) flows into the **collecting tubules** that empty urine into the calyces.

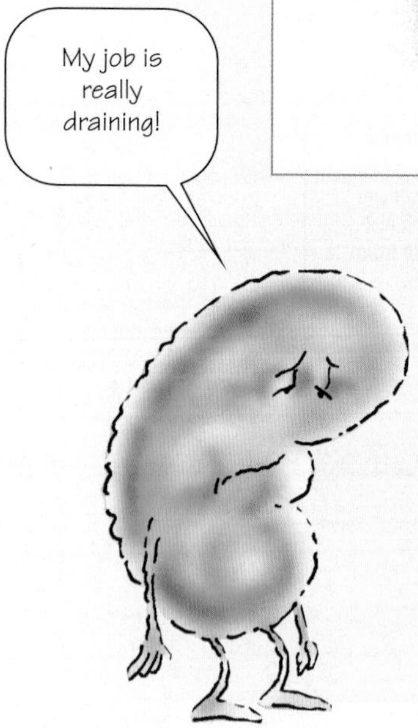
My job is really draining!

10

Reproductive system

Just the facts

In this chapter, you'll learn:

- terminology related to the structure and function of the reproductive system
- terminology needed for physical examination
- tests that help diagnose common reproductive disorders
- reproductive system disorders and their treatments.

Reproductive structure and function

Essential terminology related to the structure and normal function of the male and female reproductive systems and associated organs is presented here. A clear understanding of these systems will help you remember the terminology. (See *Pronouncing key reproductive system terms*, page 220.)

The male reproductive system produces sperm and some male sex hormones.

Male reproductive system

The male reproductive system consists of the organs that produce, transfer, and introduce mature sperm into the female reproductive tract, where **fertilization** occurs. In addition to producing male sex cells, the male reproductive system secretes some of the male sex hormones. The male reproductive organs include the penis, scrotum and testes, duct system, and accessory reproductive glands.

Pump up your pronunciation

Pronouncing key reproductive system terms

Below is a list of key terms related to the reproductive systems along with the correct ways to pronounce them.

Adnexa	ADD-NEK-SUH
Ballottement	BAHL-OT-MAW
Dyspareunia	DIS-PEH-ROO-NEE-UH
Epididymis	EP-UH-DID-UH-MISS
Gonadotropin	GOH-NEH-DOH-TROH-PIN
Leydig's cells	LAY-digz SELLZ
Oophorectomy	OH-OFF-UH-REK-TOH-MEE
Symphysis pubis	SIM-FUH-SIS PYOU-BIS

Penis

The **penis** deposits **sperm** (mature male germ cells) into the female reproductive tract through copulation and acts as the terminal duct for the urinary tract.

Column^3

The cylindrical penile shaft contains three columns of spongy vascular tissue that respond to sexual stimulation by becoming engorged with blood. Two of the three columns of this erectile tissue are bound together by heavy fibrous tissue and form the **corpora cavernosa,** the major part of the penis. The third column, on the underside of the shaft, is called the **corpus spongiosum.** It encases the urethra. (See *Caves and sponges.*)

So sensitive

The **glans penis,** at the distal end of the shaft, is a cone-shaped structure formed from the corpus spongiosum. Its lateral margin forms a ridge of tissue known as the **corona.** The glans is highly sensitive to sexual stimulation.

Beyond the dictionary

Caves and sponges

The terms **corpora cavernosa** and **corpus spongiosum** describe the columns of spongy vascular tissue in the penile shaft that respond to sexual stimulation.

Latin roots

Corpora is simply the plural of ***corpus,*** a Latin word for the main part of a bodily structure. ***Cavernosa*** is a *cave* or *cavity.* ***Spongiosum*** relates to a sponge, which is made up of little cavities.

Nearest exit

Thin, loose skin covers the penile shaft. The **urethral meatus** opens through the glans to allow urination and ejaculation. (See *Structures of the male reproductive system*, page 222.)

Scrotum and testes

The **scrotum,** meaning *pouch,* contains the primary male sex organs and joins with the penis at the **penoscrotal junction.** A thin layer of skin covers the scrotum, overlying a tighter, muscular layer. Within the scrotum are two sacs that each contain a testis, an epididymis, and a spermatic cord. The seam where the two sacs join is called the **median raphe** and is visible on the exterior of the scrotum. (See *The rap on the median raphe*, page 223.)

Totally tubular

The **testes,** also called the **testicles,** are two egg-shaped glands within the scrotum. Enclosed in a fibrous white capsule, each testicle is divided into numerous compartments, or **lobules.** The lobules contain **seminiferous tubules,** where **spermatogenesis** (sperm formation) takes place. This begins when a male reaches puberty and continues throughout life. Stimulated by male sex hormones, sperm continuously form within these tubules.

Anatomically speaking

Structures of the male reproductive system

The male reproductive system consists of the penis, the scrotum and its contents, the prostate gland, and the inguinal structures. These structures are illustrated below.

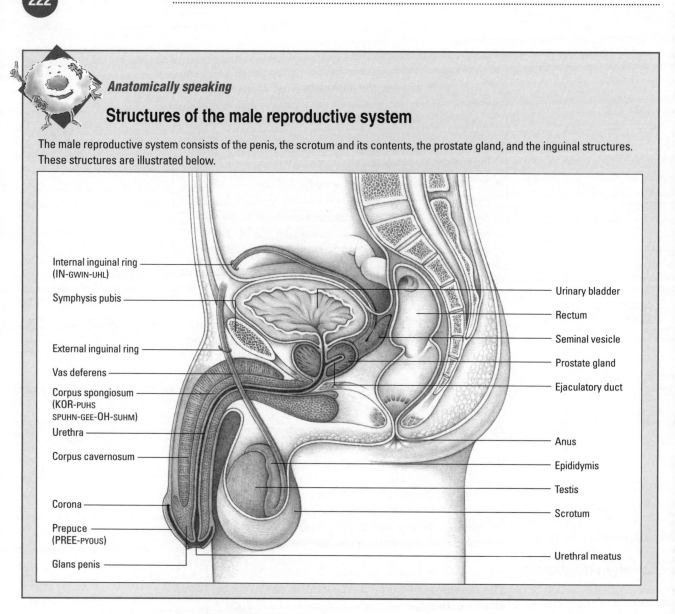

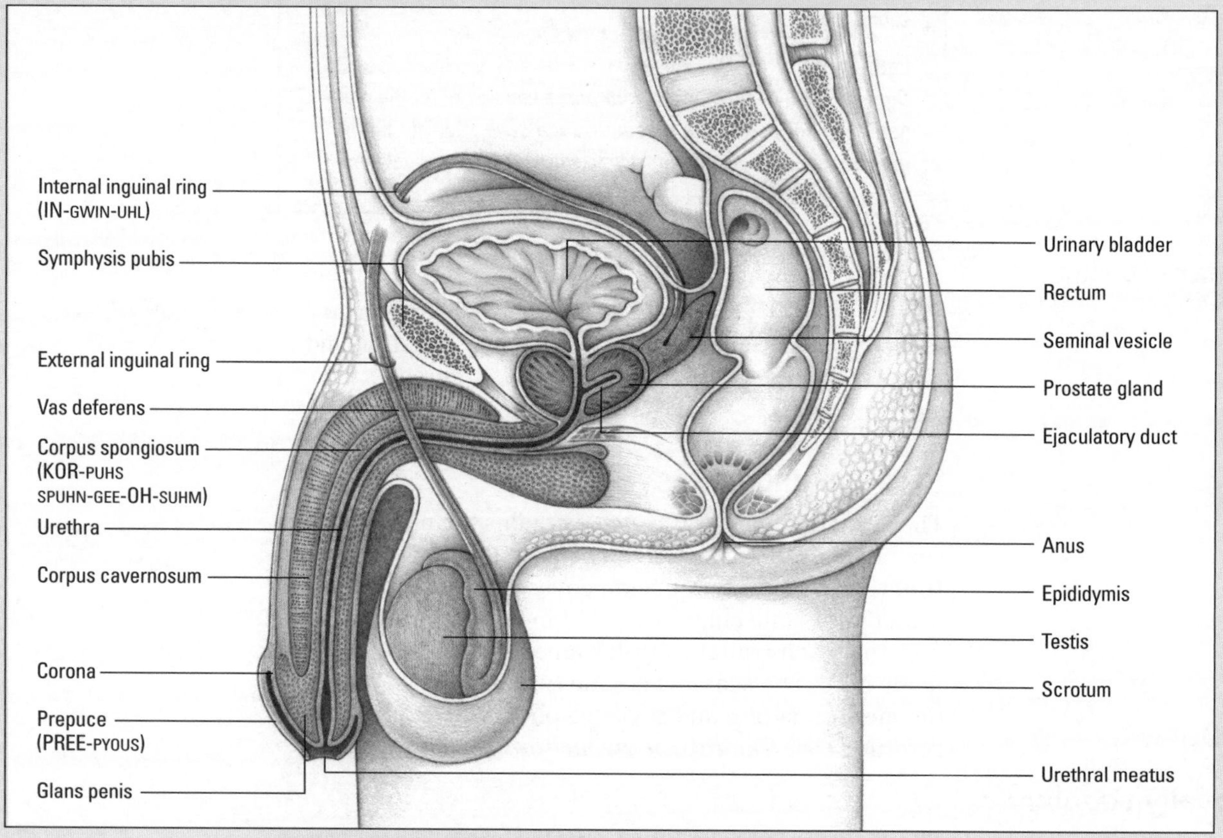
Internal inguinal ring (IN-GWIN-UHL)
Symphysis pubis
External inguinal ring
Vas deferens
Corpus spongiosum (KOR-PUHS SPUHN-GEE-OH-SUHM)
Urethra
Corpus cavernosum
Corona
Prepuce (PREE-PYOUS)
Glans penis
Urinary bladder
Rectum
Seminal vesicle
Prostate gland
Ejaculatory duct
Anus
Epididymis
Testis
Scrotum
Urethral meatus

Duct system

The male reproductive system includes a complicated duct system that delivers sperm from the testes to the ejaculatory ducts near the bladder. This system consists of the epididymides, the vas deferens, and the ejaculatory ducts.

Riding the epididymides

The **epididymides** (singular: **epididymis**) are coiled, tubular reservoirs that store sperm before ejaculation, secrete some of the seminal fluid, and serve as passageways for sperm. One epididymis is located along the border of each testicle.

Bundle of nerves

Mature sperm travel from the epididymis to the **vas deferens,** or **ductus deferens.** These two tubes begin at the epididymides, pass through the **inguinal canal** (formed by the pelvic girdle), and enter the ejaculatory duct inside the prostate gland. Each vas deferens is enclosed by a **spermatic cord,** a compact bundle of vessels, nerves, and muscle fibers.

Ready for discharge

The **ejaculatory ducts** are two short tubes formed by the vas deferens and the ducts of the seminal vesicles. They pass through the prostate gland and enter the urethra. The **seminal vesicles,** two pouches located along the bladder's lower edge, produce most of the liquid part of semen (the thick, whitish secretion that's discharged during ejaculation). The seminal vesicles also produce **prostaglandins,** potent hormonelike fatty acids.

Prostate gland

The walnut-sized **prostate gland** is located under the bladder and surrounds the urethra. It conists of three lobules: the left and right lateral lobes and the median (middle) lobe. These lobules continuously secrete **prostatic fluid**—a thin, milky substance that comprises about one-third of the semen volume and activates the sperm.

Hormones

Male sex hormones, called **androgens,** are produced in the testes and adrenal glands.

Beyond the dictionary

The rap on the median raphe

The seam where the two scrotal sacs join, called the **median raphe,** is visible on the exterior of the scrotum. **Median** comes from the Latin term ***medianus,*** meaning *in the midline of a structure.* ***Raphe*** is the Greek word for *seam.*

How did **prostaglandin** get its name?

Doctors used to think it was produced in the **prostate gland.** Think ***prosta + gland + in.***

It takes testosterone

Interstitial cells, called **Leydig's cells,** are found in tissue between the **seminiferous tubules** (the tubules that produce and conduct sperm). Leydig's cells secrete **testosterone,** the most important male sex hormone. A man's body needs testosterone for development of the sex organs, secondary sex characteristics (such as facial hair), and sperm formation.

Two other hormones—**luteinizing hormone (LH),** also known as **interstitial cell–stimulating hormone**, and **follicle-stimulating hormone (FSH)**—directly affect testosterone secretion.

Female reproductive system

The **ovaries** are the basic organs of female reproduction. Internal and external female reproductive organs include the fallopian tubes, uterus, vagina, and mammary glands.

External structures

As in males, the **mons pubis** in females is a triangular pad of tissue that's covered by skin and pubic hair and is located over the **symphysis pubis,** the joint formed by the union of the pubic bones.

Just for her

The external female genitals, sometimes referred to as the **pudendum,** are contained in the region called the **vulva.** (See *Addendum on the pudendum.*)

Two **labia majora** form the sides of the vulva. The **labia minora,** two moist mucosal folds, lie within and alongside the labia majora.

The **perineum** consists of muscles, fasciae, and ligaments between the **anus** and vulva. (See *External structures of the female reproductive system.*)

Small, but important

The **clitoris** is a small, erectile organ located at the anterior of the vulva. Less visible are the multiple openings of **Skene's glands,** mucus-producing glands found on both sides of the **urethral meatus. Bartholin's glands,** other mucus-producing glands, are located on each side of and behind the vaginal opening. The **hymen,** a tissue mem-

Beyond the dictionary

Addendum on the pudendum

The term **pudendum** derives from the Latin word ***pudendus.*** This means, literally, *that of which one is to be ashamed.* In late classical and Latin and early Christian writings, the word came to refer to the external genitalia of both sexes. Now, it more commonly refers to just female genitalia.

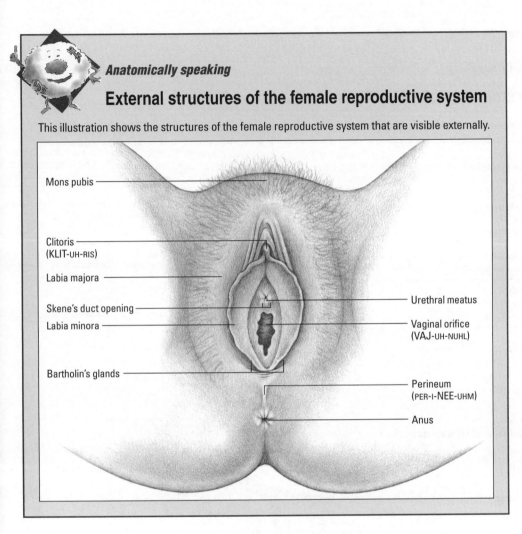

Anatomically speaking

External structures of the female reproductive system

This illustration shows the structures of the female reproductive system that are visible externally.

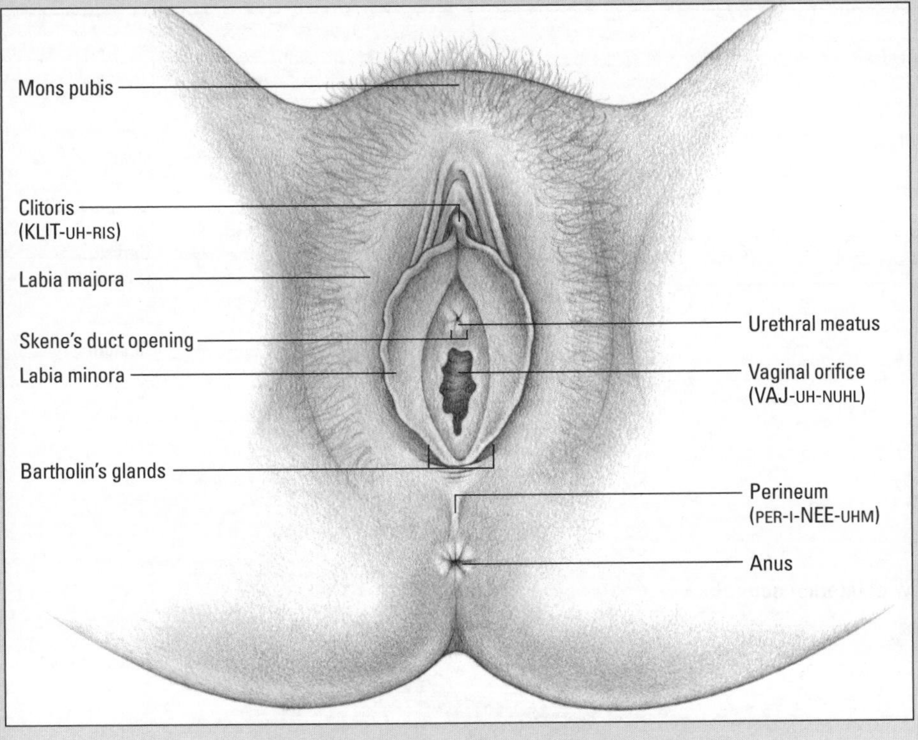
Mons pubis
Clitoris (KLIT-uh-ris)
Labia majora
Skene's duct opening
Labia minora
Bartholin's glands
Urethral meatus
Vaginal orifice (VAJ-uh-nuhl)
Perineum (per-i-NEE-uhm)
Anus

brane varying in size and thickness, can sometimes completely cover the vaginal opening.

Internal organs

The **vagina** is a highly elastic muscular tube located between the urethra and the rectum. A mucous membrane lining lubricates the vagina during sexual activity. **Rugae,** folds of tissue in the vaginal walls, allow the vagina to stretch. (See *Internal structures of the female reproductive system*, page 226.)

Anatomically speaking

Internal structures of the female reproductive system

These illustrations provide a lateral and anterior cross-sectional view of the internal structures of the female reproductive system.

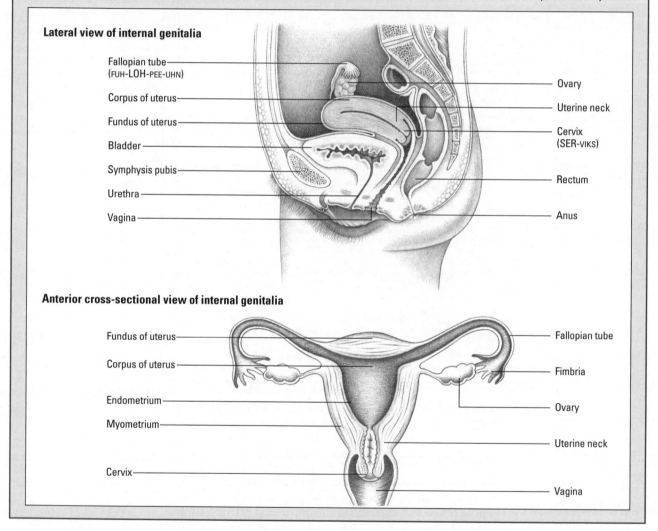

Lateral view of internal genitalia

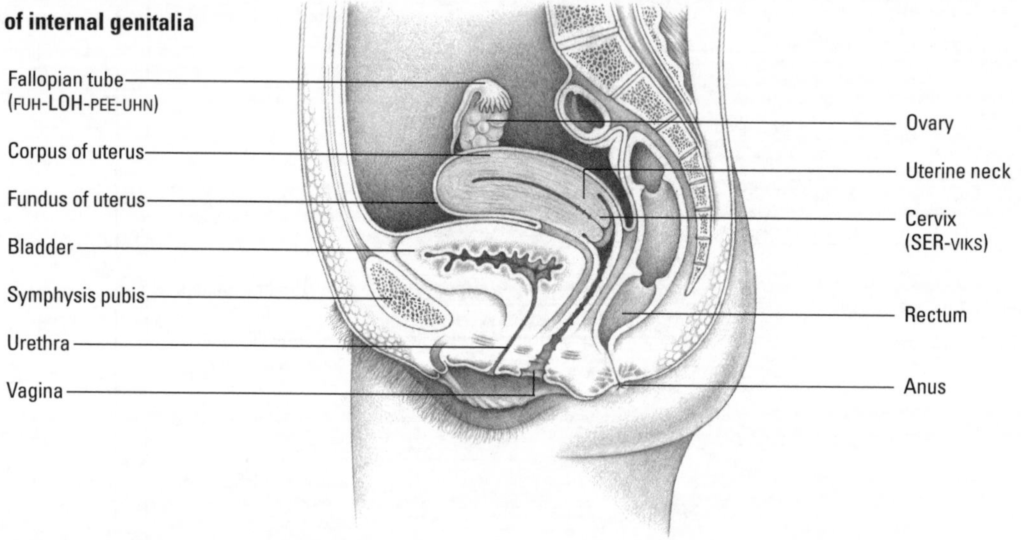
Fallopian tube
(FUH-LOH-PEE-UHN)
Corpus of uterus
Fundus of uterus
Bladder
Symphysis pubis
Urethra
Vagina
Ovary
Uterine neck
Cervix
(SER-VIKS)
Rectum
Anus

Anterior cross-sectional view of internal genitalia

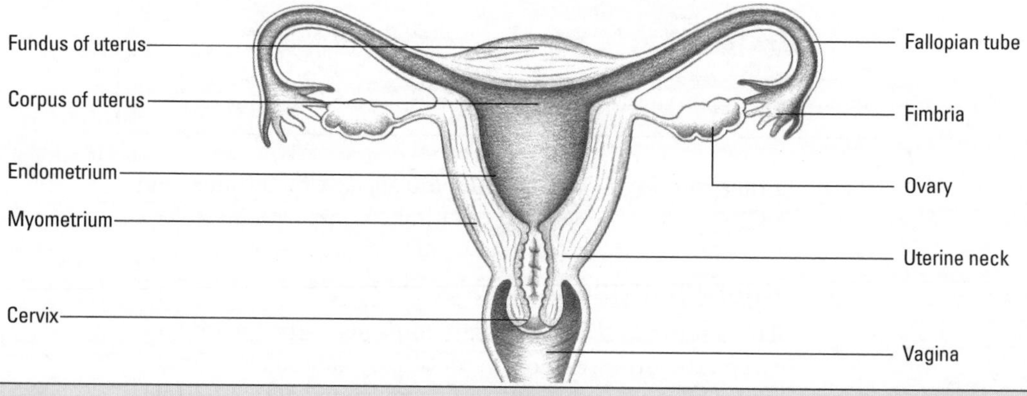
Fundus of uterus
Corpus of uterus
Endometrium
Myometrium
Cervix
Fallopian tube
Fimbria
Ovary
Uterine neck
Vagina

The pear-fect uterus

The vagina leads to the **uterus,** a small, firm, pear-shaped muscular organ resting between the bladder and rectum. The uterus usually lies at a 90-degree angle to the vagina.

The mucous membrane that lines the uterus is called the **endometrium.** The muscular layer is called the **myometrium.** (See *Metrium matters.*)

The uterine neck, or **isthmus,** joins the upper uterus, or **fundus,** to the **cervix,** the part of the uterus that extends into the vagina. The fundus and isthmus make up the **corpus,** or main body of the uterus.

Beyond the dictionary

Metrium matters

The mucous membrane that lines the uterus is called the **endometrium.** The muscular layer is called the **myometrium.**

The root of these words, ***metrium,*** refers to the uterus. It comes from the Greek word ***meter,*** which is related to and has the same meaning as the English word *mother.*

Certainly the cervix

The mouth of the cervix is called the ***os,*** a Latin term for a body orifice. The **internal os** opens from the cervix into the cervical canal, and the **external os** leads from the cervical canal to the vagina. A mucous membrane called the **endocervix** lines the cervical canal.

Fundamentally fallopian

The **fallopian tubes** are a pair of ducts attached to the uterus at the upper angles of the fundus. These long, narrow, muscular tubes have fingerlike projections, called **fimbriae** (pronounced: FIHM-BREE-EE), on their free ends that partially surround the ovaries. (See *Fallopian facts.*)

Fertilization of the **ovum** (egg), or female sex cell, usually occurs in the outer third of the fallopian tube.

Obviously ovarian

The **ovaries** are two almond-shaped organs. One ovary is located on each side of the pelvis and is connected to the uterus by a ligament. The main function of the ovaries is to produce mature ova.

At birth, each ovary contains approximately 50,000 **graafian follicles,** mature ovarian vesicles that each

Beyond the dictionary

Fallopian facts

Although the correct function of the fallopian tubes had been known for more than 2,000 years, these structures received their name from Gabrielle Fallopio, a 16th-century Italian surgeon. He described and named the tubes in his book *Observationes Anatomicae* (published in 1562), which corrected a number of widely held false ideas about anatomy.

contain an ovum. During childbearing years, one of these graafian follicles produces a mature ovum during the first half of each menstrual cycle.

Her hormones

At puberty, the ovaries release **progesterone** and the female sex hormone **estrogen.** They also release a mature egg during the menstrual cycle. When expelled from the ovary, ova are caught by the fimbriated ends of the fallopian tubes.

The ovarian cycle

The Latin word ***menstrualis*** means *monthly.* The average **menstrual cycle** occurs over 28 days, roughly 1 month. Regulated by fluctuating, reciprocating hormones, this monthly cycle is divided into three phases: menstrual, proliferative, and luteal.

Phase I—stimulate

The **menstrual,** or **preovulatory,** phase begins on the first day of menstruation. As the cycle begins, low estrogen and progesterone levels in the bloodstream stimulate the hypothalamus to secrete **gonadotropin-releasing hormone.** In turn, this substance stimulates the anterior pituitary gland to secrete FSH and LH. When FSH level rises, LH output increases.

Mensis is the Latin word for *month.* It's closely related to the English word **moon,** which has a monthly cycle, too.

Phase II—proliferate and ovulate

The **proliferative,** or **follicular,** phase lasts from day 6 to day 14. During this time, LH and FSH act on the ovarian follicle containing the ovum and stimulate estrogen secretion. After 14 days, estrogen production decreases, the follicle matures, and ovulation occurs. Normally, one follicle matures and is released from the ovary during each cycle.

Luteal phase—going down

During the **luteal phase,** which lasts about 14 days, FSH and LH levels drop. Estrogen levels decline at first. After the follicle ruptures and produces progesterone, the yellow structure called the ***corpus luteum*** (Latin for *yellow body*) begins to function, and estrogen and progesterone levels rise.

During this phase, the endometrium responds to progesterone by becoming thicker and preparing to nourish a fertilized ovum. About 10 to 12 days after ovulation, the corpus luteum diminishes as progesterone and estrogen levels drop. When a fertilized ovum isn't present and hormone levels can't sustain the thickened endometrium, the lining is shed. The process of shedding the lining is known as **menses.**

Lactos is Latin for *milk.* ***Genesis*** is a Greek word that means *creation.* Put it together and you can tell that **lactogenesis** means *milk production.*

Fat-free

Breasts

The **mammary glands,** or **breasts,** are milk-producing structures. Breast development is controlled by estrogen and progesterone, hormones secreted by the ovaries. Each breast contains ducts surrounded by **acini** (milk-secreting cells). Individual ducts join with others to form larger ducts, which encircle the **nipple** and end in tiny openings on the nipple surface. The anterior lobe of the pituitary gland produces a lactogenic hormone called **prolactin** to stimulate **lactogenesis** (milk production).

The **areola** is the pigmented area (in Latin, the word means *a little open space*) around the nipple. (See *The female breast*, page 230.)

Menopause

Most women cease menstruation between ages 40 and 55. The term **menopause** applies if a menstrual period hasn't occurred for 1 year. **Climacteric** refers to a woman's transition from reproductive fertility to infertility. This transitional phase can occur over a period of several years and is also referred to as **perimenopause.**

At the onset of menopause, estrogen and progesterone levels begin to decrease and testosterone secretion increases. The body compensates for estrogen deficiency by producing **estrone,** a weaker form of estrogen.

The female breast

Here's a closer look at terms related to the female breast.

Structures of the female breast

The **areola**—the pigmented area in the center of the breast—contains the **nipple.** Pigmented erectile tissue in the nipple responds to cold, friction, and sexual stimulation. The interior of each breast is composed of glandular and fibrous tissues. Glandular tissue contains 15 to 20 lobes made up of clustered **acini,** tiny saclike duct terminals that secrete milk. Fibrous **Cooper's ligaments** support the breasts.

Milk production and drainage

Acini draw the ingredients needed to make milk from the blood in surrounding capillaries. **Lactiferous ducts** and **sinuses** store milk during lactation, conveying it to and through the nipples.

Glands on the areolar surface, called **Montgomery's tubercles,** produce sebum that lubricates the areola and nipple during breastfeeding.

Lateral cross section

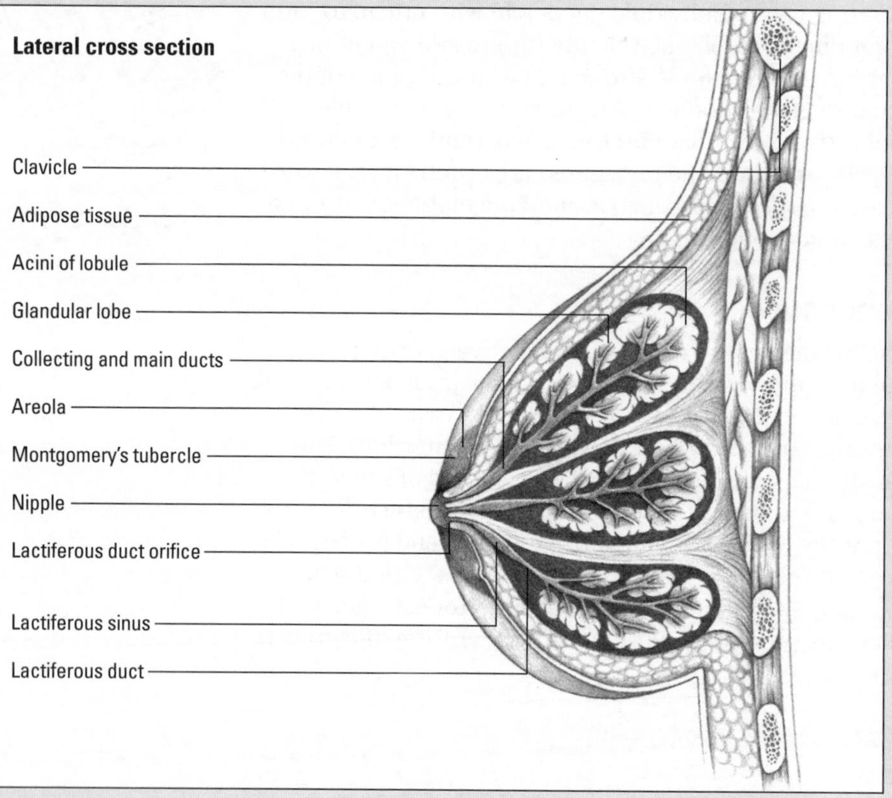
Clavicle
Adipose tissue
Acini of lobule
Glandular lobe
Collecting and main ducts
Areola
Montgomery's tubercle
Nipple
Lactiferous duct orifice
Lactiferous sinus
Lactiferous duct

Take a closer look at the body's milk-producing system.

Physical examination terms

Here are terms associated with physical examination of the male and female reproductive systems:

- **Anorchism** is the absence of one or two testes.
- **Anovulation** is the absence of ovulation
- **Azoospermia** is semen without live sperm.
- **Ballottement** is a physical examination hand manuever used to evaluate the shape and size of a deep structure or organ.
- **Bimanual examination** is the palpation of the uterus and ovaries using gloved fingers inside the vagina and the other hand outside of the body on the pelvic area.
- **Coitus** is sexual union.
- **Detumesence** is the subsiding of blood-engorged tissue after orgasm.
- **Digital rectal exam** is the examination of the prostate using a gloved finger inserted into the rectum.
- **Dysmenorrhea** refers to painful menstruation. This occurs at least occasionally in nearly all women. (See *Dissecting* dysmenorrhea *and more.*)
- **Dyspareunia** is a condition in women in which sexual intercourse is difficult or painful.
- **Frigidity** is the lack of sexual response.
- **Gynecology** is the branch of medicine concerned with the health care of women, including sexual and reproductive functions and diseases of the reproductive organs.

Beyond the dictionary

Dissecting *dysmenorrhea* and more

Dysmenorrhea means *painful menstruation.* The term is easier to remember if you dissect it. ***Dys-*** means *difficult or painful.* ***Meno*** literally means *monthly* and refers to menstruation. The third element, ***-rrhea,*** another common Greek word element, means *flow.* So, **dysmenorrhea** is painful menstrual flow.

One root, many terms

Add a few different letters to ***meno*** and you can describe other types of menstrual flow, such as:

- **amenorrhea** (***a-*** means *absence;* amenorrhea is, thus, an *absence of menstrual flow*)
- **menorrhagia** (***-rhagia*** derives from a Greek verb meaning *to burst out* and describes an excessive flow; menorrhagia is, thus, *profuse menstruation*)
- **menostasis** (***-stasis*** means *stoppage*, so this word has the same meaning as amenorrhea)
- **oligomenorrhea** (***oligo-*** means *scant* or *little*, so oligomenorrhea is *scant menstrual flow* or *scant menstruation*).

- **Gynecomastia** is abnormal enlargement or development of the male breast.
- **Hypospadias** is the opening of the male urethra on the underside of the penis.
- **Infertile** means a diminished capacity to produce offspring. An infertile man or woman isn't necessarily sterile.
- **Introitus** is the entrance into a canal such as the vagina.
- **Leukorrhea** is a white or yellowish discharge from the vagina.
- **Libido** is sexual desire.
- **Lithotomy position** is a supine position with the hips and knees fully flexed. It's used to perform female internal pelvic examinations.
- **Mastalgia** is pain in the breast.
- **Menarche** is the time when the first menstrual cycle begins.
- **Metrorrhagia** is abnormal uterine bleeding, especially between menstrual periods.
- **Orgasm** is the climax of sexual excitement.
- **Priapism** is a persistent, abnormal erection of the penis that isn't accompanied by sexual desire.
- **Rectovaginal palpation** is the examination of the posterior portion of the uterus and pelvic cavity by simultaneously inserting a gloved finger into the rectum and vagina.
- **Speculum** is an instrument used to enlarge the vaginal canal opening during a female pelvic examination.
- **Sterile** means that the patient is unable to reproduce due to an abnormality, such as the absence of spermatogenesis in a man or fallopian tube blockage in a woman.
- **Supernumerary nipples** are more than one nipple located on a breast.

Leukorrhea is a white discharge— that makes sense. ***Leuk*** is Greek for *white* and ***-rrhea*** means *flow.*
white

Diagnostic tests

Diagnostic tests associated with the reproductive system include blood and fluid tests as well as radiologic and other imaging procedures.

Blood and fluid tests

Here are some common blood and fluid tests associated with the reproductive system:

- A **darkfield examination** is a microscopic test of fluid taken from a lesion in suspected primary syphilis. A special microscope makes the syphilis organism appear bright against a dark background (therefore, the term **darkfield**).
- A **Papanicolaou (Pap) smear** is widely used for early detection of cervical cancer and inflammatory tissue changes. (See *Pap smear.*)
- A **prostate-specific antigen (PSA)** blood test is used to detect increases in PSA, a normally occurring substance that can indicate prostate disease.
- The **prostatic acid phosphatase test** measures the level of phosphatase enzymes, usually found in the prostate. Above-normal levels are suspicious for prostate cancer.
- **Semen analysis** is an examination of seminal fluid to evaluate male fertility. The procedure includes measuring the volume of seminal fluid, counting sperm, and performing microscopic examination.
- A **serum alpha-fetoprotein (AFP)** study measures the glycoprotein AFP. An above-normal level may indicate testicular cancer. In a fetus, an above-normal level may indicate a neural tube defect.
- In a **urine culture,** a common culture medium is used to detect infectious microorganisms in urine.
- A **Venereal Disease Research Laboratory (VDRL)** test confirms a diagnosis of syphilis.

The real world

Pap smear

What everyone commonly refers to as a **Pap smear** or **Pap test** is formally called a **Papanicolaou test**.

It was named after George Papanicolaou (1883-1962), a Greek doctor who immigrated to the United States and developed the test.

Radiologic and other imaging procedures

Here are some common radiologic and other imaging procedures associated with the reproductive system:

- During **colposcopy,** the examiner studies the vulva, cervix, and vagina with a **colposcope,** an instrument containing a magnifying lens and light.
- **Hysterosalpingography** allows visualization of the uterine cavity, the fallopian tubes, and the peritubal area. (See *Making sense of* hysterosalpingography, page 234.)

Beyond the dictionary

Making sense of *hysterosalpingography*

The Greek word ***hystero*** means *uterus*. ***Salpingo*** is the Greek term for *fallopian tube*, and ***-graphy*** is the term for *a recording.* So, **hysterosalpingography** means *examination of the uterus and fallopian tubes.*

Sometimes the Greeks got it wrong
Hysteros, the Greek word for the *uterus* or *womb,* also provided the root for another Greek word: ***hysteria.*** It seems the ancient Greeks had the notion that only women became extremely emotionally upset. They attributed this perceived difference from men to the presence of the uterus.

- **Laparoscopy** allows visual inspection of organs in the peritoneal cavity by inserting a fiber-optic telescope **(laparoscope)** through the abdominal wall.
- A **mammogram** uses low-dose X-rays to detect breast malignancies and evaluate masses.
- A **pelvic ultrasound** passes sound waves through the pelvic area, creating electronic images of internal structures. This test can help to diagnose pelvic disease or examine a developing fetus.
- **Sentinel node biopsy** uses radionuclide imaging to identify the first lymph node to receive drainage from a tumor. It's used in breast tumors and melanoma.
- **Transrectal ultrasound** of the prostate is a scan of the prostate performed by placing an ultrasound transducer into the rectum and imaging through the rectal wall. It may also be used to guide a biopsy of the prostate.
- **Urethrogram** is an X-ray of the prostate and urethra.

Disorders

Common disorders associated with the reproductive system are usually gender specific. Sexually transmitted diseases (STDs), however, can affect either gender.

Female reproductive disorders

PMS always makes me feel fat and irritable.

Here are some common disorders associated with the female reproductive system:

- **Dermoid cysts** are generally benign ovarian cysts consisting of displaced embryonic tissue.
- **Endometriosis** refers to a condition in which endometrial tissue appears outside the lining of the uterine cavity.
- **Oligo-ovulation** is irregular ovulation.
- **Ovarian cysts** are noncancerous sacs containing fluid or semisolid material.
- **Pelvic inflammatory disease (PID)** is an infection of the oviducts and ovaries.
- **Premenstrual syndrome (PMS)** is characterized by varying symptoms appearing 7 to 10 days before menses and usually subsiding with its onset. The effects of PMS range from minimal discomfort to severe disruptive symptoms that can include nervousness, irritability, depression, and multiple somatic complaints.
- **Rectovaginal fistula** is an abnormal communication (passage) between the vagina and the rectum.
- **Salpingitis** is inflammation of a fallopian tube.
- **Uterine leiomyomas,** also called **myomas, fibromyomas,** or **fibroids,** are the most common **neoplasms** (tumors) occurring among women. They're usually found in the uterus or cervix.
- **Vaginismus** is an involuntary, spastic constriction of the lower vaginal muscles.
- **Vesicovaginal fistula** is an abnormal communication between the vagina and the bladder.

Male reproductive disorders

Here are some common disorders associated with the male reproductive system:

- **Cryptorchidism** is a condition in which one or both testes fail to descend into the scrotum and remain in the abdomen, in the **inguinal** canal, or at the external inguinal ring.
- **Epididymitis** is inflammation of the epididymis.
- **Peyronie disease** is the buildup of fibrous tissue in the corpus cavernosum that causes a curvature of the penis and pain that worsens with erection.

• **Premature ejaculation** refers to a man's inability to control the ejaculatory reflex during intercourse, resulting in persistently early ejaculation.
• **Prostatitis** refers to a chronic inflammation of the prostate gland, usually from infection.

Impotence

Impotence is also known as **erectile dysfunction.** A man with this problem can't attain or maintain sufficient penile erection to complete intercourse. There are two types of impotence:
• **primary impotence,** in which the patient has never been able to achieve a sufficient erection to complete intercourse
• **secondary impotence,** in which the patient has succeeded in completing intercourse in the past.

Testicular torsion is abnormal twisting of the spermatic cord that's caused by rotation of the testes.

Testicular torsion

Testicular torsion is abnormal twisting of the spermatic cord that's caused by rotation of the testis. Two types of testicular torsion are:
• **extravaginal torsion,** caused by loose attachment of the tunica to the scrotal lining which, in turn, causes spermatic cord rotation above the testis.
• **intravaginal torsion,** resulting from an abnormal tunica or from narrowing of the muscular support. Normally, the tunica vaginalis envelops the testis and attaches to the epididymis and spermatic cord; in intravaginal torsion, testicular twisting may result from an anomaly of the tunica in which the testis is abnormally positioned or from narrowing of the muscular support.

Other reproductive disorders

Here are some other common reproductive disorders:
• **Adenomyosis of the uterus** is a condition in which endometrial tissue invades the muscular layer of the uterus.
• **Benign prostatic hyperplasia** refers to an enlargement of the prostate gland.
• In **hematocele,** blood collects in a body cavity, such as the scrotum, testis, or pelvis.
• **Hydrocele** is a collection of clear fluid in a testis.

• **Hyperplasia of the endometrium** is the overdevelopment of the uterine lining.
• **Mastitis** is an inflammation of the mammary glands that commonly occurs with breast-feeding.
• **Oligospermia** is a condition in which the amount of sperm in semen is low.
• **Phimosis** is a constriction of the foreskin over the penis that makes it unable to be drawn back over the glans.
• **Precocious puberty** is the early onset of pubertal changes, such as breast development and menstruation before age 9 (in females). Males with the disorder begin to sexually mature before age 10.
• **Prolapse of the uterus** is the protrusion of the uterus thought the vaginal opening.
• **Pruritus vulvae** is intense itching of the vulva.
• **Salpingocele** is a hernial protrusion of the fallopian tube. (See *Salpingocele story.*)
• **Spermatocele** is a cyst containing sperm cells that occurs near the epididymis.
• A **varicocele** is an abnormal condition characterized by dilation of the veins of the spermatic cord.

Beyond the dictionary

Salpingocele story

Salpingocele is a herniation of the fallopian tube. The Greek word ***salpinex,*** for *trumpet* (a tubular instrument), gives us ***salpingo-,*** which refers to the fallopian tubes. The ***-cele*** means *cavity* and, thus, refers to a hernia.

Sexually transmitted diseases

Here are the names of some common STDs and conditions that accompany them:
• **Chancroid,** also called **soft chancre,** is a venereal disorder marked by painful genital ulcers and inguinal lymph node inflammation.
• **Chlamydia** is the most common STD in the United States. This group of infections—which includes **urethritis** (inflammation of the urethra) in men and urethritis and **cervicitis** (cervical inflammation) in women—is linked to the *Chlamydia trachomatis* organism.
• **Genital herpes,** also known as **herpes simplex virus, herpes type 2,** or **venereal herpes,** is an acute, inflammatory infection that causes fluid-filled vesicles on the genitalia. The vesicles rupture and develop into shallow, painful ulcers.
• **Genital warts,** also called **condylomata acuminata,** consist of painless **papillomas** (noncancerous skin tumors) with fibrous tissue overgrowth that commonly have a cauliflower-like appearance.

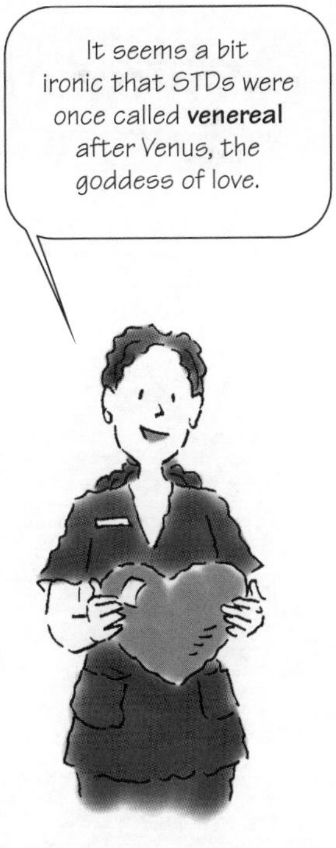
It seems a bit ironic that STDs were once called **venereal** after Venus, the goddess of love.

• **Gonorrhea** is a common disease caused by the *Neisseria gonorrhoeae* organism. This STD typically affects the urethra and cervix.
• **Syphilis** is a chronic, infectious STD that begins in the mucous membranes and quickly moves through the body by spreading to nearby lymph nodes and the bloodstream. The untreated disease process has four stages:

Primary syphilis occurs within 3 weeks of original contact. Patients may develop lymph node tenderness and **chancres** (small sores) on the body.

Secondary syphilis occurs from a few days to 8 weeks after the appearance of sores. Patients develop a rash, white lesions, and flulike symptoms.

Latent syphilis is characterized by an absence of symptoms.

Late syphilis, also called **tertiary syphilis,** involves other organs, such as those in the cardiovascular and central nervous systems.
• **Trichomoniasis** is a protozoal infection of the lower urinary tract and reproductive system.

Treatments and procedures

Here are terms related to surgeries and other treatments of the male and female reproductive systems:
• **Artificial insemination** is the placement of seminal fluid into the patient's vaginal canal or cervix. The procedure is coordinated with ovulation.
• A **cervicectomy** is removal of the cervix.
• **Circumcision** is the removal of all or part of the **prepuce** (foreskin) of the glans penis.
• In **dilatation and curettage (D&C),** a doctor dilatates (expands) the cervix to access the endocervix and uterus. A **curette** (an instrument with sharp edges) is used to scrape away endometrial tissue. (See *Just say "D&C."*)
• In **dilatation and evacuation,** suction is used to remove the uterine contents. This procedure is typically used to perform elective abortions.

The real world

Just say "D&C"

In the "real world," **dilatation** of the uterine cervix and **curettage** of the endometrium is known as a "D and C." A **dilatation and evacuation,** in which suction is used to remove the uterine contents, is referred to as a "D and E."

• With **in vitro fertilization,** an ovum is removed from the body and fertilized with sperm in a laboratory culture medium. The resulting embryo is then transferred into the woman's uterus.
• **Kegel exercises** are performed by contracting and relaxing the perineal muscles in order to strengthen the pelvic floor muscles. Kegel exercises are helpful in treating female urinary incontinence.
• In a **laparoscopy,** surgical instruments are inserted through a laparoscope to remove small lesions or perform other diagnostic and therapeutic procedures.
• A **laparotomy** is a surgical incision through the abdomen made to provide access to the peritoneal cavity.
• **Oophorectomy** is excision of one or both ovaries. Bilateral oophorectomy results in surgically induced menopause in women who are still in the reproductive phase of life.
• An **orchiectomy** is removal of one of the testes.
• **Orchiopexy** is the fixation of an undescended testis in the scrotum.
• **Penile prosthesis** is an implanted device used to provide penile erection.
• **Tubal ligation** is the interruption of both fallopian tubes to prevent conception.
• **Vasectomy** is excision of the vas deferens. When done bilaterally, this results in sterility.
• **Vasovasotomy** is the restoration of the vas deferens after a vasectomy in order to regain fertility.

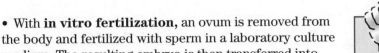

Memory jogger

Both "laparoscopy" and "laparotomy" are surgical procedures, but to help distinguish their meanings remember that lapar**oscop**y involves using a "scope" (laparoscope) and *lapa*ro**tomy** involves a surgical incision through the "tummy."

Hysterectomy

Hysterectomy is removal of the uterus. There are four types:
• **Total hysterectomy,** also called a **panhysterectomy,** is removal of all female reproductive organs, including the uterus, cervix, fallopian tubes, and ovaries. It's called a panhysterectomy because a rectangular "pan" is used during surgery to collect all the excised organs.
• **Subtotal hysterectomy** is removal of only part of the uterus. The cervix is left intact.
• **Radical hysterectomy** is removal of all of the reproductive organs and supporting structures.
• **Vaginal hysterectomy** is excision of the uterus through the vagina.

Remember, the word **hystero-** means *uterus* and **-ectomy** means *surgical removal.* Therefore, a **hysterectomy** is removal of the uterus.

systole

Vocabulary builders

At a crossroads

Completing this crossword puzzle will help you produce the correct terms for the reproductive system. Good luck!

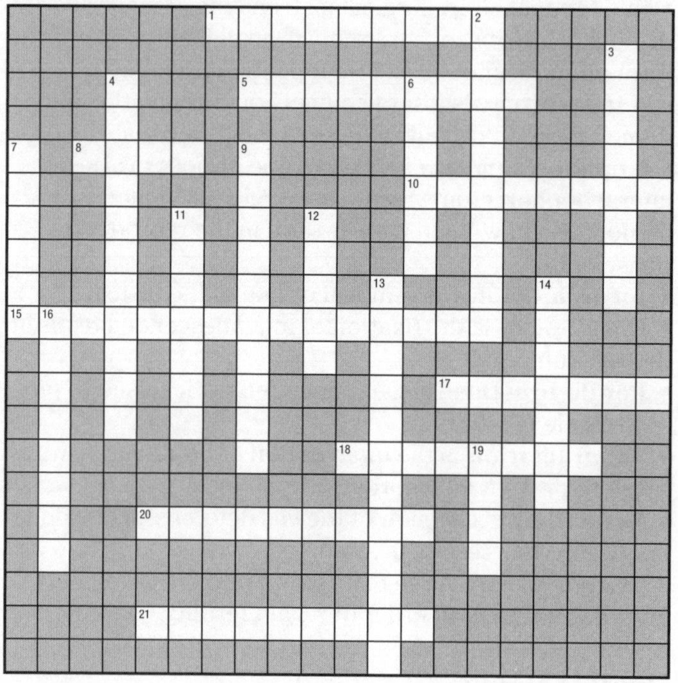

Across

1. Erectile dysfunction
5. Lactogenic hormone
8. Abbreviation for a venereal disease test
10. Visible female genitals
15. Sperm formation
17. Hormone produced after menopause
18. Female sex hormone
20. Two egg-shaped glands within the scrotum
21. Male sex hormones

Down

2. A duct system in the testes
3. An instrument used to enlarge the vaginal canal opening during a female pelvic examination
4. Lining of the uterus
6. Main body of the uterus
7. Upper uterus
9. The abnormal dilation of the veins of the spermatic cord
11. Mammary glands
12. Tissue covering the vaginal opening
13. Male sex hormone
14. Two almond-shaped female organs
16. Area between the anus and the vulva
19. Female sex cell

Answers are on page 242.

Match game

Match each description of a reproductive disorder or condition to its name.

Clues	Choices
1. Testicular torsion _____	A. Constriction of the foreskin
2. Endometriosis _____	B. Enlargement of the male breast
3. Leiomyoma _____	C. Fibroid tumor
4. Trichomoniasis _____	D. Ectopic uterine tissue
5. Papillomas _____	E. Genital warts
6. Gynecomastia _____	F. Twisting of the spermatic cord
7. Phimosis _____	G. Protozoal infection

Finish line

Fill in the blanks below with the appropriate word(s).

1. Each _______ ______ is enclosed by a spermatic cord.
2. _________ stimulates milk production.
3. Surgical removal of the uterus is called a ________.
4. A procedure to visualize pelvic organs is called a _______.
5. The process of uniting a sperm and an egg in a culture dish is known as _________ fertilization.
6. The process of instilling seminal fluid into a patient's vaginal canal is called ________ insemination.
7. An ________ is surgical removal of one of the testes.

Answers are on page 242.

Answers

At a crossroads

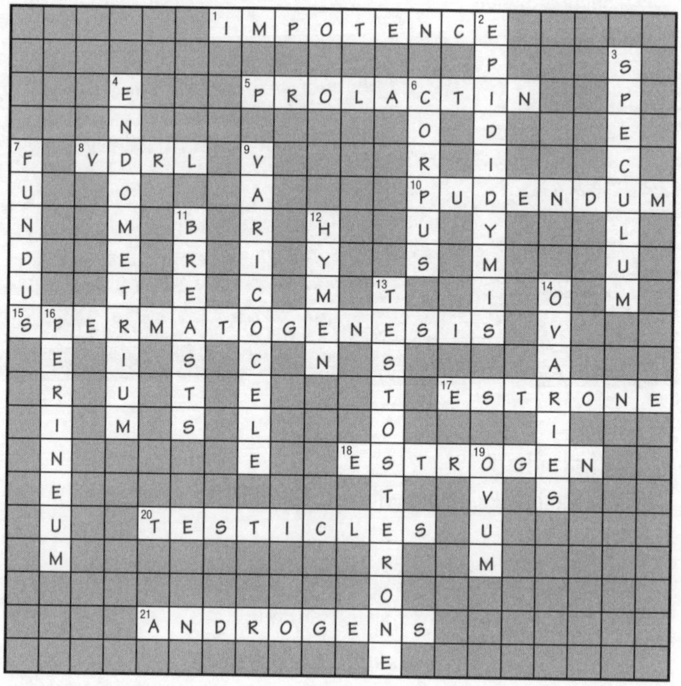
1 IMPOTENCE
2 EPIDIDYMIS
3 SPECULUM
4 ENDOMETRIUM
5 PROLACTIN
6 CORPUS
7 FUNDUS
8 VDRL
9 VARICOCELE
10 PUDENDUM
11 BREASTS
12 HYMEN
13 TESTOSTERONE
14 OVARIES
15 SPERMATOGENESIS
16 PERINEUM
17 ESTRONE
18 ESTROGEN
19 OVUM
20 TESTICLES
21 ANDROGENS

Match game

1. F; 2. D; 3. C; 4. G; 5. E; 6. B; 7. A

Finish line

1. Vas deferens; 2. Prolactin; 3. Hysterectomy; 4. Laparoscopy; 5. In vitro; 6. Artificial; 7. Orchiectomy

11

Maternal health

Just the facts

In this chapter, you'll learn:

- terminology related to pregnancy and fetal development
- terminology needed for physical examination of the pregnant woman and her fetus
- tests that help diagnose common pregnancy-related problems
- pregnancy-related disorders and their treatments.

Pregnancy-related structures and functions

Pregnancy results when a female's egg and a male's sperm unite. This chapter focuses on the terminology associated with pregnancy. (See *Pronouncing key maternal health terms*, page 244.)

Conception

Pregnancy begins with **conception,** also called **fertilization.** Conception occurs when an ovum in the fallopian tube is penetrated by a **spermatozoon** (sperm cell). The spermatozoon and the ovum unite to form a single new cell.

Only the strong survive

Although a single ejaculation deposits several hundred million spermatozoa, many are destroyed by acidic vaginal secretions. However, when spermatozoa enter the

Pump up your pronunciation

Pronouncing key maternal health terms

Below is a list of key terms related to maternal health along with the correct way to pronounce them.

Abruptio placentae	UHB-RUHP-SHEE-OH PLAH-SEN-TAY
Amenorrhea	AH-MEN-OR-REE-UH
Ballottement	BAHL-OT-MAW
Conception	KON-CEP-SHUHN
Epididymis	EP-UH-DID-UH-MISS
Fertilization	FER-TIL-UH-ZAY-SHUHN
Gestation	JES-TAY-SHUHN
Lochia	LOH-KEE-AH
Placenta	PLAH-SEN-TAH
Zygote	ZIGH-GOTE

cervical canal they're able to survive because cervical mucus protects them. Spermatozoa are typically viable (able to fertilize the ovum) for up to 2 days after ejaculation, but they can survive in the reproductive tract for up to 4 days.

Movin' right along

Spermatozoa travel through the female reproductive tract by means of **flagellar** movements (whiplike movements of the tail). After spermatozoa pass through the cervical mucus, however, the female reproductive system assists them on their journey with rhythmic uterine contractions that help them penetrate the fallopian tubes.

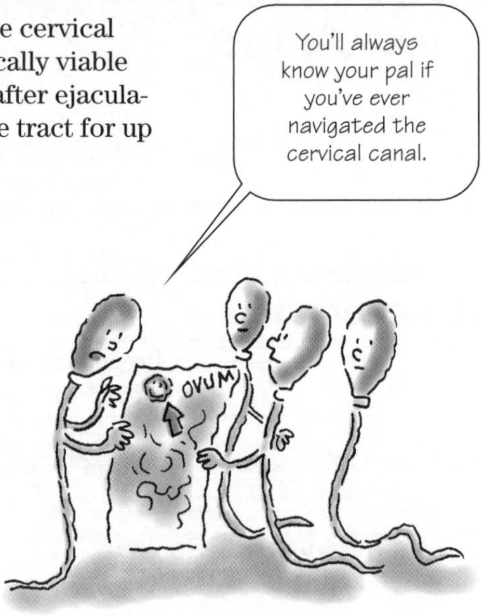
You'll always know your pal if you've ever navigated the cervical canal.
OVUM

Break on through to the other side

Before a spermatozoon can penetrate the ovum, it must disperse the ovum's granulosa cells (estrogen-producing cells) and penetrate the **zona pellucida,** the thick, transparent layer surrounding the incompletely developed ovum. Enzymes in the spermatozoon's **acrosome** (head cap) permit this penetration.

Divide and fuse

After penetration, the ovum completes its second meiotic division and the zona pellucida prevents penetration by other spermatozoa. The spermatozoon's head then fuses with the ovum nucleus, creating a cell nucleus with 46 chromosomes. (See *How fertilization occurs*, page 246.)

Plant me and watch me grow

The fertilized ovum, or **zygote,** immediately forms a rounded mass of cells and travels from the fallopian tube to the uterus. In the uterus, it implants itself in the uterine lining and begins growing.

Gestation

Gestation, or the period of pregnancy that begins with conception and ends with childbirth, typically lasts 38 to 40 weeks. During this time, the zygote divides continuously, and a complex sequence of pre-embryonic, embryonic, and fetal developments transforms the zygote into a full-term fetus.

Sizing it up

Because the uterus grows throughout pregnancy, uterine size serves as a rough estimate of gestation. However, the expected delivery date is typically calculated from the beginning of the pregnant woman's last menses using **Nägele's rule:**

First day of the last menstrual period – 3 months + 7 days = estimated date of birth.

Because the fertilization date is rarely known, a woman's expected delivery date is typically calculated using **Nägele's rule.**
S M T W T F S

Anatomically speaking

How fertilization occurs

Fertilization begins when the spermatozoon is activated upon contact with the ovum. Here's what happens.

The **spermatozoon,** which has a covering called the **acrosome,** approaches the **ovum.**

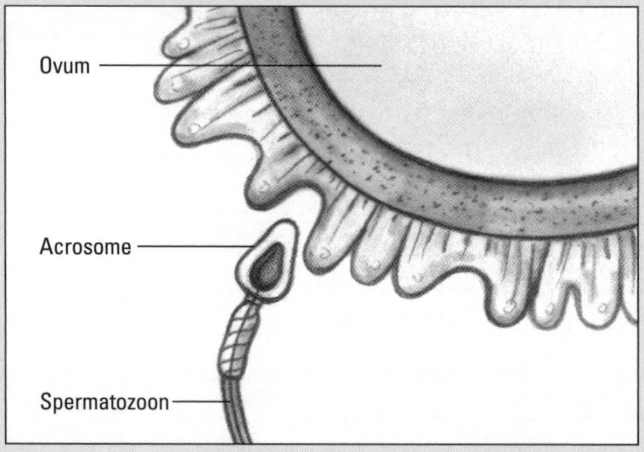
Ovum
Acrosome
Spermatozoon

The acrosome develops small perforations through which it releases enzymes necessary for the sperm to penetrate the protective layers of the ovum before fertilization.

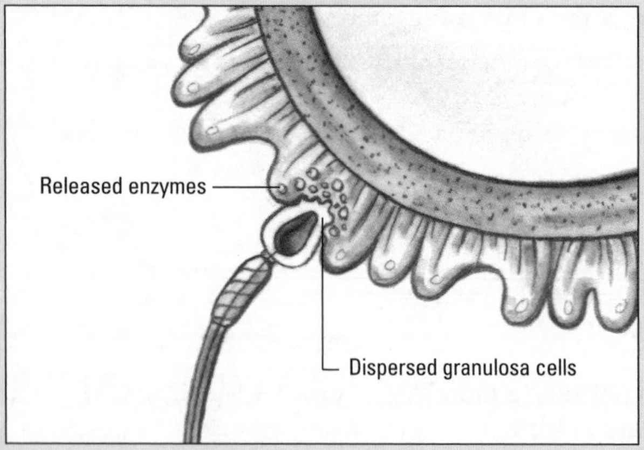
Released enzymes
Dispersed granulosa cells

The spermatozoon then penetrates the **zona pellucida** (the inner membrane of the ovum). This movement triggers the ovum's second meiotic division (following meiosis), making the zona pellucida impenetrable to other spermatozoa.

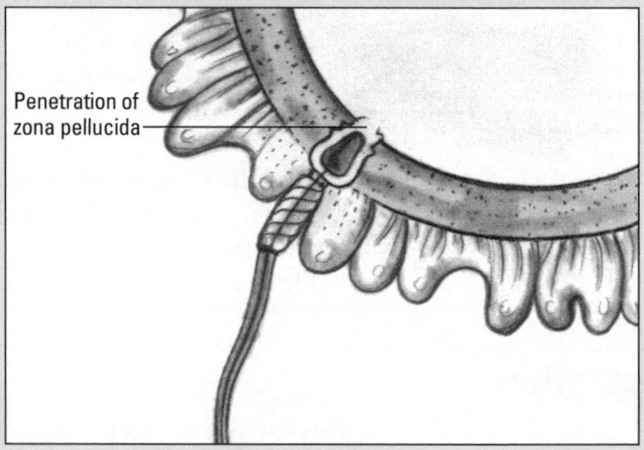
Penetration of zona pellucida

After the spermatozoon penetrates the ovum, its nucleus is released into the ovum, its tail degenerates, and its head enlarges and fuses with the ovum's nucleus. This fusion provides the fertilized ovum, called a **zygote,** with 46 chromosomes.

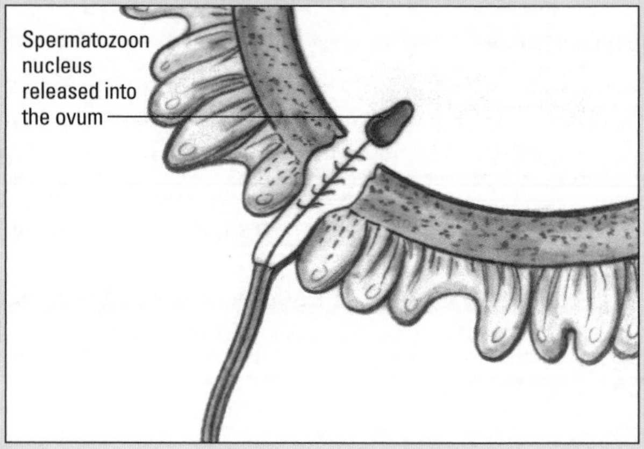
Spermatozoon nucleus released into the ovum

Fetal development

How did I get my start? Well, it all began in the pre-embryonic period...

During pregnancy, the fetus undergoes three major stages of development:

- **pre-embryonic period** (the first 3 weeks after fertilization)
- **embryonic period** (weeks 2 to 8)
- **fetal period** (end of week 8 through birth).

Pre-embryonic period

The pre-embryonic period starts with ovum fertilization and lasts about 3 weeks. As the zygote passes through the fallopian tube, it undergoes a series of mitotic divisions, or **cleavage.** (See *Pre-embryonic development*, page 248.)

Embryonic period

During the **embryonic period** (beginning at the end of the second week through the eighth week of gestation), the developing zygote starts to take on a human shape and is now called an **embryo.** The growing embryo floats within the **amnion,** a thin, clear sac filled with **amniotic** fluid. Early in this period, the **chorion,** or outer cells of the rounded cell mass, joins with the endometrium to form the **placenta.** This vital structure provides nutrients for and removes wastes from the embryo via the chorion and the embryo's **umbilical cord.**

Layer up

During the embryonic period, three germ layers develop. Each germ layer—the **ectoderm, mesoderm,** and **endoderm**—eventually forms specific tissues in the embryo. (See *Embryonic development*, page 249.)

All systems go!

Organ systems form during the embryonic period. During this time, the embryo is particularly vulnerable to injury from such factors as maternal drug use and certain maternal infections.

(Text continues on page 250.)

Anatomically speaking

Pre-embryonic development

The pre-embryonic period lasts from conception until about the end of the third week of development.

Zygote formation...

As the fertilized ovum advances through the fallopian tube toward the uterus, it undergoes mitotic division, forming daughter cells, initially called **blastomeres.** Each blastomere contains the same number of chromosomes as the parent cell. The first cell division ends about 30 hours after fertilization; subsequent divisions occur rapidly.

The **zygote,** as it's now called, develops into a small mass of cells called a ***morula,*** which reaches the uterus at about the third day after fertilization. Fluid that amasses in the center of the morula forms a central cavity.

...into blastocyst

The structure is now called a **blastocyst.** The blastocyst consists of a thin trophoblast layer, which includes the blastocyst cavity, and the inner cell mass. The trophoblast develops into fetal membranes and the placenta. The inner cell mass later forms the embryo **(late blastocyst).**

Getting attached: Blastocyst and endometrium

During the next phase, the blastocyst stays within the zona pellucida, unattached to the uterus. The zona pellucida degenerates and, by the end of the first week after fertilization, the blastocyst attaches to the endometrium. The part of the blastocyst adjacent to the inner cell mass is the first part to become attached.

The trophoblast, in contact with the endometrial lining, proliferates and invades the underlying endometrium by separating and dissolving endometrial cells.

Letting it all sink in

During the next week, the invading blastocyst sinks below the endometrium's surface. The penetration site seals, restoring the continuity of the endometrial surface.

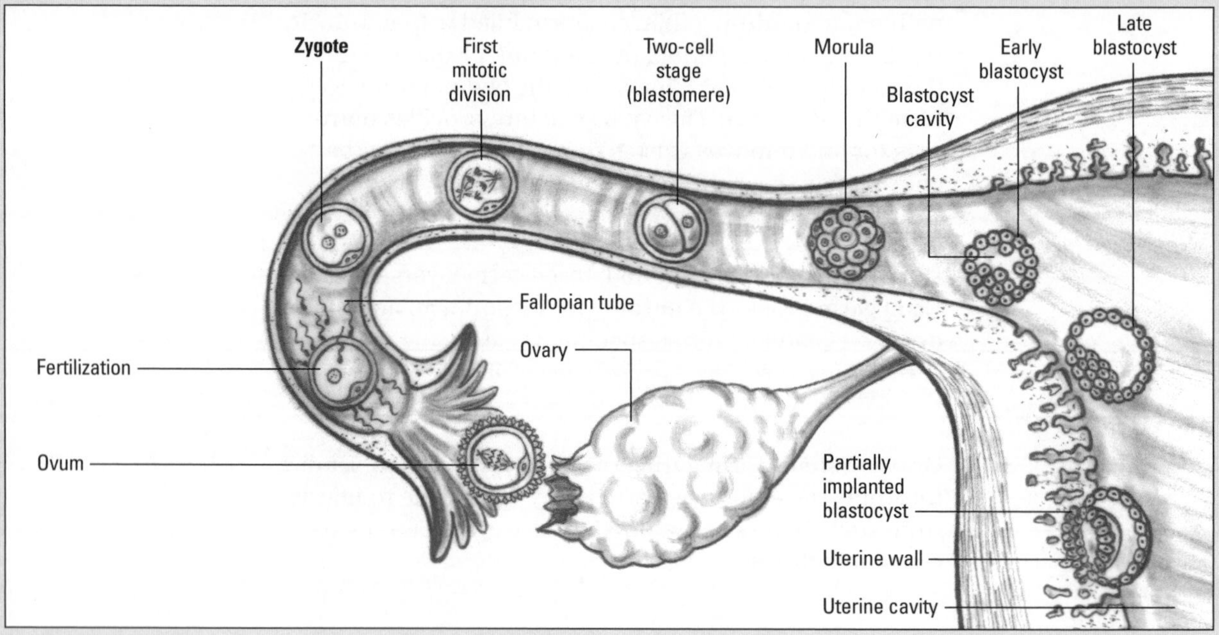
Zygote
First mitotic division
Two-cell stage (blastomere)
Morula
Early blastocyst
Late blastocyst
Blastocyst cavity
Fallopian tube
Ovary
Fertilization
Ovum
Partially implanted blastocyst
Uterine wall
Uterine cavity

Anatomically speaking

Embryonic development

Each of the three germ layers—ectoderm, mesoderm, and endoderm—forms specific tissues and organs in the developing embryo.

Ectoderm

The ectoderm, the outermost layer, develops into the:
- epidermis
- nervous system
- pituitary gland
- tooth enamel
- salivary glands
- optic lens
- lining of lower portion of anal canal
- hair.

Mesoderm

The mesoderm, the middle layer, develops into:
- connective and supporting tissue
- the blood and vascular system
- musculature
- teeth (except enamel)
- the mesothelial lining of pericardial, pleural, and peritoneal cavities
- the kidneys and ureters.

Endoderm

The endoderm, the innermost layer, becomes the epithelial lining of the:
- pharynx and trachea
- auditory canal
- alimentary canal
- liver
- pancreas
- bladder and urethra
- prostate.

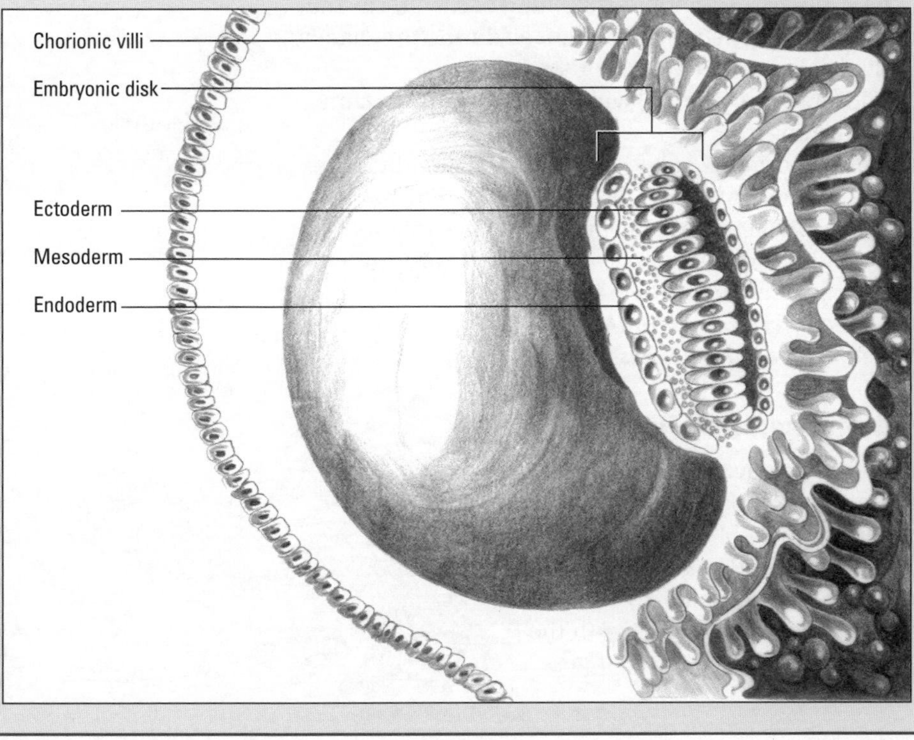
Chorionic villi
Embryonic disk
Ectoderm
Mesoderm
Endoderm

During the embryonic period, three germ layers develop—the **ectoderm, mesoderm,** and **endoderm.**

Fetal period

The fetal period lasts from the end of the eighth week until birth. During this period, the embryo enlarges, grows heavier, and becomes known as a **fetus.** The fetus's head is disproportionately large compared to its body at this time. (This feature changes after birth as the neonate grows.) The fetus also lacks subcutaneous fat. (Fat starts to accumulate shortly after birth.)

Structural changes related to pregnancy

Pregnancy changes the usual development of the corpus luteum and results in the development of these structures:

- decidua
- amniotic sac and fluid
- yolk sac
- placenta.

Decidua

The **decidua** is the endometrial lining of the uterus that undergoes hormone-induced changes during pregnancy. Decidual cells secrete these substances:

- the hormone **prolactin,** which promotes **lactation** (breast-feeding)
- a peptide hormone called **relaxin,** which induces relaxation of the connective tissue of the symphysis pubis and pelvic ligaments and promotes cervical dilation
- a potent hormonelike fatty acid, **prostaglandin,** which mediates several physiologic functions. (See *Development of the decidua and fetal membranes.*)

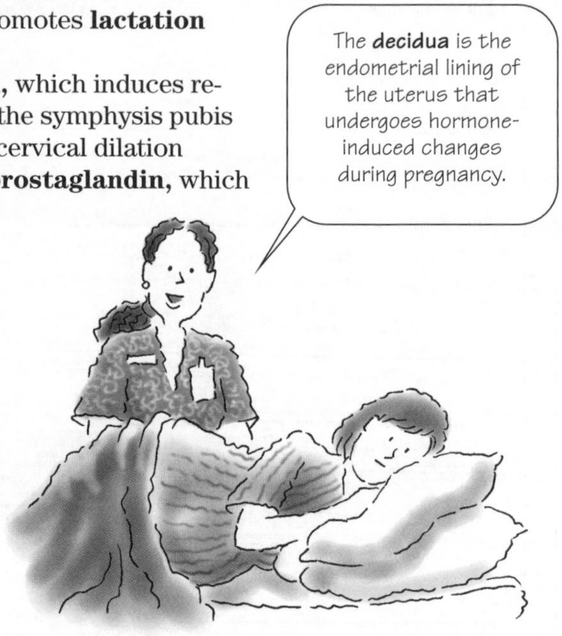
The **decidua** is the endometrial lining of the uterus that undergoes hormone-induced changes during pregnancy.

Amniotic sac and fluid

The **amniotic sac,** enclosed within the chorion, gradually grows and surrounds the embryo. As it enlarges, the amniotic sac expands into the chorionic cavity, eventually filling the cavity and fusing with the chorion by the eighth week of gestation.

Anatomically speaking

Development of the decidua and fetal membranes

Specialized tissues support, protect, and nurture the embryo and fetus throughout its development. Among these tissues are the decidua and fetal membranes, which begin to develop shortly after conception.

Decidua

During pregnancy, the endometrial lining is called the **decidua.** It provides a nesting place for the developing ovum and has some endocrine functions.

Based primarily on its position relative to the embryo, the decidua may be known as the **decidua basalis,** which lies beneath the chorionic vesicle; the **decidua capsularis,** which stretches over the vesicle; or the **decidua parietalis,** which lines the remainder of the endometrial cavity.

Fetal membranes

The **chorion** is a membrane that forms the outer wall of the blastocyst. Vascular projections, called **chorionic villi,** arise from its periphery. As the chorionic vesicle enlarges, villi arising from the superficial portion of the chorion, called the **chorion laeve,** atrophy, leaving this surface smooth. Villi arising from the deeper part of the chorion, called the **chorion frondosum,** proliferate, projecting into the large blood vessels within the decidua basalis through which the maternal blood flows.

Blood vessels that form within the growing villi become connected with blood vessels that form in the chorion, body stalk, and within the body of the embryo. Blood begins to flow through this developing network of vessels as soon as the embryo's heart starts to beat.

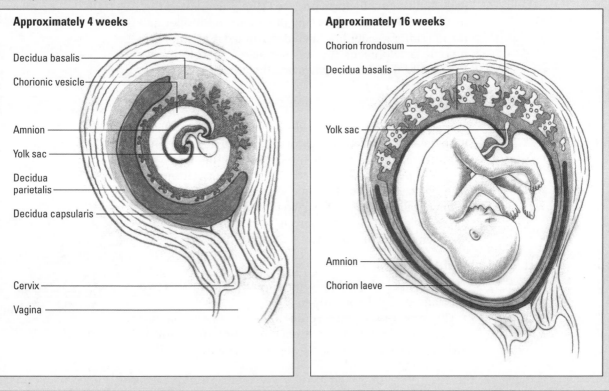

Approximately 4 weeks

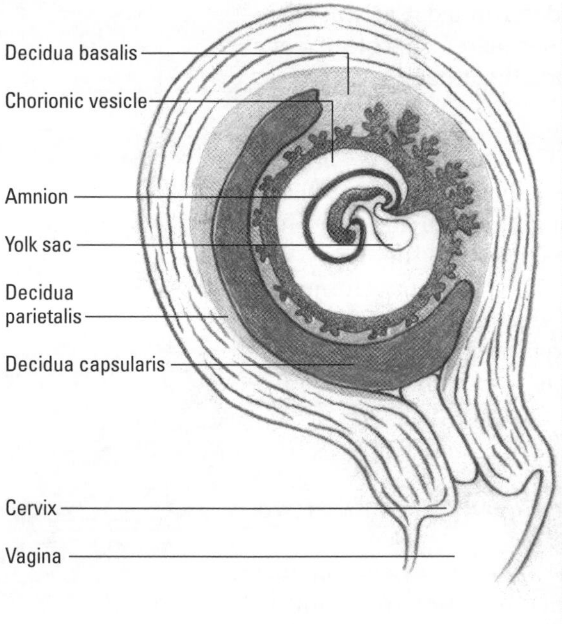
Decidua basalis
Chorionic vesicle
Amnion
Yolk sac
Decidua parietalis
Decidua capsularis
Cervix
Vagina

Approximately 16 weeks

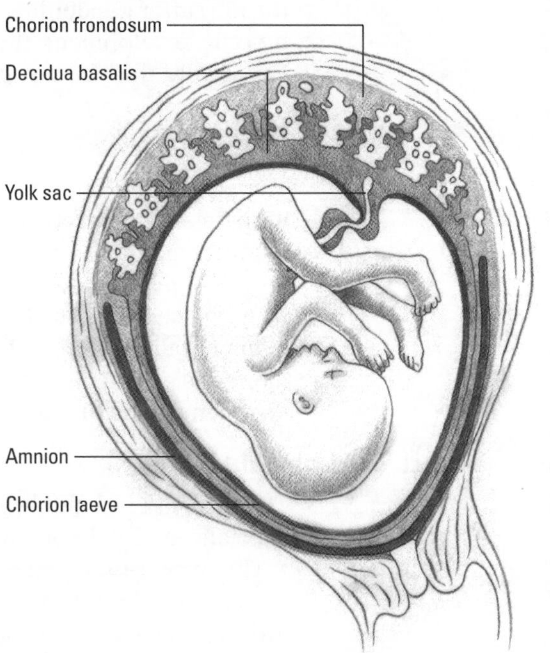
Chorion frondosum
Decidua basalis
Yolk sac
Amnion
Chorion laeve

Fluid facts

Ah! This is the life! This amniotic fluid is keeping me warm and buoyant. I may never want to leave!

Amniotic fluid comes from maternal and fetal sources. The amount of fluid in the amniotic sac is usually balanced with the amount lost through the fetal GI tract. The fluid is absorbed into the fetal circulation from the fetal GI tract; some of it's transferred from the fetal circulation to the maternal circulation and excreted in maternal urine.

Amniotic fluid serves the fetus in two ways. During gestation, the fluid gives the fetus a buoyant, temperature-controlled environment. Later, amniotic fluid serves as a fluid wedge that helps to open the cervix during birth.

Yolk sac

The **yolk sac** forms next to the endoderm. A portion of this sac incorporates into the developing embryo and forms the GI tract. Another portion of it develops into primitive germ cells, which travel to the developing gonads and eventually form **oocytes** (the precursor of the ovum) or **spermatocytes** (the precursor of the spermatozoon) after gender has been determined. Early in embryonic development, the yolk sac also forms blood cells. Eventually, this sac atrophies and disintegrates.

The placenta plays a key role in hormone production during pregnancy.

Placenta

The **placenta** is a flattened, disk-shaped structure that uses the umbilical cord as a conduit to provide nutrients to and remove wastes from the fetus from the third month of pregnancy until birth. The placenta is formed from the chorion, its chorionic villi, and the adjacent decidua basalis. It plays a key role in producing such hormones as estrogen, progesterone, and human placental lactogen during pregnancy.

Talkin' about two circulations

The placenta is a highly vascular organ and contains two specialized circulatory systems:

- The **uteroplacental circulation** carries oxygenated arterial blood from the maternal circulation to the **intervillous spaces** (large spaces separating chorionic villi in the placenta).

• The **fetoplacental circulation** transports oxygen-depleted blood from the fetus to the chorionic villi by the umbilical arteries and returns oxygenated blood to the fetus through the umbilical vein.

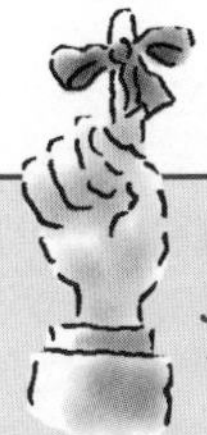

Memory jogger

To stay sharp on the phases of the first stage of labor, remember **E FLAT.**

Effacement

Latent phase

Active phase

Transition phase

Labor and birth

Labor is the process by which birth of the fetus is achieved. During this time, the cervix **dilates** and the uterus **contracts** to expel the fetus from the uterus.

Stages of labor

Labor is typically divided into four stages. The first stage, when **effacement** (thinning and shortening of the cervix) and dilation occur, begins with the onset of true uterine contractions and ends when the cervix is fully dilated. This stage may be further divided into three phases:

• **latent** phase, which begins with the onset of regular contractions; the cervix dilates from 0 to 3 cm and becomes fully effaced

• **active** phase, which is characterized by strong, regular, recurrent contractions, cervical dilation from 4 to 7 cm, and fetal descent through the pelvis

• **transition** phase, which is characterized by maximally intense uterine contractions, cervical dilation from 8 to 10 cm, and complete cervical effacement.

The stage is set

The other stages of labor are:

• second stage, which encompasses the actual birth; it begins when the cervix is fully dilated and ends with the birth of the **neonate**

• third stage, also called the **placental** stage, which begins immediately after the birth of the neonate and ends when the placenta is delivered

• fourth stage, which begins after delivery of the placenta; during this stage, homeostasis is reestablished.

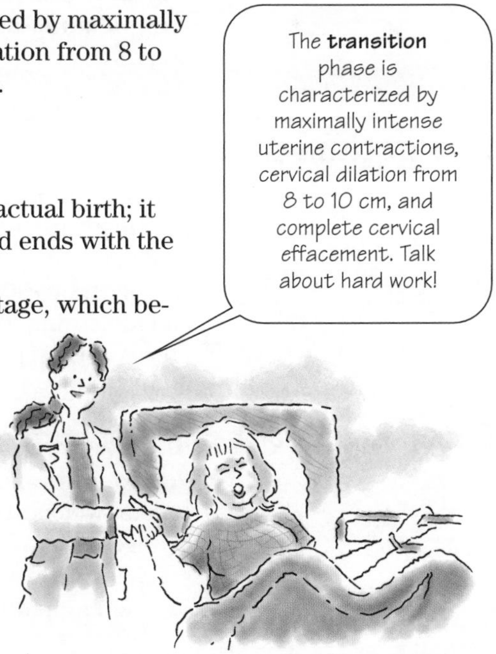
The **transition** phase is characterized by maximally intense uterine contractions, cervical dilation from 8 to 10 cm, and complete cervical effacement. Talk about hard work!

Cardinal movements of labor

With labor, the fetus must pass through the birth canal. To do so, the fetus must change position through various movements because of the size of the fetal head in relation to the irregularly shaped maternal pelvis. Specific, deliberate, and precise, the various movements allow the smallest diameter of the fetal head to pass through the corresponding diameter of the woman's pelvis. These movements include:

- **descent,** the downward movement of the fetus to reach the posterior vaginal floor
- **flexion,** the bending forward of the head so that the chin is pressed to the chest that occurs as a result of the resistance of the fetal head against the pelvic floor
- **internal rotation,** the movement of the head to a transverse (right to left) position
- **extension,** the movement of the head as it passes through the pelvis, with the **occiput** (back part of the head) emerging from the vagina and the back of the neck under the symphysis pubis
- **external rotation** (also called **restitution**), the movement of the head to face one of the mother's inner thighs
- **expulsion,** the birth of the remainder of the fetus's body.

The cardinal movements of labor allow the smallest diameter of the fetal head to pass through the corresponding diameter of the woman's pelvis.

Postpartum period

The time frame after the birth of the neonate is called the **postpartum period.** During this period, the mother's reproductive tract begins to return to its former condition through a process called **involution.** The uterus shrinks quickly during the first 2 weeks after childbirth. As the uterus contracts, the woman may experience pain, commonly referred to as **afterpains.**

Discharge after being discharged

Postpartum vaginal discharge, called **lochia,** persists for several weeks. The color and consistency of the lochia changes.

- **Lochia rubra** is a bloody discharge that appears 1 to 4 days after childbirth.

- **Lochia serosa** is a pinkish brown serous discharge that appears 5 to 7 days after childbirth.
- **Lochia alba** is a grayish white or colorless discharge that appears 1 to 3 weeks after childbirth.

Mama's milk

A postpartum woman's breasts undergo changes in preparation for breast-feeding. If the woman chooses to breast-feed, the first milk produced is called **colostrum.** It's a thick, sticky, golden yellow, easy-to-digest fluid that contains protein, sugar, fat, water, minerals, vitamins, and maternal antibodies. Colostrum is replaced by mature breast milk by about the second to fourth postpartum day.

Physical examination terms

Here are terms associated with physical examination of the maternal patient:

- **Ballottement** is passive fetal movement that occurs in response to pushing against the lower portion of the uterus. (See *Ball toss.*)
- **Bloody show** refers to the vaginal discharge that occurs as the cervix thins and begins to dilate, allowing passage of the mucus plug that seals the cervical canal during pregnancy.
- **Braxton Hicks** contractions are episodes of light, painless, irregular tightening of the uterus during pregnancy. They may occur during the first trimester and increase in duration and intensity by the third trimester.
- **Chadwick's sign** is a bluish coloration of the vulva and vagina that may occur after the sixth week of pregnancy as a result of local venous congestion.
- **Engorgement** is the feeling of tightness, fullness, and tenderness in the postpartum woman's breasts most likely resulting from venous and lymphatic stasis and accumulation of milk in the breast alveoli.
- **Goodell's sign,** softening of the cervix, is an indication of probable pregnancy.
- **Gravida** refers to a pregnant female. A woman is called gravida 1 during the first pregnancy, gravida 2 in the second pregnancy, and so on.

Beyond the dictionary

Ball toss

Ballottement is the passive fetal movement that occurs in response to pushing against the lower portion of the uterus. It's a combination of the French word ***ballotter,*** meaning *to toss about,* and the Italian word ***ballotta,*** meaning *ball.*

• **Hegar's sign,** softening of the lower portion of the uterus, occurs around the seventh week of pregnancy. It's considered a sign of possible pregnancy.
• **Lightening** is a subjective sensation reported by some women as the fetus descends into the pelvic inlet and changes the shape and position of the uterus near term.
• **Linea nigra** is a line of dark pigment that appears on a pregnant woman's abdomen.
• **Melasma** refers to the darkened areas that may appear on the face, especially on the cheeks and across the nose; it's also known as **chloasma** or the mask of pregnancy.
• **Obstetrics** is the branch of surgical medicine involving pregnancy and childbirth. It includes care of the mother and fetus throughout pregnancy, childbirth, and the postpartum period.
• **Para** refers to a mother who has produced viable—but not necessarily living—offspring. The numerals used after the term (for example, para 1 or para 2) indicate the number of pregnancies that have produced viable offspring.
• **Primigravida** refers to a woman who's pregnant for the first time (also called gravida 1).
• **Primipara** refers to a woman who has had one pregnancy that resulted in a viable offspring or a woman who's pregnant for the first time (also called para 1).
• **Quickening** refers to the first noticeable fetal movement in utero. It usually occurs at 16 to 20 weeks' gestation.
• **Ripening** refers to the process in which the cervix softens to prepare for dilation and effacement.
• **Striae gravidarum,** also called **stretch marks,** are red streaks that appear on a pregnant woman's abdomen.
• **True labor** is characterized by the uterine contractions that lead to cervical effacement and dilation, bloody show, and rupture of the membranes.

Melasma, also known as **chloasma,** refers to the darkened areas that may appear on a pregnant woman's face, especially on the cheeks and across the nose.

Striae gravidarum, also called ***stretch marks,*** are red streaks that appear on a pregnant woman's abdomen.

The fetal picture

Here are some terms associated with the physical examination involving the fetus:
• **Attitude** is the degree of flexion and the relationship of the fetal body parts to one another.
• **Breech presentation** indicates that the fetus is in a head-up position with the buttocks (frank breech), feet (incomplete or footling breech), or

buttocks and feet (complete breech) as the presenting parts.

- **Cephalic presentation** indicates that the fetal head is the first part to contact the cervix and be expelled from the uterus during birth.
- **Engagement** occurs when the presenting part of the fetus passes into the pelvis to the point where the presenting part is at the level of the ischial spines. (See *Fetal engagement and station.*)
- **Lie** refers to the relationship of the fetal spine to the maternal spine.
- **Position** is the relationship of the presenting part of the fetus to a specific quadrant of the mother's pelvis. It's designated using three letters: The first letter denotes whether the presenting part is facing the woman's right or left side (R or L). The second letter denotes the presenting part as occiput (O); mentum, or chin (M); sacrum

Anatomically speaking

Fetal engagement and station

The extent of the fetal presenting part into the pelvis is referred to as **fetal engagement. Station** refers to where the fetal presenting part lies in relation to the maternal ischial spines. Station grades range from –3 (3 cm above the maternal ischial spines) to +4 (4 cm below the maternal ischial spines, causing the perineum to bulge). A zero station indicates that the presenting part lies level with the ischial spines.

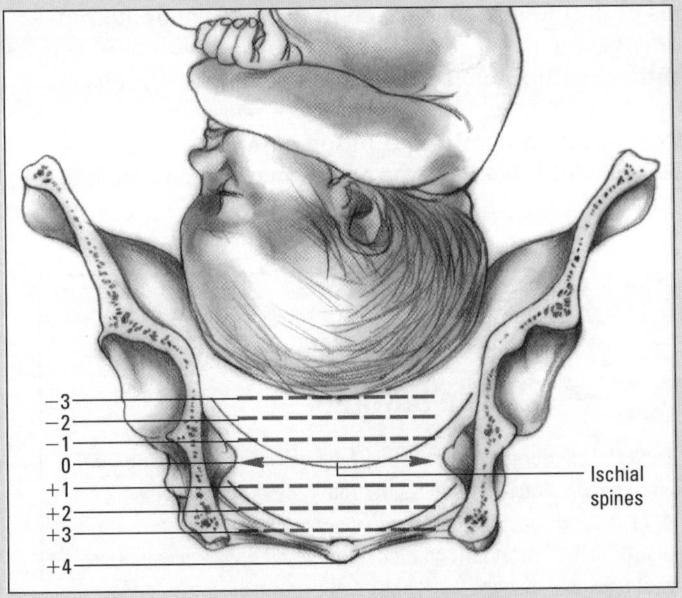
–3
–2
–1
0
+1
+2
+3
+4
Ischial spines

(Sa), or shoulder (A). The third letter denotes whether the presenting part points to the anterior (A), posterior (P), or transverse section of the mother's pelvis (T).

- **Presentation** is the portion of the fetus that first enters the birth canal.
- **Station** is the relationship of the presenting part of the fetus to the mother's ischial spines.

Diagnostic tests

Diagnostic tests associated with maternal health include blood and fluid tests as well as imaging and other tests.

Blood and fluid tests

Here are some common blood and fluid tests associated with maternal and fetal health:

- **Amniocentesis** involves the withdrawal of a sample of amniotic fluid by transabdominal puncture and needle aspiration. (See *Quite a bowlful.*)
- **Chorionic villus sampling** is a biopsy in which a minute amount of the chorionic villi (fingerlike projections of the chorion that attach to maternal endometrial tissues) is removed.
- **Indirect Coombs' test** is a blood test that screens maternal blood for red blood cell antibodies.
- **Percutaneous umbilical blood sampling** is an invasive procedure that involves insertion of a spinal needle

Beyond the dictionary

Quite a bowlful

The term **amniocentesis** derives from two Greek words: ***amnion*** and ***kentsis. Amnion*** means *bowl* and ***kentsis*** means *the act of pricking.* The "bowl" refers to the membrane that envelops the fetus. Put it all together and *amniocentesis* means the withdrawal of a sample of amniotic fluid from the amniotic sac by transabdominal puncture and needle aspiration.

into the umbilical cord to obtain a fetal blood sample or to transfuse the fetus in utero.

- **Serum alpha-fetoprotein** (AFP) measures the glycoprotein AFP. An above-normal level in an adult may indicate testicular cancer. In a fetus, an above-normal level may indicate a neural tube defect.
- A **triple screen** is a blood test performed between 15 and 20 weeks' gestation to determine whether a fetus is at increased risk for Down syndrome, a neural tube defect, or other chromosomal abnormalities.
- A **quadruple screen** includes the triple screen blood test as well as an inhibin A test to more accurately predict the likelihood of Down syndrome. This test, however, isn't available in all facilities.

Screens aren't just for football, ya know. A **triple screen** is a blood test that determines whether a fetus is at increased risk for Down syndrome, a neural tube defect, or other chromosomal abnormalities.
50
12

Imaging and other diagnostic tests

Here are some common imaging and other diagnostic tests associated with maternal and fetal health:

- **Amniography** is an X-ray of a pregnant woman's uterus. A contrast medium is injected into the amniotic sac to visualize its contents.
- **External electronic monitoring** is an indirect, noninvasive procedure using two devices that are placed on the pregnant abdomen—an ultrasound transducer that detects the baby's heart rate and a tocotransducer that records the pressure of uterine contractions. Together they help to evaluate fetal well-being and uterine contractions during labor.
- **Internal electronic monitoring,** also called **direct monitoring,** is an invasive procedure that uses a spiral electrode attached to the presenting fetal part to detect fetal heartbeat and convert it to a fetal electrocardiogram waveform.
- The **nonstress test** is a noninvasive test used to detect fetal heart accelerations in response to fetal movement.
- The **oxytocin challenge test** evaluates the fetus's ability to withstand an oxytocin-induced contraction. The test requires nipple stimulation or I.V. administration of oxytocin in increasing doses until three high-quality uterine contractions occur within a 10-minute period.
- A **pelvic ultrasound** passes sound waves through the pelvic area, creating electronic images of internal structures. This test is used to examine a developing fetus.

• The **vibroacoustic stimulation** test is a noninvasive test using 1 to 5 seconds of vibration and sound to induce fetal reactivity during a nonstress test. Vibration is produced by an artificial larynx or fetal acoustic stimulator that's placed above the head of the fetus.

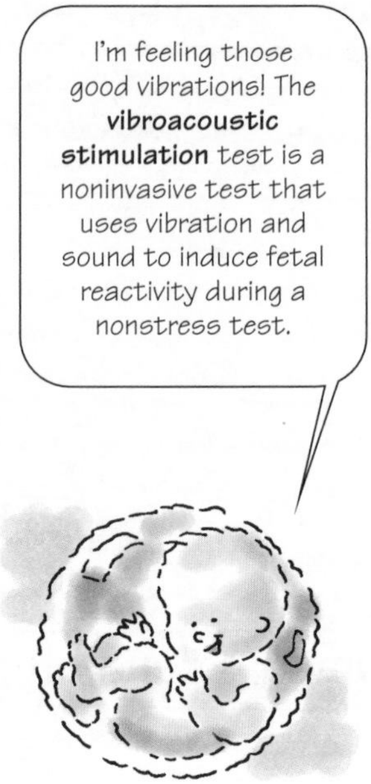
I'm feeling those good vibrations! The **vibroacoustic stimulation** test is a noninvasive test that uses vibration and sound to induce fetal reactivity during a nonstress test.

Disorders associated with pregnancy, labor, and birth

• **Abruptio placentae** is the premature separation of a normally positioned placenta in a pregnancy of at least 20 weeks' gestation. This separation may occur before or during labor but always occurs before delivery. The classic symptom is painful "rupturing" accompanied by bleeding.
• **Battledore placenta** occurs when the umbilical cord attaches to the placenta marginally rather than centrally.
• **Cephalopelvic disproportion** is a disproportion between the size of the fetal head and the maternal pelvic diameters, usually due to a narrowing or contraction of the birth canal, resulting in a failure to progress in labor.
• **Dystocia** involves the failure or inability to progress through the stages of labor. (See *How do I say* dystocia?)
• **Eclampsia** refers to the development of seizures in a woman with gestational hypertension.
• **Ectopic pregnancy** is the implantation of a fertilized ovum outside the uterine cavity, usually in a fallopian tube.

Pump up your pronunciation

How do I say *dystocia?*

The term describing the failure or inability to progress through the stages of labor—dystocia—is pronounced DIS-TOH-SHUH. The three parts of the word are all derived from Greek terms. ***Dys*** means *bad;* ***toc*** (from the word ***tokos***) means *childbirth;* and ***ia*** means a state or condition.

- **Gestational diabetes** refers to diabetes that emerges during pregnancy and may lead to the birth of a large fetus, possibly weighing more than 10 lb (4.5 kg).
- **Gestational hypertension** is hypertension that usually develops after the 20th week of pregnancy and isn't accompanied by protein in the urine.
- **Hydatidiform mole** is an uncommon chorionic tumor of the placenta. Women with this type of tumor have a good chance of developing cancer later in life. It's also called **gestational trophoblastic disease** or **molar pregnancy.**
- **Hydramnios** refers to an excess amount of amniotic fluid.
- **Hydrorrhea gravidarum** is the discharge of thin, watery fluid from the uterus during pregnancy.
- **Hyperemesis gravidarum** is severe and unremitting nausea and vomiting after the first 12 weeks of pregnancy.
- **Isoimmunization,** also called Rh incompatibility, refers to a condition in which the pregnant woman is Rh-negative but the fetus is Rh-positive. If this condition is left untreated, the neonate can develop hemolytic disease.
- **Oligohydramnios** is a condition in which a less-than-normal amount of amniotic fluid is present in the amnion during pregnancy. (See *Taking apart* oligohydramnios.)
- **Placenta previa** is a placenta that develops in the lower segment of the uterus. It's characterized by painless bleeding, which differentiates this disorder from abruptio placentae.
- **Precipitous labor** occurs when uterine contractions are so strong that the woman gives birth with only a few rapidly occurring contractions. It's commonly defined as labor lasting less than 3 hours.
- **Preeclampsia** refers to the nonconvulsive form of hypertension, manifested by the development of hypertension after the 20th week of gestation and accompanied by protein in the urine. It may progress to eclampsia.
- **Premature labor,** also called **preterm labor,** is the onset of rhythmic uterine contractions that produce cervical changes after fetal viability but before fetal maturity (usually between 20 and 37 weeks' gestation).

Hyperemesis gravidarum is severe and unremitting nausea and vomiting after the first 12 weeks of pregnancy.

Beyond the dictionary

Taking apart *oligohydramnios*

Oligohydramnios is a less-than-normal amount of amniotic fluid. The word ***oligo-*** means *few* or *scanty.* ***Hydro-*** means *water* or *fluid,* and ***-amnios*** refers to the *amnion.* Thus, **oligohydramnios** means *little fluid in the amnion.*

- **Premature rupture of membranes** (**PROM**) is a spontaneous break or tear in the amniotic sac before the onset of regular contractions.
- **Spontaneous abortion** is the premature expulsion of an embryo or nonviable fetus from the uterus.
- **Umbilical cord prolapse** occurs when a loop of the umbilical cord slips down in front of the fetal presenting part. It may occur at any time after the membranes rupture, especially if the presenting part isn't fitted firmly into the cervix.

PROM is a spontaneous break or tear in the amniotic sac before the onset of regular contractions.

Treatments and procedures

Here are terms related to treatments and procedures associated with pregnancy, labor, and birth.

- **Abortion** is the termination of a pregnancy. It can be spontaneous (from natural causes), elective (performed as a result of a choice to terminate the pregnancy), or therapeutic (performed to preserve the woman's life or when serious birth defects are expected). Controversial partial birth abortions are those performed late in pregnancy.
- **Amniotomy** requires the use of an instrument such as an amniohook to mechanically rupture the membranes.
- **Artificial insemination** is the placement of seminal fluid into the patient's vaginal canal or cervix. The procedure is coordinated with ovulation.
- **Cervical suturing,** also called **cerclage,** is the use of a purse-string suture to reinforce the cervix.
- **Cesarean birth** involves an incision made through the abdominal and uterine walls to deliver a neonate.
- In **dilatation and evacuation,** suction is used to remove the uterine contents. This procedure is typically used to perform elective abortions.
- **Episiotomy** is an incision made in the vulva to prevent tearing during birth of a neonate.
- **Gamete intrafallopian transfer** is a reproductive technology that involves placing ova collected from the ovaries transvaginally into a catheter filled with sperm. The contents of the catheter are injected into the end of the fallopian tube via a laparoscope. This technique allows fertilization and implantation to occur naturally.

• With **in vitro fertilization,** an ovum is removed from the woman's body and fertilized with sperm in a laboratory culture medium. The resulting embryo is then transferred into the woman's uterus.
• **Labor induction** involves stimulating the onset of uterine contractions by medical or surgical methods before the woman begins labor spontaneously.
• **RhoGAM administration** is the administration of Rh_0 (D) immune globulin containing Rh_0 (D) antibodies to a woman who is Rh-negative. This procedure keeps the mother from producing active antibody responses and forming anti-Rh_0 (D) to Rh-positive fetal blood cells.
• **Tocolytic therapy** involves using medications to quiet the contracting uterus when preterm labor occurs.
• **Zygote intrafallopian tube transfer** is a reproductive technology that involves fertilization of the ovum outside the mother's body followed by reimplantation of the zygote into the fallopian tube via laparoscopy.

Feeling lucky? Try your hand at winning games about maternal health on the next page.

systole

Vocabulary builders

At a crossroads

Test your maternal instincts by completing this crossword puzzle of maternal health terms.

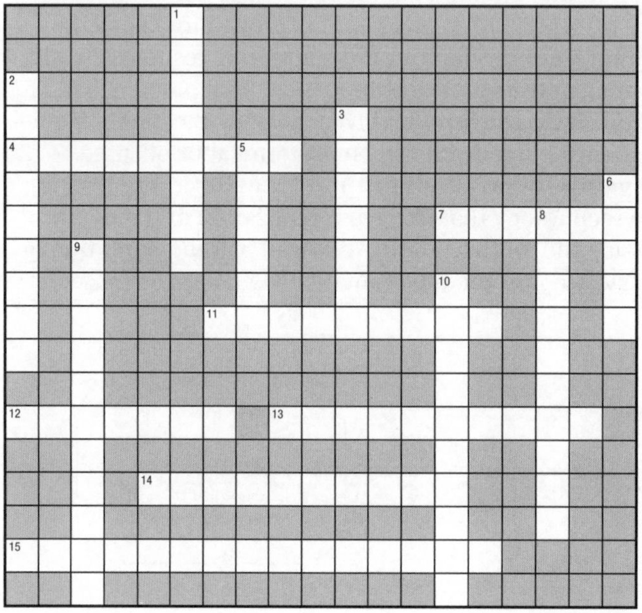

Across

4. Breast-feeding
7. Postpartum vaginal discharge
11. Period of pregnancy that begins with conception and ends with childbirth
12. A pregnant female
13. The first noticeable fetal movement in utero
14. Thinning and shortening of the cervix
15. Rh incompatibility

Down

1. The termination of a pregnancy
2. First milk produced after childbirth
3. Endometrial lining of the uterus
5. Precursor of the ovum
6. Process by which birth of the fetus is achieved
8. An excessive amount of amniotic fluid
9. Cells that move by means of flagellar movements
10. Also called fertilization

Answers are on page 266.

Finish line

Fill in the blanks with the appropriate terms.

1. ___________________ contractions are episodes of light, painless, irregular uterine tightening during pregnancy.

2. The degree of flexion and the relationship of the fetal body parts to one another is called ________________.

3. ________________________ involves the withdrawal of a sample of amniotic fluid by transabdominal puncture and needle aspiration.

4. The implantation of a fertilized ovum outside the uterine cavity, usually in a fallopian tube, is called an ___________ pregnancy.

5. _______________________ involves using medications to quiet the contracting uterus when preterm labor occurs.

Match game

Match each description of a disorder, condition, or treatment to its name.

Clues

1. Occurs when a loop of the umbilical cord slips down in front of the fetal presenting part ___

2. An incision made in the vulva to prevent tearing during birth of a neonate ____

3. The use of suction to remove the uterine contents ___

4. Premature separation of a normally positioned placenta in a pregnancy of at least 20 weeks' gestation ___

5. The use of an instrument to mechanically rupture the membranes ___

6. An uncommon chorionic tumor of the placenta ___

7. The use of a purse-string suture to reinforce the cervix ___

Choices

A. Abruptio placentae

B. Hydatidiform mole

C. Umbilical cord prolapse

D. Cervical suturing

E. Dilatation and evacuation

F. Episiotomy

G. Amniotomy

Answers are on page 266.

Answers

At a crossroads

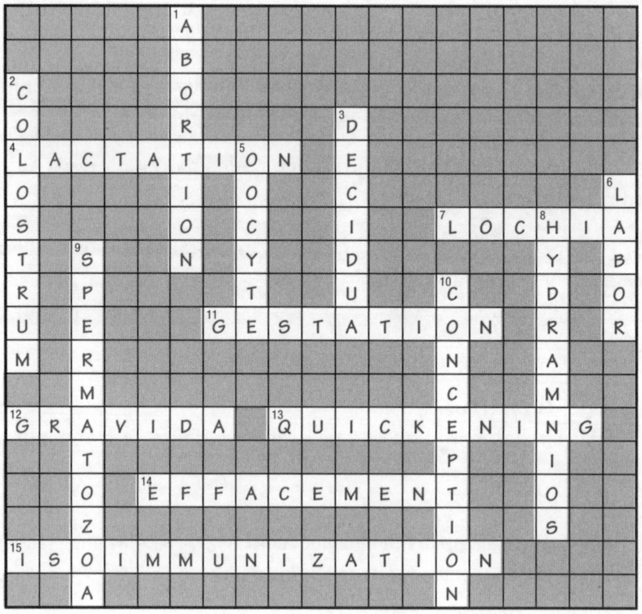

Finish line

1. Braxton Hicks; 2. Attitude; 3. Amniocentesis; 4. Ectopic; 5. Tocolytic therapy

Match game

1. C; 2. F, 3. E; 4. A; 5. G; 6. B; 7. D

12

Neurologic system

Just the facts

In this chapter, you'll learn:

- terminology related to the structure and function of the neurologic system
- terminology needed for physical examination
- tests that help diagnose common neurologic disorders
- neurologic system disorders and their treatments.

Neurologic structure and function

The neurologic system, also called the **nervous system,** coordinates all body functions, enabling a person to adapt to changes in internal and external environments. It has two main types of cells (neurons and neuroglia) and two main divisions (the **central nervous system [CNS]** and **peripheral nervous system**). (See *Pronouncing key neurologic system terms*, page 268.)

Cells of the nervous system

The nervous system is packed with intertwined cells.

Neurons—the naked truth

Neurons, the primary functional unit of the nervous system, respond to stimuli and transmit responses by means of electromechanical messages.

The main parts of a neuron are the **cell body** (which contains the nucleus [plural: **nuclei**]) and the **cytoplasm.** This is the metabolic center of the neuron. One

Pump up your pronunciation

Pronouncing key neurologic system terms

Below is a list of key terms related to the neurologic system along with the correct ways to pronounce them.

Choroid plexus	KOR-OYD PLEK-SEHS
Echoencephalography	EK-OH-EN-SEF-UH-LAWG-RUH-FEE
Guillain-Barré syndrome	GEE-LAYN BAHR-RAY SIN-DROHM
Gyri	JEYE-REYE
Neuroglia	NEW-RoG-GLEE-UH
Sulci	SUHL-KEYE
Trigeminal neuralgia	TREYE-JEM-UH-NUHL NEW-RAL-JEE-UH
Ventriculoperitoneal shunt	VEN-TRIK-YOU-LOH-PER-UH-TOH-NEE-UHL SHUHNT

axon and several **dendrites** project from each cell body. (See *Parts of a neuron.*) In a typical neuron, one axon and many dendrites extend from the cell body.

Shipping and receiving

Axons conduct nerve impulses away from the cell body. **Dendrites** conduct impulses toward the cell body.

The main function of the axon is to send or transmit signals to other cells. The highly specialized neuron cells can't replace themselves but will attempt to repair themselves if damage is limited to the axon.

Axons can vary in length from quite short to very long—up to 3¼′ (1 m). A typical axon has **terminal branches** and is wrapped in a white, fatty, segmented covering called a **myelin sheath.** The myelin sheath is produced by **Schwann cells,** made up of **phagocytic cells** (cells capable of engulfing and digesting microorganisms and cellular debris) separated by gaps called **nodes of Ranvier.** (See *Schwann and Ranvier,* page 270.)

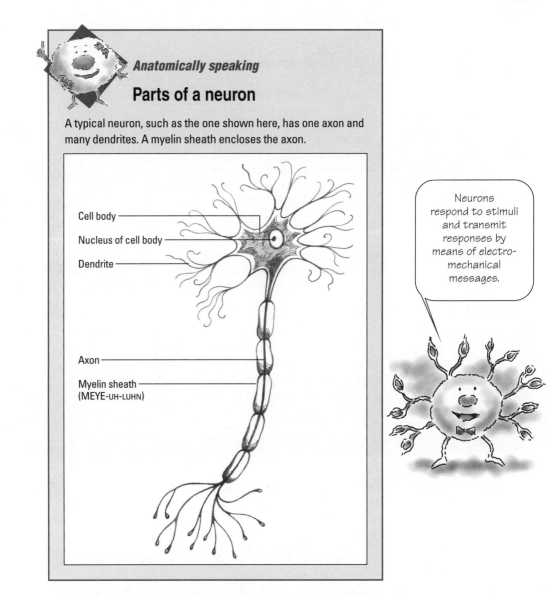

Anatomically speaking

Parts of a neuron

A typical neuron, such as the one shown here, has one axon and many dendrites. A myelin sheath encloses the axon.

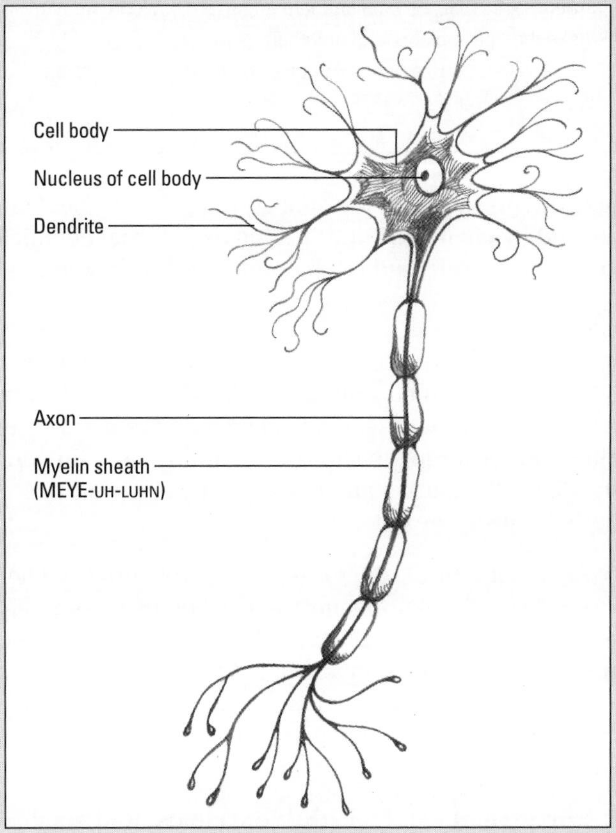
Cell body
Nucleus of cell body
Dendrite
Axon
Myelin sheath
(MEYE-UH-LUHN)

Neurons respond to stimuli and transmit responses by means of electro-mechanical messages.

Dendrites are short, thick, diffusely branched extensions that receive impulses arriving at the neuron from other cells.

Being impulsive

The purpose of a neuron is to initiate, receive, and process messages through electrochemical conduction of impulses, also known as **neurotransmission.** Neuron activity can be provoked by mechanical stimuli, such as

Guten morgen.

Beyond the dictionary

Schwann and Ranvier

Schwann cells are named after Theodor Schwann, a 19th-century German anatomist and physiologist who studied muscular activity. In 1837, he published an important book on the workings of the cell in plants and animals.

Louis Antoine Ranvier, a French pathologist, first described the nodes of Ranvier in 1878.

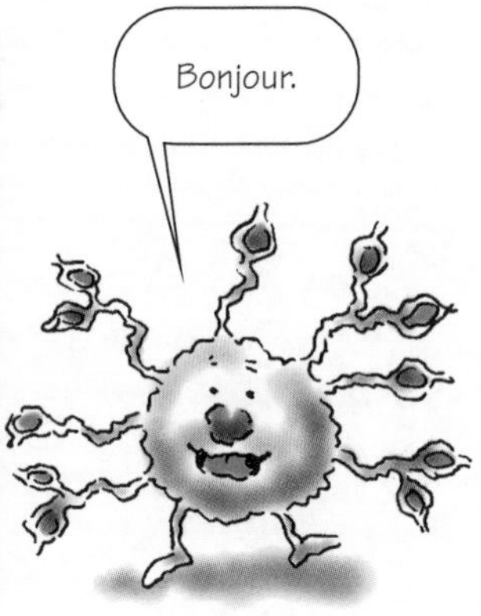
Bonjour.

touch and pressure; by thermal stimuli, such as heat and cold; and by chemical stimuli, such as external chemicals and chemicals released by the body, such as histamine.

Neuro-glue

The supportive structures of the nervous system, **neuroglia,** are also called **glial cells. Glial** is derived from the Greek word for *glue;* these cells hold the neurons together and form roughly 40% of the brain's bulk. In addition, glial cells nourish and protect the neurons. Four types of neuroglia exist:

1. **Astroglia,** or **astrocytes,** exist throughout the nervous system. They supply nutrients to neurons and help them maintain their electrical potential. Astrocytes also form part of the **blood-brain barrier** that separates CNS tissue from the bloodstream and guards against invasion by disease-causing organisms and other harmful substances.

2. **Ependymal cells** line the **ventricles,** four small cavities in the brain, as well as the **choroid plexuses,** vascular structures that form a network in the pia mater of the brain and project into the third, lateral, and fourth ventricles. These cells help produce **cerebrospinal fluid (CSF).**

3. **Microglia** are phagocytic cells that ingest and digest microorganisms and waste products from injured neurons, giving them an important role in host defense.

4. **Oligodendroglia** support and electrically insulate CNS axons by forming protective myelin sheaths.

Brain

The CNS includes the spinal cord and the brain. The brain consists of the **cerebrum, cerebellum,** brain stem, and primitive structures that lie below the cerebrum—the **diencephalon,** limbic system, and reticular activating system. (See *Major structures in the brain,* page 272.)

You're so cerebral

The cerebrum has right and left hemispheres. The **corpus callosum—**a mass of nerve fibers—bridges the hemispheres, allowing communication between corresponding centers in each. The rolling surface of the cerebrum is made up of **gyri** (convolutions) and **sulci** (creases or fissures). The thin surface layer, the **cerebral cortex,** consists of **gray matter** (unmyelinated nerve fibers). Within the cerebrum lie **white matter** (myelinated nerve fibers) and islands of internal gray matter.

Name that lobe

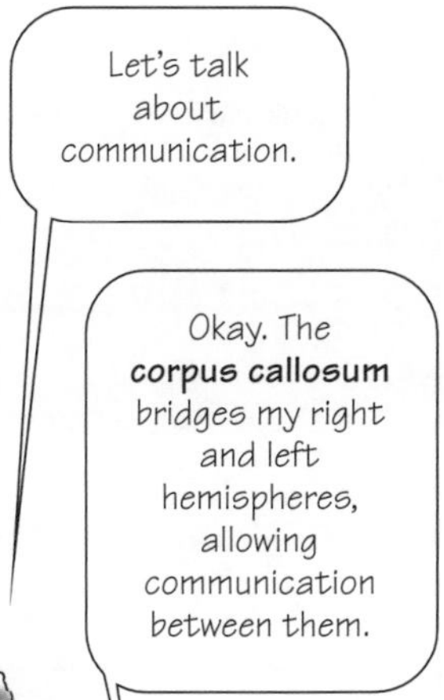
Let's talk about communication.
Okay. The **corpus callosum** bridges my right and left hemispheres, allowing communication between them.

Each cerebral hemisphere is divided into four lobes, based on anatomic landmarks and functional differences. The lobes are named for the cranial bones that lie over them—frontal, temporal, parietal, and occipital:

- The **frontal lobe** influences personality, judgment, abstract reasoning, social behavior, language expression, and movement.
- The **temporal lobe** controls hearing, language comprehension, and storage and recall of memories (although memories are stored throughout the entire brain).
- The **parietal lobe** interprets and integrates sensations, including pain, temperature, and touch. It also interprets size, shape, distance, and texture. The parietal lobe of the nondominant hemisphere is especially important for awareness of one's own body shape.
- The **occipital lobe** functions primarily to interpret visual stimuli.

Celebrating the cerebellum

The **cerebellum,** the second largest brain region, lies posterior and inferior to the cerebrum. Like the cerebrum, it has two hemispheres, an outer cortex of gray matter and

Anatomically speaking

Major structures in the brain

These illustrations show the two largest structures of the brain—the cerebrum and cerebellum. Also note the locations of the four cerebral lobes, the sensory cortex, and the motor cortex. The bottom illustration shows a cross section of the brain, from its outermost portion (cerebrum) to its innermost (diencephalon).

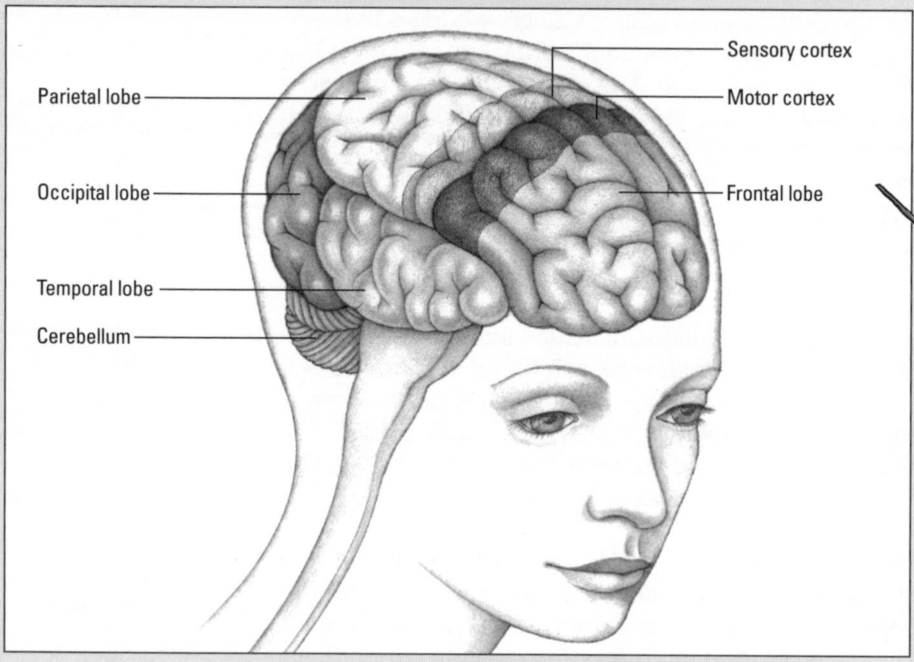
Sensory cortex
Parietal lobe
Motor cortex
Occipital lobe
Frontal lobe
Temporal lobe
Cerebellum

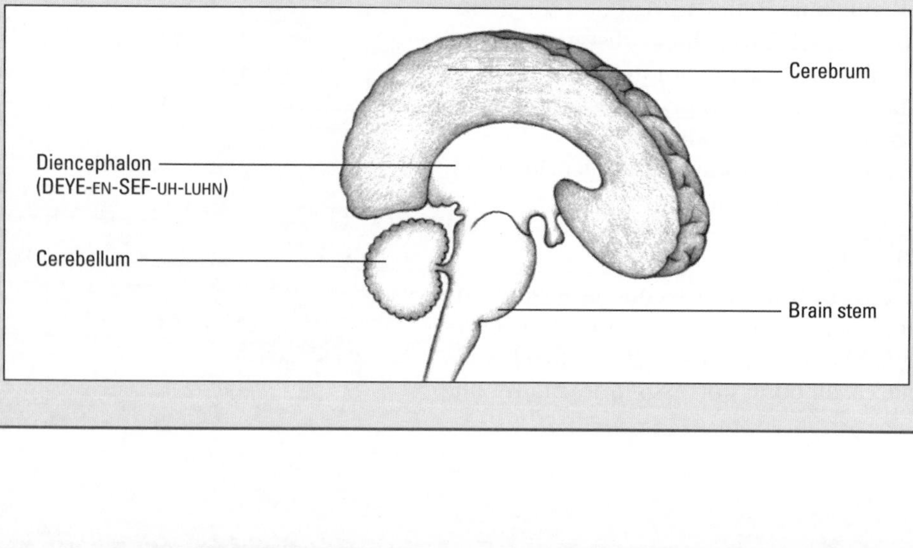
Cerebrum
Diencephalon
(DEYE-EN-SEF-UH-LUHN)
Cerebellum
Brain stem

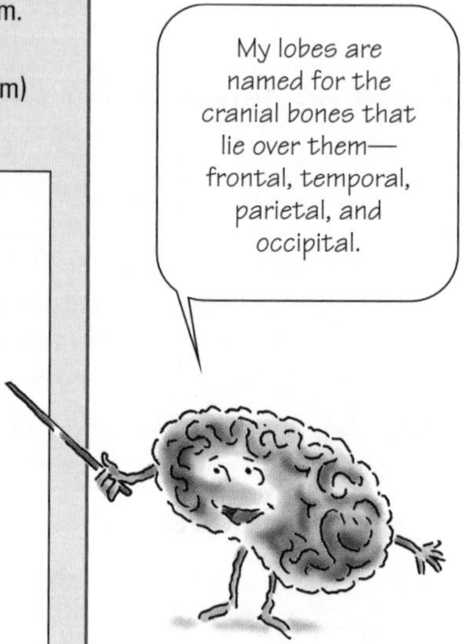
My lobes are named for the cranial bones that lie over them—frontal, temporal, parietal, and occipital.

an inner core of white matter. The cerebellum functions to maintain muscle tone, coordinate muscle movement, and control balance.

Memory jogger

To distinguish the locations of the "cerebrum" and the "cerebellum," look at the "BR" in "cereBRum" and think "BRow," meaning that the cerebrum is the top (the outermost) part of the brain.

For "cerebellum," look at the "BEL" in "cereBELlum" and think "BELow" because the cerebellum is below and behind the cerebrum.

Brain stem

The **brain stem** lies immediately inferior to the cerebrum, just anterior to the cerebellum. It's continuous with the cerebrum superiorly and with the spinal cord inferiorly.

Composed of the midbrain, pons, and medulla oblongata, the brain stem relays messages between the parts of the nervous system. It has three main functions:

1. It produces the rigid autonomic behaviors necessary for survival, such as increasing heart rate and respiratory rate and stimulating the adrenal medulla to produce epinephrine.
2. It provides pathways for nerve fibers between higher and lower neural centers.
3. It serves as the origin for 10 of the 12 pairs of cranial nerves.

The **reticular activating system (RAS),** a diffuse network of hyperexcitable neurons, fans out from the brain stem through the cerebral cortex. After screening all incoming sensory information, the RAS channels it to appropriate areas of the brain for interpretation. RAS activity also stimulates wakefulness or arousal of consciousness.

Where nerves volunteer

The **midbrain** connects dorsally with the cerebellum and extends from the pons to the hypothalamus. It contains large voluntary motor nerve tracts running between the brain and spinal cord.

The pons pathway

It makes perfect sense. The *pons* acts as a pathway, and *pons* is the Latin term for bridge.

The **pons** connects the cerebellum with the cerebrum and links the midbrain to the medulla oblongata. It houses two of the brain's respiratory centers that work with those in the medulla to produce a normal breathing rhythm. The pons also acts as a pathway between brain centers and the spinal cord and serves as the exit point for cranial nerves V, VI, and VII.

Inferior, not unimportant

The **medulla oblongata,** the most inferior portion of the brain stem, is a small, cone-shaped structure. It joins the spinal cord at the level of the **foramen magnum,** an opening in the occipital portion of the skull. The medulla oblongata serves as an autonomic reflex center to maintain homeostasis, regulating respiratory, vasomotor, and cardiac functions.

Primitive structures

The **diencephalon** consists of the thalamus and hypothalamus, which lie beneath the surface of the cerebral hemispheres. The **thalamus** relays all sensory stimuli (except olfactory) as they ascend to the cerebral cortex. Its functions include primitive awareness of pain, screening of incoming stimuli, and focusing of attention. The **hypothalamus** controls or affects body temperature, appetite, water balance, pituitary secretions, emotions, and autonomic functions (including sleep and wake cycles).

Note to hypothalamus: Please adjust your thermostat!

Limbo with the limbic system

The **limbic system** is a primitive brain area deep within the temporal lobe. In addition to initiating basic drives, such as hunger, aggression, and emotional and sexual arousal, the limbic system screens all sensory messages traveling to the cerebral cortex. (See *Limbic system and brain stem.*)

Spinal cord

A cylindrical structure in the vertebral canal, the **spinal cord** extends from the foramen magnum at the base of the skull to the upper lumbar region of the vertebral column. The spinal nerves arise from the cord. At the cord's inferior end, nerve roots cluster in the **cauda equina.**

Horn of sensation, horn of activity

Within the spinal cord, the H-shaped mass of gray matter is divided into horns, which consist mainly of neuron cell bodies. Cell bodies in the **posterior horn** primarily relay sensations; those in the **anterior horn** play a part in voluntary and involuntary (reflex) motor activity. White matter surrounding the outer part of these horns consists of

Anatomically speaking

Limbic system and brain stem

The major structures of the limbic system and brain stem, shown here, are associated with emotions and responses such as anger, fear, and sexual arousal.

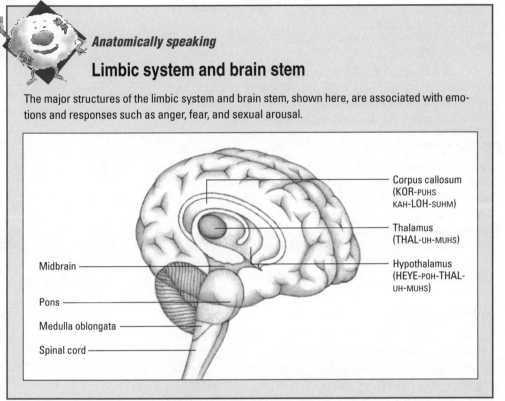

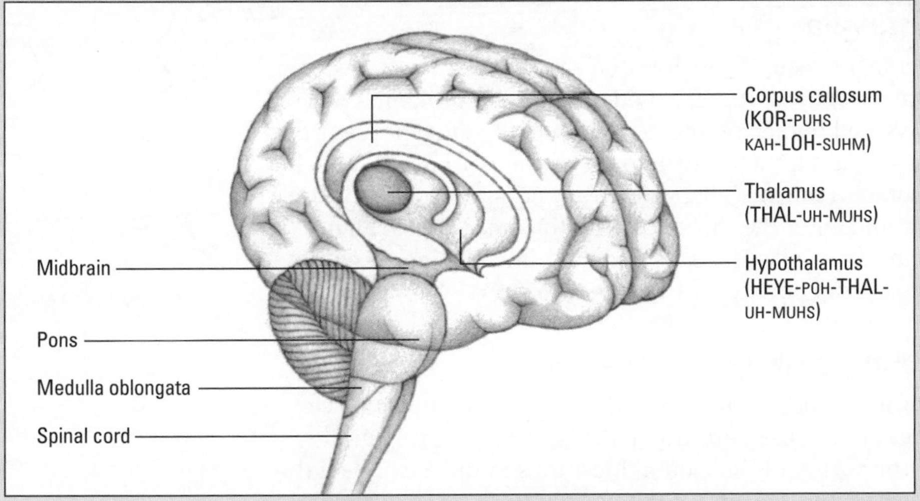
Corpus callosum
(KOR-PUHS KAH-LOH-SUHM)
Thalamus
(THAL-UH-MUHS)
Hypothalamus
(HEYE-POH-THAL-UH-MUHS)
Midbrain
Pons
Medulla oblongata
Spinal cord

myelinated nerve fibers grouped functionally in vertical columns, or **tracts.**

Impulse conductor

The spinal cord conducts sensory nerve impulses to the brain and conducts motor impulses from the brain. It also controls such reflexes as the knee-jerk (patellar) reaction to a reflex hammer.

Pathways in the brain

Nerve impulses to the brain follow sensory pathways. Nerve impulses from the brain—those that control body function and movement—follow motor pathways.

Sensory pathways

Sensory impulses travel via the **afferent,** or **ascending,** neural pathways to the brain's sensory cortex in the parietal lobe, where they're interpreted. These impulses use two major pathways.

Ouch! I shouldn't have touched that hot pan! Better alert the spinothalamic tract.

Ouch!

Pain and temperature sensations enter the spinal cord through the dorsal horn. After immediately crossing over to the opposite side of the cord, these stimuli then travel to the thalamus via the **spinothalamic tract.**

Touchy-feely with the ganglia

Tactile, pressure, and vibration sensations enter the spinal cord via relay stations called **ganglia** (knotlike masses of nerve cell bodies on the dorsal roots of spinal nerves). These stimuli then travel up the spinal cord in the dorsal column to the medulla, where they cross to the opposite side and enter the thalamus. The thalamus relays all incoming sensory impulses (except olfactory impulses) to the sensory cortex for interpretation.

Motor pathways

Motor impulses travel from the brain to the muscles via **efferent,** or **descending,** pathways. Originating in the motor cortex of the frontal lobe, these impulses reach the lower motor neurons of the peripheral nervous system via **upper motor neurons.** Upper motor neurons originate in the brain and form two major systems:

Just an impulse

- The **pyramidal system,** also called the **corticospinal tract,** is responsible for fine motor movements of skeletal muscle. Impulses in this system travel from the motor cortex, through the internal capsule, and to the medulla, where they cross to the opposite side and continue down the spinal cord.
- The **extrapyramidal system,** or **extracorticospinal tract,** controls gross motor movements. Impulses originate in the premotor area of the frontal lobe and travel to the pons, where they cross to the opposite side. Then the impulses travel down the spinal cord to the anterior horn, where they're relayed to the lower motor neurons. These neurons, in turn, carry the impulses to the muscles.

It's all automatic

Reflex responses occur automatically, without any brain involvement, to protect the body. Spinal nerves, which have both sensory and motor portions, mediate **deep tendon reflexes**—involuntary contractions of a muscle after brief stretching caused by tendon percussion—and **superficial reflexes**—withdrawal reflexes elicited by noxious or tactile stimulation of the skin, cornea, or mucous membranes.

A simple reflex, such as the **knee-jerk reflex,** requires an **afferent** (sensory) neuron and an **efferent** (motor) neuron. (See *Patellar reflex arc.*)

Patellar reflex arc

Spinal nerves—which have sensory and motor portions—control deep tendon and superficial reflexes. A simple reflex arc requires a sensory (or afferent) neuron and a motor (or efferent) neuron. The knee-jerk, or patellar, reflex illustrates the sequence of events in a normal reflex arc.

First, a sensory receptor detects the mechanical stimulus produced by the reflex hammer striking the patellar tendon. Then the sensory neuron carries the impulse along its axon by way of the spinal nerve to the dorsal root, where it enters the spinal column.

Next, in the anterior horn of the spinal cord, shown below, the sensory neuron joins with a motor neuron, which carries the impulse along its axon by way of the spinal nerve to the muscle. The motor neuron transmits the impulse to muscle fibers through stimulation of the motor end plate. This triggers the muscle to contract and the leg to extend.

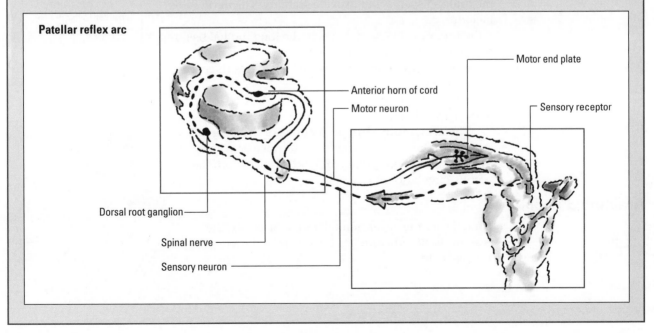

Patellar reflex arc

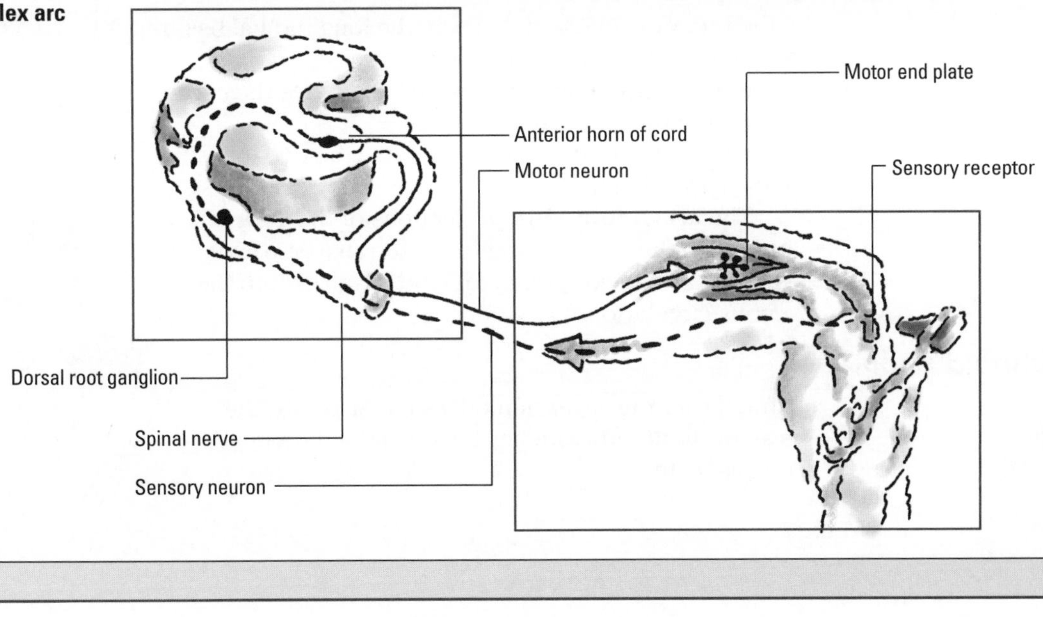
Motor end plate
Anterior horn of cord
Motor neuron
Sensory receptor
Dorsal root ganglion
Spinal nerve
Sensory neuron

Protective structures of the CNS

The brain and spinal cord are protected from shock and infection by bones, the meninges, several additional cushioning layers, and CSF.

Bones

The **skull,** formed of cranial bones, completely surrounds the brain. It opens at the foramen magnum, where the spinal cord exits.

The **vertebral column** protects the spinal cord. Its 30 vertebrae are separated from one another by an intervertebral disk that allows flexibility.

Meninges

The **meninges** cover and protect the cerebral cortex and spinal column. They consist of three layers of connective tissue: the dura mater, arachnoid membrane, and pia mater. (See *Protective membranes of the CNS.*)

The dura mater truly matters

The **dura mater** is a fibrous membrane that lines the skull and forms reflections, or folds, that descend into the brain's fissures and provide stability. The dural folds include:

- the **falx cerebri,** which lies in the longitudinal fissure and separates the cerebral hemispheres
- the **tentorium cerebelli,** which separates the cerebrum from the cerebellum
- the **falx cerebelli,** which separates the two lobes of the cerebellum.

The **arachnoid villi,** projections of the dura mater into the superior sagittal and transverse sinuses, serve as the exit points for CSF drainage into the venous circulation.

Guess what, little one. ***Pia mater*** is the Latin term for *gentle mother.* ***Dura mater*** is Latin for *tough mother.*

Arachnoid phobia?

A fragile, fibrous layer of moderate vascularity, the **arachnoid membrane** lies between the dura mater and pia mater.

Anatomically speaking

Protective membranes of the CNS

Three membranes—the dura mater, arachnoid membrane, and pia mater—help protect the central nervous system (CNS). The arachnoid villi project from the arachnoid membrane into the superior sagittal and transverse sinuses. The subarachnoid space, filled with cerebrospinal fluid, separates the arachnoid membrane from the pia mater.

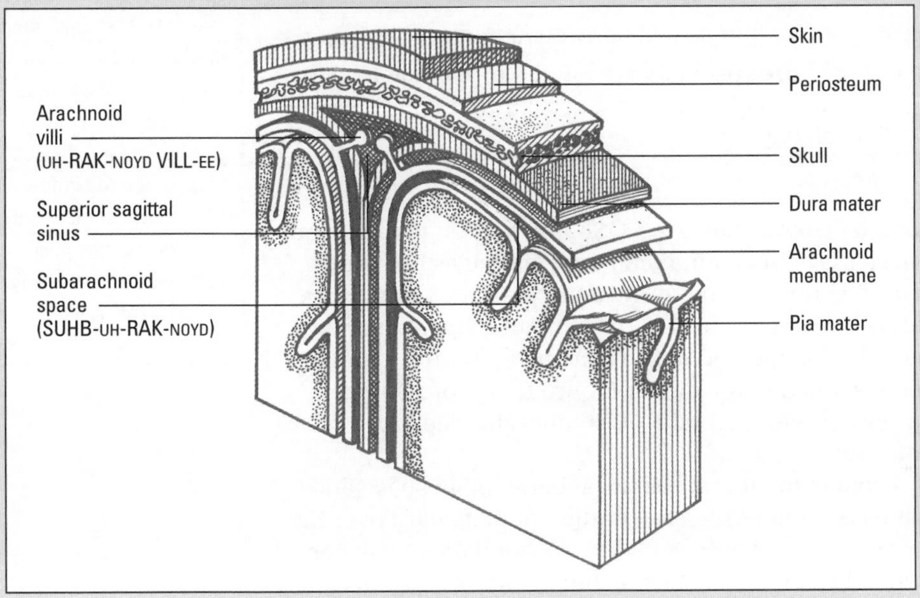
Skin
Periosteum
Skull
Dura mater
Arachnoid membrane
Pia mater
Arachnoid villi (UH-RAK-NOYD VILL-EE)
Superior sagittal sinus
Subarachnoid space (SUHB-UH-RAK-NOYD)

Thin and rich

The extremely thin **pia mater,** the innermost layer, has a rich blood supply. It adheres to the brain's surface and extends into its fissures.

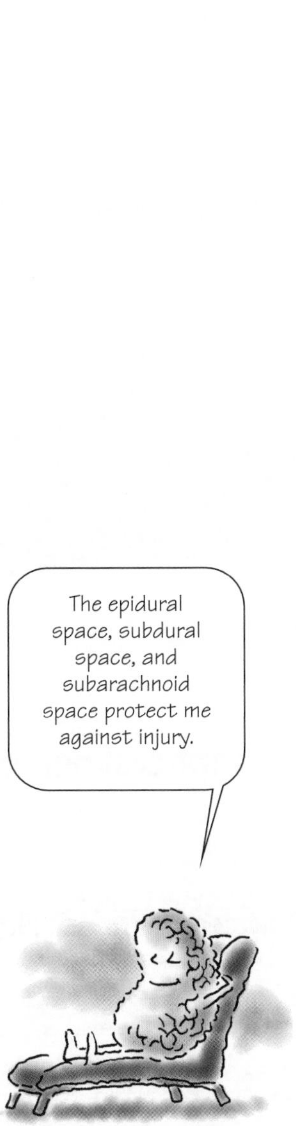
The epidural space, subdural space, and subarachnoid space protect me against injury.

Cushioning layers

Three layers of space further cushion the brain and spinal cord against injury. The **epidural space** (actually, a potential space) lies over the dura mater. The **subdural space** is situated between the dura mater and arachnoid membrane. This closed area—typically the site of hemorrhage after head trauma—offers no escape route for accumulated blood. The **subarachnoid space,** filled with CSF, separates the arachnoid membrane and pia mater.

Cerebrospinal fluid

CSF is a colorless fluid that arises from blood plasma and has a similar composition. It cushions the brain and spinal cord, nourishes cells, and transports metabolic waste.

Fluid factory

CSF forms continuously in clusters of capillaries called the **choroid plexuses,** located in the roof of each ventricle. The choroid plexuses produce approximately 500 ml of CSF each day.

Open to flow

From the lateral ventricles, CSF flows through the **interventricular foramen,** commonly known as the **foramen of Monro,** to the third ventricle of the brain. **Foramen** is a term used to describe a natural opening or passage. The foramen of Monro is named after the man who first described it: Alexander Monro II, a professor of anatomy at the University of Edinburgh. (See *Three men of Monro.*)

From there, it reaches the subarachnoid space and then passes under the base of the brain, upward over the brain's upper surfaces, and down around the spinal cord. Eventually, it reaches the arachnoid villi, where it's reabsorbed into venous blood at the venous sinuses on top of the brain.

Beyond the dictionary

Three men of Monro

The foramen of Monro is named after Alexander Monro II (1733–1817), the man who first described it. Monro was the second professor of anatomy at the University of Edinburgh (and the second named Alexander Monro). He succeeded his father in this position and was succeeded by his own son, Alex III.

Peripheral nervous system

The peripheral nervous system consists of the cranial nerves, spinal nerves, and **autonomic nervous system (ANS).**

Message lines: Neck and above

The 12 pairs of **cranial nerves** transmit motor or sensory messages, or both, primarily between the brain or brain stem and the head and neck. All cranial nerves, except the olfactory and optic nerves, exit from the midbrain, pons, or medulla oblongata of the brain stem. (See *A look at the 12 cranial nerves.*)

A look at the 12 cranial nerves

As this illustration reveals, 10 of the 12 pairs of cranial nerves (CNs) exit from the brain stem. The remaining two pairs—the olfactory and optic nerves—exit from the forebrain.

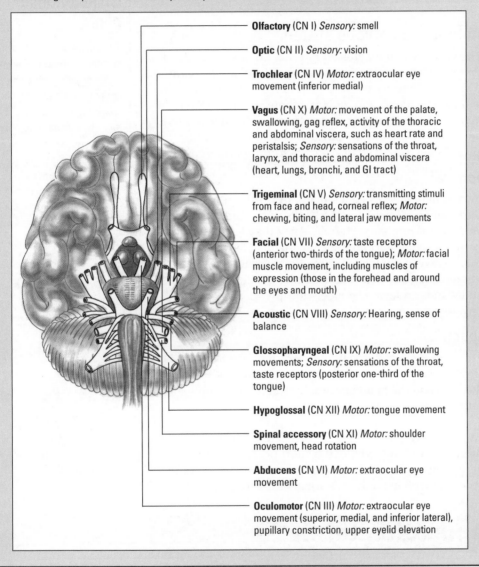

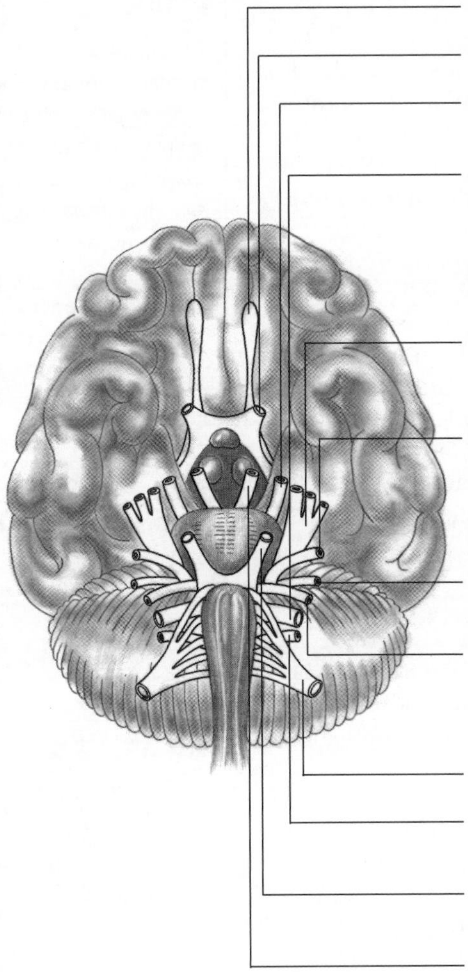
Olfactory (CN I) *Sensory:* smell
Optic (CN II) *Sensory:* vision
Trochlear (CN IV) *Motor:* extraocular eye movement (inferior medial)
Vagus (CN X) *Motor:* movement of the palate, swallowing, gag reflex, activity of the thoracic and abdominal viscera, such as heart rate and peristalsis; *Sensory:* sensations of the throat, larynx, and thoracic and abdominal viscera (heart, lungs, bronchi, and GI tract)
Trigeminal (CN V) *Sensory:* transmitting stimuli from face and head, corneal reflex; *Motor:* chewing, biting, and lateral jaw movements
Facial (CN VII) *Sensory:* taste receptors (anterior two-thirds of the tongue); *Motor:* facial muscle movement, including muscles of expression (those in the forehead and around the eyes and mouth)
Acoustic (CN VIII) *Sensory:* Hearing, sense of balance
Glossopharyngeal (CN IX) *Motor:* swallowing movements; *Sensory:* sensations of the throat, taste receptors (posterior one-third of the tongue)
Hypoglossal (CN XII) *Motor:* tongue movement
Spinal accessory (CN XI) *Motor:* shoulder movement, head rotation
Abducens (CN VI) *Motor:* extraocular eye movement
Oculomotor (CN III) *Motor:* extraocular eye movement (superior, medial, and inferior lateral), pupillary constriction, upper eyelid elevation

It says here that most of the cranial nerves transmit either **motor** or **sensory** information. A few, such as the **vagus nerve,** do both.

Can you hear me now?

The 31 pairs of **spinal nerves** are named for the vertebra immediately below each nerve's exit point from the spinal cord; thus, they're designated from top to bottom as C1 through S5 and the coccygeal nerve. Each spinal nerve consists of afferent and efferent neurons, which carry messages to and from particular body regions called **dermatomes.**

Autonomic nervous system

The vast ANS innervates all internal organs. Sometimes known as **visceral efferent nerves,** the nerves of the ANS carry messages to the viscera from the brain stem and neuroendocrine regulatory centers. The ANS has two major subdivisions: the **sympathetic (thoracolumbar)** nervous system and the **parasympathetic (craniosacral)** nervous system. (See *On autonomic pilot.*)

Beyond the dictionary

On autonomic pilot

The autonomic nervous system innervates all internal organs. **Autonomic** comes from two Greek words: ***auto,*** meaning *self,* and ***nomos,*** meaning *law.* So, this nervous system operates according to its own law, or without conscious control.

Think of the autonomic nervous system as being on autopilot.

System response: General

Sympathetic nerves called **preganglionic neurons** exit the spinal cord between the levels of the first thoracic and second lumbar vertebrae. After they leave the spinal cord, these nerves enter small ganglia near the spinal cord. The ganglia form a chain that spreads the impulse to **postganglionic neurons,** which reach many organs and glands and can produce widespread, generalized physiologic responses.

System response: Specific

Fibers of the parasympathetic nervous system leave the CNS by way of the cranial nerves from the midbrain and medulla and the spinal nerves between the second and fourth sacral vertebrae (S2-S4).

After leaving the CNS, the long preganglionic fiber of each parasympathetic nerve travels to a ganglion near a particular organ or gland; the short postganglionic fiber enters the organ or gland. This creates a more specific response, involving only one organ or gland.

Physical examination terms

Here are terms associated with procedures and observations one might encounter in a physical examination relating to the neurologic system:

- **Absence seizure** (also known as a **petit mal seizure**) is marked by a sudden, momentary loss of conscious-

(Text continues on page 283.)

Incredibly Easy miniguide: The brain

The cerebrum has right and left hemispheres. Each cerebral hemisphere is divided into four lobes.

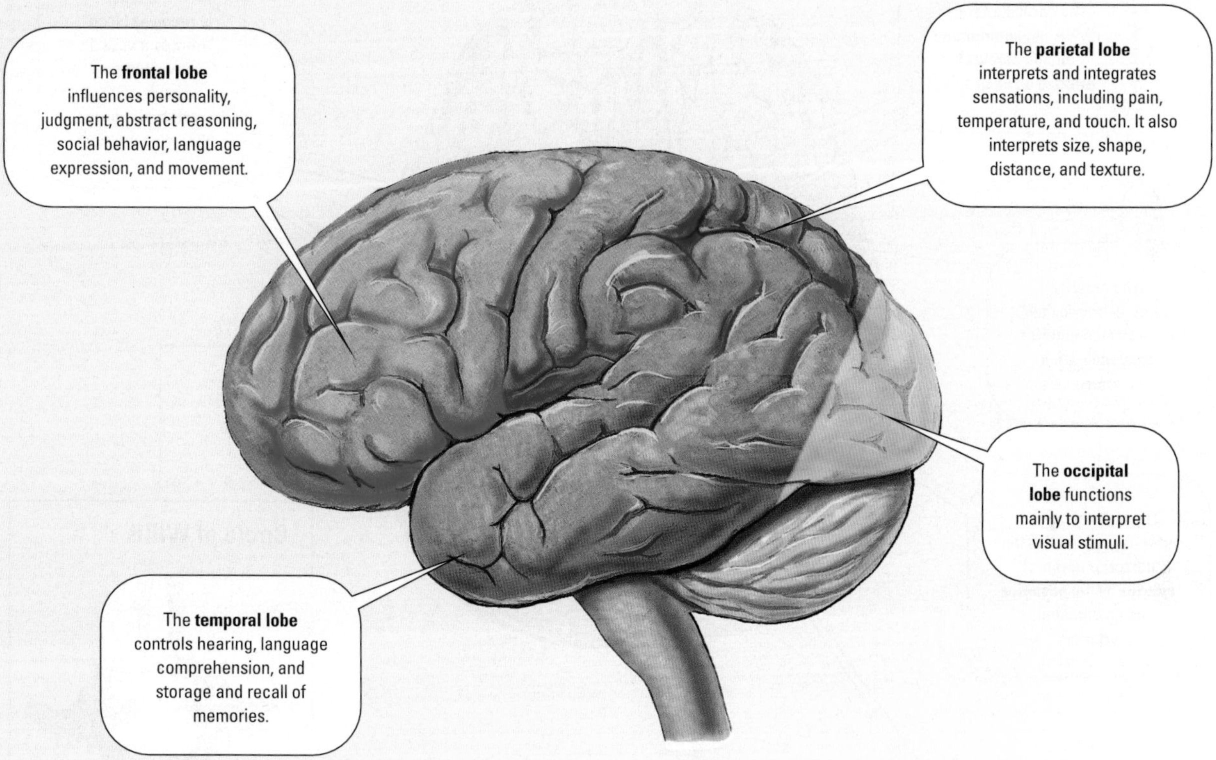
The **frontal lobe** influences personality, judgment, abstract reasoning, social behavior, language expression, and movement.
The **parietal lobe** interprets and integrates sensations, including pain, temperature, and touch. It also interprets size, shape, distance, and texture.
The **occipital lobe** functions mainly to interpret visual stimuli.
The **temporal lobe** controls hearing, language comprehension, and storage and recall of memories.

You really can't understand me unless you're willing to look at my lobes.

Incredibly Easy miniguide: The brain

This illustration of the inferior surface of the brain shows the anterior and posterior arteries, which join with smaller arteries to form the circle of Willis.

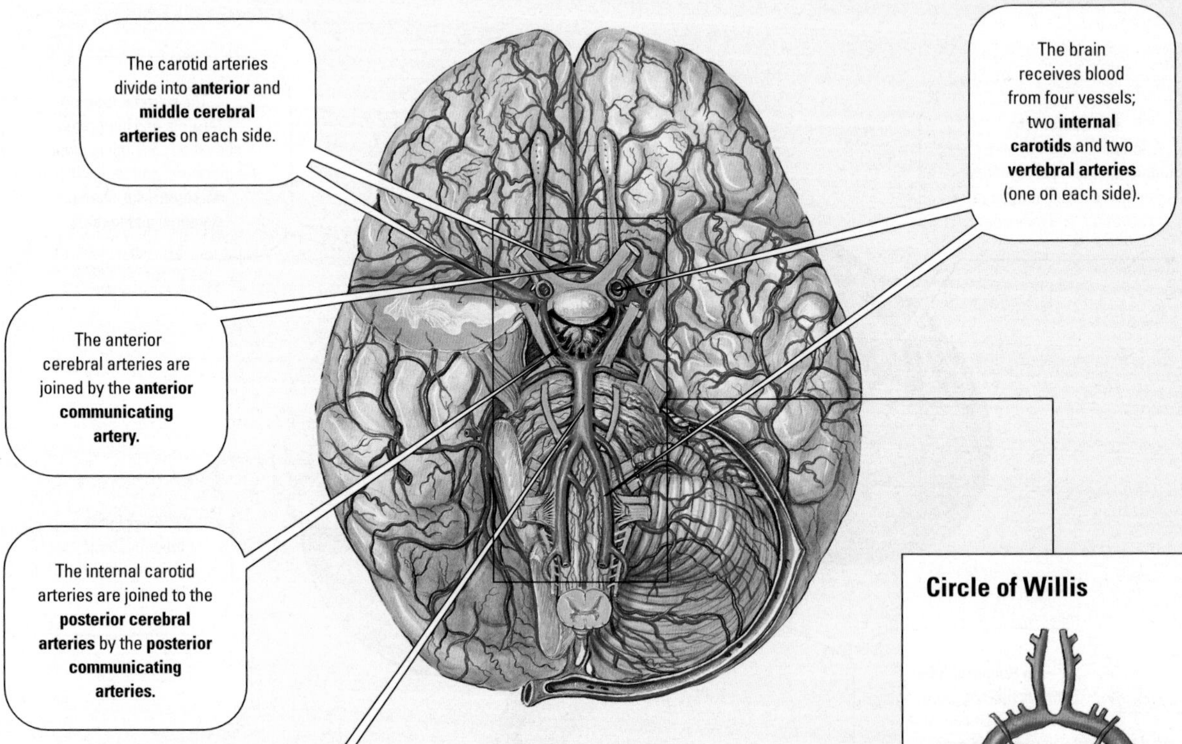
The carotid arteries divide into **anterior** and **middle cerebral arteries** on each side.
The brain receives blood from four vessels; two **internal carotids** and two **vertebral arteries** (one on each side).
The anterior cerebral arteries are joined by the **anterior communicating artery.**
The internal carotid arteries are joined to the **posterior cerebral arteries** by the **posterior communicating arteries.**
The vertebral arteries join centrally to form the **basilar artery.**

Circle of Willis

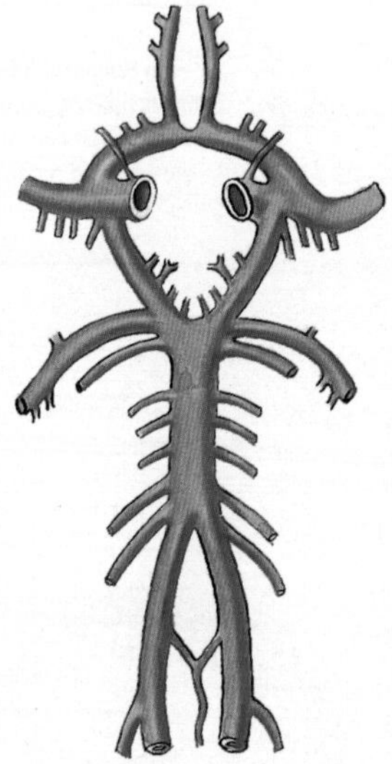

This circle of arteries is known as the circle of Willis.

Incredibly Easy miniguide: The brain

The meninges cover and protect the brain. They consist of three layers of connective tissue—the dura mater, arachnoid, and pia mater.

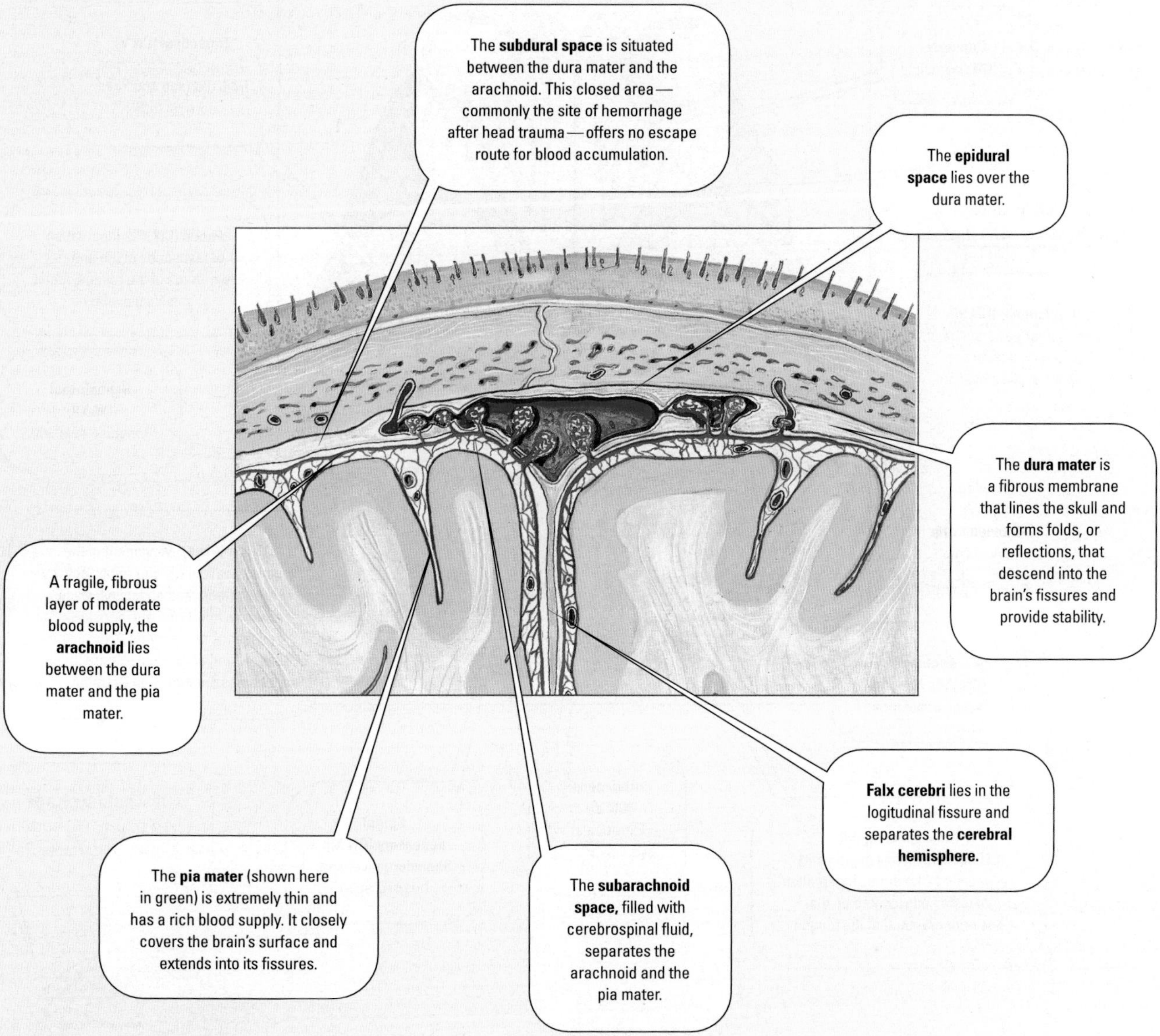
The **subdural space** is situated between the dura mater and the arachnoid. This closed area—commonly the site of hemorrhage after head trauma—offers no escape route for blood accumulation.
The **epidural space** lies over the dura mater.
The **dura mater** is a fibrous membrane that lines the skull and forms folds, or reflections, that descend into the brain's fissures and provide stability.
A fragile, fibrous layer of moderate blood supply, the **arachnoid** lies between the dura mater and the pia mater.
Falx cerebri lies in the logitudinal fissure and separates the **cerebral hemisphere.**
The **pia mater** (shown here in green) is extremely thin and has a rich blood supply. It closely covers the brain's surface and extends into its fissures.
The **subarachnoid space,** filled with cerebrospinal fluid, separates the arachnoid and the pia mater.

Incredibly Easy miniguide: The brain

The 12 pairs of cranial nerves transmit motor messages, sensory messages, or both, primarily between the brain or brainstem and the head and neck.

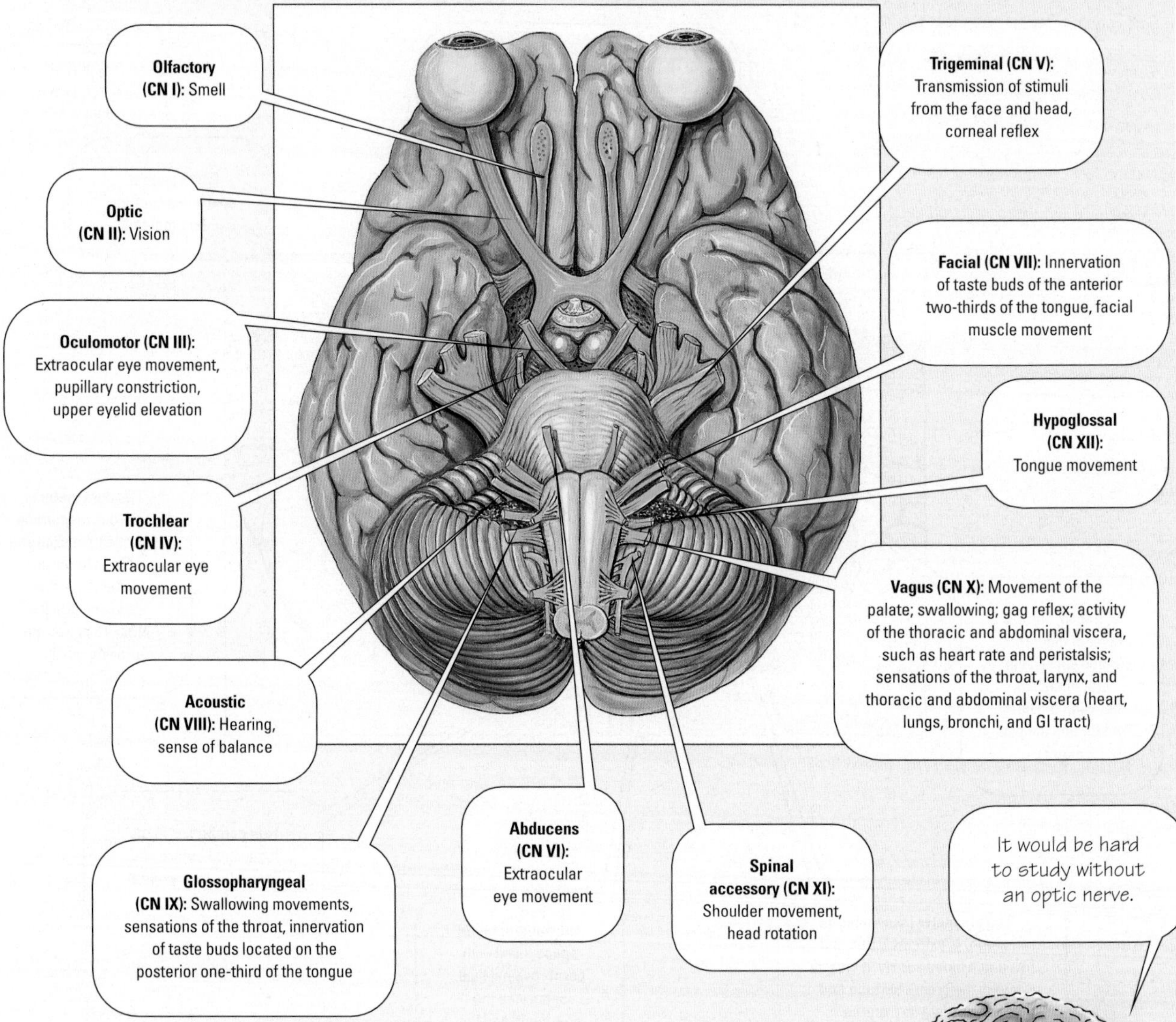
Olfactory (CN I): Smell
Optic (CN II): Vision
Oculomotor (CN III): Extraocular eye movement, pupillary constriction, upper eyelid elevation
Trochlear (CN IV): Extraocular eye movement
Acoustic (CN VIII): Hearing, sense of balance
Glossopharyngeal (CN IX): Swallowing movements, sensations of the throat, innervation of taste buds located on the posterior one-third of the tongue
Abducens (CN VI): Extraocular eye movement
Spinal accessory (CN XI): Shoulder movement, head rotation
Trigeminal (CN V): Transmission of stimuli from the face and head, corneal reflex
Facial (CN VII): Innervation of taste buds of the anterior two-thirds of the tongue, facial muscle movement
Hypoglossal (CN XII): Tongue movement
Vagus (CN X): Movement of the palate; swallowing; gag reflex; activity of the thoracic and abdominal viscera, such as heart rate and peristalsis; sensations of the throat, larynx, and thoracic and abdominal viscera (heart, lungs, bronchi, and GI tract)

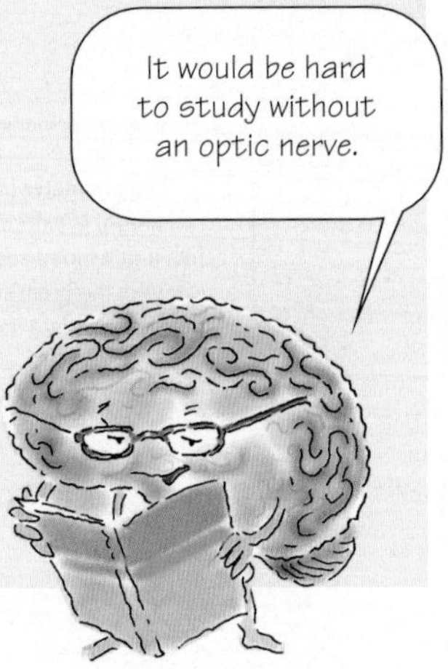
It would be hard to study without an optic nerve.

ness, typically accompanied by loss of muscle control or spasms, and a vacant facial expression. The patient may experience many seizures per day.

- **Aphasia** is loss or impairment of the ability to communicate through speech, written language, or signs. It typically results from brain disease or trauma.
- **Aphonia** is loss of the ability to speak.
- **Apraxia** is complete or partial inability to perform purposeful movements in the absence of sensory or motor impairment.
- **Ataxia** is impairment of the ability to coordinate voluntary muscle movement.
- **Ataxic speech** is characterized by faulty formation of sounds. It's typically caused by neuromuscular disease.
- **Athetosis** is a condition characterized by constant, slow, writhing, involuntary movements of the extremities, especially the hands.
- **Aura** is the word for the sensations that occur before a paroxysmal attack, such as a seizure or migraine headache.
- **Battle's sign** is discoloration of the skin behind the ear following the fracture of a bone in the lower skull.
- **Biot's respiration** is an abnormal, unpredictable breathing pattern characterized by irregular periods of apnea alternating with periods of four or five breaths of the same depth. Biot's respiration indicates meningitis, a lesion in the medulla, or increased intracranial pressure.

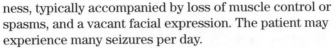

Biot's respiration, pronounced BEE-OHZ, is named after Camille Biot, a 19th-century French doctor.

- **Bradylalia** refers to abnormally slow speech, caused by a brain lesion.
- **Brudzinski's sign** is flexion of the hips and knees in response to passive flexion of the neck. A positive Brudzinski's sign signals meningeal irritation.
- **Coma** is a state of unconsciousness from which the patient can't be aroused.
- **Decerebrate posturing** is associated with a lesion of the upper brain stem or severe bilateral lesions in the cerebrum. The patient typically lies with legs extended, head retracted, arms adducted and extended, wrists pronated, and the fingers, ankles, and toes flexed.
- **Decorticate posturing** is associated with a lesion of the frontal lobes, cerebral peduncles, or internal capsule. The patient lies with arms adducted and flexed, wrists

and fingers flexed on the chest, legs stiffly extended and internally rotated, and feet plantar flexed.

- **Delirium** is a disorientation to time and place; the patient may also experience illusions and hallucinations.
- **Dementia** is an organic mental syndrome marked by general loss of intellectual abilities, with chronic personality disintegration, confusion, disorientation, and stupor. It doesn't include states of impaired intellectual functioning resulting from delirium or depression.
- **Dysphagia** is difficulty swallowing.
- **Dysphasia** is impairment of speech involving failure to arrange words in their proper order, usually resulting from injury to the speech area in the cerebral cortex.

Dysphasia
failure words is proper order in arrange to.

- **Dyspraxia** is a partial loss of the ability to perform coordinated movements, with no associated defect in motor or sensory functions.
- **A generalized tonic-clonic (grand mal) seizure** is an **epileptic seizure** that may be preceded by an aura. This type of seizure is characterized by loss of consciousness and muscle spasms (tonic phase), followed by convulsive movement of the limbs (clonic phase).
- The **Glasgow Coma Scale** is commonly used to assess a patient's level of consciousness (LOC). It was designed to help determine a patient's chances for survival and recovery after a head injury. The scale scores three observations — eye opening response, best motor response, and best verbal response. Each response receives a point value. If a patient is alert, can follow simple commands, and is well-oriented, his score will total 15 points. If the patient is comatose, his score will be 7 or less. The lowest possible score, 3, indicates deep coma and a poor prognosis.

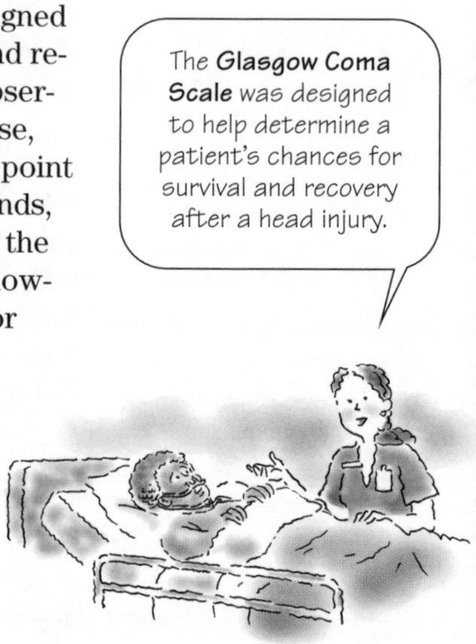
The Glasgow Coma Scale was designed to help determine a patient's chances for survival and recovery after a head injury.

- **Headache** is diffuse pain that occurs in different portions of the head and is not confined to any nerve distribution area.
- **Hemiparesis** refers to paralysis or muscular weakness affecting only one side of the body.
- **Hemiplegia** is paralysis of one side of the body.
- **Intracranial pressure (ICP)** is the pressure created by CSF in the subarachnoid space between the skull and brain. ICP may increase as a result of head trauma, brain tumor, stroke, or infection in the brain.
- **Kernig's sign** refers to resistance and hamstring muscle pain that occur when an examiner attempts to extend

a patient's knee while the hip and knee are both flexed 90 degrees. This sign is usually present in a patient with meningitis or subarachnoid hemorrhage.

- **Neuralgia** is severe pain in a nerve or nerves.

Reflexes

Reflexes, involuntary responses to stimuli, are discussed here:

- **Achilles tendon reflex** produces plantar flexion when the Achilles tendon is tapped.
- **Babinski's reflex** is dorsiflexion of the big toe in response to scraping the sole of the foot.
- **Biceps reflex** causes contraction of the biceps muscles when the tendon is tapped.
- **Brachioradialis reflex** is flexion and supination of the elbow or visible contraction of the brachioradialis muscle when the radius is tapped 1⅛″ to 2″ (3 to 5 cm) above the wrist while the arm is relaxed.
- **Corneal reflex** is closure of the eyelids when the cornea is touched.
- A negative **oculocephalic reflex,** also known as an absent **doll's eye sign,** is an indicator of brain stem dysfunction. The absence of the doll's eye sign is detected by rapid, but gentle, turning of the patient's head from side to side. The eyes remain fixed in an abnormal straight-ahead position instead of moving in the direction opposite to which the head is turned.
- **Gag reflex** is elicited by touching the soft palate or the back of the pharynx. The normal response is elevation of the palate, retraction of the tongue, and contraction of the constrictor muscle of the pharynx.
- **Knee-jerk reflex** is a kick reflex produced by sharply tapping the patellar ligament. It's also known as the **patellar reflex.**
- **Pupillary reflex** is contraction of the pupils in response to light.
- **Triceps reflex** is visible contraction of the triceps or extension of the arm when the triceps tendon is tapped above the elbow while the arm is flexed.

Sorry!

Diagnostic tests

Diagnostic tests associated with the neurologic system include radiographic and imaging studies, electrophysiologic studies, and CSF and blood tests.

Radiographic and imaging studies

Here are some common radiographic and imaging studies:

- **Cerebral angiography** is a radiographic procedure in which radiopaque contrast is injected into blood vessels to allow visualization of the vascular system of the brain.
- **Computed tomograph (CT)** combines radiography and computer analysis of tissue density. When used to diagnose neurologic disorders, it produces images of the structures inside the skull and spinal cord.
- **Digital subtraction angiography (DSA)** traces the cerebral vessels by means of a type of computerized fluoroscopy. The technician takes an image of the area being studied and stores it in the computer's memory. Additional images are taken after the patient receives a contrast medium. By subtracting the original picture from the later images, the computer produces high-resolution images for interpretation.
- **Echoencephalography** is a diagnostic technique that involves the use of ultrasound waves to study structures within the brain.
- **Magnetic resonance angiography (MRA)** is a noninvasive method of scanning that allows visualization of blood flowing through the cerebral vessels.
- **Magnetic resonance imaging (MRI),** also called **nuclear magnetic resonance,** is a noninvasive method of scanning with an electromagnetic field and radio waves. It provides visual images of structures on a computer screen.
- In **myelography,** dye or air is injected into the patient's subarachnoid space after lumbar puncture. X-rays are then taken.
- **Pneumoencephalography (PEG)** enables visualization the fluid-filled structures of the brain after CSF is intermittently withdrawn through lumbar puncture and replaced by air, oxygen, or helium. (See *Getting around PEG.*)

The root ***echo*** in **echoencephalography** tells you that this test uses sound waves.

Beyond the dictionary

Getting around PEG

Pneumoencephalography is a long word, but it can easily be broken down.

Pneumo- means *air.* The prefix ***en-*** means *within,* and ***-cephal-*** is a Greek term for *head.* So ***-encephal-*** literally means *within the head* and thus refers to the brain. The suffix ***-graphy*** refers to a method of recording, in this case X-ray photography. So, the term means *X-ray photography of air (or gas) in the brain.*

• A **positron emission tomography (PET)** scan is used to determine the brain's metabolic activity after the infusion of radioactive materials.
• In **skull X-rays,** high-energy radiography is used to detect fractures, bony tumors, or vascular abnormalities. They're typically taken from two angles: **anteroposterior** and **lateral. Waters' projection** is used to examine the frontal and maxillary sinuses, facial bones, and eye orbits. **Towne's projection** is used to examine the occipital bone.
• **Spinal X-rays** are obtained to detect spinal fractures, displacement of the spine, destructive lesions, structural abnormalities, and other conditions.
• **Stereotaxic neuroradiography** is an X-ray procedure used during neurosurgery to guide a needle or electrodes into a specific area of the brain. (See *Understanding stereotaxic neuroradiography.*)

Beyond the dictionary

Understanding stereotaxic neuroradiography

Stereotaxic neuroradiography is easy to understand when you break it down into its components. ***Stereo-*** is a familiar term from the Greek language that refers to something that's *solid,* meaning it has three dimensions. **Taxic** refers to *movement in response to a stimulus.* **Neuro-** refers to the nervous system. **Radiography** is *an X-ray study.* Thus, **stereotaxic neuroradiography** involves movement (of a needle or electrode) in three dimensions accompanied by X-ray photography of the brain.

Electrophysiologic studies

Here are some common electrophysiologic studies associated with the neurologic system:
• **Electroencephalography,** also called **EEG,** records the brain's continuous electrical activity.
• **Evoked potential testing** evaluates the integrity of visual, somatosensory, and auditory nerve pathways by measuring evoked potentials—the brain's electrical response to stimulation of the sensory organs or peripheral nerves. This type of testing is used to detect neurologic lesions and to evaluate multiple sclerosis as well as various vision and hearing disorders.
• **Magnetoencephalography** is a noninvasive test that directly measures the magnetic fields produced by electrical currents in the brain.

CSF and blood tests

CSF analysis is performed on CSF that's removed during a lumbar puncture (aspiration of CSF by insertion of a needle into the L3-4 or L4-5 interspace). Three common tests of CSF and blood are described here:
• The **amyloid beta-protein precursor test** checks CSF for levels of a substance that produces the protein

plaques seen in the brains of patients with Alzheimer's disease.

- **Coccidioidomycosis antibodies** is a blood test to identify a fungal infection that affects CNS and other areas of the body.
- **CSF analysis** is used to detect the presence of blood, infection, and other abnormalities.

Disorders

This section discusses brain and spinal cord disorders, cranial nerve disorders, degenerative disorders, head trauma, vascular disorders, and miscellaneous neurologic disorders.

Brain and spinal cord disorders

Here are some common brain and spinal cord disorders, including CNS infections and neural tube defects:

- **Cerebral palsy** is a chronic disorder of motor function resulting from nonprogressive brain damage or a brain lesion.
- **Epilepsy** refers to a group of neurologic disorders marked by uncontrolled electrical discharge from the cerebral cortex and typically manifested by seizures with clouding of consciousness. **Status epilepticus** describes a continuous seizure state, which is life-threatening.
- **Hydrocephalus** is a condition marked by excess CSF within the brain's ventricles. Two types exist; they're named according to their causes. **Noncommunicating hydrocephalus** results from obstruction of CSF flow. **Communicating hydrocephalus** is caused by faulty reabsorption of CSF. (See *Too much water*.)
- **Migraine headache** is a very painful, throbbing headache commonly associated with sensitivity to light and sound. In some people, the headache is preceded by an aura.
- A **subarachnoid hemorrhage** is an intracranial hemorrhage into the subarachnoid space.
- **Subdural hematoma** is accumulation of blood in the subdural space.

Beyond the dictionary

Too much water

Hydrocephalus is a condition marked by excess cerebrospinal fluid within the brain's ventricles. The term **hydrocephalus** originates from the Greek words ***hydro,*** meaning *water* or *fluid,* and ***kephale,*** meaning *head.*

CNS infections

CNS infections include encephalitis, meningitis, rabies, and others:

- **Brain abscess,** also known as an **intracranial abscess,** is a free or encapsulated collection of pus, usually found in the temporal lobe, cerebellum, or frontal lobe.
- **Encephalitis** is an inflammatory disorder of the brain that's commonly caused by the bite of an infected mosquito.
- **Meningitis** refers to the inflammation of the meninges of the brain and spinal cord caused by bacterial, viral, or fungal infection.
- **Myelitis** is an inflammation of the spinal cord.
- **Poliomyelitis** is an acute viral infection and inflammation of the gray matter of the spine, usually caused by poliovirus.
- **Rabies** is an acute, usually fatal CNS disease spread by animals to people through contaminated saliva, blood, or tissue. (See *Afraid of the water.*)

Beyond the dictionary

Afraid of the water

Rabies is also called **hydrophobia**—meaning *fear of water*—because this condition produces muscle spasms in the throat when the patient drinks water.

Neural tube defects

Neural tube defects are serious birth defects involving the spine or brain. They result from failure of the neural tube to close approximately 28 days after conception.

The most common forms of neural tube defects are spina bifida, anencephaly, and encephalocele:

- In **anencephaly,** part of the top of the skull and all or part of the brain are missing.
- In **encephalocele,** a saclike portion of the meninges and brain protrudes through a defective opening in the skull.
- **Spina bifida cystica** is incomplete closure of one or more vertebrae, which causes spinal contents to protrude in an external sac. The spinal cord is usually normal.
- **Spina bifida with meningocele** is a form of spina bifida in which the sac contains meninges and CSF.
- **Spina bifida with myelomeningocele (meningomyelocele)** is a form of spina bifida in which the sac contains meninges, CSF, and a portion of the spinal cord or nerve roots.

Remember, -itis refers to inflammation. So meningitis is an inflammation of the meninges.

Cranial nerve disorders

Cranial nerve disorders include Bell's palsy and trigeminal neuralgia:

- **Bell's palsy** is a unilateral facial paralysis of sudden onset, attributable to a lesion of the facial nerve. It's generally not permanent.
- **Trigeminal neuralgia,** also called **tic douloureux,** is a painful disorder affecting one or more branches of the fifth cranial (trigeminal) nerve. With stimulation of a trigger zone, the patient experiences paroxysmal attacks of excruciating facial pain.

Degenerative disorders

Degenerative disorders of the brain include Alzheimer's disease, multiple sclerosis, Parkinson's disease, and others:

- **Alzheimer's disease** produces three hallmark features in the brain: neurofibrillary tangles, neuritic plaques, and granulovascular degeneration. Early signs progress to severe deterioration in memory, language, and motor function.
- **Amyotrophic lateral sclerosis,** also called **Lou Gehrig disease,** is an incurable disease affecting the spinal cord and the medulla and cortex of the brain. It's characterized by progressive degeneration of motor neurons. This degeneration leads to weakness and wasting of the muscles, increased reflexes, and severe muscle spasms. Death typically occurs within 2 to 5 years.
- **Huntington's disease,** also called **Huntington's chorea,** is a hereditary disorder that causes degeneration in the cerebral cortex and basal ganglia. Degeneration leads to chronic, progressive **chorea** (rapid, jerky movements) and mental deterioration and ends with dementia and death.
- **Multiple sclerosis** is a progressive demyelination of the white matter of the brain and spinal cord that results in weakness, incoordination, paresthesia, speech disturbances, and visual complaints.
- **Myasthenia gravis** is abnormal muscle weakness and fatigability, especially in the muscles of the face and throat, resulting from a defect in the conduction of nerve impulses at the myoneural junction.

Asthenia is the Greek word for *weakness*. **Myasthenia gravis** is abnormal muscle weakness, particularly in the face and throat.

• **Parkinson's disease** is a slow-progressing, degenerative neurologic disorder that produces muscle rigidity, akinesia, and involuntary tremor.

Head trauma

Head trauma can range from concussion to tentorial herniation:

• **Cerebral contusion** is a bruising of the brain tissue as a result of a severe blow to the head. More severe than a concussion, a contusion disrupts normal nerve function in the bruised area and may cause loss of consciousness, hemorrhage, edema, and even death.

• **Concussion,** the most common head injury, results from a blow to the head that's hard enough to jostle the brain and cause it to strike the skull. This causes temporary neural dysfunction and a change in LOC.

• An **epidural hematoma** is the rapid accumulation of blood between the skull and dura mater.

• **Tentorial herniation** occurs when injured brain tissue swells and squeezes through the tentorial notch (an area that contains the midbrain), constricting the brain stem.

Vascular disorders

Vascular disorders include cerebral aneurysm, cerebrovascular accident, and others:

• **Arteriovenous malformation (AVM)** is a congenital malformation characterized by a tangled mass of dilated cerebral vessels that form an abnormal communication between the arterial and venous systems.

• A **cerebral aneurysm** is a localized dilation (ballooning) of a cerebral artery caused by weakness in the arterial wall.

• **Cerebrovascular accident (CVA)** is a condition of sudden onset in which a cerebral blood vessel is occluded by an embolus or cerebrovascular hemorrhage. The resulting ischemia of brain tissue normally perfused by the affected vessel may lead to permanent neurologic damage. (See *CVA substitutes.*)

• A **transient ischemic attack (TIA)** is a recurrent neurologic episode lasting less than 1 hour. It doesn't cause permanent or long-lasting neurologic deficit but is

The real world

CVA substitutes

A **cerebrovascular accident (CVA)** is rarely referred to by its proper name in the real world. Rather, it's referred to as a "stroke" or "brain attack."

usually considered a warning sign of an impending stroke.

Miscellaneous neurologic disorders

Other neurologic disorders include Reye's syndrome, tetanus, and Tourette syndrome:

- **Guillain-Barré syndrome** is an acute, febrile polyneuritis that sometimes occurs after a viral infection. It's marked by rapidly ascending paralysis that begins as weakness and paresthesia of the legs.
- **Neurofibromatosis** is a genetic trait characterized by the presence of multiple neurofibromas (fibrous tumors of peripheral nerves, resulting from abnormal proliferation of Schwann cells) of the nerves and skin, café-au-lait (light, coffee-colored) spots on the skin and, sometimes, developmental anomalies of the muscles, bones, and visceral tissue.
- **Reye's syndrome** is usually an acute childhood illness that causes fatty infiltration of the liver with concurrent elevated blood ammonia levels, encephalopathy, and increased ICP. Although a definitive cause hasn't been determined, it's associated with the use of aspirin-containing medications in the treatment of viral illnesses.
- **Tetanus** is an acute, commonly fatal infection caused by the anaerobic bacillus *Clostridium tetani*, which usually enters the body through a contaminated puncture wound.
- **Tetany** is hyperexcitability of nerves and prolonged contraction of muscles caused by low calcium levels.
- **Tourette syndrome** is a condition characterized by facial and vocal tics, generalized lack of coordination, and rarely **coprolalia** (an uncontrollable urge to utter obscenities).

Treatments

The terminology discussed here describes treatments (including surgeries) that may be employed when caring for a patient with a neurologic disorder.

Brain treatments and monitoring tools

Treatments include craniotomy, lobotomy, placement of a ventriculoperitoneal shunt, and different methods of ICP monitoring:

- **Cerebellar stimulator implantation** involves the surgical implantation of electrodes into a patient's brain to regulate uncoordinated neuromuscular activity using electrical impulses. This treatment has also been used to prevent seizures.
- **Craniectomy** is removal of a part of the skull.
- A **craniotomy** is the creation of a surgical incision into the skull to expose the brain for treatment.
- **Hemicraniectomy** is the removal of the skull to expose half of the brain in preparation for surgery.
- **Intracranial hematoma aspiration** is performed to reduce high ICP caused by a collection of blood around the surface of the brain. A craniotomy must be performed to access the brain.
- **Lobectomy** is removal of a lobe of the brain.
- **Lobotomy** is incision into the frontal lobe of the brain through holes drilled into the skull.
- **Stereotactic surgery** provides three-dimensimal images that guide the surgeon in removal of small brain tumors and abscesses drainage of hematomas, repair of AVMs, and ablation for Parkinson's disease.
- A **ventriculoperitoneal shunt** is a surgical treatment for hydrocephalus in which a catheter drains CSF from the ventricular system for absorption. The shunt extends from the cerebral ventricle to the scalp, where it's tunneled under the skin and drains into the peritoneal cavity. Shunting lowers ICP and prevents brain damage by draining excess CSF or relieving blockage.
- In **volumetric interstitial brachytherapy**, radioactive materials are implanted into the skull and left in place for several days to deliver radiation to a brain tumor.

Lobectomy or lobotomy? I'm confused.

In a **lobectomy**, a lobe of the brain is **exc**ised. **Lobotomy** involves incision, not excision.

Intracranial pressure monitoring

ICP monitoring is an important part of neurologic treatment because increased ICP can lead to fatal brain herniation. Invasive ICP monitoring is accomplished in one of several ways:

- An **epidural probe** is a tiny fiber-optic sensor inserted in the brain's epidural space through a burr hole (a hole drilled into the skull).
- A **subarachnoid screw** is a small, hollow, steel screw with a sensor tip that's inserted through a burr hole. It's used to monitor pressure in the subarachnoid space.
- A **ventricular catheter,** consisting of a small polyethylene cannula and an external drainage and collection system, is inserted through a burr hole into a lateral ventricle.

Spinal and nerve surgery

Here are some common surgeries performed on the spine or spinal nerves:

- **Chordotomy** is any operation on the spinal cord.
- **Gamma knife surgery** is a noninvasive procedure that uses beams of gamma radiation to precisely target and treat brain lesions such as brain tumors, vascular malformations, and functional disorders such as trigeminal neuralgia.
- **Myelomeningocele repair** is performed to correct a congenital spinal defect as a means of preventing infection. The surgeon isolates neural tissue from the rest of the myelomeningocele sac and fashions a flap from surrounding tissue.
- **Neurectomy** is removal of part of a nerve.
- **Neuroplasty** is surgical repair of a nerve.
- In **sympathectomy,** a surgeon resects a sympathetic nerve or ganglion.
- **Vagotomy** is transection of the vagus nerve.

Other neurologic treatments

Here are some other common neurologic treatments:

- **AVM embolization** is a minimally invasive technique that's used to treat AVMs when surgery isn't an option. To lower the risk of rupture and hemorrhage, a flexible catheter is threaded into the AVM site, and small, heat-resistant silicon beads or a rapid-setting plastic polymer is inserted. The beads or polymer lodge in the feeder artery and occlude blood flow to the AVM.
- An induced **barbiturate coma** is a treatment of last resort for a patient experiencing sustained or acute episodes

of high ICP. The patient receives large doses of a short-acting barbiturate, such as pentobarbital, to induce a coma. The drug reduces the metabolic rate and cerebral blood volume, possibly reducing ICP and protecting cerebral tissue.

- **Drug therapy** for neurologic disorders includes the use of **anticonvulsants** to control seizures, **corticosteroids** to decrease inflammation and edema, **osmotic diuretics** to promote diuresis and reduce cerebral edema, and **antibiotics** to treat infection.
- **Plasmapheresis** is a process by which the blood is cleansed of harmful substances. In this procedure, plasma is removed from withdrawn blood, and the formed blood elements are reinfused after being mixed with a plasma replacement solution. In some methods, the plasma is filtered to remove a specific disease mediator and is then returned to the patient. Plasmapheresis is used to treat Guillain-Barré syndrome, multiple sclerosis, and myasthenia gravis.

Okay, listen up. You anticonvulsants, corticosteroids, osmotic diuretics, and antibiotics may be needed to treat neurologic disorders.

systole

Vocabulary builders

At a crossroads

Completing this crossword puzzle will help test your nerve with the nervous system. Good luck!

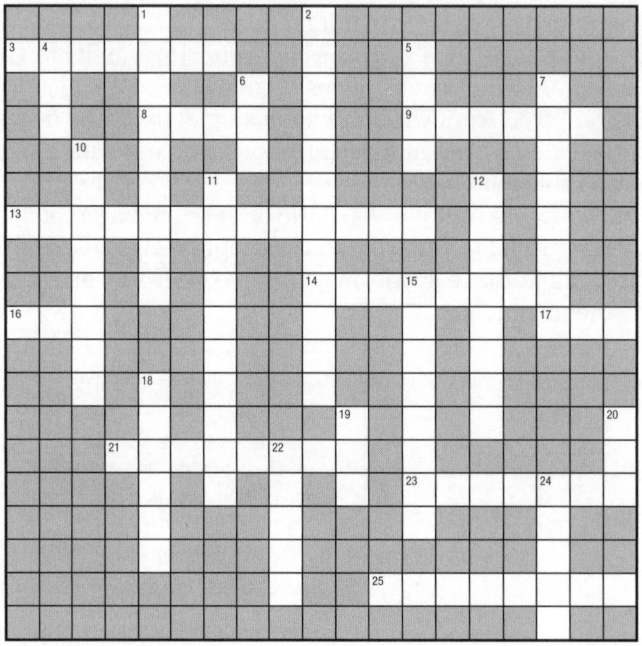

Across

3. Neurons outside the brain
8. Carries impulses away from the cell
9. Plural of **nucleus**
13. "Water on the brain"
14. Another name for **sensory neurons**
16. Acronym for the medical term for *stroke*
17. Records the brain's electrical activity
21. Membranes enclosing the CNS
23. Basic cells of the nervous system
25. Type of headache preceded by an aura

Down

1. First cranial nerve
2. Controls body temperature
4. **Arteriovenous malformation** abbreviation
5. Serves as a bridge
6. **Central nervous system** abbreviation
7. Carries impulses to the cell
10. Another name for **mesencephalon**
11. Infection of the meninges
12. Largest part of the brain
15. Another name for **motor neurons**
18. Sheath covering nerve cells
19. **Cerebrospinal fluid** abbreviation
20. The brain's switchboard
22. Gluelike cells
24. Second cranial nerve

Answers are on page 298.

Finish line

Fill in the blanks below with the appropriate word(s).

1. The most common head injury is a _____.
2. A patient who loses the ability to speak or write has _____.
3. Patients commonly experience an _____ just before a migraine headache.
4. Creation of a surgical incision into the skull is a _____.
5. Holes drilled into the skull are known as _____ holes.
6. A subarachnoid screw is used to monitor a patient's __________ __________.
7. __________ __________ is the surgical treatment of hydrocephalus.
8. Plasmapheresis is the therapeutic removal of _____ from the patient's body.

I get a lot of support, nourishment, and protein from my nonneuronal buddy cells. Do you know which ones I mean?

Talking in circles

Use the clues below to fill in the blanks with the appropriate word. Then unscramble the circled letters to find the answer to the question posed at left.

1. _ _ _ _ _ (_)
2. _ _ _ _ (_) _ _
   _ _ _ _ _ (_) _ _ _
3. _ _ _ (_) _ _ _ _
4. _ _ _ (_) _ _ _ _ _ _ (_) _
5. (_) _ _ _ _ _
6. (_) _ _ _ _ _ (_) _ _ _ _ _

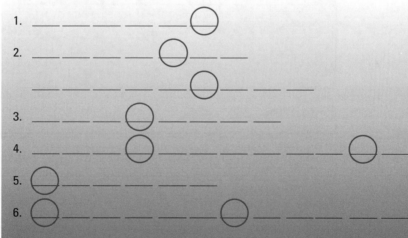

1. Highly specialized cell that detects and transmits stimuli electromechanically
2. Autonomic reflex center that maintains homeostasis, regulating respiratory, vasomotor, and cardiac functions
3. Cover and protect the cerebral cortex and spinal column
4. Controls or affects body temperature, appetite, water balance, pituitary secretions, and emotions
5. Acute, usually fatal CNS disease spread by animals to people through contaminated saliva, blood, or tissue
6. An inflammatory disorder of the brain commonly caused by the bite of an infected mosquito

Answers are on page 298.

Answers

At a crossroads

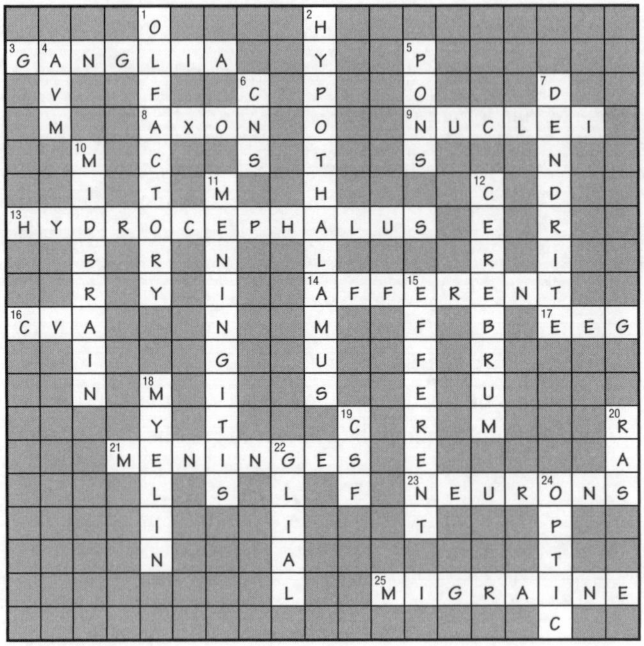

Finish line

1. Concussion; 2. Aphasia; 3. Aura; 4. Craniotomy; 5. Burr; 6. Intracranial pressure; 7. Ventricular shunting; 8. Plasma

Talking in circles

1. Neuron; 2. Medulla oblongata; 3. Meninges; 4. Hypothalamus; 5. Rabies; 6. Encephalitis
Answer to puzzle—Neuroglia

My brain got a great workout from this chapter!

13

Endocrine system

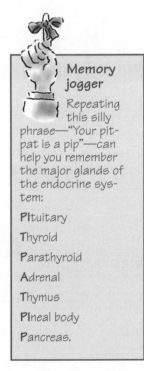

Just the facts

In this chapter, you'll learn:

- terminology related to the structure and function of the endocrine system
- terminology needed for physical examination
- tests that help diagnose common endocrine disorders
- endocrine system disorders and their treatments.

Endocrine structure and function

The endocrine system controls complicated body activities by secreting chemical substances into the circulatory system. The major components of the endocrine system are **glands** (specialized cell clusters or organs) and **hormones** (chemical substances secreted by the glands in response to stimulation). (See *Pronouncing key endocrine system terms*, page 300.)

Glands in a major key

The major glands of the endocrine system are the:

- pituitary gland
- thyroid gland
- parathyroid glands
- adrenal glands
- pancreas
- pineal body
- thymus. (See *Endocrine system structures*, page 301.)

Memory jogger

Repeating this silly phrase—"Your pit-pat is a pip"—can help you remember the major glands of the endocrine system:

PItuitary

Thyroid

Parathyroid

Adrenal

Thymus

PIneal body

Pancreas.

Pump up your pronunciation

Pronouncing key endocrine system terms

Below is a list of key terms related to the endocrine system along with the correct ways to pronounce them.

Acromegaly	ACK-ROH-MEG-UH-LEE
Adenohypophysis	ADD-EH-NOH-HEYE-PAHF-IH-SIS
Hyperaldosteronism	HEYE-PER-AL-DOS-TER-OHN-IZM
Luteinizing hormone	LOO-TEE-I-NEYE-ZING HOR-MOHN
Oxytocin	OCH-SEE-TOE-SIN
Radioimmunoassay	RAY-DEE-OH-IM-YOU-NOH-AHS-SAY
Thymopoietin	THEYE-MOH-POY-EH-TIN
Thyrotoxicosis factitia	THEYE-ROH-TOK-SI-KOH-SIS FAK-TISH-SHUH
Triiodothyronine	TREYE-EYE-O-DOH-THEYE-ROH-NEEN

Pituitary gland

The **pituitary gland,** also known as the **hypophysis,** is no larger than a pea and lies at the base of the brain in a depression of the sphenoid bone called the **sella turcica.**

Cover and connection

The **pituitary diaphragm,** an extension of the dura mater (the membrane covering the brain), extends over the pituitary gland and protects it. The **pituitary stalk,** a stemlike structure, provides a connection to the hypothalamus.

Hypo- means *beneath*; -***physis*** means *to grow.*
So…the **hypophysis** (pituitary gland) "grows" beneath me?

Master gland

The pituitary gland is also called the "master gland" because it controls all the other glands. It's divided into two regions: the anterior pituitary lobe and the posterior pituitary lobe.

Anatomically speaking

Endocrine system structures

Endocrine glands secrete hormones directly into the bloodstream to regulate body function. This illustration shows the locations of most of the major endocrine glands.

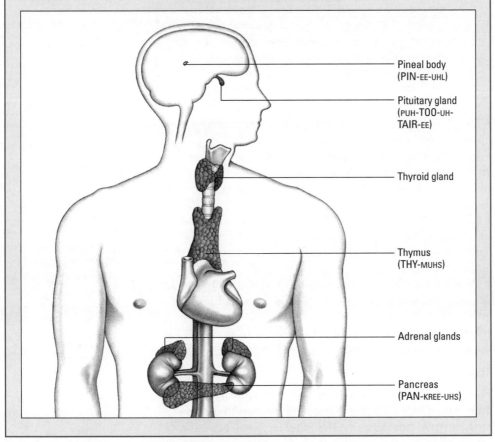

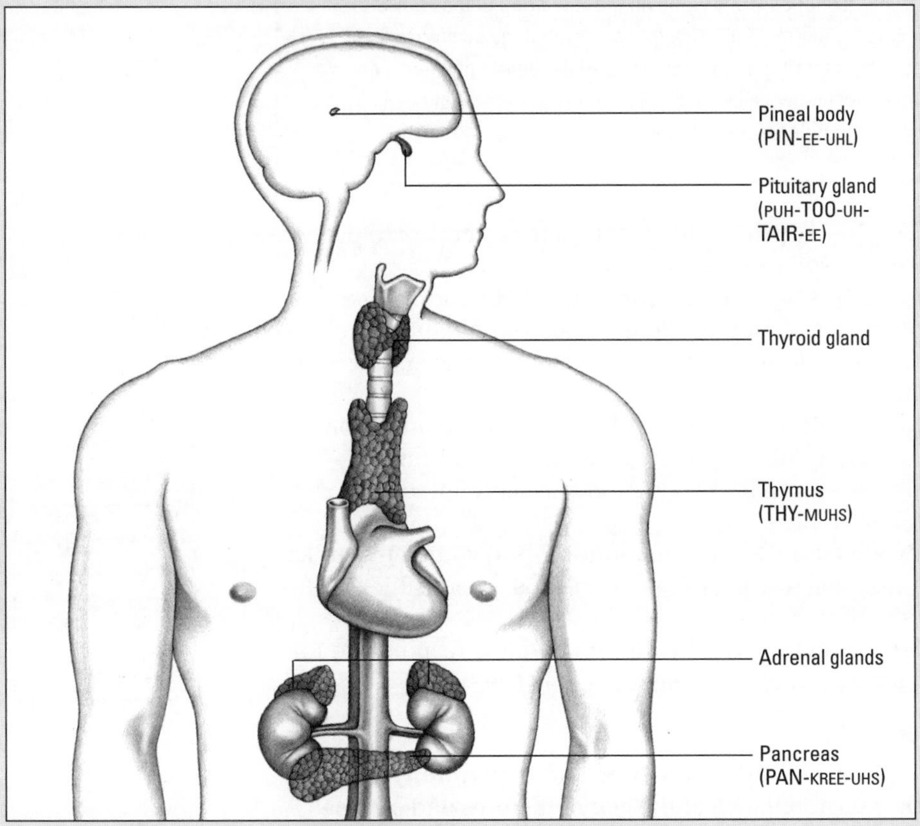
Pineal body
(PIN-EE-UHL)
Pituitary gland
(PUH-TOO-UH-TAIR-EE)
Thyroid gland
Thymus
(THY-MUHS)
Adrenal glands
Pancreas
(PAN-KREE-UHS)

Courtesy of the anterior pituitary

The largest region of the pituitary gland, the **anterior pituitary lobe (adenohypophysis)** produces at least seven hormones. (See *The history of* pituitary, page 302.) These are:

- **Growth hormone (GH),** or **somatotropin,** promotes the growth of bony and soft tissues.
- **Thyrotropin,** or **thyroid-stimulating hormone (TSH),** influences secretion of thyroid hormone.

Beyond the dictionary

The history of *pituitary*

The word **pituitary** derives from the Latin word ***pituita,*** which means *phlegm (mucus)* and was based on the belief that phlegm was produced by this gland. In the "Doctrine of the Four Humors," a theory of physiology and psychology commonly held during the 17th century, too much of the humor phlegm in one's body resulted in a listless, cold, apathetic personality—in other words, a **phlegmatic** individual.

- **Corticotropin** stimulates the adrenal cortex to produce cortisol. (See *Turning on to* tropins.)
- **Follicle-stimulating hormone (FSH)** stimulates the growth of **graafian follicles.** It also stimulates estrogen secretion in females and the development of sperm cells in males.
- **Luteinizing hormone (LH)** stimulates maturation of the ovarian follicle and the ovum and ovulation in females. It stimulates production and secretion of testosterone in males.
- **Prolactin (PRL),** or **mammotropin,** stimulates breast development during pregnancy and is responsible for the production of milk.
- **Melanocyte-stimulating hormone** is responsible for the formation of melanin pigment in the skin.

Thyroid literally means *shield-shaped* and refers to the shields that ancient Greek soldiers carried.

The posterior plays its part

The **posterior pituitary lobe (neurohypophysis)** makes up about 25% of the gland. It stores and releases **antidiuretic hormone (ADH)** and oxytocin after they're produced by the hypothalamus. ADH, also called **vasopressin,** stimulates water resorption by the kidneys to limit the production of large volumes of urine. **Oxytocin** stimulates the ejection of breast milk into the mammary ducts. It also stimulates contraction of the uterus during labor.

Thyroid gland

The **thyroid gland** lies directly below the larynx and partially in front of the trachea. Its two lobes are joined by a narrow tissue bridge called the **isthmus,** which gives the thyroid its butterfly shape.

Two lobes as one

The lobes function as one unit to produce the thyroid hormones **thyroxine (T_4), triiodothyronine (T_3),** and **thyrocalcitonin (calcitonin).** T_3 and T_4 are collectively known as **thyroid hormones.** They influence many metabolic processes, including cellular heat production, protein synthesis, and carbohydrate metabolism. Calcitonin lowers blood calcium and phosphate levels by blocking the resorption of bone, where calcium and phosphate are stored.

Too much of a good thing

Iodine is an essential element of thyroid hormones; many thyroid disorders are caused by overproduction of thyroid hormones and the iodine-containing substances they contain. The iodine within thyroid hormones combines with a protein in the blood to form **protein-bound iodine.** The components separate, however, when the hormone enters the tissues.

Beyond the dictionary

Turning on to *tropins*

The word **tropin,** or **trophin,** appears in the names of a number of hormones produced by the pituitary gland (for example, *somatotropin* and *mammotropin*). The word derives from a Greek word meaning *to turn.* In reference to a hormone, the sense is that a tropin turns or changes something.

Parathyroid glands

Four parathyroid glands lie on the posterior surface of the thyroid, one on each corner. (***Para-*** means *alongside.*)

Checking calcium

Like the thyroid lobes, the parathyroid glands work together as a single unit, producing **parathyroid hormone (PTH).** This hormone regulates the calcium and phosphorus content of the blood and bones. PTH increases blood calcium and phosphate levels through bone resorption. It antagonizes (works against) the hormone calcitonin. Together, these two hormones maintain calcium balance in the blood.

Adrenal glands

The two **adrenal glands** sit on top of the two kidneys. Each gland contains two distinct structures that function as separate endocrine glands.

Mandatory medulla

The inner portion, or **medulla,** produces the catecholamines **epinephrine** and **norepinephrine.** Because these hormones are vital to the autonomic nervous system, the **adrenal medulla** is also considered a neuroendocrine structure. The adrenal medulla is essential to life, but the **cortex,** the much larger outer layer, isn't.

Zoning in

The cortex has three zones and produces hormones called **corticoids:**

- The outermost zone is the **zona glomerulosa,** which produces mineralocorticoid hormones, primarily aldosterone.
- The **zona fasciculata,** the middle and largest zone, produces glucocorticoids and small amounts of the sex hormones estrogen and androgen.
- The inner zone, the **zona reticularis,** produces mainly glucocorticoids as well as some sex hormones.

Get me some glucocorticoids. They specialize in helping me recover from injury.

Classifying corticoids

The corticoid hormones are classified into three groups:

- **Glucocorticoids** are secreted mainly by the zona fasciculata and include **cortisol (hydrocortisone)** and **corticosterone.** These hormones affect all cells in the body but specialize in controlling the metabolism of carbohydrates, fats, and proteins; stress resistance; antibody formation; lymphatic functions; and recovery from injury and inflammation.
- **Mineralocorticoids** are secreted by the cortex and control the regulation and secretion of sodium and potassium. **Aldosterone** is the principle mineralocorticoid and is responsible for electrolyte and water balance.
- **Sex hormones** are secreted by the zona reticularis and the zona fasciculata. They include small amounts of the male hormone **androgen** (also present in smaller amounts in females), which promotes such secondary sex characteristics as facial hair and a low-pitched voice.

No corticotropin? Can't secrete.

The adrenal cortex can't secrete androgens and cortisol without the pituitary hormone corticotropin.

Pancreas

The **pancreas** lies along the posterior of the abdominal wall in the upper left quadrant behind the stomach. The **islets of Langerhans,** which perform the endocrine functions of this gland, contain specialized cells that secrete hormones.

The islets of Langerhans are named for Paul Langerhans, the German pathologist who first described these structures in 1869.

Products of the pancreas

Pancreatic hormones include:

- **insulin,** the hormone responsible for the storage and use of carbohydrates and for decreasing the body's blood glucose levels; it's produced by **beta cells** in the pancreas
- **glucagon,** which increases blood glucose levels and is produced by **alpha cells** in the pancreas
- **somatostatin**, a neurotransmitter released by **delta cells** in the pancreas that inhibits the release of glucagon and insulin.

Pineal body

The tiny **pineal body** lies at the back of the third ventricle of the brain and is a neuroendocrine gland. (See *Pining away for the pineal body.*)

Makin' melatonin

This gland produces the hormone **melatonin,** which is involved in the reproductive system and the body's **circadian** (24-hour) rhythms.

Thymus

Located below the sternum, the **thymus** contains lymphatic tissue.

Extra! Extra! Get your T cells here

Although the thymus produces the hormones **thymosin** and **thymopoietin,** its major role involves the immune system. T cells, important in cell-mediated immunity, are created within the thymus.

Beyond the dictionary

Pining away for the pineal body

The name **pineal** is derived from the structure's resemblance to a pine cone.

Physical examination terms

Ack!
Polydipsia is
excessive
thirst.

These physical findings are significant in the diagnosis of endocrine disorders:

- **Buffalo hump** is an accumulation of **cervicodorsal fat** (fat in the neck and back). The condition may indicate hypercortisolism or Cushing's syndrome.
- **Exophthalmos** is the abnormal protrusion of one or both eyeballs. The condition is sometimes the result of thyrotoxicosis (hyperthyroidism).
- A **goiter** is an enlarged thyroid gland, usually evident as swelling in the front of the neck.
- **Hirsutism** is an excessive growth of dark hair. Its occurrence on a woman's body results from excessive androgen production.
- **Moon face,** usually caused by hypercortisolism, results in marked roundness of the face, double chin, and a fullness in the upper lip.
- **Polydipsia** is excessive thirst, a symptom of diabetes mellitus.
- **Polyphagia** is excessive hunger, also a symptom of diabetes mellitus.
- **Polyuria** is the increased excretion of urine by the kidneys; it's a sign of diabetes mellitus and diabetes insipidus.

Diagnostic tests

Many diagnostic tests and studies are available to asses the function of the endocrine system and to detect related disorders. These tests include serum studies, urine studies, and radiologic and other imaging tests.

Serum studies

Specific tests are used to measure the blood levels of hormones and other substances and to monitor the function of endocrine glands:

- A **fasting plasma glucose** test is used to measure plasma glucose levels after a 12-hour fast. This test is commonly used to screen for diabetes mellitus.

• **Glycosylated hemoglobin** monitoring provides information about the average blood glucose level during the preceding 2 to 3 months. This test requires one venipuncture every 3 to 6 months to evaluate long-term effectiveness of diabetes therapy. This test is also known as **hemoglobin A_{1C}**, or **HbA_{1C}**.
• The **oral glucose tolerance** test measures plasma and urine glucose levels hourly for 3 hours after ingestion of glucose. This test assesses insulin secretion and the body's ability to metabolize glucose.
• Quantitative analysis of **plasma catecholamines** is used to test for adrenal dysfunction.
• Quantitative analysis of **plasma cortisol** levels is used to test for pheochromocytoma or adrenal medullary tumors.
• The **plasma LH** test, typically ordered for anovulation and infertility studies in women, is a quantitative analysis of plasma LH.
• **Provocative testing** stimulates an underactive gland or suppresses an overactive gland, depending on the patient's suspected disorder. A hormone level that doesn't increase despite stimulation confirms primary hypofunction. Hormone secretion that continues after suppression confirms hyperfunction.
• **Radioimmunoassay (RIA)** is the technique used to determine most hormone levels. In this test, blood or urine (or a urine extract) is incubated with the hormone's antibody and a radiolabeled hormone tracer (antigen). Antibody-tracer complexes can then be measured. (See *Dissecting* radioimmunoassay.)
• **Serum calcium** analysis measures blood levels of calcium to detect bone and parathyroid disorders.
• **Serum FSH** analysis measures gonadal function, especially in women.

Indirect tests measure the substance a particular hormone controls, rather than the hormone itself.

Beyond the dictionary

Dissecting *radioimmunoassay*

The word **radioimmunoassay** can be broken down into three readily understandable units: ***radio-*** refers to the radioactive tracer, ***-immuno-*** refers to the hormone's antibody (which creates an immunologic response), and ***assay*** means *test.*

• The **serum human growth hormone (hGH)** test is a quantitative analysis of plasma hGH levels that detects hyposecretion or hypersecretion of this hormone.
• **Serum phosphate** analysis measures serum levels of phosphate, the primary anion in intracellular fluid.
• **Serum PTH** measurement evaluates parathyroid hormone function.
• **Serum TSH** levels are measured by RIA, which can detect primary hypothyroidism and determine whether the hypothyroidism results from thyroid gland failure or from pituitary or hypothalamic dysfunction.
• **T_3** measurement determines total serum content of T_3 to investigate thyroid dysfunction.
• **T_4** measurement determines the total circulating T_4 level, which helps diagnose thyroid disorders.

Get this man some water. He's scheduled for a catecholamine analysis.

Urine studies

These tests are used to analyze urine samples for evidence of endocrine dysfunction:
• **Catecholamine** analysis utilizes a 24-hour urine specimen to measure levels of the major catecholamines—epinephrine, norepinephrine, and dopamine—to assess adrenal medulla function.
• **17-hydroxycorticosteroid (17-OHCS)** tests measure urine levels of 17-OHCS—metabolites of the hormones that regulate glyconeogenesis.
• **17-ketosteroid (17-KS)** assays determine urine levels of 17-KS. This test is used to diagnose adrenal dysfunction.

Radiologic and other imaging tests

These tests are used to create images of body structure and assess function:
• **Computed tomography (CT) scanning** provides high-resolution, three-dimensional images of a gland's structure by registering radiation levels absorbed by tissues.
• **Magnetic resonance imaging (MRI)** uses magnetic and radiofrequency waves. The deflection of the waves is interpreted by computer to provide detailed, three-dimensional images of soft tissues.

• A **radioactive iodine uptake** test evaluates thyroid function by measuring the amount of orally ingested iodine isotope that accumulates in the thyroid.
• In **radionuclide thyroid imaging,** the thyroid is studied with a gamma camera after the patient receives a radioisotope.
• **Thyroid ultrasonography** is a noninvasive procedure used to detect cysts and tumors of the thyroid by directing ultrasonic waves at the gland.

Disorders

Endocrine problems are caused by **hyperfunction,** resulting in excess hormone effects, or **hypofunction,** resulting in hormone deficiency. **Primary dysfunction** is caused by disease within an endocrine gland. **Secondary dysfunction** occurs when endocrine tissue is affected by dysfunction of a nonendocrine organ. **Functional hyperfunction** or **functional hypofunction** results from disease in a nonendocrine tissue or organ.

Pituitary disorders

Here are some of the terms used to describe pituitary dysfunction:
• **Adiposogenital dystrophy** is marked by increased body fat and underdevelopment of secondary sex characteristics in males. This disorder is caused by damage to the hypothalamus, which causes decreased secretion of gonadotropic hormones from the anterior pituitary gland.
• **Diabetes insipidus** is caused by deficiency of circulating ADH, or vasopressin. ADH deficiency leads to extreme polyuria. Patients can urinate up to 30 L of dilute urine per day because the kidneys can't concentrate urine.
• **Hypopituitarism** may cause dwarfism as a result of decreased levels of GH when it begins in childhood. It's a complex syndrome that leads to metabolic problems, sexual immaturity, and growth retardation. These complications are caused by a deficiency of hormones secreted by the anterior pituitary gland.
• **Panhypopituitarism** refers to a generalized condition caused by partial or total failure of all six of the pituitary

gland's vital hormones: corticotropin, TSH, LH, FSH, GH, and PRL.

Here's the long and short of it—a malfunctioning pituitary gland can lead to dwarfism or gigantism.

Gonadotrophic hormone excess

Gonadotrophic hormone excess is a chronic, progressive disease marked by excess GH, tissue overgrowth, and hyperpituitarism. It appears in two forms:

- **Gigantism** begins while the bones are still growing and causes proportional overgrowth of all body tissues.
- **Acromegaly** occurs after bone growth is complete, causing bones and organs to thicken. Bones of the face, jaw, and extremities gradually enlarge in a patient with this condition.

Thyroid disorders

Two types of thyroid dysfunction, hyperthyroidism and hypothyroidism, are described here.

Hyperthyroidism

Hyperthyroidism results from excess thyroid hormone. The most common cause is **Graves' disease,** which increases T_4 production, enlarges the thyroid gland **(goiter),** and causes metabolic changes.

Stormy forecast

Forms of hyperthyroidism include:

- **functioning metastatic thyroid carcinoma,** a rare disease that causes excess production of thyroid hormone
- **silent thyroiditis,** a self-limiting form of hyperthyroidism with no inflammatory symptoms
- **subacute thyroiditis,** a viral inflammation of the thyroid gland, which produces short-term hyperthyroidism associated with flulike symptoms
- **thyroid storm,** an acute exacerbation of hyperthyroidism that's a medical emergency and may lead to cardiac failure
- **thyrotoxicosis factitia,** which results from chronic ingestion of thyroid hormone, sometimes by a person who's trying to lose weight
- **toxic adenoma,** a small, benign nodule in the thyroid gland that secretes thyroid hormone

• **TSH-secreting pituitary tumor,** which causes overproduction of thyroid hormone.

Hypothyroidism

Hypothyroidism results from low serum thyroid hormone or cellular resistance to thyroid hormone. It's caused by insufficiency of the hypothalamus, pituitary gland, or thyroid gland. Here are two related terms:
• **Hashimoto's thyroiditis** is an inflammation of the thyroid gland caused by antibodies to thyroid antigens in the blood. It causes inflammation and lymphocytic infiltration of the thyroid, leading to thyroid tissue destruction and hypothyroidism.
• **Myxedema coma** is a life-threatening complication of hypothyroidism marked by depressed respirations, decreased cardiac output, and hypotension.

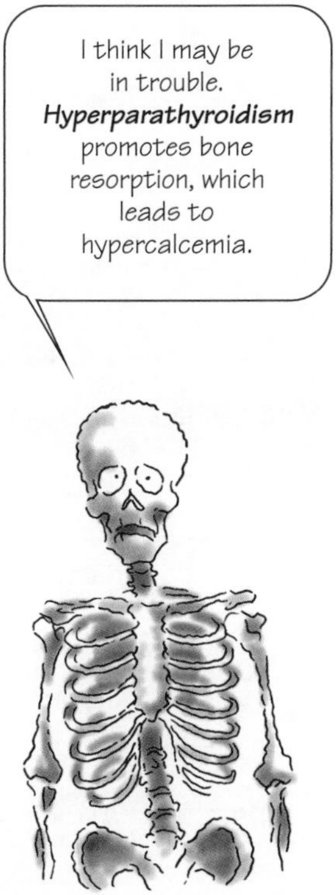
I think I may be in trouble. *Hyperparathyroidism* promotes bone resorption, which leads to hypercalcemia.

Parathyroid disorders

Here's a list of parathyroid disorders:
• **Hypoparathyroidism** is caused by PTH deficiency or decreased effectiveness of PTH on target tissues. Because PTH regulates calcium balance, PTH deficiency causes **hypocalcemia** (low blood levels of calcium), which leads to neuromuscular symptoms, such as **paresthesia** (tingling of the extremities) and **tetany** (muscle rigidity).
• **Hyperparathyroidism,** overactivity of one or more of the parathyroid glands and production of excess PTH, promotes bone resorption, which leads to **hypercalcemia. Hypophosphatemia** results from increased kidney excretion of phosphate. With **primary hyperparathyroidism,** the glands enlarge. In **secondary hyperparathyroidism,** the glands produce excessive PTH to compensate for low calcium levels in the blood caused by some other abnormality.

Pancreatic disorders

These diseases are associated with the pancreas:
• **Diabetes mellitus** is a chronic insulin deficiency or resistance to insulin by the cells. This form of diabetes causes problems with carbohydrate, protein, and fat me-

Beyond the dictionary

Distinguishing mellitus from insipidus

Diabetes mellitus and **diabetes insipidus** are two distinct diseases with similar symptoms, including especially profuse urine excretion. The word ***mellitus*** derives from the Latin word for *honey*—diabetes mellitus refers to the sweet smell of a patient's urine due to excess amounts of glucose. Diabetes insipidus produces no such sweetness and is therefore called **insipidus,** meaning *bland.*

Gestational diabetes is a form of diabetes mellitus that occurs during pregnancy.

tabolism. Diabetes mellitus is classified as type 1 (insulin-dependent) or type 2 (non-insulin-dependent). Type 2 diabetes is the more prevalent form. (See *Distinguishing mellitus from insipidus.*)

• **Gestational diabetes** is a form of diabetes mellitus that occurs during pregnancy. Usually, the patient's condition returns to normal after delivery, but she may have an increased risk of developing type 2 diabetes later in life.

When diabetes gets complicated

A number of complications can occur with diabetes:

• **Diabetic ketoacidosis** is a life-threatening form of metabolic acidosis that can arise as a complication of uncontrolled diabetes mellitus. Due to a lack of available insulin, accumulation of ketone bodies leads to urinary loss of water, potassium, ammonium, and sodium, resulting in hypovolemia, electrolyte imbalances, an extremely high blood glucose level and, commonly, coma.

• **Hyperosmolar hyperglycemic nonketotic syndrome (HHNS)** is a complication of diabetes mellitus in which the level of blood glucose is increased but, because some insulin is present, ketosis doesn't occur. Coma results when the high concentration of blood glucose causes dehydration of brain tissues.

• **Hypoglycemia** is characterized by an abnormally low blood glucose level. This condition occurs when glucose is utilized too rapidly, when the rate of glucose release falls behind demand, or when excess insulin enters the bloodstream.

Adrenal disorders

Here are names of important adrenal gland disorders:

- **Addisonian crisis,** an acute adrenal crisis, occurs when the body's stores of glucocorticoids and mineralocorticoids are exhausted, leading to hypotension, hypoglycemia, electrolyte imbalances, cardiac arrhythmias and, ultimately, death.
- **Adrenal hyperfunction,** also called **Cushing's syndrome,** results from excessive levels of adrenocortical hormones, especially cortisol. This condition can be caused by hypersecretion of corticotropin by the pituitary gland, an corticotropin-secreting tumor of another organ, or the use of glucocorticoid medications.
- **Adrenal hypofunction,** also called **Addison's disease,** is the most common sign of adrenal insufficiency, seen when 90% of the gland is destroyed. In this autoimmune process, circulating antibodies react against adrenal tissue, leading to decreased secretion of androgens, glucocorticoids, and mineralocorticoids. (See *Addison and Cushing.*)
- **Hyperaldosteronism** results when the adrenal cortex secretes excess amounts of aldosterone. It can be a primary disease of the adrenal cortex or a response to other disorders. Excessive aldosterone in the bloodstream prompts the kidneys to reabsorb too much sodium and water, excreting too much potassium. The fluid retention

Beyond the dictionary

Addison and Cushing

Addison's disease is named after the British doctor Thomas Addison (1793–1860), who described this form of adrenal insufficiency in 1849. Harvey Cushing (1869–1939), an American physiologist, was the first to note the changes in body appearance—development of fat deposits on the face, neck, and trunk and purple striae (streaks) on the skin—associated with pituitary tumors **(Cushing's syndrome).**

Beyond the dictionary

Focus on *pheochromocytoma*

Pheochromocytoma is a vascular tumor of the chromaffin tissue found in the adrenal medulla. To better understand pheochromocytoma, break down the word:

- **pheo-** means *dusky*
- -**chromo**- means *color*
- **-cyt-** refers to *cell*
- **-oma** is a suffix that means *tumor.*

Thus, **pheochromocytoma** is *a tumor of the dusky-colored cells of the adrenal glands.*

and hypokalemia caused by this disorder lead to hypertension, decreased hematocrit, muscle weakness, tetany, excess thirst, and many other symptoms.

- **Pheochromocytoma** refers to a vascular tumor of the chromaffin tissue found in the adrenal medulla. This condition is characterized by secretion of epinephrine and norepinephrine, causing hypertension associated with attacks of palpitations, nausea, headache, dyspnea, anxiety, pallor, and profuse sweating. (See *Focus on* pheochromocytoma.)

Treatments

Treatments for endocrine disorders include surgery, radiation therapy, and drug therapy.

Surgery

Surgeries to correct diseases affecting the endocrine systems are described here:

- **Adrenalectomy** is a resection or removal of one or both adrenal glands.
- **Hypophysectomy** is the surgical removal of the pituitary gland. In a procedure called **transsphenoidal hypophysectomy,** the gland is removed by entering the inner aspect of the upper lip through the sphenoid sinus.

- **Pancreatectomy** is removal of the pancreas. This procedure is performed only after more conservative treatment measures have failed.
- **Parathyroidectomy** is the surgical removal of one or more of the four parathyroid glands. It's used to treat hyperparathyroidism. The number of glands removed depends on the underlying cause of the excessive hormone secretion.
- A **subtotal thyroidectomy** is surgical removal of a portion of the thyroid gland.
- **Total bilateral adrenalectomy,** excision of both adrenal glands, eliminates the body's reserve of corticosteroids (which are synthesized in the adrenal cortex). Adrenalectomy is performed only when treatment of the pituitary gland is impossible.
- **Total parathyroidectomy** is removal of all of the parathyroid glands. In such cases, the patient requires lifelong treatment for hypoparathyroidism.
- In **total thyroidectomy,** the entire thyroid gland is removed.

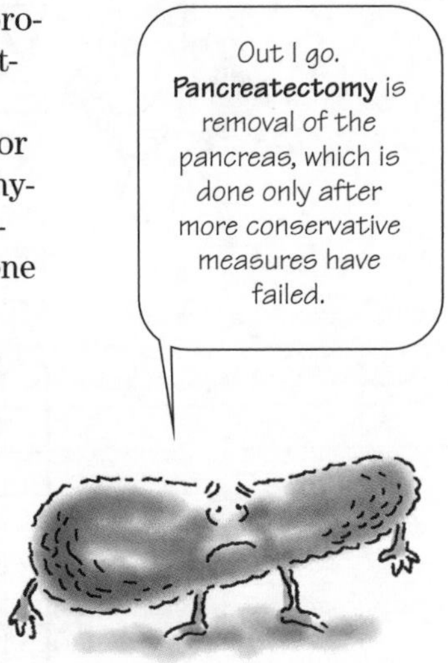
Out I go. Pancreatectomy is removal of the pancreas, which is done only after more conservative measures have failed.

Radiation therapy

There are two types of radiation treatment for endocrine disorders:

- **^{131}I administration** uses an isotope of iodine to treat hyperthyroidism or thyroid cancer. It shrinks functioning thyroid tissue, decreases levels of thyroid hormone in the body, and destroys malignant cells.
- **Pituitary radiation** controls the growth of a pituitary tumor or relieves its signs and symptoms.

Get ready for some fun and games!

Drug therapy

Here are some common drug therapies for endocrine disorders:

- **Corticosteroids** and **hormone replacements** are administered to combat hormone deficiencies.
- **Insulin** or **oral antidiabetic agents** may be administered to control glucose levels.

systole

Vocabulary builders

At a crossroads

Completing this crossword puzzle will help stimulate your excretion of correct endocrine system terms. Good luck!

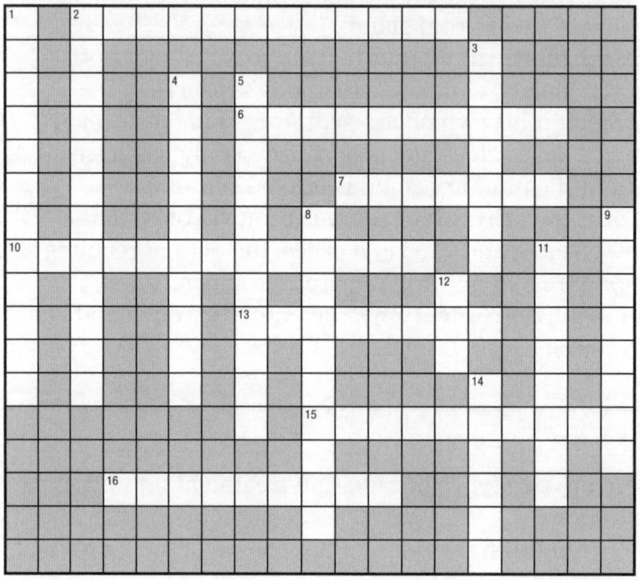

Across

2. Enlarged spleen
6. Also known as the **pituitary gland**
7. Inner portion of the adrenal gland
10. Stimulates the adrenal cortex
13. Stimulates the ejection of breast milk into the mammary ducts
15. Excessive hunger
16. Proportional overgrowth of body tissues

Down

1. Condition characterized by abnormally low blood glucose level
2. Promotes the growth of bony and soft tissues
3. Hormone that decreases blood glucose levels
4. Hormones produced by the adrenal cortex
5. Influences secretion of thyroid hormone
8. Excessive thirst (a sign of diabetes mellitus)
9. Organ that lies along the posterior surface of the abdominal wall behind the stomach
11. Hormone that increases blood glucose levels
12. Abbreviation for **radioimmunoassay**
14. Gland located below the sternum

Answers are on page 318.

Match game

As with many medical terms, some endocrine terms go by more than one name. Match each hormone or organ below with its alternate name.

Clues	**Choices**
1. Pituitary gland ____	A. Somatotropin
2. Growth hormone ____	B. Prolactin
3. Antidiuretic hormone ____	C. Hypophysis
4. Mammotropin ____	D. Vasopressin

Finish line

Fill in the blanks below with the appropriate treatment or surgical intervention.

1. Removal of the entire thyroid gland is known as ______ ______.
2. ______ is a surgery that's used to remove the pancreas after more conservative treatment measures have failed.
3. The resection or removal of one or both adrenal glands is known as ______.
4. ______ ______ controls the growth of a pituitary tumor or relieves its signs and symptoms.
5. When only a portion of the thyroid gland is surgically removed it's called a ______ ______.
6. The surgical removal of the pituitary gland is known as ______.

I'm frazzled. Is it my hormones or these questions?

Answers are on page 318.

Answers

At a crossroads

1 H		2 S	P	L	E	N	O	M	E	G	A	L	Y					
Y		O												3 I				
P		M			4 C		5 T							N				
O		A			O		6 H	Y	P	O	P	H	Y	S	I	S		
G		T			R		Y							U				
L		O			T		R			7 M	E	D	U	L	L	A		
Y		T			I		O		8 P					I				9 P
10 C	O	R	T	I	C	O	T	R	O	P	I	N		N		11 G		A
E		O			O		R		L				12 R			L		N
M		P			I		13 O	X	Y	T	O	C	I	N		U		C
I		I			D		P		D				A			C		R
A		N			S		I		I					14 T		A		E
							N		15 P	O	L	Y	P	H	A	G	I	A
									S					Y		O		S
			16 G	I	G	A	N	T	I	S	M			M		N		
									A					U				
														S				

Match game

1. C; 2. A; 3. D; 4. B

Finish line

1. Total thyroidectomy; 2. Pancreatectomy; 3. Adrenalectomy; 4. Pituitary radiation; 5. Subtotal thyroidectomy; 6. Hypophysectomy

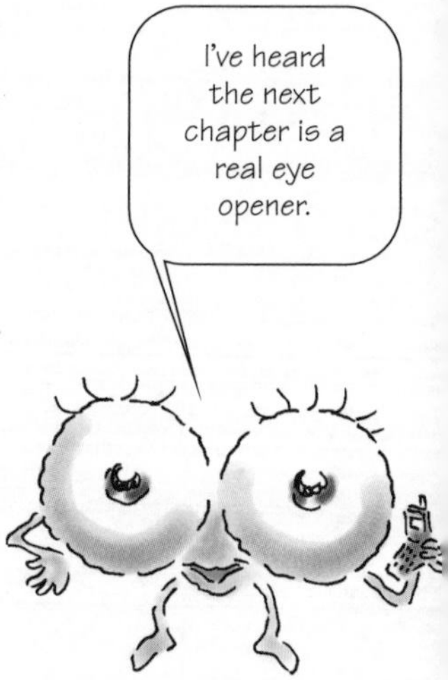
I've heard the next chapter is a real eye opener.

14

Blood and the lymphatic system

Just the facts

In this chapter, you'll learn:

- terminology related to the structure and function of the blood and the lymphatic system
- terminology needed for physical examination of the blood and lympathic system
- tests that help diagnose blood and lymphatic system disorders
- common blood and lymphatic system disorders and their treatments.

Did you know that the average person has 5 to 6 L of circulating blood, which makes up about 5% to 7% of the body's weight?

Blood and lymphatic structure and function

The circulatory system consists of blood, which is pumped through blood vessels by the heart, and lymphatic fluid, which moves through lymph channels and tissues passively. Blood and the lymphatic system are interconnected. Lymph fluid passes into the veins through the lymphatic and thoracic ducts. (See *Pronouncing key blood and lymphatic system terms*, page 320.)

Fancy fluids

The liquid portion of blood is called **plasma**. In the lymphatic system, the liquid portion is called **lymph fluid.** Both fluid types are high in water content, but they differ in their distribution of fats and proteins.

Pump up your pronunciation

Pronouncing key blood and lymphatic system terms

Here's a list of key terms related to blood and the lymphatic system, along with the correct ways to pronounce them.

Hemolysis	HEE-MAHL-EH-SIS
Hemorrhage	HEM-EH-REHJ
Immunoelectrophoresis	IM-YOU-NOH-EE-LEK-TROH-FOH-REE-SIS
Lymphadenopathy	LIM-FAD-UH-NOP-UH-THEE
Phagocytosis	FAG-OH-SEYE-TOH-SIS
Splenomegaly	SPLEE-NO-MEG-UH-LEE
Thymus	THEYE-MUHS
Trabeculae	TRAH-BEK-YOU-LEE

Shared traits

Blood and the lymphatic system share some similar functions. For example, both collect and transport vital substances and both are involved in protecting and healing the body.

They're special, so special

Blood and the lymphatic system each contain specialized cells suspended in fluid. Most of these cells are produced by the bone marrow. The specialized cells help the body protect itself, working as part of the immune system.

Cells

Cells specific to the blood and lymphatic system include **erythrocytes** (also known as **red blood cells** [RBCs]), **leukocytes** (also known as **white blood cells** [WBCs]), **thrombocytes** (also known as **platelets**), and **pluripotential stem cells.**

Seeing red

RBCs account for 99% of the circulating elements in blood and transport oxygen and carbon dioxide. The average RBC lives about 120 days and then is **phagocytized** (destroyed and digested) by cells in the spleen and liver. Iron from the hemoglobin on the RBCs is recovered and recycled.

The ABCs of WBCs

WBCs are active in the immune system. The various types of WBCs are classified into two categories according to how they appear when stained and viewed under a microscope:

- **granular leukocytes** (having a grainlike appearance)
- **nongranular leukocytes** (having few or no granular particles).

Although some WBCs constantly circulate, others remain in the tissues of the lymph system, bone marrow, spleen, and other organs.

First responders

Platelets are small cell fragments that circulate in blood and respond to injuries by starting the clotting process and providing **hemostasis** (stoppage of bleeding).

To stem cells and beyond!

Pluripotential stem cells are located in the bone marrow. They develop into immune system and blood cells through a process called **hematopoiesis.** (See *Breaking down blood formation.*)

Some stem cells destined to produce immune system cells serve as sources of **lymphocytes** (a type of WBC), whereas others develop into **phagocytes** (cells that engulf and digest microorganisms and cellular debris). Those that become lymphocytes are differentiated to become either B cells (which mature in the bone marrow) or T cells (which travel to the thymus and mature there).

B cells and T cells are distributed throughout the **lymphoid** organs, especially the lymph nodes and spleen.

Beyond the dictionary

Breaking down blood formation

Hematopoiesis may seem like a difficult word at first glance, but break it down and the difficulty disappears.

In Greek, ***hematos*** is the word for *blood* and ***poiesis*** means *formation.* Together they form the word for *blood formation*—**hematopoiesis.**

I'm a pluripotential stem cell. That means I have the potential to take many (pluri-) forms.
Helper
Suppressor
Killer

Basic T-cell training

In the **thymus** (a lymph structure located in the mediastinum), T cells undergo a process called **T-cell education,** in which the cells are "trained" to recognize other cells from the same body **(self cells)** and distinguish them from all other cells **(nonself cells).**

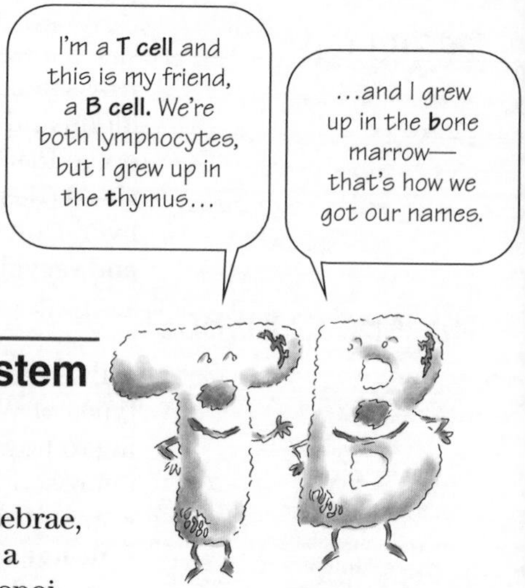
I'm a **T cell** and this is my friend, a **B cell.** We're both lymphocytes, but I grew up in the **t**hymus...
...and I grew up in the **b**one marrow— that's how we got our names.

Organs and tissues of blood and the lymphatic system

Bone marrow

Bone marrow is found in the cranial bones, vertebrae, ribs, pelvis, sternum, and femurs. It's the site of a process called **erythropoiesis,** in which erythropoietin (a potent hormone secreted by the kidneys) stimulates the bone marrow to produce RBCs. Platelets also originate from stem cells in the bone marrow.

The term **lymphoid** is used to refer to organs and tissues of the lymphatic system because they're all involved in some way in the growth, development, and dissemination of lymphocytes. (See *How* nymph *became* lymph.)

Lymph nodes

The small, kidney-shaped **lymph nodes** contain **lymphatic tissue** and are located along a network of lymphatic channels. They release lymphocytes, the primary cells of the immune system, and help remove and destroy antigens circulating in the blood and lymphatic vessels. Each lymph node is surrounded by a fibrous capsule that extends **trabeculae** (bands of connective tissue) into the node.

Function is an emphatic issue for lymphatic tissue

When lymph fluid enters the node, it's filtered through sinuses before draining into the single exit vessel. The filtration process removes bacteria and other foreign bodies or particles, including malignant cells.

Another function of lymph nodes is **phagocytosis,** the destruction of invading cells or particles. Lymphatic tissue is also the site of final maturation for lymphocytes that migrate from the bone marrow.

Beyond the dictionary

How *nymph* became *lymph*

Lymph fluid is a clear, transparent liquid that's found in the **lymphatic vessels,** which take their name from this substance. In Greek, ***nymph*** was the name for a goddess of lower rank usually associated with a river or lake. In turn, the Greeks applied the term to young women, "pure as a virgin river," of marriageable age. Latin borrowed the term, but the ***n*** mutated to an ***l*** and it became applied to a fluid thought to be as pure and clear as the nymphs of long ago.

Location, location, location

Lymph nodes are classified according to their locations, including:

- **axillary**—underarm and upper chest
- **cervical**—neck
- **inguinal**—groin area
- **popliteal**—behind the knee
- **submandibular**— floor of the mouth and lower jaw.

Lymphatic fluid

Lymphatic fluid (also **lymph fluid** or **lymph**) is a transparent, usually slightly yellow liquid found within the lymphatic vessels. It's collected from all parts of the body and returned to the blood after filtration in the lymph nodes.

The word **lacteal** probably reminds you of the word **lactate,** which means *to produce milk.* Lacteals produce a "milky" lymph fluid.

Lymphatic vessels

Lymphatic vessels intertwine with blood vessels and distribute lymphatic fluid throughout the body. They remove proteins and water from the interstitial spaces and return them to the bloodstream.

Lymphatic vessels located in the small intestine are called **lacteals.** They absorb fats and other nutrients, producing a milky lymph fluid called **chyle** (from the Greek word ***chylos,*** or *juice*).

Spleen

The **spleen** is a lymphoid organ located in the left upper quadrant of the abdomen beneath the diaphragm. The largest structure of the lymphatic system, the spleen initiates an immune response, filters and removes bacteria and other foreign substances from the bloodstream, destroys worn-out blood cells **(hemolysis),** and serves as a blood reservoir. (See *History of* spleen, page 324.)

Accessory lymphoid organs and tissues

The tonsils, adenoids, appendix, thymus, and Peyer's patches remove foreign debris in much the same way lymph nodes do. They're located in food and air passages—areas where microbial access is more likely to occur.

Immunity

Immunity is the body's capacity to resist invading organisms and toxins, thereby preventing tissue and organ damage. The immune system's cells and organs are designed to recognize, respond to, and eliminate foreign substances, including bacteria, viruses, and parasites. The immune system also preserves the body's internal environment by scavenging dead or damaged cells and by patrolling antigens.

Getting specific

All foreign substances elicit the same response in general host defenses. In contrast, particular microorganisms or molecules activate specific immune responses and initially can involve specialized sets of immune cells. Such specific responses, classified as either humoral immunity or cell-mediated immunity, are produced by lymphocytes (B cells and T cells).

Humoral immunity

In **humoral immunity,** an invading antigen causes B cells to divide and differentiate into plasma cells. Each plasma cell, in turn, produces and secretes large amounts of antibodies (immunoglobulin molecules that interact with a specific antigen) into the bloodstream. Antibodies destroy bacteria and viruses, thereby preventing them from entering host cells.

Five major classes of immunoglobulin exist:

- **Immunoglobulin (Ig) G** makes up 80% of plasma antibodies. It appears in all body fluids and is the major antibacterial and antiviral antibody.
- **IgM** is the first immunoglobulin produced during an immune response. It's too large to easily cross membrane barriers and is usually present only in the vascular system.
- **IgA** is found mainly in body secretions, such as saliva, sweat, tears, mucus, bile, and colostrum. It defends against pathogens on body surfaces, especially those that enter the respiratory and GI tracts.
- **IgD** is present in plasma and is easily broken down. It's the predominant antibody on the surface of B cells and is mainly an antigen receptor.

Beyond the dictionary

History of *spleen*

Since ancient times, the word **spleen** has been used to designate the largest lymphatic organ. The word probably first appeared in its modern form between 1250 and 1300, having been derived from the Latin word ***splen.*** The origins of the word go back even further, to the ancient Sanskrit ***plihan.***

Spleen: Cheerful or gloomy?

The spleen was considered to be the seat of various emotions or attributes. Some were positive, linking the spleen with cheerfulness, courage, and spirit. At other times, the spleen was thought to be the site of negative attributes, such as a bad temper and a spiteful or gloomy nature.

• **IgE** is the antibody involved in immediate hypersensitivity reactions (or allergic reactions) that develop within minutes of exposure to an antigen. IgE stimulates the release of mast cell granules, which contain histamine and heparin.

Another part of humoral immunity, the **complement system,** is a major mediator of the inflammatory response. It consists of 20 proteins circulating as functionally inactive molecules. In most cases, an antigen-antibody reaction is necessary for the complement system to activate to destroy invading cells.

Cell-mediated immunity

In **cell-mediated immunity,** T cells respond directly to antigens (foreign substances such as bacteria or toxins that induce antibody formation). This response involves destruction of target cells—such as virus-infected cells and cancer cells—through the secretion of lymphokines (lymph proteins). Organ rejection is an example of cell-mediated immunity.

Acquired immunity

The body readily develops long-term immunity to specific antigens, including pollen, dust, mold, and invading organisms. There are four types of acquired immunity:

I'm a natural, thanks to passive immunity!

Natural, active immunity occurs when the immune system responds to a harmful agent and develops long-term immunity. This type of immunity is the most effective and longest lasting. For example, people develop immunity to measles after having the disease once.

Natural, passive immunity is the transfer of antibodies from a mother to a fetus (through the placenta) or to a breast-fed infant. This type of transmission provides temporary, partial immunity.

Artificial, active immunity is obtained by vaccination with weakened or dead infectious agents introduced into the body to alert the immune system.

Artificial, passive immunity is provided by substances that offer immediate but temporary immunity, such as antibiotics, gamma globulin, and interferon.

Physical examination terms

The following conditions may be encountered when performing a physical examination of blood and the lymphatic system:

- **Angioedema** is a subcutaneous and dermal eruption that produces deep, large, raised sections of skin (usually on the hands, feet, lips, genitals, and eyelids) and diffuse swelling of the subcutaneous tissue.
- **Butterfly rash** is a classic sign of **systemic lupus erythematosus.** Lesions appear on the cheeks and bridge of the nose, creating a characteristic butterfly-shaped pattern.
- **Chills** (also called **rigors**) are extreme, involuntary muscle contractions with characteristic paroxysms of violent shivering and tooth chattering.
- **Cyanosis** is a blue to purple color of the skin, nail bed, and lips due to a lack of oxygen.
- **Ecchymosis** is another name for a bruise.
- **Epistaxis** is a profuse nosebleed.
- **Hematochezia** is the passing of bloody stools.
- **Hemoptysis** is bleeding from the lungs or bronchial tubes.
- **Hemorrhage** refers to uncontrolled bleeding.
- **Lymphadenopathy** is enlarged lymph nodes.
- **Lymphangioma** is a benign tumor caused by congenital malformation of the lymphatic system.
- **Pruritus** is also known as itching.
- **Splenomegaly** is an enlarged spleen.
- **Thrombosis** is the formation of a blood clot inside a blood vessel.
- **Urticaria** is a skin condition that's more commonly known as **hives.**

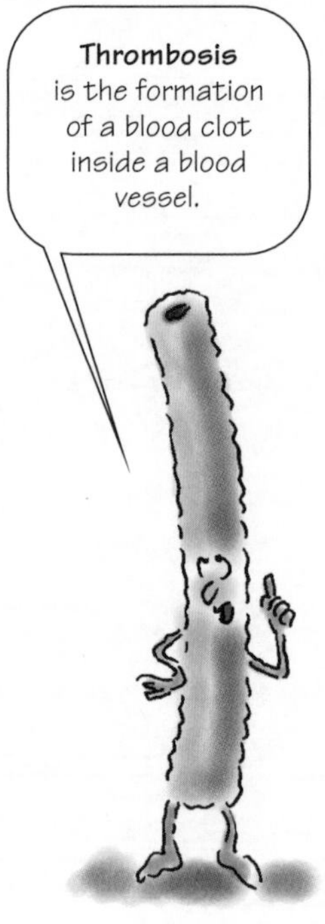
Thrombosis is the formation of a blood clot inside a blood vessel.

Diagnostic tests

Most tests use a combination of techniques to evaluate the body's immune response and break down the individual components of blood and the lymphatic system.

Laboratory tests

Here are some common laboratory tests:

- **ABO blood typing** classifies blood according to the presence of major antigens A and B on RBC surfaces and according to serum antibodies anti-A and anti-B. ABO blood typing is required before transfusion to prevent a lethal reaction.
- **Complete blood count (CBC)** measures the number of blood elements in a blood sample.
- **Crossmatching** is an antibody detection test that establishes the compatibility of a donor's and recipient's blood.
- A **direct antiglobulin test (direct Coombs' test)** demonstrates the presence of antibodies (such as antibodies to the Rh factor) or complement on circulating RBCs.
- **Enzyme-linked immunosorbent assay (ELISA)** identifies antibodies to bacteria, viruses, deoxyribonucleic acid, allergens, and substances such as immunoglobulins.
- **Erythrocyte sedimentation rate (ESR)** is the degree of erythrocyte settling in a blood sample during a specified period.
- **Hematocrit** measures the percentage of RBCs in a blood sample.
- **Hemoglobin (Hb)** is the measure of the amount of hemoglobin in a volume of blood.
- **Human leukocyte antigen test (HLA)** identifies a group of antigens that are present on the surfaces of all nucleated cells but most easily detected on lymphocytes. These antigens are essential to immunity and determine the degree of histocompatibility between transplant recipients and donors.
- **Immunoelectrophoresis** identifies immunoglobulins in a serum sample. It evaluates the effectiveness of radiation therapy or chemotherapy and detects **hypogammaglobulinemias** (abnormally low levels of gamma globulins causing increased susceptibility to infection).
- The **platelet count** indicates the number of platelets in a microliter of blood.
- **Prothrombin time (PT)** is commonly used to evaluate clotting in patients receiving oral anticoagulant therapy.

- **Rh typing** classifies blood by the presence or absence of the $Rh_0(D)$ antigen on the surface of RBCs. In this test, a patient's RBCs are mixed with serum containing anti-$Rh_0(D)$ antibodies and are observed for clamping together of antigen-bearing particles of similar size in a solution.
- **Shilling test** determines a patient's ability to absorb vitamin B_{12}, which is necessary for erythropoiesis.
- **WBC count,** also called a *leukocyte count,* is part of a complete blood count. It indicates the number of WBCs in a microliter of whole blood.
- The **WBC differential** evaluates the type, number, and condition of WBCs present in the blood. WBCs are classified as one of five major types of leukocytes—neutrophils, eosinophils, basophils, lymphocytes, and monocytes—and the percentage of each type is determined in this test.
- **Western blot test** detects the presence of specific viral proteins.

Patch and scratch allergy tests

Patch and scratch allergy tests evaluate the immune system's ability to respond to known allergens, which are applied to hairless areas of the patient's body.

A patch test shows results in 2 to 3 days. A scratch test works more quickly; results show in 30 to 40 minutes.

Patch work

In **patch testing,** a dilute solution of each allergen is placed directly on the skin and covered with gauze. In 48 to 72 hours, the appearance of redness, vesicles, itching, or swelling shows a positive reaction.

Scratching the surface

Scratch tests introduce allergens into a scratched area on the patient's skin with a special tool or needle. Test sites are examined 30 to 40 minutes later and compared with a control site; redness, itching, or swelling are considered positive reactions.

Under your skin

Intradermal skin tests evaluate the patient's immune system by injecting **recall antigens** (antigens to which the patient may have been previously sensitized) into the superficial skin layer with a needle and syringe or a sterile four-pronged lancet.

Bone marrow aspiration

In a **bone marrow aspiration** or biopsy, a small amount of bone marrow is removed and the blood elements and their precursors are evaluated. The specimen is also checked for the presence of abnormal or malignant cells.

Disorders

Bone marrow cells reproduce rapidly and are vulnerable to genetic or environmental conditions that influence cell function or the body's ability to make cells. For example, heredity may cause genetic defects in the type or amount of cells or the ability of cells to function. Environmental factors, such as nutrition, medications, radiation, and toxins, may affect bone marrow's ability to make normal cells. Additionally, the complex processes involved in host defense and immune response may malfunction. When the body's defenses are exaggerated, misdirected, absent, or depressed, a hypersensitivity disorder, autoimmunity, or immunodeficiency may result.

This section provides terminology associated with blood and lymphatic system disorders.

Blood disorders

Blood disorders may be quantitative or qualitative. Quantitative blood disorders involve abnormalities in the number of cells. These disorders may result from the bone marrow producing too few or too many cells or from processes that destroy cells. Quantitative blood disorders include certain types of anemias, such as these:

- **Aplastic anemia** results from injury to the stem cells in the bone marrow, which causes decreased production of RBCs, WBCs, and platelets.
- **Pernicious anemia** is caused by a deficiency in the absorption of vitamin B_{12} (folic acid) due to a lack of hydrochloric acid in the stomach. (Vitamin B_{12} is essential for the production of RBCs.)

• **Myeloproliferative disorders** occur when the bone marrow produces too many cells, although an excess of RBCs is rare.
• **Erythroblastosis fetalis,** also known as **Rh factor incompatibility** between a mother and her fetus, occurs when antibodies in the mother's blood destroy the fetus's RBCs, resulting in fetal anemia. Intrauterine transfusions can save about 40% of the fetuses affected.
• **Posthemorrhagic anemia** is the result of acute or chronic blood loss.

Blood disorders may result from abnormalities in the quantity or quality of cells.

Quality counts

Qualitative blood disorders involve abnormalities within the cells or plasma components. Here are some examples:
• **Sickle cell anemia** is a hereditary disease in which RBCs are abnormally "sickle" shaped and can't easily travel through the blood vessels.
• **Thalassemia** is a hereditary type of anemia in which Hb isn't produced properly.

Blood-clotting disorders

Blood-clotting, or hemorrhagic disorders result from cellular abnormalities in the clotting cycle or problems with clotting factors in the plasma. They may be hereditary or acquired.

Here's a list of some blood-clotting disorders:
• **Disseminated intravascular coagulation (DIC)** is a life-threatening disease in which the patient may suffer severe hemorrhage. It occurs when other conditions cause the circulating clotting factors and platelets to deplete, leaving the patient prone to bleeding.
• **Factor V Leiden mutation** is a relatively common inherited mutation in the factor V gene that may cause the development of inappropriate blood clots and, in young people, an increased risk of stroke.
• **Hemophilias** are a group of hereditary bleeding disorders in which there are deficiencies in the clotting factors necessary for coagulation.
• **Inherited thrombophilias** are diseases in which abnormal clotting factor traits are inherited, causing clots to form in the blood vessels inappropriately.
• **Idiopathic thrombocytopenic purpura** is caused by an abnormal immune response that destroys platelets. It

may be acute and follow a viral infection. Patients usually recover without treatment.

• **Thrombocytopenias** are the most common of the blood-clotting disorders and result from deficiencies in the number of circulating platelets.

Hyperreactivity and **hypersensitivity** share a prefix. ***Hyper-*** comes from Greek and means *in excess of.* These are disorders that cause an excessive reaction or sensitivity in the immune system.

Hypersensitivity disorders

An exaggerated or inappropriate immune response may lead to various **hypersensitivity** disorders, such as asthma, allergic rhinitis, anaphylaxis, atopic dermatitis, latex allergy, and blood transfusion reactions.

Asthma

Asthma is a chronic, reactive airway disorder leading to episodes of airway obstruction with bronchospasms, increased mucus secretion, and mucosal swelling. (See *How do I [pant] say* asthma?)

Take a deep breath

Here are a few types of asthma:

• **Acute asthma** is an attack that can begin either dramatically with severe symptoms or slowly with gradual symptoms.

• **Extrinsic asthma** results from sensitivity to pollen, animal dander, mold, or other sensitizing substances.

• **Intrinsic asthma** is diagnosed when no extrinsic allergen can be identified.

• **Status asthmaticus** is a persistent, intractable asthma attack that can lead to acute respiratory failure.

Pump up your pronunciation

How do I (pant) say *asthma?*

Asthma derives from Greek and means *gasping* or *panting.* The grouping of consonants in its middle makes it look more difficult to pronounce than it actually is. The ***th*** is silent, making the word easily pronounceable: AZ-MAH.

Allergic rhinitis

Allergic rhinitis is a reaction to airborne (inhaled) allergens. The resulting runny nose, itching, nasal obstruction, and congestion can be seasonal, as in **hay fever,** or year-round, as in **perennial allergic rhinitis.**

Anaphylaxis

Anaphylaxis is a dramatic, acute reaction marked by the sudden onset of rapidly progressive hives and respiratory distress. It can be a life-threatening situation if treatment isn't initiated immediately.

Atopic dermatitis

Atopic dermatitis is a chronic skin disorder characterized by superficial skin inflammation and intense itching.

Latex allergy

Latex allergy is a hypersensitivity reaction to products that contain natural latex, which is derived from the sap of a rubber tree. Hypersensitivity reactions to latex range from local dermatitis to life-threatening anaphylactic reaction.

Hypersensitivity reactions to latex range from local dermatitis to life-threatening anaphylactic reaction.

Blood transfusion reactions

Mediated by immune or nonimmune factors, a **transfusion reaction** happens during or after the administration of blood components. Symptoms can be mild (fever and chills) or severe (acute renal failure or complete vascular collapse and death), depending on the amount of blood transfused, the type of reaction, and the patient's general health.

Poorly made matches

Hemolytic reactions follow transfusions of mismatched blood. When this occurs, RBCs clump together and break down, leading to kidney damage.

Less worrisome

Allergic reactions to transfused blood are fairly common and only occasionally serious. Patients may experience transient hives, itching, chills, and fever. Symptoms resolve quickly when the transfusion is stopped.

More common

Febrile nonhemolytic reactions, the most common type of reaction, apparently develop when antibodies in the patient's plasma attack antigens on lymphocytes, granulocytes, or plasma cells of the transfused blood.

Autoimmune disorders

Autoimmune disorders occur when a misdirected immune response causes the body's defenses to become self-destructive. Here are some types of autoimmune disorders:

- **Ankylosing spondylitis** is a chronic, usually progressive, inflammatory disease that primarily affects the sacroiliac, apophyseal, and costovertebral joints and adjacent soft tissue.

- **Rheumatoid arthritis** is a chronic, systemic inflammatory disease that primarily attacks peripheral joints and surrounding muscles, tendons, ligaments, and blood vessels.
- **Scleroderma** is a diffuse connective tissue disease characterized by fibrotic, degenerative, and occasionally inflammatory changes in the skin, blood vessels, synovial membranes, skeletal muscles, and internal organs.
- **Sjögren's syndrome,** the second most common rheumatoid disorder, is marked by decreased secretions from the lacrimal and salivary glands.
- **Systemic lupus erythematosus (SLE)** is a chronic inflammatory disorder of the connective tissue. It affects multiple organ systems, is characterized by remissions and exacerbations, and can be fatal.
- **Vasculitis** includes a broad spectrum of disorders characterized by inflammation and necrosis of blood vessels.

Immunodeficiency disorders

In immunodeficiency, the immune system is absent or depressed, resulting in increased susceptibility to infection.

Opportunity knocks

Also known as **AIDS, acquired immunodeficiency syndrome** causes progressive damage to the body's immune response and gradual destruction of cells—including T cells. The retrovirus **human immunodeficiency virus (HIV)** causes AIDS.

Major immunity missing

DiGeorge syndrome is a congenital aplasia or hypoplasia of the thymus that's caused by a missing gene on chromosome 22. This abnormality leads to a deficiency of T lymphocytes and compromises cell-mediated immunity.

Chemo complication

Iatrogenic immunodeficiency is a deficiency in the immune response that occurs as a complication of chemotherapy and other medical treatment.

Lupus is Latin for *wolf.* It was first used as a medical term because disorders such as **systemic lupus erythematosus** were thought to devour the body like a hungry wolf.

Treatments

Various methods are used to combat disorders of blood and the lymphatic system, including drug therapy, radiation therapy, surgery, and bone marrow transplantation.

Drugs are one way to treat blood and lymphatic system disorders.

Drug therapy

Here's a list of drugs commonly used to treat blood and lymphatic system disorders:

- **Anticoagulants** are drugs given to inhibit blood clotting.
- **Antilymphocyte serum,** or **antithymocyte globulin,** is an anti-T-cell antibody that reduces the number and function of T cells. This suppresses cell-mediated immunity. The drug is used to prevent rejection of tissue grafts or transplants.
- **Corticosteroids** are adrenocortical hormones widely used to treat immune disorders because of their anti-inflammatory and immunosuppressant effects. These drugs stabilize the vascular membrane, blocking tissue infiltration by neutrophils and monocytes and thus inhibiting inflammation.
- **Cytotoxic drugs** kill cells while they're replicating. However, most cytotoxic drugs aren't selective and, therefore, interfere with all rapidly growing cells. As a result, they reduce the number of lymphocytes as well as phagocytes.
- **Cyclosporine** is an immunosuppressant drug that selectively suppresses T-helper cells, resulting in depressed immunity. It's used to prevent organ rejection in kidney, liver, bone marrow, and heart transplants.
- **Thrombolytic drugs** are given to break apart blood clots.
- **Iron supplements** may be given to patients with anemia after the cause of the anemia is determined.

Radiation therapy

Radiation therapy is the use of a radioactive substance to treat a disease. Radiation therapy of all major lymph node areas—known as **total nodal radiation**—is used to treat certain disorders, such as Hodgkin's disease.

Surgery

Surgeries for lymphatic and immune system disorders include the removal of a lymph node, a lymph vessel, the spleen, or the thymus:

- **Lymphadenectomy** is surgical removal of a lymph node.
- **Lymphangiectomy** is surgical removal of a lymph vessel.
- **Splenectomy,** or removal of the spleen, causes an increased risk of infection, especially from such bacteria as *Streptococcus pneumoniae.*
- **Thymectomy** is surgical removal of the thymus.

Bone marrow transplantation

Bone marrow transplantation begins with the collection of marrow cells from a donor. The cells are then transferred to an immunosuppressed patient. There are four types of bone marrow transplant:

- **Allogeneic transplant** uses bone marrow from a compatible donor, usually a sibling.
- **Autologous transplant** uses marrow tissue that's harvested from the patient before he receives chemotherapy and radiation therapy, or while he's in remission, and is frozen for later use.
- **Stem cell transplant** involves the transfusion of stem cells, which can develop into RBCs, WBCs, and platelets. Stem cells are typically donated by the patient before chemotherapy.
- **Syngeneic transplant** refers to the transplantation of marrow between identical twins.

Memory jogger

To remember the difference between an "allogeneic" transplant and "autologous" transplant, visualize the "gene" in allo**gene**ic and think "the gene pool that's your family." For **auto**logous, remember that "auto" = self, meaning you can donate blood to yourself.

Blood transfusions

A **blood transfusion** is a procedure in which blood or blood products are introduced into the patient's bloodstream. Here are two types of blood transfusions:

- **Autologous transfusion** involves a patient donating blood so it can be stored for his own later use.
- **Homologous transfusion** is when blood is voluntarily donated by one person and given to a compatible recipient.

systole
parietal
aorta

Vocabulary builders

At a crossroads

Completing this crossword puzzle will help you ward off an attack by incorrect blood and lymphatic system terms. Good luck!

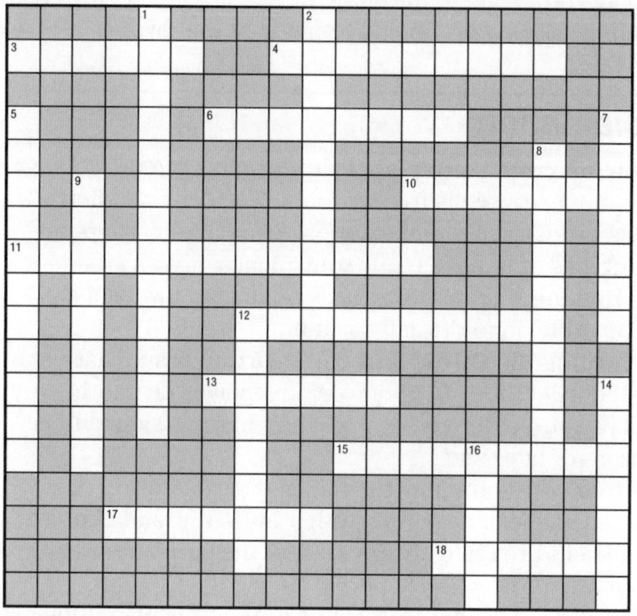

Across

3. The largest structure of the lymphatic system
4. Term indicating *location behind the knee*
6. Term used to refer to immune system organs and tissues
10. Eponym for the second most common autoimmune rheumatoid disorder
11. Process by which stem cells develop into blood cells or immune system cells
12. Immunodeficiency introduced by a medical treatment
13. Response activated by microorganisms
15. The type of transplant of marrow between identical twins
17. Tests that introduce allergens to the skin using a special tool, with results examined 30 to 40 minutes later
18. A chronic, reactive airway disorder

Down

1. The "S" in **ESR**
2. A group of 20 protein compounds that activate to destroy invading cells
5. Exaggerated systemic reaction of the immune system
7. Masses of lymphatic tissue located at the back of the mouth and throat
8. Bands of connective tissue
9. Reactions that follow transfusion of mismatched blood
12. The body's capacity to resist invading organisms and toxins
14. Lymphatic vessel located in the small intestine
16. Acronym for test that identifies antibodies to bacteria, among others

Answers are on page 338.

Match game

The long-term immunity the body develops to specific antigens is called *acquired immunity.* Match the following types of acquired immunity to their definitions.

Clues

1. Natural, passive ____
2. Artificial, active ____
3. Natural, active ____
4. Artificial, passive ____

Choices

A. When the immune system responds to a harmful agent and develops long-term resistance

B. The transfer of antibodies from a mother to her fetus or breast-fed infant, providing temporary, partial resistance

C. Obtained by vaccination with weakened or dead infectious agents

D. Provided by substances that give immediate but temporary immunity, such as antibiotics, gamma globulin, and interferon

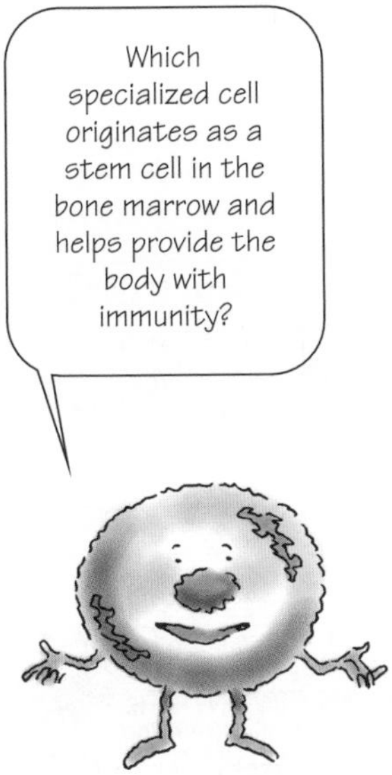
Which specialized cell originates as a stem cell in the bone marrow and helps provide the body with immunity?

Talking in circles

Use the clues below to fill in the blanks with the appropriate word. Then unscramble the circled letters to find the answer to the question posed at left.

1. ___ ___ ___ ___ (◯) ___ ___ ___
2. ___ ___ ___ (◯) ___ ___ ___ ___
3. ___ ___ ___ ___ (◯) ___ ___ ___ ___
   ___ ___ ___ ___
4. (◯) ___ ___ ___ ___
5. ___ (◯) ___ ___ ___ ___ ___ ___ ___ ___

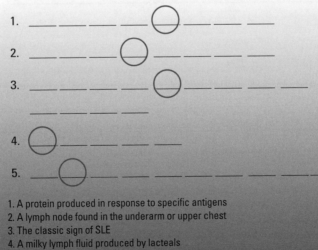

1. A protein produced in response to specific antigens
2. A lymph node found in the underarm or upper chest
3. The classic sign of SLE
4. A milky lymph fluid produced by lacteals
5. A type of transplant that uses bone marrow from a compatible donor

Answers are on page 338.

Answers

At a crossroads

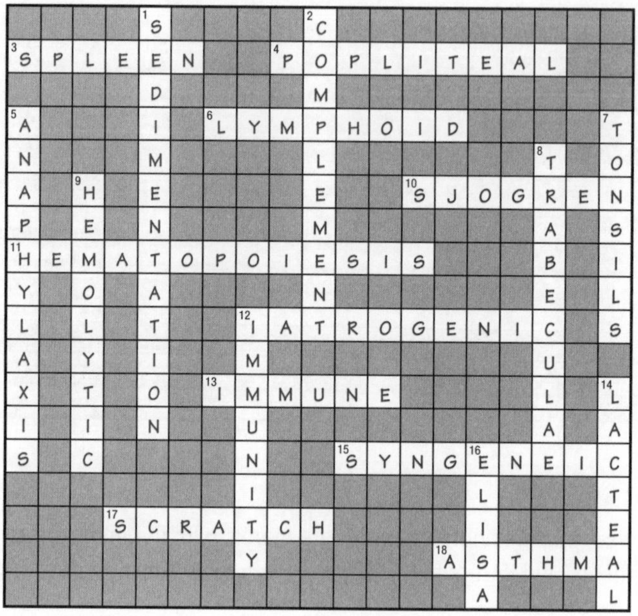
1 SEDIMENTATION
2 COMPLEMENT
3 SPLEEN
4 POPLITEAL
5 ANAPHYLAXIS
6 LYMPHOID
7 TONSILS
8 TRABECULA
9 HEMOLYTIC
10 SJOGREN
11 HEMATOPOIESIS
12 IATROGENIC
12 IMMUNITY
13 IMMUNE
14 LACTEAL
15 SYNGENEIC
16 ELISA
17 SCRATCH
18 ASTHMA

Match game

1. B; 2. C; 3. A; 4. D

Talking in circles

1. Antibody; 2. Axillary; 3. Butterfly rash; 4. Chyle; 5. Allogeneic
Solution to puzzle—B cell

I sense the next chapter will be of great interest!

15

Sensory system

DETECTIVE

Just the facts

In this chapter, you'll learn:

- terminology related to the structure and function of the sensory system
- terminology needed for physical examination of the sensory system
- tests that help diagnose common sensory system disorders
- common sensory system disorders and their treatments.

Sensory structure and function

Sensory stimulation allows the body to interact with the environment. The brain receives stimulation from the sense organs—the eyes, the ears, and the **gustatory** (taste) and **olfactory** (smell) organs located in the nose and mouth. (See *Pronouncing key sensory system terms*, page 340.)

Vision

The **eye** is the sensory organ of sight and transmits visual images to the brain for interpretation. The eyeball occupies the **bony orbit,** a skull cavity formed by bones of the face. The term **optic,** as well as the prefixes ***oculo-*** and ***ophthalmo-***, refers to the eye. (See *Eye terms*, page 340.)

Pump up your pronunciation

Pronouncing key sensory system terms

Here's a list of key terms related to the sensory system, along with the correct ways to pronounce them.

Auricle	AW-RIH-KUHL
Choanae	KOH-AY-NEE
Cilia	SILL-EE-AH
Eustachian	YOU-STAY-SHEE-UHN
Optesthesia	AHP-TEHS-THEE-ZYUH
Tinnitus	TIHN-IH-TEHS or TIH-NEYE-TEHS

Beyond the dictionary

Eye terms

Many eye terms are derived from Greek or Latin roots. Recognizing these roots will help you quickly understand many eye terms.

Eye know Greek
The term **optic** means *pertaining to the eye or sight* and derives from the Greek word of the same meaning, ***optikos.*** The **optic disk,** therefore, is a round area within the eye. The ***opt-*** of "optic" is used as a prefix to form other terms pertaining to the eye, such as **optometry,** *the science of treating the human eye.*

Ophthalmo-, from the Greek word for eye, ***ophthalmos,*** also forms "eye words" such as **ophthalmoscope,** *an instrument used for examining the inner eye.*

Eye know Latin
The root ***oculo-,*** from the Latin word for eye, ***oculus,*** is also used to form many terms that refer to the eye; for example, **intraocular,** which means *within the eyeball*—as in **intraocular structures.**

The outer eye

Six cranial nerves serve the eye, the ocular muscles, and the **lacrimal apparatus.** The coordinated action of six muscles controls eye movement. Extraocular structures—the **eyelids, conjunctivae,** and lacrimal apparatus—protect and lubricate the eye.

Eye protectors

The **eyelids,** also called **palpebrae,** are loose folds of skin covering the front of the eye. They provide protection from foreign bodies, regulate the entrance of light, and distribute tears over the eye by blinking. The lid margins contain hair follicles, which in turn contain eyelashes **(cilia)** and sebaceous glands.

Conjunctivae are transparent mucous membranes that protect the eye from foreign bodies. The **palpebral conjunctiva** lines the eyelids and appears shiny and pinkish red. The **bulbar conjunctiva** joins the palpebral portion and covers the sclera up to the limbus. A small, fleshy elevation called the **caruncle** sits at the nasal aspect of the conjunctivae.

These crying eyes

The **lacrimal apparatus** lubricates and protects the eye with tears produced by **lacrimal glands.** After washing across the eyeball, tears drain through the **punctum,** a tiny opening at the junction of the upper and lower eyelids. From there, tears flow through **lacrimal canals** into the **lacrimal sac.** They then drain through the **nasolacrimal duct** and into the nose.

Lacrimal comes from the Latin word for a teardrop, ***lacrima.***

The inner eye

The **sclera** is the white part of the eyeball. Composed of fibrous tissue and fine elastic fibers, it's covered by the conjunctiva and bathed by tears from the lacrimal glands.

The light of the eye

The **cornea** is a smooth, transparent portion of the eyeball through which light enters the eye. It bulges slightly with a domelike protrusion and lacks blood vessels. The cornea is very sensitive to touch.

Looking straight in the eye

The **iris** is a circular disk in the center of the eye with the ability to contract. The **anterior** and **posterior chambers** of the iris are filled with a clear watery fluid called **aqueous humor.** This fluid drains through the trabecular meshwork into **Schlemm's canal** (a sinus at the junction of the cornea and the iris). **Intraocular pressure (IOP)** is the balance of pressure between secretion and removal of fluid.

The lens of a camera takes its name from the lens in our eyes. They perform the same function: refracting and focusing light.

Focus on this

The **pupil,** or central opening of the iris, is black in color. By expanding and contracting, it regulates the amount of light admitted to the **lens.** Enclosed in an elastic capsule directly behind the iris, the lens acts like a camera lens, refracting and focusing light onto the retina.

The reception area

The **retina** receives visual stimuli and sends them to the brain.

Optical equipment

The **optic disk** is a well-defined, round, yellow to pink disk within the nasal portion of the retina. It allows the optic nerve to enter the retina at the **nerve head.**

Photoreceptors called **rods** and **cones**, named for their shape, are the visual receptors of the retina and are responsible for vision. The rods, located toward the outside of the retina, respond to low-intensity light and shades of gray. The cones are concentrated in the center and respond to bright light and color.

It's all clear here

Located to the side of the optic disk is the **macula,** which is slightly darker than the rest of the retina. A region in the macula called the **fovea centralis** is the site of clearest vision, where cones are most concentrated and no rods are found. Because the fovea centralis contains the heaviest concentration of cones, it's a main receiver of vision and color.

Focusing on convergence

The process called **accommodation** allows the eyes to focus on light rays that are close or far away. The eyeballs are **converged** (move together) by muscles attached to the eyeball and the bones of the orbit.

Hearing

The **ear** is a sensory organ that enables hearing and maintains equilibrium. It's conveniently divided into the **external, middle,** and **inner ear.**

Why is the **tympanic membrane** called the eardrum? For starters, the term comes from the Greek word for *kettle drum,* **tympanon,** and most importantly, it acts like a drum when struck by sound vibrations.

The external ear

The **auricle,** or **pinna** (pinna means *wing),* is the cartilage-based outer part of the ear. The **external auditory meatus** (opening) is the short passage leading into the ear. Earwax, also called **cerumen,** lines this canal, which ends at the tympanic membrane.

Drum roll, please...

The **tympanic membrane** separates the external ear from the middle ear. Also called the **eardrum,** it picks up sound waves and transmits them to the auditory nerve in the brain.

The middle ear

The **middle ear** is located in a small, air-filled cavity in the temporal bone called the **tympanic cavity.** It lies between the tympanic membrane and the inner ear and communicates with the throat by way of the **eustachian tube,** which keeps air pressure equal on both sides of the eardrum. The tympanic membrane is so sensitive to air pressure that rapid changes in altitude can produce pain, feelings of pressure, and ringing in the ears **(tinnitus).**

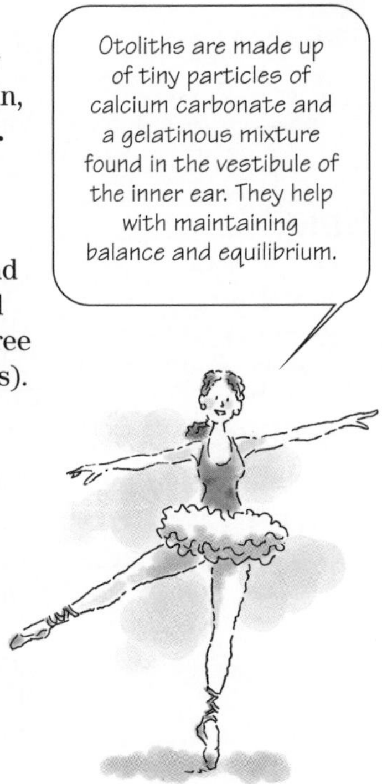
Otoliths are made up of tiny particles of calcium carbonate and a gelatinous mixture found in the vestibule of the inner ear. They help with maintaining balance and equilibrium.

A hammer, anvil, and stirrup

The middle ear contains three small bones named for their shapes—the **malleus** (hammer), **incus** (anvil), and **stapes** (stirrup). Connected by joints, their mechanical activity transmits sound waves to the inner ear. The three bones together are called the **auditory ossicles** (bones). The stapes sits in an opening called the **oval window (fenestra ovalis),** through which sound vibrations travel to the inner ear.

The inner ear

A bony labyrinth and a membrane-covered labyrinth combine to form the inner ear. It consists of the **vestibule,** a small space at the beginning of a canal, and two systems of canals, the **cochlea** and the **semicircular.**

Ear-y canals

Sensory tissue in the semicircular canals maintains the body's sense of position and equilibrium. The **cochlea** (which means *spiral* or *shell-shaped*) contains three canals separated from one another by thin membranes:

- The **vestibular canal** connects with the oval window that leads to the middle ear.
- The **tympanic canal** is connected to the **round window,** which also leads to the middle ear. Both of these canals are bony and contain **perilymph fluid.**
- The **cochlear canal** is membranous and filled with **endolymph fluid.**

Located in the cochlear canal is the **organ of Corti,** a spiral-shaped membrane made up of cells with projecting hairs that transmit sound to the cochlear branch of the acoustic nerve.

For me to hear what Polly is saying, the sound of her voice has to travel to my inner ear through **air conduction, bone conduction,** or both!

Listen up

For hearing to occur, sound waves travel through the ear by two pathways:

- **Air conduction** occurs when sound waves travel in the air through the external and middle ear to the inner ear.

Bone conduction occurs when sound waves travel through bone to the inner ear.

Smell

The sensory organ for smell, the **nose,** also warms, filters, and humidifies inhaled air. The word elements ***naso-*** and ***rhino-*** and the term **olfactory** refer to the nose, including the external parts and internal cavities.

The nose knows

The **olfactory epithelium** within the nose is the actual organ of smell, perceiving odors when its cells are stimulated. **Olfactory receptors** are located in a narrow shelf formed by the **superior nasal concha,** the upper part of the **septum,** and—bordering the **nostrils** on the lower part of each side—the winglike **alae.** Smells received by the olfactory epithelium are transmitted to the **olfactory bulb** and continue from there to olfactory centers in the brain. (See *Not that kind of factory.*)

Beyond the dictionary

Not that kind of factory

When studying the sense of smell and the nose, the term **olfactory** comes up often, as in **olfactory epithelium,** the actual organ of smell. Although the term **olfactory** suggests *a smell factory,* the term actually derives from the Latin word for *smell,* ***olfactus.***

Nosing around the inside of the nose

The upper third of the nose consists of bone, and the lower two-thirds is made of cartilage. **Cilia,** tiny hairs that filter inhaled air, line the **vestibule,** the area inside the nostrils. The **nasal septum** separates the nostrils. Grooves called **meatuses** separate the three curved, bony structures called **turbinates (superior, middle,** and **inferior),** which aid breathing by warming, filtering, and humidifying inhaled air. Posterior air passages known as **choanae** lead to the oropharynx (throat).

The nose can identify about 10,000 odors—but all result from combinations of the six basic odors: flowery, fruity, spicy, resinous, burned, and putrid. Phew!

And right out in front of your nose

The upper, narrow end of the nose is called the **root.** The **bridge** extends from the root to the **tip.** The **external nares** are the two outer openings, separated by the **nasal septum.** The **alae** flare out from either side of the nares.

Touch

The **skin** is the organ of touch, able to receive sensations of pressure, heat, cold, and pain. Touch, or light pressure perception, occurs when **dendrites** (free sensory nerve endings in the skin) are stimulated.

A light touch

Merkel's disks are **tactile corpuscles** in the epidermis that relay light touch and superficial pressure. **Meissner's corpuscles** (in the corium below the epidermis), receive light pressure sensation. Heavy pressure is transmitted by **Pacini's corpuscles,** layered sensory nerve tissues in the skin's subcutaneous layer.

Touchy to temperature changes

The skin reacts to temperature changes of even a few degrees. Although the mechanism is unknown, skin capillaries, free nerve endings, and **Ruffini's corpuscles** (in the corium) help send temperature information to the brain.

Taste

The **taste buds** are the receptors for the taste nerve fibers located in the **papillae** (small projections on the tongue). A few taste buds are found in the mucous membranes of the soft palate, the opening from the mouth to the throat, and the epiglottis. (See *A tasteful history.*)

Beyond the dictionary

A tasteful history

The term **gustatory** pertains to the sense of taste and derives from the Latin word ***gustare,*** *to taste*. Another "tasteful" English word, or rather "distasteful," that is derived from that same Latin root is ***disgust,*** which literally means *to cause nausea.*

Physical examination terms

This section will provide terms you may need to know for physical examination of the sensory system.

In the term **blepharospasm,** ***blepharo*** comes from the Greek word **blepharon,** which means ***eyelid.***

Examining vision

An **ophthalmoscope,** which contains a light, a mirror with a single hole, and several lenses, is used for examining the interior structures of the eye. This instrument is also called a **funduscope.** These terms are used in physical examination of the sense of vision:

- **anisopia**—unequal vision in two eyes
- **astigmatism**—impairment in vision due to an irregularity in the curvature of the cornea or lens
- **blepharospasm**—spasms or constant blinking of the eyelid
- **diplopia**—double vision
- **exophthalmos**—unilateral or bilateral bulging or protrusion of the eyeballs
- **floaters**—tiny clumps of vitreous gel appearing to float in the visual field (see *Keeping it simple*, page 346.)

- **monochromatism**—total color blindness
- **myopia**—nearsightedness
- **nyctalopia**—night blindness
- **optic neuritis**—inflammation of the optic nerve
- **presbyopia**—inability to focus on small print due to loss of elasticity of the lens (a normal sign of aging)
- **ptosis**—drooping of the eyelid
- **strabismus**—absence of coordinated eye movement, leading to misalignment of the eyes
- **uveitis**—inflammation of the uvea, including the iris, ciliary body, and choroid.

The real world

Keeping it simple

Not all medical terms are derived from Greek and Latin and contain many syllables. Sometimes a simple word best describes a medical phenomenon. Take, for example, the term **floaters,** a coined term for the tiny clumps of vitreous gel that appear to "float" in the eyes.

Examining hearing

An **otoscope** is a device for examining the ear, including the external ear, eardrum, and ossicles. This instrument includes a device for **insufflation** (blowing vapor or powder into a cavity), a light, and a magnifying glass. Here are terms involved with physical examination of the ear:

- **otorrhagia**—bleeding from the ear
- **otorrhea**—discharge from the ear
- **ototoxic**—a substance toxic to the eighth cranial nerve or the organs of balance and hearing
- **tinnitus**—ringing in one or both ears
- **vertigo**—a sensation of movement in which the patient feels himself revolving in space or surroundings revolving about him (may result from inner ear disease).

Examining sense of smell

The following terms are used in the physical examination of the sense of smell:

- **anosmia**—absence of the sense of smell
- **dysosmia**—a defect in or impairment of the sense of smell
- **hyperosmia**—abnormal sensitivity to odors
- **osmesthesia**—inability to perceive and distinguish odors
- **osmodysphoria**—abnormal dislike of certain odors.

Memory jogger

Here's the near and far, so to speak, of two vision examination terms:

- **myopia** (nearsightedness), vision is better for near rather than far objects.
- **hyperopia** (farsightedness), vision is better for far rather then near objects.

Examining sense of taste

The following terms are used in the physical examination of the sense of taste:

- **ageusia**—an impaired or absent sense of taste

- **dysgeusia**—abnormal or distorted sense of taste
- **hypergeusia**—unusual acuteness of taste
- **hypogeusia**—impaired sense of taste.

Diagnostic tests

Many methods are used to diagnose the origins of sensory diseases or conditions. Some tests measure an individual component's level of function in the sensory system, while others examine each component for injury. This section reviews diagnostic test terms for the sensory system.

Eye tests

Eye tests can be conducted either under direct evaluation or with radiologic and imaging equipment.

Direct evaluation

In direct evaluation, tests are applied directly to the eye by the examiner with the aid of various pieces of equipment.

Look into the light

Refraction is an examination to determine and correct refractive eye errors. The **ophthalmologist** usually performs a refraction with a **retinoscope.** In this test, the examiner uses the retinoscope to shine a light into the patient's eye. The examiner then notes the reflexive movements of the fundus.

Most enlightening! In **refraction,** the examiner uses the retinoscope to shine a light into the patient's eye. The examiner then notes the reflexive movements of the fundus.

In the spotlight

Slit-lamp examination gets its name from the piece of equipment used, an instrument equipped with a special lighting system and a binocular microscope that allows the examiner to view details of the eye, including the eyelids, eyelashes, conjunctiva, and cornea.

Eye know IOP

Tonometry permits indirect measurement of IOP.

Radiologic and imaging studies

Radiologic and imaging equipment can make the inner eye visible for closer study.

Shutter bug

Fluorescein angiography records the appearance of blood vessels inside the eye through rapid-sequence photographs of the fundus. The photographs follow the I.V. injection of **sodium fluorescein,** a contrast medium.

Sounding it out

Ocular ultrasonography transmits high-frequency sound waves through the eye and measures their reflection from ocular structures.

Eye of the storm

Other eye examinations and terms include:
- **Orbital computed tomography (CT)** reveals abnormalities that can't be seen with standard X-rays. The orbital CT scan is a series of tomograms reconstructed by a computer and displayed as anatomic slices on a screen.
- **Orbital radiography** examines the orbit (the deep-set cavity housing the eye), lacrimal gland, blood vessels, nerves, muscles, and fat.
- A **scanning laser ophthalmoscope** is a laser device used to detect abnormal retinal secretions.

Visual acuity tests

A **Snellen eye chart** is the standard chart used in eye examinations, containing block letters of decreasing size read by the patient from a distance.

Visual field tests determine the extent of the retin-al area through which the patient can perceive visual stimuli.

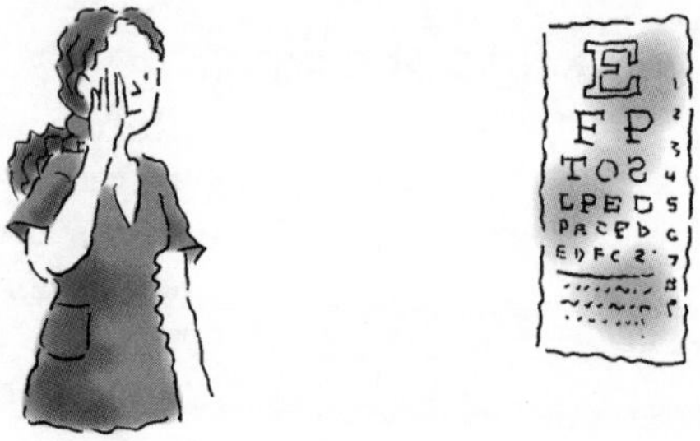

Testing the ears

When performing diagnostic tests on the sense of hearing, the examiner generally needs the participation of the patient. After all, only the individual being tested can tell the examiner whether he heard something.

First look

Otoscopy is the direct visualization of the external auditory canal and the tympanic membrane through an instrument called an **otoscope.**

Tuning fork tests

Tuning fork tests such as Weber's test and the Rinne test are quick screening tools for detecting hearing loss.

Good vibrations

Weber's test evaluates bone conduction by placing a vibrating tuning fork on top of the patient's head at the midline or in the middle of the patient's forehead. The patient should perceive the sound equally in both ears.

The **Rinne test** compares bone conduction to air conduction in both ears by placing the base of a vibrating tuning fork on the mastoid process and noting how many seconds pass before the patient can no longer hear it.

Audiometric tests

Audiometric tests are performed by **audiologists** to confirm hearing loss. **Audiometry** is the evaluation of hearing using an **audiometer,** a device that measures perception of tones at various frequencies. (See *I hear.*)

> **Beyond the dictionary**
>
> **I hear**
>
> You're probably familiar with the word **audio**. You own audio equipment (such as a radio) and maybe even consider yourself an **audiophile** *(one devoted to high-quality sound equipment).* But did you know that ***audio*** is the Latin word for *I hear?* Therefore, it makes sense that tests that examine your ability to hear are called **audiometric.**

Reaching the threshold

Pure-tone audiometry provides a record of the **thresholds**—the lowest intensity levels—at which a patient can hear a set of test tones through earphones or a bone conduction (sound) vibrator. The **test tones** are concentrated at certain frequencies labeled bone conduction thresholds and air conduction thresholds. In **Békésy audiometry,** a patient pushes a button to indicate that a tone was heard.

Going with the flow

Acoustic admittance tests evaluate middle ear function by measuring sound energy's flow into the ear (admittance) and the opposition to that flow (impedance). Two tests are used to measure admittance:

- **Tympanometry** measures middle ear admittance in response to air pressure changes in the ear canal.
- The **acoustic reflex test** measures the change in admittance produced by contraction of the stapedius muscle as it responds to an intense sound.

Electrocochleography

Electrocochleography measures the electrical current generated in the inner ear after sound stimulation. The current is measured by an electrode in the external acoustic canal. (See *Isn't there an abbreviation?*)

Electronystagmography

In **electronystagmography,** eye movements in response to specific stimuli are recorded on graph paper and used to evaluate the interactions of the vestibular system and the muscles controlling eye movement in what is known as the **vestibulo-ocular reflex.**

Pump up your pronunciation

Isn't there an abbreviation?

Generally, tests with long, hard-to-pronounce names like **electro-cochleography** are referred to by an abbreviation. In this case, maybe ECG would be appropriate; however, that abbreviation is for the term **electrocardiogram.** What do you do then? Take a deep breath and sound it out: EH-LECK-TROH-KAWK-LEE-AWG-RAH-FEE.

Tests for smell

The **Proetz test** measures the acuity of smell, using different concentrations of substances with recognizable odors.

Do you smell something?

The lowest concentration at which the patient recognizes an odor is called the **olfactory coefficient,** or **minimal identifiable odor.**

Disorders

The sensory system is a complex system with even more complicated components. This section provides terminology related to disorders of the sensory system.

The Proetz (pronounced PRHOTS) test measures the acuity of smell, using different concentrations of substances with recognizable odors.
Pepper Mint

Eye disorders

Eye disorders can range from common irritation in and around the eyes to impaired vision. Various types of eye disorders are discussed here.

Common inflammations and infections

- **Blepharitis** is a common inflammatory condition of the eyelids, lash follicles, and glands of the eyelids, characterized by swelling, redness, and crusts of dried mucus on the eyelids.
- **Conjunctivitis** is an inflammation or infection of the conjunctiva, sometimes called **pinkeye.** (See *Is pinkeye pink?*)

• **Dacryocystitis** is a common infection of the lacrimal sac caused by an obstruction (**dacryostenosis**) of the nasolacrimal duct or by trauma.
• **Keratitis** is an inflammation of the cornea, usually confined to one eye, and it may be acute or chronic, superficial or deep.

Other eye disorders

One common cause of vision loss, a **cataract** is a gradually developing opacity of the lens or lens capsule of the eye.

Here are some other eye disorders:
• **Corneal abrasion,** a scratch on the surface epithelium of the cornea, is often caused by a foreign body.
• **Macular degeneration,** the atrophy or degeneration of the macular disk, is the most common cause of blindness in adults.
• **Nystagmus** is recurring, involuntary eyeball movement that produces blurred vision and difficulty in focusing. The movement may be horizontal, vertical, rotating, or mixed.

Too much pressure

Glaucoma is a group of disorders characterized by an abnormally high IOP, which can damage the optic nerve. Left untreated, it can cause blindness. Glaucoma occurs in several forms:
• **Chronic open-angle glaucoma** results from overproduction of aqueous humor.
• **Acute angle-closure glaucoma** results from obstruction to the outflow of aqueous humor.
• **Secondary glaucoma** can result from uveitis, trauma, or drugs such as steroids.

Looking to the retina

In **retinal detachment,** the retinal layers split and create a subretinal space, which fills with fluid (called **subretinal fluid**).

A genetically transmitted disorder, **retinitis pigmentosa** causes progressive destruction of the retinal rods and leads to eventual blindness.

Noninflammatory retinal disorders, called **vascular retinopathies,** result from disruption of the eye's blood supply. The two types of this condition are:

Beyond the dictionary

Is pinkeye pink?

The inflammation caused by **pinkeye** may strike some as pink in color and therefore explain the origin of its use, but the term probably derives from the Middle English word ***pinken,*** which means *to prick.*

Pinkeye originally was used to indicate *half-shut,* or what your eye would look like after it was pricked or poked, and what it may look like if you're suffering from pinkeye.

- **Hypertensive retinopathy** results from prolonged hypertensive disease, which produces retinal vasospasm and consequently damages and narrows the arteriolar opening.
- **Diabetic retinopathy** is retinopathy that results as a complication of diabetes.

Ear disorders

Ear disorders can range from common irritation to serious hearing loss.

Hearing loss

Hearing loss (deafness) results from a dysfunction in the mechanical or nervous system that disrupts transmission of sound waves. It's classified as:

- **conductive loss**—interrupted transmission of sound impulses from the external ear to the junction of the stapes and oval window
- **mixed hearing loss**—combined conductive and sensorineural dysfunctions
- **otosclerosis**—slow growth of a spongy bone in the otic capsule, particularly at the oval window (the most common cause of progressive conductive hearing loss)
- **sensorineural loss**—impaired cochlear or acoustic nerve function that prevents transmission of sound impulses within the inner ear or brain.

The older we get

Presbycusis, an effect of aging, results from the loss of hair cells in the organ of Corti. This disorder causes sensorineural hearing loss, usually of high-frequency tones.

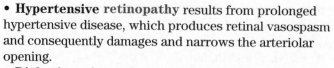

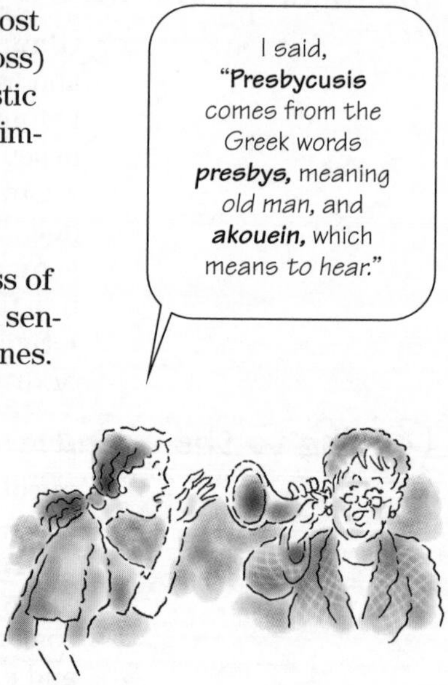
I said, "**Presbycusis** comes from the Greek words ***presbys,*** meaning old man, and ***akouein,*** which means to hear."

Ear disorders without chronic hearing loss

Here are some common disorders of the ear that generally have no long-term effect on hearing:

- **Infectious myringitis** is characterized by inflammation, hemorrhage, and effusion of fluid into the tissue and at the end of the external ear canal and tympanic membrane.
- **Labyrinthitis,** an inflammation of the labyrinth of the inner ear, frequently causes severe vertigo.

• **Mastoiditis** is a bacterial infection and inflammation of the mastoid antrum air cells and is commonly a complication of chronic or acute otitis media.
• **Ménière's disease,** also called **endolymphatic hydrops,** is a labyrinthine dysfunction known to cause violent attacks of severe vertigo lasting from 10 minutes to several hours.
• **Otitis externa** is an inflammation of the external ear canal, which may be acute or chronic.
• **Otitis media** is an inflammation of the middle ear.

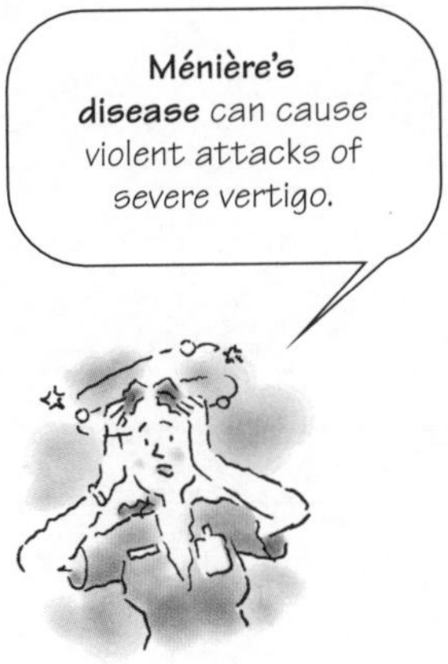
Ménière's disease can cause violent attacks of severe vertigo.

Treatments

Treatment options for sensory system disorders include drug therapy, surgery and, in some cases, a transplant replacing a damaged component.

Eye treatments

Drug therapy is a common treatment for eye disorders.

Drug therapy

The most frequently used drugs include:
• **Anti-infectives,** such as bacitracin and erythromycin, are used to treat infection.
• **Anti-inflammatory agents,** such a dexamethasone, are used to treat inflammatory conditions of the eye.
• **Artificial tears** provide moisture for the eyes when insufficient tear production is a problem.
• **Miotics** are agents that cause constriction of the pupil.
• **Mydriatics** are agents that dilate the pupil of the eye.
• **Ophthalmic anesthetics** prepare the eye for procedures, such as tonometry, suture removal from the cornea, or removal of foreign bodies.

Eye surgery

Surgery may involve the repair, removal, or transplant of a failing component of the eye. Surgeons often employ **laser surgery,** using a laser that generates focused, or monochromatic, light waves; it then magnifies their power by deflecting them off a series of mirrors. The result is a finely focused, high-energy beam.

• **Cataracts** are removed by one of two methods. In **intracapsular cataract extraction,** the entire lens is removed, most often with a **cryoprobe,** a surgical instrument that freezes and adheres to the lens, making the lens easier to remove. **Extracapsular cataract extraction** removes the patient's anterior capsule, cortex, and nucleus, leaving the posterior capsule intact. This technique uses irrigation and aspiration or **phacoemulsification.** Phacoemulsification uses an ultrasonic probe to break the lens into minute particles and aspirate them. (See *How do I say* phacoemulsification?)
• Performed by laser or standard surgery, an **iridectomy** reduces IOP by improving the drainage of aqueous humor. The procedure makes a hole in the iris, creating an opening though which the aqueous humor can flow to bypass the pupil.
• **Radial keratotomy** is a treatment for myopia (nearsightedness) that involves the creation of small radial incisions in the cornea. These incisions flatten the cornea and help properly focus light on the retina.
• **Sclerectomy** is excision of part of the sclera.
• **Scleral buckling** is surgical repair of a detached retina, in which indentations of the sclera are made over the retinal tears to promote retinal adherence to the choroid.
• **Trabeculectomy** is a surgical filtering procedure that removes part of the trabecular meshwork, allowing aqueous humor to bypass blocked channels. This procedure creates a filtering bleb or opening under the conjunctiva.
• A microsurgical procedure, **vitrectomy** removes part or all of the vitreous humor—the transparent gelatinous substance that fills the cavity behind the lens. It's also used for removal of foreign bodies and infection within the eye.

Pump up your pronunciation

How do I say *phacoemulsification?*

Phacoemulsification is the process by which an ultrasonic device disintegrates a cataract. ***Phakos*** is the Greek term for *lens,* and ***emulsification*** is the process by which something is *emulsified* or *broken down.* This word becomes easier to pronounce when you break it down phonetically: FACK-OH-EE-MULL-SIH-FIH-KAY-SHUN.

Restoring clarity

In a **corneal transplant,** healthy corneal tissue from a human donor replaces a damaged part of the cornea. The transplant can take one of two forms:

Full-thickness penetrating keratoplasty involves excision and replacement of the entire cornea.

Lamellar keratoplasty removes and replaces a superficial layer of corneal tissue.

In corneal transplantation, corneal tissue from a human donor replaces a damaged part of the cornea.

Lasik surgery (laser-assisted in situ keratomileusis) uses a laser to reshape the cornea and correct vision.

Ear treatments

Treatments for ear disorders range from drug therapy to surgical intervention.

Drug therapy

The following drugs are used to treat otic disorders:

- **Acetic acid,** or **Domeboro's Solution,** treats ear canal infections (and prevents "swimmer's ear").
- **Anesthetics** treat pain from otitis media and assist with removal of cerumen.
- **Antibiotics** treat external ear canal infection.
- **Cerumeolytics** help remove impacted cerumen.
- **Corticosteroids,** such as hydrocortisone, treat inflammation of the external ear canal.

Ear surgery

Surgical procedures can either repair or remove a failing component.

Drum repair

Myringotomy is a surgical incision into the tympanic membrane to relieve pain and drain pus or fluid from the middle ear. **Myringoplasty** is performed to repair a ruptured tympanic membrane. The surgeon approximates the edges of the membrane or applies a graft taken from the temporalis muscle.

Taking off the stirrups

Stapedectomy removes all or part of the stapes. A **total stapedectomy** involves removal of the entire bone, followed by insertion of a graft and prosthesis to bridge the gap between the incus and the inner ear.

In a **partial stapedectomy,** the surgeon removes part of the bone and rebuilds what's left with a prosthesis. **Laser stapedectomy,** a relatively new technique, is easier to perform but carries a risk of the laser beam penetrating the bone.

systole
parietal
aorta

Vocabulary builders

At a crossroads

Completing this crossword puzzle will help you come to your senses about correct sensory system terms. Good luck!

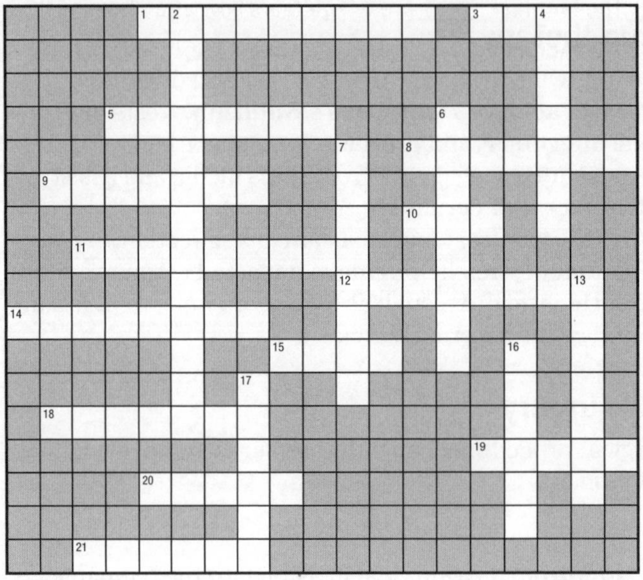
1 2 3 4 5 6 7 8 9 10 11 12 13 14 15 16 17 18 19 20 21

Across

1. Another name for **eyelids**
3. Eponym for the spiral-shaped membrane that transmits sound to the cochlear branch
5. Absence of the sense of smell
8. Latin term for *teardrop*
9. Term for *earwax*
10. Number of basic odors
11. Free sensory nerve endings
12. Particles of calcium carbonate in the small sacs of the vestibule
14. Ringing in the ears
15. Organ of touch
18. Air passages from the nose that lead to the throat
19. This test evaluates bone conduction
20. The eyeball occupies the bony ___
21. The white part of the eyeball

Down

2. Process that allows eyes to focus on light rays that are close or far away
4. Eponym for corpuscles that are involved in sending temperature information to the brain
6. Location of taste buds
7. Unequal vision in the two eyes
13. Name that lends itself to the standard eye chart
16. Test that measures the acuity of smell
17. Part of the eye that receives visual stimuli

Answers are on page 358.

Finish line

Tears protect and lubricate the eye. **Lacrimal** pertains to tears and comes from the Latin word ***lacrima***, which means *tear.* Fill in the blanks for the eye structures involved in tear production.

1. The **lacrimal** _____ lubricates and protects the eye with tears.
2. The **lacrimal** _____ produce tears.
3. The **lacrimal** _____ are where tears flow after draining through the punctum.
4. The **lacrimal** _____ is where the tears then collect.
5. The ___-**lacrimal** ___ is where tears drain through into the nose.

Talking in circles

Use the clues below to fill in the blanks with the appropriate word. Then unscramble the circled letters to find the answer to the question posed at left.

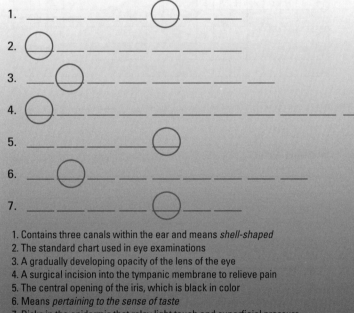

I am one of three small bones in the middle ear that hammers away at sound waves. Which bone am I?

1. ___ ___ ___ ___ (◯) ___ ___
2. (◯) ___ ___ ___ ___ ___ ___
3. ___ (◯) ___ ___ ___ ___ ___ ___
4. (◯) ___ ___ ___ ___ ___ ___ ___ ___ ___ ___
5. ___ ___ ___ ___ (◯)
6. ___ (◯) ___ ___ ___ ___ ___ ___ ___
7. ___ ___ ___ ___ (◯) ___ ___

1. Contains three canals within the ear and means *shell-shaped*
2. The standard chart used in eye examinations
3. A gradually developing opacity of the lens of the eye
4. A surgical incision into the tympanic membrane to relieve pain
5. The central opening of the iris, which is black in color
6. Means *pertaining to the sense of taste*
7. Disks in the epidermis that relay light touch and superficial pressure

Answers are on page 358.

Answers

At a crossroads

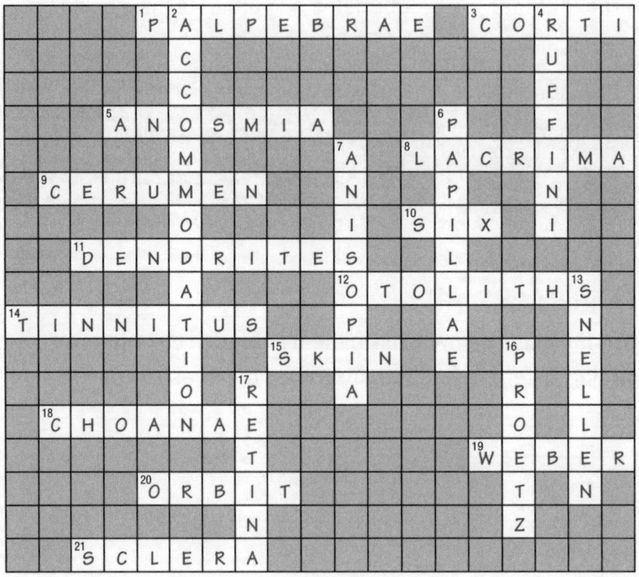
1 PALPEBRAE
2 ACCOMMODATION
3 CORTI
4 RUFFINI
5 ANOSMIA
6 PAPILLAE
7 ANISOPIA
8 LACRIMA
9 CERUMEN
10 SIX
11 DENDRITES
12 OTOLITHS
13 SNELLEN
14 TINNITUS
15 SKIN
16 PROETZ
17 RETINA
18 CHOANAE
19 WEBER
20 ORBIT
21 SCLERA

I can sense without even looking that you've done a great job with this chapter.

Finish line

1. Apparatus; 2. Glands; 3. Canals; 4. Sac; 5. Naso-, Duct

Talking in circles

1. Cochlea; 2. Snellen; 3. Cataract;
4. Myringotomy; 5. Pupil; 6. Gustatory; 7. Merkel's
Solution to puzzle—Malleus

16

Clinical pharmacology

Just the facts

In this chapter, you'll learn:

- terminology related to the fundamentals of clinical pharmacology
- terminology associated with drug administration
- medications that affect each body system.

Pharmacology basics

Pharmacology is the scientific study of the origin, nature, chemistry, effects, and uses of medications. The term **pharmacology** originated from the Greek root ***pharmako,*** which means *medicine.* (See *Pronouncing key pharmacology terms*, page 360.)

Pharmacology contains three main branches:

1. **Pharmacokinetics** refers to the absorption, distribution, metabolism, and excretion of a drug in a living organism.
2. **Pharmacodynamics** is the study of the biochemical and physical effects of drugs and the mechanisms of drug actions in living organisms.
3. **Pharmacotherapeutics** refers to the use of drugs to prevent and treat diseases.

There's a lot to know when it comes to pharmacology.

Pharmacokinetics

The term **kinetics** means *movement;* therefore, **pharmacokinetics** refers to a drug's movement through the body, including how the drug is:

Pump up your pronunciation

Pronouncing key pharmacology terms

Here's a list of key pharmacology terms, along with the correct ways to pronounce them.

Antiemetics	AN-TEE-EH-MET-IKS
Bioavailability	BEYE-OH-EH-VAYL-EH-BIHL-IH-TEE
Catecholamines	KAT-UH-KOH-LAH-MEENZ
Iatrogenic effects	EYE-AT-ROH-JEN-IK EH-FEKS
Lipodystrophy	LIHP-OH-DIHS-TROH-FEE
Palliative therapy	PAL-EE-AY-TIV THER-UH-PEE
Parasympathomimetic	PAR-UH-SIM-PUH-THOH-MI-MEH-TIK
Pharmacodynamics	FAR-MAH-KOH-DEYE-NAM-IKS
Pharmacogenetics	FAR-MAH-KOH-JEH-NEHT-IKS
Pharmacokinetics	FAR-MAH-KOH-KUH-NET-IKS
Pharmacotherapeutics	FAR-MAH-KOH-THER-UH-PYOU-TIKS

- absorbed
- distributed
- metabolized
- excreted.

In passive transport, a drug moves from an area of higher concentration to one of lower concentration.

Absorption

The process of drug **absorption** covers the progress of a drug from the time it's administered, through the time it passes to the tissues, until it becomes available for use by the body. On a cellular level, drugs are primarily absorbed through passive or active transport.

No energy required

Passive transport requires no cellular energy because the drug moves from an area of higher concentration to one of lower concentration. It occurs when small molecules diffuse across membranes. **Diffusion** (movement from a higher concentration to a lower concentration) stops when drug concentration on both sides of the membrane equalizes.

Active transport requires energy.

Energy required

Active transport requires cellular energy to move the drug from an area of lower concentration to one of higher concentration. Active transport is used to absorb electrolytes, such as sodium and potassium.

Distribution

Drug **distribution** is the process by which a drug is delivered to the tissues and fluids of the body. Distribution of an absorbed drug within the body depends on blood flow, solubility, and protein binding.

Go with the flow

After a drug reaches the bloodstream, its distribution in the body depends on blood flow. The drug is quickly distributed to organs with a large supply of blood, such as the heart, liver, and kidneys.

Drug crossing

The ability of a drug to cross a cell membrane depends on whether the drug is water soluble or lipid soluble. **Lipid-soluble** drugs (those capable of dissolving in fat) easily cross through cell membranes, while **water-soluble** drugs (those capable of dissolving in water) can't.

Ties that bind

As a drug travels through the body, it comes in contact with proteins such as the plasma protein albumin. The drug can either remain free or bind to the protein. The portion of a drug that's **protein bound** is inactive and can't produce a therapeutic effect. Only the free (or unbound) portion remains active.

Metabolism

Drug metabolism, also known as **biotransformation**, refers to the body's ability to change a drug from its dosage form to a more water-soluble form that can later be excreted.

Excretion

Drug **excretion** refers to the elimination of a drug from the body. Most drugs are excreted by the kidneys and leave the body through urine. However, drugs can also be excreted through the lungs, exocrine glands (sweat, salivary, or mammary glands), skin, and intestinal tract.

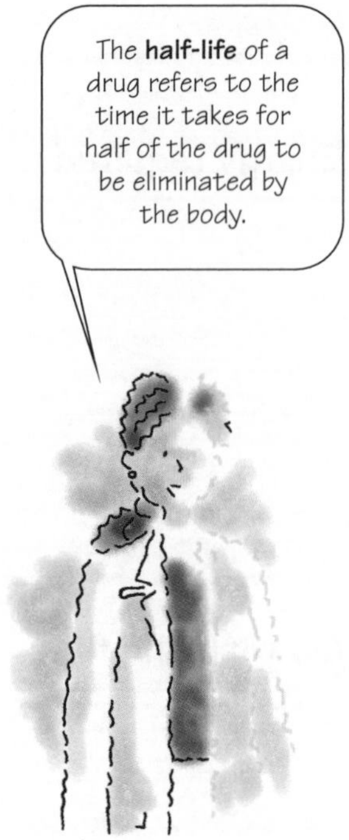
The **half-life** of a drug refers to the time it takes for half of the drug to be eliminated by the body.

Half and half

The **half-life** of a drug refers to the time it takes for half of the drug to be eliminated by the body. Knowing how long a drug remains in the body helps determine how frequently a drug should be administered.

Onset, peak, and duration

In addition to absorption, distribution, metabolism, and excretion, three other factors play important roles in a drug's pharmacokinetics:
- onset of action
- peak concentration
- duration of action.

Lights, camera...action!

Onset of action refers to the time interval that starts when the drug is administered and ends when the therapeutic effect actually begins. Rate of onset varies depending on the route of administration and other pharmacokinetic properties.

Peak performance

As the body absorbs more of a drug, blood concentration levels of that drug rise. The **peak concentration** level is reached when the absorption rate equals the elimination rate.

Total effect

The **duration of action** is the total length of time the drug produces its therapeutic effect.

Pharmacodynamics is the study of drug mechanisms that produce biochemical or physiologic changes in the body.

Pharmacodynamics

Pharmacodynamics is the study of drug mechanisms that produce biochemical or physiologic changes in the body. Interaction at the cellular level represents **drug ac-**

tion. The response resulting from this drug action is referred to as the **drug effect.**

That's stimulating

Many drugs work by stimulating or blocking drug **receptors** (a specialized location on a cell membrane or inside a cell). A drug that's attracted to a receptor displays an affinity—or attraction—for that receptor. When a drug displays an affinity for a receptor and stimulates it, the drug acts as an **agonist.** The drug's ability to initiate a response after binding with the receptor is referred to as **intrinsic activity.**

Memory jogger

Here's a tip for remembering the difference between **agonist** and **antagonist:** Think, "**Ago**nists are **a go,**" meaning that they give the go-ahead for a drug to stimulate a receptor.

Response buster

If a drug has an affinity for a receptor but displays no intrinsic activity (in other words, it doesn't stimulate the receptor), it's called an **antagonist.** The antagonist prevents a response from occurring.

On-site competition

Antagonists can be competitive or noncompetitive. A **competitive antagonist** competes with the agonist for receptor sites. Because this type of receptor binds reversibly to the receptor site, increased doses of an agonist can overcome the antagonist's effects. A **noncompetitive antagonist** binds to receptor sites and blocks the effects of the agonist.

Any one will do

If a drug acts on a variety of receptors, it's said to be **nonselective** and can cause multiple and widespread effects. Some receptors are further classified by their specific effects. For example, **beta receptors** typically produce increased heart rate and bronchial relaxation as well as other systemic effects.

It's got the power

Drug potency refers to the relative amount of a drug required to produce a desired response. Drug potency is also used to compare two drugs.

Safety margin

Most drugs produce a range of multiple effects. The relationship between a drug's desired therapeutic effect and its adverse effect is called the drug's **therapeutic index.**

Pharmacotherapeutics

Pharmacotherapeutics is the use of drugs to treat disease. When choosing a drug to treat a particular condition, health care providers consider the drug's effectiveness along with other factors, such as the type and duration of therapy the patient will receive.

Therapy, not always the same

The type of therapy a patient receives depends on the severity, urgency, and prognosis of the patient's condition. A patient may receive:
- **acute therapy,** which is used for those who are symptomatically ill and require therapy to correct an underlying condition
- **empiric therapy,** which is based on practical experience rather than on pure scientific data
- **maintenance therapy,** which is used to treat chronic conditions that can't be cured
- **supplemental** or **replacement therapy,** in order to replenish or substitute missing substances, such as enzymes or hormones, in the body
- **supportive therapy,** which doesn't effectively treat the cause of the disease but maintains other threatened body systems until a patient's condition improves or resolves
- **palliative therapy,** which is used to treat end-stage or terminal diseases to make the patient as comfortable as possible.

In **drug dependence,** a patient displays physical or psychological need for the drug.
Drug tolerance occurs when a patient shows a decreased response to a particular drug over time.

Different reactions

Certain drugs have a tendency to create drug tolerance and drug dependence. **Drug tolerance** occurs when a patient shows a decreased response to a particular drug over time. The patient then requires larger doses of that drug to produce the same response.

Drug tolerance differs from **drug dependence,** in which a patient displays a physical or psychological need for the drug. **Physical dependence** produces withdrawal symptoms when the drug is stopped, while **psychological dependence** causes drug-seeking behaviors.

Drug interactions

Drugs can interact with other drugs or with food.

Drug interactions can occur between drugs or between drugs and foods. Interactions may impede the results of a laboratory test or produce physical or chemical incompatibilities. The risk of drug interactions increases in relation to the amount of drugs a patient receives. Potential drug interactions include:
- additive effects
- synergistic effects
- antagonistic effects.

Two drugs are better than one

An **additive effect** can occur when two drugs with similar actions are administered to a patient. The effects are equivalent to the sum of the effects of either drug administered alone in higher doses.

Teamwork

A **synergistic effect,** also called **potentiation**, occurs when two drugs that produce the same effect are given together and one drug potentiates (enhances the effect of) the other drug. The combined effect is greater than either drug can produce when taken alone—for example, the effect produced by taking fentanyl (Sublimaze) and midazolam (Versed) concomitantly.

Duking it out

An **antagonistic effect** occurs when the combined response of two drugs is less than the response produced by either drug alone.

Adverse drug reactions

An **adverse drug reaction** (also called a **side effect** or **adverse effect**) is a harmful, undesirable response to a drug. Adverse reactions can range from mild ones that disappear when the drug is discontinued to debilitating diseases that become chronic. Adverse drug reactions are classified as dose-related or patient sensitivity–related. Dose-related reactions include:
- secondary effects
- hypersusceptibility
- overdose
- iatrogenic effects.

Special effects

In addition to its major therapeutic effect, a drug typically produces additional **secondary effects** that are either beneficial or adverse. For example, morphine used to relieve pain may cause respiratory depression as an undesirable secondary effect. Diphenhydramine used as an antihistamine may produce the adverse effect of drowsiness; therefore, it's sometimes prescribed as a sleep aid.

Hyped-up action

Even when the correct therapeutic dose is determined, a patient may experience an excessive therapeutic response called **hypersusceptibility.** Hypersusceptibility typically results from altered pharmacokinetics leading to higher-than-expected blood concentration levels.

An **overdose** occurs when an excessive dose of a drug is taken either intentionally or by accident, So don't abuse me!

Over the top

An **overdose** occurs when an excessive dose of a drug is taken either intentionally or by accident. The result is an exaggerated response (or **toxic reaction**) to the drug that causes transient changes or more serious reactions, such as cardiovascular collapse, respiratory depression, or death.

Simon says

Some adverse reactions, known as **iatrogenic effects,** can mimic pathologic disorders. For example, propranolol can induce asthma.

Too sensitive

Patient sensitivity–related reactions aren't as common as dose-related reactions. Sensitivity-related reactions result from a patient's unusual and extreme sensitivity to a drug. These adverse reactions arise from a unique tissue response rather than from an exaggerated pharmacologic action. Extreme patient sensitivity can occur as a drug allergy.

A **drug allergy** occurs when a patient's immune system identifies a drug, a drug metabolite, or a drug contaminant as a dangerous foreign substance that must be neutralized or destroyed. Previous exposure to the drug or to one with a similar chemical characteristic sensitizes the patient's immune system, and subsequent exposure causes an **allergic reaction** (hypersensitivity) to occur.

Silent but deadly

The allergic reaction can vary in intensity from an immediate life-threatening **anaphylactic reaction** (a dramatic, acute reaction marked by sudden onset of rapidly progressive hives and respiratory distress) to a mild rash and itching. (See *What's behind an anaphylactic reaction.*)

> **Beyond the dictionary**
>
> **What's behind an anaphylactic reaction**
>
> An anaphylactic reaction is characterized by a sudden onset of progressive hives and respiratory distress in response to a drug. ***Ana-*** comes from the Greek words ***an-,*** meaning *not,* and ***phylaxis,*** meaning *protection.*

Drug administration

Because prescribing and administering drugs is a critical responsibility for health care providers, it's important to understand the terminology associated with drug administration.

Drug orders

In an outpatient setting, a doctor or health care provider who's licensed to prescribe drugs writes an order on a special pad and gives it directly to the patient. This is known as a **prescription.**

Drug orders in the inpatient setting differ. The following drug orders are used in inpatient settings:

- **Standard written orders** are written by the health care provider and apply indefinitely until another order is written to discontinue or alter the first one.
- **Single orders** are orders written for a medication that's given only once.
- **Stat orders** are written for medications that must be administered immediately to treat an urgent patient problem.
- Prescribers write **p.r.n. orders** for drugs that are to be given as needed. (See *As needed.*)
- **Standing orders,** also known as **protocol orders,** establish guidelines for treating a particular disease or set of symptoms.
- **Verbal orders** are medication orders that are given orally in urgent situations.
- **Telephone orders** are verbal orders prescribed over the telephone. This type of drug order is usually only given in urgent situations.

> **Beyond the dictionary**
>
> **As needed**
>
> The abbreviation **p.r.n.** is derived from the Latin phrase ***pro re nata,*** meaning *as the occasion arises.* Prescribers write p.r.n. orders for medications that are to be given when needed.

Drug forms

Drugs are manufactured in many different forms, such as solids, liquids, suppositories, and inhalants. Other drug forms include sprays, which are used with several administration routes; creams, lotions, and patches, which are administered topically; and lozenges, which are used to treat local effects.

A tablet is a drug that's been compressed into a certain shape. Tablets come in different forms.

Solidifying solids

Solid drug forms include capsules and tablets. **Capsules** are hard or soft gelatin shells that contain the drug in a powder, in sustained-release beads, or in a liquid form.

A **tablet** is a drug that's been compressed to form a certain shape. Some tablets are uncoated, while others differ in composition:

- **Enteric-coated tablets** have a thin coating that allows the tablet to pass through the stomach and disintegrate or dissolve in the small intestine, where the drug is absorbed.
- **Osmotic pump tablets** release the drug through a single tiny hole in the tablet.
- **Wax matrix tablets** distribute the drug through a honeycomb-like material made of wax.

Liquefying liquids

Liquid medications are usually given orally or parenterally. Orally administered liquids contain the drug mixed with some type of fluid and are classified as:

- **syrups**—drugs mixed in a sugar-water solution
- **suspensions**—finely divided drug particles suspended in a suitable liquid medium
- **tinctures**—hydroalcoholic drug solutions
- **elixirs**—hydroalcoholic solutions that contain glycerin, sorbitol, or other sweeteners.

Packaging parenterals

Parenteral is a term that literally means *outside the intestines.* Drugs given parenterally are administered outside the GI tract and are available in three package styles:

- **vials**—bottles sealed with a rubber diaphragm that contain a single dose or several doses
- **ampules**—glass containers with a thin neck that's typically scored so it can be snapped off easily

• **prefilled system**—a single dose of a drug contained in a plastic bag or a prefilled syringe.

Supposing suppositories

Suppositories deliver medications in a solid base that will melt at body temperature. They can be administered rectally or vaginally.

Inhaling inhalants

Inhalants are drugs that are administered in powdered or liquid form using the respiratory route. Inhalants are absorbed by the rich supply of capillaries in the lungs.

There are many ways to take drugs. Inhalants are administered via the respiratory system.

Routes of administration

The GI tract provides a fairly safe (but relatively slow-acting) site for drug absorption. When a drug is administered using the GI tract, it's called **enteral administration.** A drug administered by any other route is referred to as **parenteral administration.**

Enteral administration

Oral, sublingual, buccal, and rectal preparations are administered by the GI tract:

• Drugs administered by the **oral route** are placed in the patient's mouth and swallowed. Tablets, capsules, liquids, and lozenges are administered this way.

• The **sublingual route** involves placing an uncoated tablet under the tongue, where it disintegrates and dissolves.

• A drug administered by the **buccal route** is placed between the cheek and gum, where it disintegrates and dissolves.

• Suppositories and **enemas** (a solution introduced into the rectum or colon) are administered by the **rectal route.** This route is commonly used when the oral route is prohibited, such as in a patient with nausea or vomiting.

Parenteral administration

Drugs may be administered parenterally through four types of direct injections:

• **intradermal**—injected directly into the skin

• **subcutaneous**—injected into the subcutaneous tissue

- **intramuscular**—injected directly into a muscle
- **intravenous**—injected into a vein.

Under my skin...

Intradermal (I.D.) injections are used for skin tests such as tuberculin. The **ventral** (anterior portion) forearm is the site of choice for I.D. injections.

Simplifying subcutaneous

Subcutaneous injections provide a slow, sustained release of medication and a longer duration of action. Subcutaneous injections are used when the total volume injected is less than 1 ml of liquid. Drugs commonly administered by the subcutaneous route include insulin, heparin, and epinephrine. (See *Sub cue injections.*)

Subcutaneous injection sites include the area over the scapula, the lateral aspects of the upper arm and thigh, and the abdomen.

> *The real world*
>
> **Sub cue injections**
>
> In practice, you may hear a subcutaneous injection referred to as a **sub cue** injection—for example, "Administer this dose of insulin **sub cue**."

Mr. Muscle

Intramuscular (I.M.) injections are given when rapid absorption of medication is desired. The onset of action usually occurs within 10 to 15 minutes after the I.M. injection. A larger amount of fluid (between 2 ml and 5 ml, depending on the site) can be administered using I.M. rather than S.C. injections.

Commonly used I.M. injection sites include the **dorsogluteal muscle** (in the back of the buttocks), **ventrogluteal muscle** (in the anterior portion of the buttocks), **vastus lateralis muscle** (in the lateral thigh), **rectus femoris muscle** (in the upper thigh), and **deltoid muscle** (the upper arm muscle that covers the shoulder prominence).

I.V. meds pack a punch!

I.V. intro

Medications are administered by the **intravenous (I.V.) route** to obtain an immediate onset of action, to attain the highest possible blood concentration level of a drug, or to treat conditions that require constant **titration** (increase or decrease of dosage according to the patient's response).

I.V. medications can be administered by several methods:

- **direct bolus**—the medication is injected directly into the I.V. catheter over a recommended time interval

- **intermittent infusion**—the medication is infused through an I.V. catheter at various time intervals
- **continuous infusion**—the medication is infused through an I.V. catheter for a prolonged period.

Other routes

Other routes that are used for medication administration include the intrathecal, epidural, intra-articular, dermal, ophthalmic, otic, nasal, sinus, and respiratory routes.

Into the great intrathecal space

Intrathecal administration involves introducing a catheter into the intrathecal space of the spinal canal for drug administration. Drugs are delivered by bolus or continuous infusion. Chemotherapeutic agents are sometimes administered by this route.

Epidural space travel

Epidural administration occurs when a catheter is introduced into the epidural space of the spinal column for drug administration. Drugs are delivered by bolus or continuous infusion. Pain medications are commonly administered by this route.

Joint relief

Intra-articular administration is characterized by injecting a drug directly into a joint. Patients with severe joint inflammation sometimes receive intra-articular injections of steroids.

Over the top

Medications given by **dermal** or **topical administration** are applied directly to the skin. Medications administered by this route include creams, lotions, ointments, powders, and patches.

Eye it up

Ophthalmic administration involves instilling liquid or ointment medications topically into the eye.

Friends, Romans...lend me your ear

Medications given by **otic administration** are administered topically into the ear.

Nosing around

Nasal or **sinus administration** refers to the administration of liquid or powdered forms of the drug into the patient's nose and sinuses by instillation or by an atomizer (a device that changes a jet of liquid into a spray).

On the fast tract

Respiratory administration refers to the delivery of medications directly into the respiratory tract. Almost all of the drugs administered by this route have a **systemic effect,** which means that they affect the entire body because of the rich blood supply in the lungs. The drug forms commonly administered by this route are gas and liquid.

Nebulization is one method commonly used to administer drugs by the respiratory route. There are three types of nebulizers:

- The **ultrasonic nebulizer** uses a small volume of medication combined with normal saline solution. Air forced into the nebulizer delivers the medication in a fine mist.
- A **metered-dose inhaler** requires a nebulizer that's prefilled by the manufacturer with several doses of the drug.
- A **dry-powder inhaler** is similar to a metered-dose inhaler. It's activated by an inhaled breath, and a precise amount of medication is then delivered.

Drug classifications

Drugs that share similar characteristics are grouped together as a pharmacologic class or family. Terminology associated with drugs in each pharmacologic class is broken down according to the body system that's affected.

Nervous system drugs

Many drugs affect the nervous system. They include cholinergic drugs, cholinergic blocking drugs, adrenergic drugs, adrenergic blocking drugs, skeletal muscle relaxants, neuromuscular blocking drugs, and anticonvulsant drugs.

Copy cats

Cholinergic drugs promote the action of **acetylcholine** (a neurotransmitter). These drugs are also called **parasympathomimetic drugs** because they produce effects that mimic parasympathetic nerve stimulation.

There are two major classes of cholinergic drugs:

- **Cholinergic agonists** mimic the action of the neurotransmitter acetylcholine.
- **Anticholinesterase drugs** block the action of the enzyme acetylcholinesterase (which breaks down acetylcholine) at cholinergic receptor sites, preventing the breakdown of acetylcholine.

Cholinergic busters

Cholinergic blocking drugs interrupt parasympathetic nerve impulses in the central and autonomic nervous systems. These drugs are also referred to as **anticholinergic drugs** because they prevent acetylcholine from stimulating cholinergic receptors.

Similar to the sympathetic

Adrenergic drugs are also called **sympathomimetic drugs** because they create effects similar to those produced by the sympathetic nervous system. Adrenergic drugs are classified into two groups based on their chemical structure: **catecholamines** (which stimulate the nervous system, constrict peripheral blood vessels, increase heart rate, and dilate the bronchi) and **noncatecholamines** (which have many effects on the body, including local or system constriction of blood vessels, nasal and eye decongestion, bronchiole dilation, and smooth muscle relaxation).

Adrenergic drugs are also called sympathomimetic drugs because they create effects similar to those produced by the sympathetic nervous system.

Adrenergic drugs are also divided by their mechanism of action:

- **Direct-acting adrenergics** act directly on the organ or tissue that's **innervated** (supplied with nerves or nerve impulses) by the sympathetic nervous system.
- **Indirect-acting adrenergics** trigger the release of a neurotransmitter, typically norepinephrine.
- **Dual-acting adrenergics** have both direct and indirect actions.

The road to disruption

Adrenergic blocking drugs (also called **sympatholytic drugs**) are used to disrupt the function of the sympathetic nervous system. These drugs work by blocking impulse transmission at adrenergic receptor sites.

Adrenergic blocking drugs are classified according to their site of action:

- **Alpha-adrenergic blockers** work by interrupting the actions of the catecholamines epinephrine and norepinephrine at alpha receptor sites.
- **Beta-adrenergic blockers** prevent stimulation of the sympathetic nervous system by inhibiting the action of catecholamines at beta-adrenergic receptors. (See *Taking out the* adrenergic.)

> *The real world*
>
> **Taking out the *adrenergic***
>
> In practice, the most widely used adrenergic blockers are beta-adrenergic blockers, simply referred to as **beta blockers.**

Muscle R and R

Skeletal muscle relaxants are used to relax skeletal muscles and treat acute pain or muscle spasticity associated with multiple sclerosis.

Motor end plate stopper

Neuromuscular blocking drugs relax skeletal muscles by disrupting the transmission of nerve impulses at the motor end plate (the branching terminals of a motor nerve axon).

Seizure silencers

Anticonvulsants, also known as **antiseizure drugs,** inhibit neuromuscular transmission in order to prevent seizure activity.

Pain medications

Drugs used to control pain range from mild, over-the-counter preparations, such as acetaminophen, to potent general anesthetics. Here's a list of drugs commonly used to treat pain:

- **Nonopioid analgesics** are drugs that don't contain opioids but that still control pain. Some of these drugs also exhibit an **antipyretic** action, which means they control fever.
- **Nonsteroidal anti-inflammatory drugs (NSAIDs)** control pain by combating inflammation.

- **Opioid agonists** are opium derivatives and synthetic drugs with similar properties used to relieve or decrease pain without causing the person to lose consciousness.
- **Opioid antagonists** block the effects produced by opioid agonists to reverse adverse drug reactions.
- **Anesthetic drugs** depress the central nervous system (CNS) and produce loss of consciousness, loss of responsiveness to sensory stimulation (including pain), and muscle relaxation.

Cardiovascular system drugs

Types of drugs used to improve cardiovascular function include cardiac glycosides and **phosphodiesterase** (PDE) inhibitors, antiarrhythmics, and antianginal drugs.

Cardiac glycosides and PDE inhibitors

Antiarrhythmic drugs help me keep my rhythm.

Cardiac glycosides and **PDE inhibitors** increase the force of the heart's contractions. This is known as a positive **inotropic effect** (affecting the force or energy of muscular contractions).

Changing the rhythm

Antiarrhythmic drugs are used to treat **arrhythmias** (disturbances in normal heart rhythm).

Stopping heart pain

Antianginal drugs are used to treat **angina** (chest pain) by reducing the amount of oxygen the heart needs to do its work, increasing the supply of oxygen to the heart, or both.

There are three commonly used classes of antianginal drugs:

Nitrates are the drugs of choice for relieving acute anginal pain. Nitrates cause smooth muscles of the veins and arteries to relax and dilate. When the vessels dilate, blood flow to the myocardium increases, which relieves the pain.

Beta-adrenergic blockers are drugs used for long-term prevention of angina. Beta-adrenergic blockers decrease blood pressure and block beta-adrenergic receptor sites in the heart muscle and conduction system. They work by decreasing heart rate and reducing the force of the heart's contractions, which results in a lower demand for oxygen.

Calcium channel blockers are used only for long-term prevention of angina. They prevent the passage of calcium ions across the myocardial cell membrane and vascular smooth muscle cells. This causes dilation of the coronary and peripheral arteries, which decreases the force of the heart's contractions and reduces the workload of the heart.

Pressure droppers

Antihypertensive drugs act to reduce blood pressure. Three types of commonly used antihypertensive drugs include:

- **sympatholytic drugs**—which reduce blood pressure by inhibiting or blocking the sympathetic nervous system
- **vasodilating drugs**—which relax peripheral vascular smooth muscle, causing vessels to dilate, thereby lowering blood pressure
- **angiotensin-converting enzyme (ACE) inhibitors**—which reduce blood pressure by interrupting the renin-angiotensin-aldosterone system.

Antihypertensive drugs can help bring a patient's blood pressure down.

Water works

Diuretics are used to promote the excretion of water and electrolytes by the kidneys. Major diuretics include thiazide and thiazide-like diuretics, loop diuretics, and potassium-sparing diuretics:

- **Thiazide** and **thiazide-like diuretics** work by preventing sodium resorption in the kidneys.
- **Loop diuretics** act primarily on the loop of Henle to increase the secretion of sodium, chloride, and water.
- **Potassium-sparing diuretics** conserve potassium and exert weaker diuretic and antihypertensive effects.

Lower lipid levels

Antilipemic drugs lower abnormally high blood levels of lipids, such as cholesterol, triglycerides, and phospholipids.

Clot stoppers

Anticoagulant drugs are used to reduce the ability of the blood to clot. **Antiplatelet drugs** are administered to prevent arterial thromboembolism, particularly in patients at risk for myocardial infarction, stroke, and arteriosclerosis (hardening of the arteries). **Antithrombolytic drugs** are used to dissolve a preexisting clot or thrombus, commonly in an acute or emergency situation.

Respiratory system drugs

Drugs used to improve respiratory function include methylxanthines, expectorants, antitussives, mucolytics, and decongestants.

Breathing gone awry

Methylxanthines are used to treat breathing disorders. They work by decreasing airway reactivity and relieving bronchospasm by relaxing the bronchial smooth muscle.

Thinner and smoother

Expectorants thin mucus so it can be cleared more easily out of airways. They also soothe mucous membranes in the respiratory tract.

Suppress and inhibit

Antitussive drugs suppress or inhibit coughing.

H_2-receptor antagonists block histamine from stimulating acid secretion.

Mucus movers

Mucolytics act directly on mucus, breaking down sticky, thick secretions to make them easier to eliminate.

Oh, what a relief

Decongestants relieve the symptoms of swollen nasal membranes resulting from hay fever, allergic rhinitis, sinusitis, and the common cold.

GI system drugs

Some classes of drugs that are used to improve GI function include histamine-2 (H_2)-receptor antagonists, proton pump inhibitors, antiemetics, and emetics.

Histamine halters

H_2-receptor antagonists are commonly prescribed as antiulcer drugs. They block histamine from stimulating the acid-secreting parietal cells of the stomach.

Chemical disruption

Protein pump inhibitors disrupt chemical binding in stomach cells to reduce acid production, lessening irritation and allowing peptic ulcers to heal.

Opposites don't always attract

Antiemetics and **emetics** represent two groups of drugs with opposing actions. Antiemetic drugs decrease nausea, reducing the urge to vomit. Emetic drugs do just the opposite—they produce vomiting.

Reproductive system drugs

Various drugs may be used to address sexual dysfunction, fertility, and contraception.

When ED comes to visit

Phosphodiesterase type 5 inhibitors such as sildenafil (Viagra) are used to treat penile erectile dysfunction (ED). These drugs increase smooth-muscle relaxation, promoting the flow of blood into the corpus cavernosum of the penis.

A helping hand for women

Here are some examples of drugs that help women with fertility and its associated conditions:

- Danazol (Danocrine), a **synthetic steroid,** is used to treat endometriosis, a condition that may decrease fertility. The drug suppresses the hormonal cycle and decreases the inflammation associated with endometriosis.
- **Chlorotrianisene derivatives** such as clomiphene citrate (Clomid) are used to stimulate ovulation.
- **Progestins** such as progesterone gel (Prochieve) improve fertility by supplementing progesterone and improving the cervical mucus environment.

There's nothing wrong with a little improvement. Men with hypogonadism may need drugs such as HCG to improve sperm quality.

A helping hand for men

For men with hypogonadism secondary to pituitary or hypothalamic failure, treatment to improve sperm quality may include administering **human menopausal gonadotropins (hMGs), human chorionic gonadotropin (HCG),** or **pulsatile gonadotropin-releasing hormone (Gn-RH)**.

Preventive medicine

Contraceptives are hormonal drugs consisting of synthetic estrogen and progesterone that are used to prevent conception or impregnation. The estrogen suppresses production of follicle-stimulating hormone and luteinizing hormone, which then acts to suppress ovulation. Contraceptives may be administered orally or I.M., or through transdermal patches, subdermal implants, and vaginal rings.

Spermicides are inserted into the vagina to kill the sperm before they enter the cervix. Spermicides are available as gels, creams, films, and suppositories.

Maternal health drugs

Several drugs may be used to treat complications of pregnancy and labor. Drugs that are known to cause fetal anomalies are called **teratogens.** These drugs should be avoided unless the benefits of the drug outweigh the risks. (See *Tackling* teratogen.)

Here are some common maternal health drugs:

- **Folic acid** is a B vitamin that is essential for RBC formation and DNA synthesis. Adequate intake of folic acid during pregnancy has been shown to reduce the incidence of fetal neural tube defects.
- **Tocolytic drugs** are used to manage labor or prevent preterm labor by decreasing uterine muscle contractions.
- **Uterotropic drugs** improve uterine contractions by stimulating the smooth muscle of the uterus.

Beyond the dictionary

Tackling *teratogen*

A **teratogen** is anything (such as a drug, an infection, or an environmental factor) that interferes with normal fetal growth, causing abnormal prenatal development. It comes from the Greek words ***teras,*** which means *monster,* and ***genes,*** which means *born* or *producing.*

Anti-infective drugs

Anti-infective drugs are chosen after the infective organism is identified. Anti-infective agents are effective only against specific organisms. Anti-infective drugs include:

- **antibacterial drugs**—used mainly to treat systemic bacterial infections
- **antiviral drugs**—used to prevent or treat viral infections
- **antitubercular drugs**—used to treat tuberculosis
- **antimycotic drugs**—used to treat fungal infections.

Immune system drugs

Immune and inflammatory responses protect the body from invasive foreign substances. These responses can be modified by certain classes of drugs:

- **Antihistamines** block the effects of histamine on target tissues.
- **Corticosteroids** suppress immune responses and reduce inflammation.
- **Noncorticosteroid immunosuppressants** prevent rejection from transplanted organs and can be used to treat autoimmune disease.
- **Uricosurics** prevent or control the frequency of gouty arthritis attacks.

Psychiatric drugs

Sedatives can be used to induce sleep.

Various drugs are used to treat sleep and other psychogenic disorders, such as anxiety, depression, and psychotic disorders.

You're getting sleepy

Sedatives reduce anxiety or excitement. Some degree of drowsiness commonly accompanies sedative use. When given in large doses, sedatives are considered **hypnotics,** which induce a state that resembles natural sleep. The three main classes of synthetic drugs used as sedatives and hypnotics are:

1. **benzodiazepines,** which work on receptors in the reticular activating system of the brain (the portion associated with wakefulness and attention)
2. **barbiturates,** which depress the sensory cortex of the brain, decrease motor activity, alter cerebral function, and produce drowsiness, sedation, and hypnosis
3. **nonbenzodiazepine-nonbarbiturate drugs,** which act as hypnotics for short-term treatment of simple insomnia.

Mood modifiers

Antidepressants and **antimanic drugs** are used to treat affective disorders—such as mood disturbances—that are typically characterized by intense episodes of depression and elation.

Three drug classes are commonly used to treat affective disorders:

- **Monoamine oxidase inhibitors (MAOIs)** relieve the symptoms of depression by inhibiting the enzyme monoamine oxidase.
- **Tricyclic antidepressants (TCAs)** effectively treat episodes of major depression by increasing the amount of chemicals in the brain.
- **Selective serotonin reuptake inhibitors (SSRIs)** are used to treat major depressive episodes by inhibiting the neuronal reuptake of the neurotransmitter serotonin.

Benzodiazepines and barbiturates are the two main types of anxiolytics.

Anxiety critic

Anxiolytics, also called **antianxiety drugs,** are used primarily to treat anxiety disorders. Two of the main types are benzodiazepines and barbiturates.

Symptoms under wrap

Antipsychotic drugs control psychotic symptoms—such as delusions, hallucinations, and thought disorders—that sometimes occur with schizophrenia, mania, and other psychoses.

Endocrine system drugs

Together with the CNS, the **endocrine** system regulates and integrates the body's metabolic activities and maintains homeostasis.

Too little? Too much?

Patients who produce too little thyroid hormone (as in hypothyroidism) may need supplements such as levothyroxine. Patients who produce too much thyroid hormone (as in hyperthyroidism) may be given drugs such as propylthiouracil (PTU) to suppress thyroid function.

Sugar up...sugar down

Insulin, a pancreatic hormone, and **oral antidiabetic drugs** are classified as **hypoglycemic drugs** because they lower blood glucose levels. **Glucagon,** another pancreatic hormone, is classified as a **hyperglycemic drug** because it raises blood glucose levels.

systole
parietal

Vocabulary builders

At a crossroads

Don't get caught up in the conundrum of medication administration terms. Complete this puzzle to prove that you've received the correct dose of clinical pharmacology terminology.

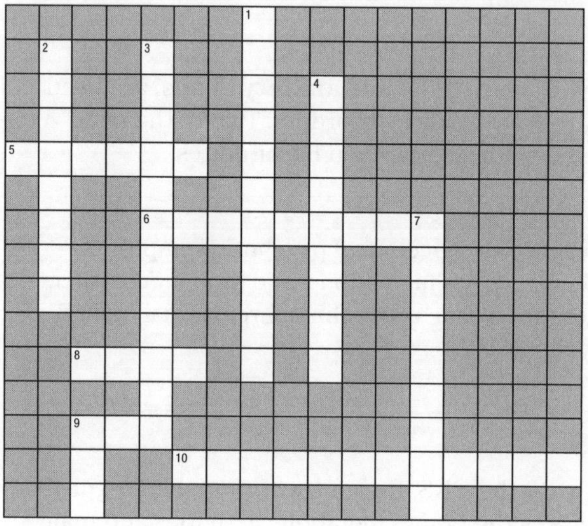

Across

5. A drug that's compressed to form a shape
6. Decreased response to a drug over time
8. Type of drug that's administered directly into the ear
9. Type of order that allows drugs to be given as needed
10. Study of drugs

Down

1. Drug that promotes the action of acetylcholine
2. Drug administered via the respiratory route
3. Drug interaction in which one drug enhances the effect of the other drug
4. Increase or decrease of drug dosage according to the patient's response
7. process by which a drug is eliminated by the body
9. Type of inhibitor that increases the force of the heart's contractions

Answers are on page 384.

Match game

For some types of drug administration, the location of administration is self-explanatory; for example, **intrathecal administration** refers to drug administration into the intrathecal space of the spinal canal. However, other terms used to describe administration routes aren't so apparent. Match the drug administration route below with its correct definition.

Clues	Choices
1. Intra-articular ____	A. Into the skin
2. Dermal ____	B. Under the tongue
3. Buccal ____	C. Into a vein
4. Ophthalmic ____	D. In the ear
5. Intradermal ____	E. Between the cheek and gum
6. Otic ____	F. Into a joint
7. Sublingual ____	H. Onto the skin
8. Intravenous ____	I. Into the eye

Finish line

The Greek root ***pharmaco*** indicates that a word has to do with drugs. Fill in the blanks below to complete the drug-related terms.

1. **Pharmaco** _____ is the use of drugs to prevent or treat diseases.
2. **Pharmaco** _____ is the study of the origin, nature, chemistry, effects, and uses of drugs.
3. **Pharmaco** _____ is the study of the biochemical and physical effects of drugs and the mechanisms of drug actions in living organisms.
4. **Pharmaco** _____ is how drugs are absorbed, distributed, metabolized, and excreted in a living organism.

Answers are on page 384.

Answers

At a crossroads

							1 C									
	2 I			3 P			H									
	N			O			O		4 T							
	H			T			L		I							
5 T	A	B	L	E	T		I		T							
	L			N			N		R							
	A			6 T	O	L	E	R	A	N	C	7 E				
	N			I			R		T			X				
	T			A			G		I			C				
				T			I		O			R				
		8 O	T	I	C		C		N			E				
				O								T				
		9 P	R	N								I				
		D			10 P	H	A	R	M	A	C	O	L	O	G	Y
		E										N				

Match game

1. F; 2. H; 3. E; 4. I; 5. A; 6. D; 7. B; 8. C

Finish line

1. Therapeutics; 2. Logy; 3. Dynamics; 4. Kinetics

17

Mental health

Just the facts

In this chapter, you'll learn:

- terminology related to the definition and assessment of mental health disorders
- terminology needed for examination of patients with mental health disorders
- tests that help diagnose mental health disorders
- terminology related to the types of mental health disorders
- mental health disorders and their treatments.

Mental health overview

The emphasis in mental health diagnoses is on observable data rather than subjective and theoretical impressions.

From teenage depression and suicide to increased substance abuse and elderly depression, the risk of mental disorders is on the rise. This chapter introduces terms associated with the diagnosis and treatment of mental health disorders. (See *Pronouncing key mental health terms*, page 386.)

DSM-IV-TR. Say what?

The American Psychiatric Association's ***Diagnostic and Statistical Manual of Mental Disorders*, Fourth Edition, Text Revision** (*DSM-IV-TR*) provides a unified system of classifying mental disorders. The system requires the health care provider to consider many aspects of the patient's behavior, mental performance, history, and culture and emphasizes using observable data rather than subjective and theoretical impressions. This approach makes psychiatric diagnoses more reliable and has lead to improvements in treating and managing mental health disorders.

Pump up your pronunciation

Pronouncing key mental health terms

Below is a list of key terms related to mental health, along with the correct way to pronounce them.

Cyclothymia	SIGH-KLOH-THIGH-MEE-UH
Echolalia	EK-OH-LAY-LEE-UH
Narcissism	NAR-SIH-SISM
Schizoid	SKIT-SOYD
Tardive dyskinesia	TAR-DIV DIS-KIH-NEE-ZHUH
Tourette syndrome	TOO-RET SIN-DROHM
Wernicke-Korsakoff syndrome	VER-NIH-KUH KOR-SEH-KOFF SIN-DROHM

Defining mental disorders

The *DSM-IV-TR* defines a **mental disorder** as a clinically significant behavioral or psychological syndrome or pattern that's associated with:

- current distress (a painful symptom) or disability (impairment in one or more important areas of functioning)
- significantly greater risk of suffering, death, pain, or disability
- an important loss of freedom.

This syndrome or pattern isn't an expected, culturally sanctioned response, such as grieving over the death of a loved one. It's considered a sign of a behavioral, psychological, or biological dysfunction.

The multiaxial approach to diagnosing mental health disorders specifies that every patient should be evaluated on each of five axes.

Five axes

The *DSM-IV-TR* uses a multiaxial approach to diagnosing mental disorders. This approach specifies that every patient should be evaluated on each of five axes, as follows:

- **Axis I: clinical disorders**—the diagnosis (or diagnoses) that best describes the presenting complaint and

that indicates the presence or absence of a major mental health disorder
- **Axis II: personality disorders and mental retardation**—determining whether these factors are present
- **Axis III: general medical conditions**—a description of concurrent medical conditions or disorders
- **Axis IV: psychosocial and environmental problems**—life events and problems that may affect the diagnosis, treatment, and prognosis of the mental health disorder
- **Axis V: global assessment of functioning (GAF)**—based on a scale of 1 to 100, evaluates the patient's overall psychological, social, and occupational function.

And now, for the diagnosis

A patient's diagnosis after being evaluated on these five axes may look like this:
- Axis I: adjustment disorder with anxious mood
- Axis II: obsessive-compulsive personality
- Axis III: Crohn's disease, acute bleeding episode
- Axis IV: recent remarriage, death of father
- Axis V: GAF = 83.

Psychological examination terms

Here are some important terms to understand when examining a patient with mental health issues.

Assessment terms

- **Attention level** refers to the ability to concentrate on a task for an appropriate length of time.
- **Behavior** includes the patient's demeanor and overall attitude, mannerisms (such as nail biting, fidgeting, or pacing), tics or tremors, and how he responds to the interviewer (for example, cooperative, friendly, hostile, or indifferent).
- **Chief complaint** is the main reason the patient has sought help and includes when symptoms began, whether symptoms are abrupt or gradual, the severity of symptoms, how long symptoms last, and how symptoms affect the patient's level of functioning.

• **Cultural and religious beliefs** include the patient's cultural background and values and how these factors affect the patient's response to illness and adaptation to hospital care. Keep in mind that certain questions or behaviors considered inappropriate in one culture may be acceptable in another.

Gathering demographic, socioeconomic, and cultural data is an important part of diagnosing mental health problems.

• **Current symptoms** are the subjective and objective symptoms that are currently affecting the patient, including their severity and persistence and whether they occurred abruptly or gradually.
• **Demographic data** includes the patient's age, sex, ethnic origin, primary language, birthplace, religion, and marital status.
• **General appearance of the patient** helps determine the patient's emotional and mental status. When evaluating a patient's appearance, include information about his dress, grooming, posture, gait, and facial expression.
• **Medication history** includes information about what drugs (including over-the-counter and herbal supplements) the patient has taken in the past and what he's currently taking. This information is important to collect because certain drugs can cause symptoms of mental illness. If the patient is taking an antipsychotic, antidepressant, anxiolytic, or antimanic drug, include information about whether symptoms have improved or adverse reactions have occurred.

During a mental health assessment, be aware of your nonverbal communication as well as the patient's.

• **Mood** refers to the internal emotional state and physical expressions of an individual's current feelings (for example, depression, crying, sweating, breathing heavily, or trembling).
• **Nonverbal communication** (body language) consists of eye contact, posture, facial expression, gestures, clothing, affect, and silence (which can convey a powerful message). In addition to observing the patient's nonverbal communication during the assessment process, you'll need to be aware of your own.
• **Patient history** helps establish a baseline for future assessments. It includes the chief complaint, current symptoms, psychiatric history, demographic and socioeconomic data, cultural and religious beliefs, medication history, and history of physical illnesses that may cause disorientation, distorted thought processes, depression, or other symptoms of mental illness.

• **Psychiatric assessment** is the process of identifying a patient's psychosocial problems, strengths, and concerns.
• **Psychiatric history** includes information about past psychiatric disturbances, such as episodes of delusions, hallucinations, violence, attempted suicide, drug or alcohol abuse, or depression, and previous psychiatric treatment.
• **Socioeconomic data** refers to the patient's economic and personal situation and how it impacts his current psychological status. Information may include educational level, housing conditions, income, and current employment status.
• **Therapeutic relationship** is a relationship between the patient and the health care provider that's based on trust. The health care provider's words and actions must communicate to the patient that his thoughts and behaviors are important.
• **Thought processes and cognitive function** are assessed based on orientation to time, place, and person and the presence of confusion or disorientation. Speech characteristics that may indicate altered thought processes include minimal monosyllabic responses, irrelevant or illogical replies to questions, convoluted or excessively detailed speech, repetitious speech patterns, a flight of ideas, and sudden silence without an obvious reason.

Acting out involves repeating certain actions to ward off anxiety without weighing the possible consequences of those actions.

Signs and symptoms

• **Acting out** involves repeating certain actions to ward off anxiety without weighing the possible consequences of those actions.
• **Compensation** (also called **substitution**) refers to an individual's attempt to make up for feelings of inadequacy or frustration in one area by excelling or overindulging in another area.
• **Compulsion** is a ritualistic, repetitive, and involuntary defensive behavior that's performed to reduce anxiety, which increases the likelihood that the behavior will recur.
• **Coping mechanisms** (also called **defense mechanisms**) are behaviors that operate on an unconscious level to protect the ego.

Excessive hand washing in a ritualistic, involuntary manner is an example of a compulsion.

- **Delusions** are false ideas or beliefs accepted as real by the patient. Delusions of grandeur, persecution, and reference are common in schizophrenia.
- **Denial** is a way of protecting oneself from unpleasant aspects of life by refusing to perceive, acknowledge, or deal with them.
- **Displacement** refers to misdirecting pent-up feelings toward something or someone that's less threatening than what triggered the response.
- **Fantasy** is the creation of unrealistic or improbable images to escape from daily pressures and responsibilities.
- **Hallucinations** are false sensory perceptions with no basis in reality. Usually visual or auditory, hallucinations also may be olfactory or tactile.
- **Identification** involves unconsciously adopting the personality characteristics, attitudes, values, and behavior of someone else as a way to alleviate anxiety
- **Intellectualization** (also called **isolation**) refers to an individual removing himself from emotional events. The patient may discuss painful events in a detached, impersonal way because describing true feelings is too difficult.
- **Introjection** refers to an individual adopting someone else's values and standards without exploring whether they're appropriate for him.
- **Obsession** is an intrusive or inappropriate recurrent idea, thought, image, or impulse that causes marked anxiety or distress.
- **Projection** is the displacement of negative feelings onto another person.
- **Rationalization** is substituting acceptable reasons for the real or actual reasons that are motivating the patient's behavior
- **Reaction formation** refers to the display of behavior that's opposite of the individual's true feelings.
- **Regression** occurs when an individual returns to an earlier developmental stage.
- **Repression** refers to unconsciously blocking out painful or unacceptable thoughts and feelings, leaving the feelings to operate in the subconscious.
- **Self-destructive behavior** is death-seeking behavior, including suicidal tendencies.

Regression occurs when a patient returns to an earlier developmental stage.

• **Sublimation** is transforming unacceptable needs into acceptable ambitions and actions. For example, a person with highly aggressive tendencies may study and excel in the martial arts.
• **Undoing** refers to an individual trying to undo the harm he feels he has done to others.
• **Withdrawal** refers to growing emotionally uninvolved by retreating and becoming passive.

Diagnostic tests

Toxicologic studies are blood and urine tests that can detect the presence of many drugs.

Various laboratory tests and psychological and mental status tests provide information about the patient's mental status and possible physical causes of signs and symptoms.

Laboratory tests

• **Toxicologic studies** are blood and urine tests that can detect the presence of many drugs and quantify the blood levels of these drugs. Patients undergoing treatment with psychotherapeutic drugs may need routine toxicology screening to ensure that they aren't receiving a toxic dose.

Psychological and mental status tests

Here are some examples of tests that evaluate the patient's mood, personality, and mental status:
• **Beck Depression Inventory** helps diagnose depression and determine its severity. This test may provide objective evidence of the need for treatment. It's also used to monitor the patient's response during treatment.
• **Cognitive Assessment Scale** measures orientation, general knowledge, mental ability, and psychomotor function.
• **Cognitive Capacity Screening Examination** measures orientation, memory, calculation, and language.
• **Eating Attitudes Test** detects patterns that suggest an eating disorder.
• **Functional Dementia Scale** measures orientation, affect, and the ability to perform activities of daily living.

• **Global Deterioration Scale** assesses and stages primary degenerative dementia based on orientation, memory, and neurologic function.
• **Minnesota Multiphasic Personality Inventory** helps assess personality traits and ego function in adolescents and adults. Test results provide information on coping strategies, defenses, strengths, gender identification, and self-esteem. The test pattern may strongly suggest a diagnostic category, point to a suicide risk, or indicate the potential for violence.
• **Mini–Mental Status Examination** measures orientation, registration (the ability of a patient to name three objects previously mentioned to him by the examiner), recall, calculation, language, and graphomotor (the movements required in writing) function.

The **Minnesota Multiphasic Personality Inventory** helps assess personality traits and ego function in adolescents and adults.

Disorders

This section provides terminology related to mental health disorders, which can affect any age-group.

Disorders of infancy, childhood, and adolescence

Here are some examples of disorders of infancy, childhood, and adolescence:
• **Anorexia nervosa** is self-imposed starvation resulting from a distorted body image and an intense and irrational fear of gaining weight, even when obviously emaciated. It mainly affects adolescents.
• **Attention deficit hyperactivity disorder** is a disorder in which the child has difficulty focusing his attention, engaging in quiet passive activities, or both. This condition is usually diagnosed after age 4 or 5.
• **Autistic disorder** is a severe, pervasive developmental disorder marked by unresponsiveness to social contact, gross deficits in cognitive and language development, ritualistic and compulsive behaviors, restricted capacity for developmentally appropriate activities and interests, and bizarre responses to the environment. Autistic disorder usually becomes apparent before age 3.
• **Bulimia nervosa** is a disorder marked by eating binges followed by feelings of guilt, humiliation, and self-deprecation. These feelings precipitate self-induced vom-

Anorexia nervosa is self-imposed starvation resulting from a distorted body image and an intense and irrational fear of gaining weight.

iting, use of laxatives or diuretics, or strict dieting or fasting to overcome the effects of the binges. As with anorexia nervosa, this condition usually affects adolescents.

• **Conduct disorder** is characterized by aggressive behavior. A child with this disorder fights, bullies, intimidates, and assaults others physically or sexually, and is truant from school at an early age.

• **Down syndrome** (also known as **mongolism** and **trisomy 21 syndrome**), is a disorder attributed to a chromosomal aberration, and characteristically produces mental retardation, abnormal facial features, and other distinctive physical abnormalities.

• **Mental retardation,** as defined by the American Association on Mental Retardation, is "significantly subaverage general intellectual function existing concurrently with deficits in adaptive behavior manifesting itself during the developmental period" (before age 18). This disorder is transmitted genetically.

• **Tic disorders** are a group of three disorders that include Tourette syndrome, chronic motor or vocal tic disorder, and transient tic disorder. They involve involuntary, spasmodic, recurrent, and purposeless motor movements or vocalizations. These disorders tend to appear before age 21.

Substance-related disorders

Substance-related disorders include alcoholism and drug abuse and dependence, which affect the central nervous system, causing physical and mental harm.

• **Alcoholism** is a chronic disorder most commonly described as the uncontrolled intake of alcoholic beverages that interferes with physical and mental health, social and familial relationships, and occupational responsibilities.

• **Drug abuse** is defined by The National Institute on Drug Abuse as the use of a legal or an illegal drug that causes physical, mental, emotional, or social harm.

Psychotic disorders

Characterized by disordered thinking, psychotic disorders include delusional disorders and schizophrenia.

• According to the *DSM-IV-TR,* **delusional disorders** (formerly called **paranoid disorders**) are characterized by false beliefs despite contradictory information. Delusional disorders are known to involve erotomanic, grandiose, jealous, or somatic themes as well as persecutory delusions. For example, an individual may believe a sexual partner is being unfaithful without any factual information to support the belief.

• **Schizophrenia** is characterized by disturbances in thought content and form, perception, affect, language, social activity, sense of self, volition, interpersonal relationships, and psychomotor behavior. The *DSM-IV-TR* recognizes catatonic, paranoid, disorganized, residual, and undifferentiated schizophrenia.

Pump up your pronunciation

How do I say *cyclothymia?*

Cyclothymia—a mild form of bipolar disorder—is pronounced SIGH-KLOH-THIGH-MEE-UH. It's a combination of two Greek words, ***kyklos,*** meaning *circle* or *recurring,* and ***thymos,*** meaning *mind.* A patient with this disorder alternates between episodes of hypomania and depression.

Mood disorders

A mood disorder involves disturbances in the regulation of a person's mood, behavior, and affect. With these disorders, a person's mood becomes so intense and persistent that it interferes with his social and psychological function.

• **Bipolar disorder** is an affective disorder marked by severe pathologic mood swings from hyperactivity and euphoria to sadness and depression. Some patients suffer from acute attacks of mania only.

• **Cyclothymia** is a variant of bipolar disorder in which numerous episodes of hypomania and depressive symptoms are too mild to meet the criteria for major depression or bipolar illness. (See *How do I say* cyclothymia?)

• **Major depression** is defined as a depressed mood on a daily basis for 2 weeks or longer. It's a syndrome of persistent sad, dysphoric mood accompanied by disturbances in sleep and appetite, lethargy, and an inability to experience pleasure (anhedonia).

Major depression is defined as a depressed mood on a daily basis for 2 weeks or longer.

Anxiety disorders

Anxiety disorders are characterized by apprehension, feelings of tension, and avoidant behavior. Here's a list of major anxiety disorders:

• **Generalized anxiety disorder** is characterized by a feeling of apprehension caused by a threat to a person or his values.

- **Obsessive-compulsive disorder** is characterized by obsessive thoughts and compulsive behaviors that represent recurring efforts to control overwhelming anxiety, guilt, or unacceptable impulses that persistently enter the consciousness.
- **Panic disorder** is characterized by recurrent and unpredictable episodes of intense apprehension, terror, and impending doom. Panic disorder involves anxiety in its most severe form.
- A **phobia** is a persistent and irrational fear of a specific object, activity, or situation that results in anxiety. A phobia causes a compelling desire to avoid the perceived hazard. Panic attacks can be triggered by the phobia. Examples of phobias include:
  - **agoraphobia** (fear of leaving familiar settings or of open space)
  - **social phobia** (fear of embarrassing oneself in public)
  - **pharmacophobia** (fear of drugs)
  - **triskaidekaphobia** (fear of the number 13). (See *Taking apart triskaidekaphobia.*)
- **Posttraumatic stress disorder** refers to a persistent psychological disturbance that occurs following a traumatic event.

Beyond the dictionary

Taking apart *triskaideka-phobia*

Triskaidekaphobia is an illogical or irrational fear of the number thirteen. Its roots are from the Greek words ***treis,*** meaning *three;* ***deka,*** meaning *ten;* and ***phobos,*** meaning *fear* or *having an aversion to.*

Somatoform disorders

The patient with a **somatoform disorder** complains of physical signs and symptoms and typically travels from doctor to doctor in search of treatment. Physical examinations and laboratory tests fail to uncover an organic basis for the patient's signs and symptoms and the somatic symptoms aren't due to the effects of alcohol or recreational or prescription drugs. Here's a list of major somatoform disorders:

- **Body dysmorphic disorder** involves a preoccupation with an imagined (or, if present, slight) defect in physical appearance.
- **Conversion disorder** (previously called **hysterical neurosis, conversion type**) allows a patient to resolve a psychological conflict through the loss of a specific physical function; for example, through paralysis, blindness, or the inability to swallow.

• **Hypochondriasis** (previously referred to as **hypochondriacal neurosis**) is an unrealistic misinterpretation of the severity and significance of physical signs or sensations. This condition leads to a preoccupation with having a serious disease. This fear persists despite medical reassurance to the contrary. (See *Feeling ill?*)

• **Pain disorder** is a persistent complaint of pain. The pain is severe enough to warrant clinical attention, and significantly impairs social, occupational, or other important areas of functioning.

• In **somatization disorder,** which primarily affects females, the patient has multiple unintentional physical complaints from different systems. The patient's complaints are typically dramatic but inconsistent. Mood changes and anxiety are common and may be the result of drug interactions.

Beyond the dictionary

Feeling ill?

Hypochondriasis is a chronic and abnormal anxiety about imaginary symptoms and ailments. The ancients thought that this condition was caused by the disturbed function of the *hypochondria,* another name for the upper abdominal regions.

Dissociative disorders

Dissociation refers to an unconscious defense mechanism that keeps troubling thoughts out of a person's awareness. The patient with a **dissociative disorder** experiences temporary changes in consciousness, identity, and motor function.

• **Depersonalization disorder** is characterized by persistent or recurrent episodes of detachment. During these episodes, self-awareness is temporarily altered or lost; the patient typically perceives this alteration in consciousness as a barrier between himself and the outside world.

• **Dissociative amnesia** is a sudden inability to recall important personal information that can't be explained by ordinary forgetfulness.

• **Dissociative identity disorder** is a complex disturbance of identity and memory characterized by the existence of two or more distinct, fully integrated personalities in the same person.

The patient with **dissociative disorder** experiences temporary changes in consciousness, identity, and motor function.

Personality disorders

The patient with a **personality disorder** possesses chronic, inflexible, and maladaptive patterns of behavior that cause social discomfort and impair social and occupational functioning. Here's a list of major personality disorders:

- **Histrionic disorder** applies to an individual who's excessively emotional and constantly seeking attention.
- **Schizoid disorder** is characterized by emotional detachment from other people. The patient is emotionally cold and distant, and he has a limited range of emotional expressions.
- **Antisocial disorder** is marked by the disregard for social norms. Patients commonly display deceitful behavior and don't show remorse or take responsibility for their actions.

Sexual disorders

These disorders affect a person's sexual ability or response, gender identity, or sexual behavior:

- **Arousal disorder** is the inability to experience sexual pleasure. It's one of the most severe forms of female sexual dysfunction.
- **Exhibitionism** is marked by sexual fantasies, urges, or behaviors involving surprise exposure of the genitals to strangers.
- **Fetishism** is characterized by sexual fantasies, urges, or behaviors that involve the use of a fetish—a nonhuman object or a nonsexual part of the body—to produce or enhance sexual arousal.
- **Frotteurism** is sexual arousal from touching or rubbing against a nonconsenting person.
- **Gender identity disorder** produces persistent feelings of gender discomfort and dissatisfaction.
- **Orgasmic disorder,** the most common type of female sexual dysfunction, is an inability to achieve orgasm. The patient may desire sexual activity and become aroused but feels inhibited as she approaches orgasm.
- **Paraphilias** are complex psychosexual disorders and are characterized by a dependence on unusual behaviors or fantasies to achieve sexual excitement. The imagery or acts may involve the use of inanimate objects (especially clothing), repetitive sexual activity that includes suffering or humiliation, or sexual behavior with nonconsenting partners.
- **Pedophilia** is marked by sexual fantasies, urges, or activity involving a child, usually age 13 or younger.

Other possible sexual disorders include **dyspareunia,** or painful intercourse, and **vaginismus,** the involuntary spastic constriction of the lower vaginal muscles. Both can lead to a woman's lack of interest in intercourse.

- **Sexual masochism** is sexual gratification from being physically or sexually abused.
- **Sexual sadism** is achieving sexual gratification by inflicting pain, cruelty, or emotional abuse on others.
- **Transvestic fetishism** involves a heterosexual male dressing in female clothes to produce or enhance sexual arousal.
- **Voyeurism** involves deriving sexual pleasure from looking at sexual objects or sexually arousing situations such as an unsuspecting couple engaged in sex.

Treatments

Assertiveness training uses positive reinforcement, shaping, and modeling to reduce anxiety.

Here's a list of common psychiatric treatments:

- **Assertiveness training** uses positive reinforcement, **shaping** (modifying existing behavior into desired behavior), and **modeling** (demonstrating desired behavior) to reduce anxiety. It teaches the patient ways to express feeling, ideas, and wishes without feeling guilty or demeaning others.
- **Aversion therapy** uses a painful stimulus to create an aversion to the obsession underlying the patient's undesirable behavior.
- **Behavior therapy** assumes that problematic behaviors are learned and through special training, these behaviors can be unlearned and replaced by acceptable behaviors. Behavior therapy may be used with an individual or with a group and may include treatments such as assertiveness training, aversion therapy, desensitization, flooding, positive conditions, response prevention, thought stopping, thought switching, and token economy.
- According to cognitive theory, depression stems from low self-esteem and belief that the future is hopeless. **Cognitive therapy** helps identify and change the patient's negative generalizations and expectations and thereby reduces depression, distress, and other emotional problems.
- **Crisis intervention** seeks to help the patient develop adequate coping skills to resolve an immediate problem. Therapy focuses on helping the patient resume their precrisis functional level. Therapy may include family members.

• **Desensitization** slowly exposes the patient to something he fears.
• **Detoxification** programs offer a relatively safe alternative to self-withdrawal after prolonged dependence on alcohol or drugs. They provide symptomatic treatment as well as counseling or psychotherapy on an individual, group, or family basis.
• **Drug therapy** includes the use of antidepressants, antianxiety agents, and antipsychotics. This therapy requires careful monitoring and possible dosage changes.
• **Electroconvulsive therapy (ECT)** is used for major depression. After the patient is anesthetized, a tiny electric current is sent to the brain for 1 second through electrodes placed above the temples. The current produces a seizure, which lasts 30 seconds to 1 minute. The prevailing theory is that ECT temporarily alters some of the brain's electrochemical processes.
• **Family therapy** aims to alter relationships within a family and change the problematic behavior of one or more of its members.
• **Flooding** (also called **implosion therapy**) involves direct exposure to an anxiety-producing situation. It also uses the idea that confrontation helps the patient overcome fear.
• **Group therapy,** guided by a psychotherapist, involves a group of people (ideally 4 to 10) who are experiencing similar emotional problems meeting to discuss their concerns.
• **Individual therapy** involves a series of therapy sessions that promote personality growth and development. It may be short- or long-term.
• **Milieu therapy** uses the patient's environment as a tool for treating mental and emotional disorders. The patient's surroundings become a therapeutic community, and the patient shares responsibility for establishing group rules and policies.
• **Positive conditioning** attempts to gradually instill a positive or neutral attitude toward a phobia. A pleasurable stimulus is introduced along with the phobic stimulus.
• **Psychotherapy** involves a range of approaches—from in-depth psychoanalysis to 1-day crisis counseling—that aims to change a patient's attitudes, feeling, or behavior. Types of psychotherapy include individual therapy, group

Drugs used to treat mental health disorders include antidepressants, antianxiety agents, and antipsychotics.

therapy, cognitive therapy, family therapy, and crisis intervention.

- **Response prevention** seeks to prevent compulsive behavior through distraction, persuasion, or redirection of activity.
- **Thought stopping** helps break the habit of fear-inducing anticipatory thoughts by focusing attention on calmness and muscle relaxation.
- **Thought switching** teaches the patient to replace fear-inducing self-instructions with competent self-instructions.
- In **token economy,** the therapist rewards acceptable behavior by giving out tokens, which the patient uses to "buy" a privilege or object.

In **thought switching,** the patient learns to replace fear-inducing self-instructions with competent self-instructions.
I CAN COPE
I CAN DO BETTER
IT'S NOT THE END OF THE WORLD
I CAN GET THROUGH THIS

systole
parietal
aorta

Vocabulary builders

At a crossroads

Completing this crossword puzzle will help you wrap your head around mental health terms.

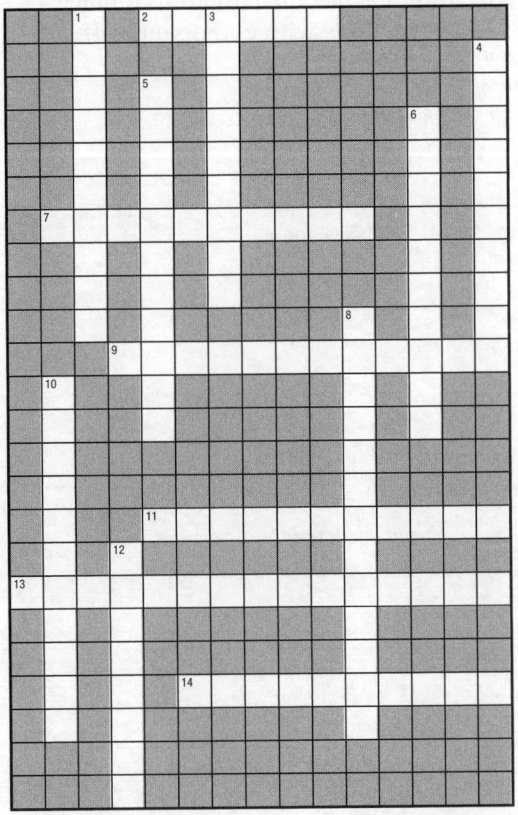

Across

2. A persistent and irrational fear of a specific object, activity or situation
7. An involuntary spastic constriction of the lower vaginal muscles
9. An unconscious defense mechanism that keeps troubling thoughts out of an individual's awareness
11. A dependence on unusual behaviors or fantasies to achieve sexual excitement
13. The process of slowly exposing the patient to something he fears
14. Uncontrolled intake of alcohol

Down

1. Growing emotionally uninvolved by pulling back and being passive
3. An intense preoccupation that interferes with daily living
4. Returning to an earlier developmental stage
5. Transforming unacceptable needs into acceptable ambitions and actions
6. Displacement of negative feelings onto another person
8. A false sensory perception with no basis in reality
10. Pain associated with intercourse
12. A false idea or belief that's accepted as real

Answers are on page 404.

Match game

Match each description of a disorder to its name.

Clues

1. Characterized by disturbances in thought content and form, perception, affect, language, social activity, sense of self, volition, interpersonal relationships, and psychomotor behavior ___
2. An uncontrolled intake of alcoholic beverages that interferes with physical and mental health, social and familial relationships, and occupational responsibilities ___
3. Self-imposed starvation resulting from a distorted body image and an intense and irrational fear of gaining weight ___
4. Involuntary, spasmodic, recurrent, and purposeless motor movements or vocalizations ___
5. Characteristically produces mental retardation, abnormal facial features, and other distinctive physical abnormalities ___
6. Characterized by recurrent and unpredictable episodes of intense apprehension, terror, and impending doom ___
7. Characterized by aggressive behavior ___
8. Allows a patient to resolve a psychological conflict through the loss of a specific physical function ___

Choices

A. Anorexia nervosa

B. Conduct disorder

C. Tic disorders

D. Schizophrenia

E. Panic disorder

F. Conversion disorder

G. Alcoholism

H. Down syndrome

I'm thinking.
I'm thinking.

Answers are on page 404.

Finish line

Fill in the blanks below with the appropriate word(s).

1. ________ includes emotional and physical expressions of current feelings, such as depression, crying, sweating, breathing heavily, or trembling.

2. Repeating certain actions to ward off anxiety without weighing the possible consequences of those actions is called ________ __________.

3. An ______________ is an intense preoccupation that interferes with daily living.

4. Transforming unacceptable needs into acceptable ambitions and actions is called ________________.

5. ___________ is returning to an earlier developmental stage.

Done! Done! Done!
I'm really in the mood
to celebrate!

Answers are on page 404.

Answers

At a crossroads

		1 W		2 P	H	3 O	B	I	A					
		I				B								4 R
		T		5 S		S								E
		H		U		E						6 P		G
		D		B		S						R		R
		R		L		S						O		E
	7 V	A	G	I	N	I	S	M	U	S		J		S
		W		M		O						E		S
		A		A		N						C		I
		L		T						8 H		T		O
			9 D	I	S	S	O	C	I	A	T	I	O	N
	10 D			O						L		O		
	Y			N						L		N		
	S									U				
	P									C				
	A			11 P	A	R	A	P	H	I	L	I	A	S
	R		12 D							N				
13 D	E	S	E	N	S	I	T	I	Z	A	T	I	O	N
	U		L							T				
	N		U							I				
	I		S		14 A	L	C	O	H	O	L	I	S	M
	A		I							N				
			O											
			N											

Great job!

Match game

1. D; 2. G; 3. A; 4. C; 5. H; 6. E; 7. B; 8. F

Finish line

1. Mood; 2. Acting out; 3. Obsession; 4. Sublimation; 5. Regression

Selected references

American Psychiatric Association Diagnostic and Statistical Manual of Mental Disorders, 4th ed., Text Revision. Arlington, VA: American Psychiatric Publishing, Inc., 2000.

Anatomy and Physiology Made Incredibly Easy, 3rd ed. Philadelphia: Lippincott Williams & Wilkins, 2008.

Bickley, L. *Bates' Guide to Physical Examination and History Taking*, 9th ed. Philadelphia: Lippincott Williams & Wilkins, 2007.

Cohen, B. *Memmler's The Human Body in Health and Disease*, 10th ed. Philadelphia: Lippincott Williams & Wilkins, 2005.

Craven, R.F. *Fundamentals of Nursing: Human Health and Function*, 5th ed. Philadelphia: Lippincott Williams & Wilkins, 2007.

Fox, F.I. *A Laboratory Guide to Human Physiology: Concepts and Clinical Applications*, 12th ed. Boston: McGraw-Hill Higher Education, 2008.

Guide to Clinical Preventative Services. Recommendations of the US Preventative Task Force. Rockville, MD: Agency for Healthcare Research and Quality, 2006.

JNC Express. *The Seventh Report of the Joint National Committee on Prevention, Detection, Evaluation and Treatment of High Blood Pressure.* NIH Publication Number 03-5233, 2003.

Lippincott Manual of Nursing Practice Series: Diagnostic Tests. Philadelphia: Lippincott Williams & Wilkins, 2007.

Lynn-McHale Wiegand, D.J., and Carlson, K.K., eds. *AACN Procedure Manual for Critical Care*, 5th ed. St. Louis: Saunders, 2005.

Maternal-Neonatal Nursing Made Incredibly Easy, 2nd ed. Philadelphia: Lippincott Williams & Wilkins, 2008.

Nursing Procedures, 4th ed. Philadelphia: Lippincott Williams & Wilkins, 2004.

Nursing 2007 Drug Handbook, 27th ed. Philadelphia: Lippincott Williams & Wilkins, 2007.

Orshan, S. *Maternity, Newborn, & Women's Health Nursing: Comprehensive Care Across the Lifespan.* Philadelphia: Lippincott Williams & Wilkins, 2008.

Professional Guide to Diagnostic Tests. Philadelphia: Lippincott Williams & Wilkins, 2005.

Professional Guide to Pathophysiology, 2nd ed. Philadelphia: Lippincott Williams & Wilkins, 2007.

Sadock, B.J., and Sadock, V.A., eds. *Kaplan and Sadock's Comprehensive Textbook of Psychiatry*, 8th ed. Philadelphia: Lippincott Williams & Wilkins, 2005.

Smeltzer, S.C., and Bare, B.G., eds. *Brunner & Suddarth's Textbook of Medical-Surgical Nursing*, 11th ed. Philadelphia: Lippincott Williams & Wilkins, 2008.

Stedman's Medical Dictionary, 28th ed. Philadelphia: Lippincott Williams & Wilkins, 2005.

Stuart, G., and Laraia, M. *Principles and Practice of Psychiatric Nursing*, 8th ed. St. Louis: Mosby, 2005.

Taylor, C., et al., eds. *Fundamentals of Nursing: The Art and Science of Nursing Care*, 6th ed. Philadelphia: Lippincott Williams & Wilkins, 2008.

Index

i refers to an illustration; t refers to a table; boldface refers to color pages.

i refers to an illustration; t refers to a table; boldface refers to color pages.

i refers to an illustration; t refers to a table; boldface refers to color pages.

i refers to an illustration; t refers to a table; boldface refers to color pages.

RRS1506